THE
American Jewish Experience

THE
American Jewish Experience

Edited with Introduction and Notes by
JONATHAN D. SARNA

HM
Holmes & Meier
NEW YORK / LONDON

This volume is issued in conjunction with the Center for the Study of the American Jewish Experience, Hebrew Union College—Jewish Institute of Religion

First published in the United States of America 1986 by
Holmes & Meier Publishers, Inc.
30 Irving Place
New York, N.Y. 10003

Great Britain:
Holmes & Meier Limited
Pindar Road
Hoddesdon, Hertfordshire EN11 0HF
England

Library of Congress Cataloging in Publication Data

The American Jewish experience.

"This volume is issued in conjunction with the
Center for the Study of the American Jewish Experience,
Hebrew Union College—Jewish Institute of Religion."
  Bibliography: p.
  Includes index.
  1. Jews—United States—History. 2. United States—
Ethnic relations. I. Sarna, Jonathan D. II. Hebrew
Union College—Jewish Institute of Religion. Center
for the Study of the American Jewish Experience.
E184.J5A34 1986   973'.04924   86-7579
ISBN 0-8419-0934-2
ISBN 0-8419-0935-0 (pbk.)

Book design by Ellen Foos

Manufactured in the United States of America

SOURCES

The American Colonial Jew: A Study in Acculturation
Reprinted with permission of Jacob R. Marcus from *The American Colonial Jew;* the B. G. Rudolph Lectures in Judaic Studies, Syracuse University, copyright © 1967 by Jacob R. Marcus.

The Impact of the American Revolution on American Jews
Reprinted with minor revisions and without accompanying footnotes from *Modern Judaism* 1 (1981), pp. 149–160, copyright © 1981 by Jonathan D. Sarna and Johns Hopkins University Press; by permission of *Modern Judaism*.

The 1820s: American Jewry Comes of Age

Reprinted with minor revisions and without accompanying footnotes from *A Bicentennial Festschrift for Jacob Rader Marcus*, edited by Bertram Wallace Korn (New York: KTAV Publishing House, 1976), pp. 539–549, copyright © 1976 by KTAV Publishing House, Inc.; by permission of KTAV Publishing House.

German-Jewish Identity in Nineteenth-Century America

Reprinted with permission of Transaction, Inc., and without accompanying footnotes from *Toward Modernity: The European Jewish Model*, ed. Jacob R. Katz, copyright © 1986 by Transaction, Inc.

Ulysses S. Grant and the Jews

Reprinted with permission and without accompanying footnotes from "Candidate Grant and the Jews," *American Jewish Archives* 17 (April 1965), pp. 3–15, copyright © 1965 by the American Jewish Archives.

A Business Elite: German-Jewish Financiers in Nineteenth-Century New York

Reprinted in somewhat abridged form and without accompanying footnotes from *Business History Review* 31 (Summer 1957), pp. 143–178, copyright © 1957 by the President and Fellows of Harvard College; by permission of *Business History Review* and Barry E. Supple.

Reform Judaism and the Unitarian Challenge

Reprinted in somewhat revised form and without accompanying footnotes from the *Journal of Ecumenical Studies*, 23 (Winter 1986), copyright © 1985 by Benny Kraut; by permission of Benny Kraut.

Immigrant Jews on the Lower East Side of New York: 1880–1914

Reprinted without accompanying footnotes and charts from "Health Conditions of Immigrant Jews on the Lower East Side of New York: 1800–1914," *Medical History* 25 (1981), pp. 1–18, copyright © 1981 by the Wellcome Institute for the History of Medicine; by permission of the Wellcome Institute and Deborah Dwork.

Germans versus Russians

Reprinted by permission and without accompanying footnotes from Moses Rischin, *The Promised City* (Cambridge, MA: Harvard University Press, 1962), copyright © 1962 by the President and Fellows of Harvard College.

Immigrant Women and Consumer Protest: The New York City Kosher Meat Boycott of 1902

Reprinted by permission and without accompanying footnotes from *American Jewish History* 70 (September 1980), pp. 91–105, copyright © 1980 by the American Jewish Historical Society.

The Kehillah Vision and the Limits of Community

Reprinted by permission and without accompanying footnotes from Arthur A. Goren, *New York Jews and the Quest for Community* (New York: Columbia University Press, 1970), copyright © 1970 by the Columbia University Press.

The Jewishness of the Jewish Labor Movement in the United States
Reprinted by permission from *A Bicentennial Festschrift for Jacob Rader Marcus*, edited by Bertram Wallace Korn (New York: KTAV Publishing House, 1976), pp. 121–130, copyright © 1976 by KTAV Publishing House, Inc.

Henry Ford and **The International Jew**
Reprinted in abridged form and without accompanying footnotes from *American Jewish History* 69 (June 1980), pp. 437–477, copyright © 1980 by the American Jewish Historical Society; by permission of the American Jewish Historical Society and Leo P. Ribuffo.

The Emergence of the American Synagogue
Reprinted by permission and without accompanying footnotes from Jeffrey S. Gurock, *When Harlem Was Jewish* (New York: Columbia University Press, 1979), copyright © 1979 by Columbia University Press.

Zionism: An American Experience
Reprinted by permission and without accompanying footnotes from *American Jewish Historical Quarterly* 63 (March 1974), pp. 261–282, copyright © 1974 by the American Jewish Historical Society.

The Midpassage of American Jewry
Reprinted by permission and without accompanying footnotes from *The Midpassage of American Jewry, 1929–1945*, The Fifth Annual Feinberg Memorial Lecture (May 13, 1982), copyright © 1982 by the Judaic Studies Program, University of Cincinnati.

Who Shall Bear Guilt for the Holocaust: The Human Dilemma
Reprinted by permission and without accompanying footnotes from *American Jewish History* 68 (March 1979), pp. 261–282, copyright © 1979 by the American Jewish Historical Society.

At Home in America
Reprinted by permission and without accompanying footnotes from Deborah Dash Moore, *At Home in America* (New York: Columbia University Press, 1981), copyright © 1981 by Columbia University Press.

The Jew Who Didn't Get Away: On the Possibility of an American Jewish Culture
Reprinted from *Judaism* 31 (Summer 1982), pp. 274–286, copyright © 1982 by the American Jewish Congress; by permission of *Judaism* and Robert Alter.

American Jews: Their Story Continues
Reprinted by permission from *Jewish Life in America: Fulfilling the American Dream* (New York: Anti-Defamation League of B'nai B'rith, 1983), copyright © 1983 by the Anti-Defamation League of B'nai B'rith.

CONTENTS

Introduction   xiii
Jonathan D. Sarna

PART ONE: THE AMERICAN JEWISH COMMUNITY TAKES
     SHAPE

1. The American Colonial Jew: A Study in Acculturation   6
Jacob R. Marcus
2. The Impact of the American Revolution on American Jews   20
Jonathan D. Sarna
3. The 1820s: American Jewry Comes of Age   31
Malcolm H. Stern

For Further Reading   38

PART TWO: THE "GERMAN PERIOD" IN AMERICAN
     JEWISH HISTORY

4. German-Jewish Identity in Nineteenth-Century America   45
Michael A. Meyer
5. Ulysses S. Grant and the Jews   62
Joakim Isaacs
6. A Business Elite: German-Jewish Financiers in
     Nineteenth-Century New York   73
Barry E. Supple
7. Reform Judaism and the Unitarian Challenge   89
Benny Kraut

For Further Reading   97

PART THREE: THE ERA OF EAST EUROPEAN
     IMMIGRATION

8. Immigrant Jews on the Lower East Side of New York:
     1880–1914   102
Deborah Dwork
9. Germans versus Russians   120
Moses Rischin

10. Immigrant Women and Consumer Protest: The New York
    City Kosher Meat Boycott of 1902   135
    Paula E. Hyman

11. The Kehillah Vision and the Limits of Community   149
    Arthur A. Goren

12. The Jewishness of the Jewish Labor Movement in the
    United States   158
    Lucy S. Dawidowicz

For Further Reading   167

PART FOUR: COMING TO TERMS WITH AMERICA

13. Henry Ford and *The International Jew*   175
    Leo P. Ribuffo

14. The Emergence of the American Synagogue   193
    Jeffrey S. Gurock

15. Zionism: An American Experience   211
    Melvin I. Urofsky

16. The Midpassage of American Jewry   224
    Lloyd P. Gartner

For Further Reading   234

PART FIVE: THE HOLOCAUST AND BEYOND

17. Who Shall Bear Guilt for the Holocaust? The Human
    Dilemma   240
    Henry L. Feingold

18. At Home in America   260
    Deborah Dash Moore

19. The Jew Who Didn't Get Away: On the Possibility of an
    American Jewish Culture   269
    Robert Alter

20. American Jews: Their Story Continues   284
    Stephen J. Whitfield

For Further Reading   294

Appendix 1: The Growth of the American Jewish Population   296

Appendix 2: A Century of Jewish Immigration to the United
    States   297

Reference Sources in American Jewish History   298

Index   300

To Jacob Rader Marcus
Teacher, mentor, friend

Acknowledgments

This volume is another in a series of texts issued in conjunction with the Center for the Study of the American Jewish Experience to increase public awareness of American Jewry's past and present, and to enhance the teaching of American Jewish history and life, particularly at the college level. When it began to take shape six years ago, this volume was no more than a collection of photocopied articles prepared for my students at Hebrew Union College–Jewish Institute of Religion in Cincinnati. Several years' worth of student comments and criticisms have improved my selections (not to speak of my ideas), and I am pleased to express my gratitude. I am also grateful to all of my colleagues at the College-Institute, the American Jewish Archives, and the Center for the Study of the American Jewish Experience for their friendship and encouragement, and particularly to Drs. Jacob R. Marcus, Benny Kraut, Alexandra S. Korros, Abraham J. Peck, Murray Friedman and Rabbi Lance Sussman for specific suggestions, and for reading earlier drafts. The late Professor Julius Weinberg generously shared with me his ideas about a reader, and might have been a collaborator on this volume but for his premature death. I am also particularly appreciative to President Alfred Gottschalk of Hebrew Union College-Jewish Institute of Religion for his ongoing support of my research, to Louise Stern whose copyediting of this volume resulted in numerous improvements, to my parents, brother and sister-in-law for their love, and to Ruth Langer, who came into my life just as this volume was being completed, and who is responsible for the fact that a new chapter in my life is about to begin.

Once again, the Memorial Foundation for Jewish Culture generously underwrote some of the costs connected with this volume. The Foundation's support has done much to further both my personal scholarship and the broader work of the Center for the Study of the American Jewish Experience, and I am pleased to acknowledge its contribution here.

I have dedicated this volume to my teacher, colleague, and friend Dr. Jacob Rader Marcus, now in his ninetieth year. As a rabbi, scholar, teacher, and active participant in American Jewish affairs, Dr. Marcus, the dean of American Jewish historians, has devoted his entire adult life to the American Jewish experience. This dedication represents but a small token of my esteem for all that he has done, and cannot do justice to my deep personal indebtedness to him for favors far too numerous to mention. Happy birthday, Dr. Marcus! May you continue to bless us with your happy returns for a great many years to come.

Introduction

Jonathan D. Sarna

American Jewish history weds together two great historical traditions: one Jewish, dating back to the Patriarchs, the Prophets, and the rabbis of the Talmud, the other American, dating back to the Indians, Columbus, and the heroes of the Revolution. Bearing the imprint of both, it nevertheless forms a distinctive historical tradition of its own, now more than three centuries old. It is a tradition rooted in ambivalence, for American Jews are sometimes pulled in two different directions at once. Yet it is also unified by a common vision, the quest to be fully a Jew and fully an American, both at the same time. It is closely tied to Jews worldwide, and just as closely tied to Americans of other faiths. It is perpetuated generation after generation by creative men and women, who grapple with the tensions and paradoxes inherent in American Jewish life, and fashion from them what we know as the American Jewish experience—a kaleidoscope of social, religious, cultural, economic, and political elements that makes up the variegated, dynamic world of the American Jew.

In this volume, leading students of American Jewish life explore how the American Jewish experience developed and changed over time, from the colonial period down to the present. Organized chronologically, the selections highlight critical moments and issues in the past that helped to shape the present, as well as broader themes—the central tensions of American Jewish life—that recur like a familiar refrain generation after generation. No effort has been made here to be encyclopedic, to cover every name or every fact. Instead, the articles selectively profile the American Jewish experience, emphasizing essential features and trends, with detailed bibliographies appended for those who wish to fill out the larger picture.

The basic outline of this volume follows the traditional periodization of American Jewish history, and is organized into five parts: early American Jewry, the "German Period," the era of East European

Jewish immigration, the inter-war years, and the contemporary period ("the Holocaust and beyond"). This periodization serves to underscore the basic unity of the modern Jewish world, for it shows how currents of American Jewish life have been affected by events taking place far beyond the nation's shores. Within each of the five parts, attention is also paid to the American dimension of American Jewish history. Individual articles make the case both for American influence on American Jewish life and for American Jewish influence on American life, recognizing that American Jews, however strong their links to world Jewry, have still been integrally and intimately involved with the society in which they live.

In dealing with all of these historical periods, events, and influences, it is easy to lose sight of the overarching themes that characterize American Jewish history, distinguishing it both from the historical experience of other Americans, and from that of Jews in other times and places. Generalizations covering the entire American Jewish experience must obviously be approached with caution, and can never be considered definitive. <u>Still, there are four broad characteristic features and five ongoing challenges that seem to me to be critical to any serious effort at understanding what Jewish life in America, especially since the Revolution, has been all about.</u> They are summarized here in brief outline:

Belief in the promise of American life. The promise of American life—freedom, equality, opportunity—was what originally drew most Jews to America's shores, and for many it has proved a continuing inspiration. Jewish immigrants dreamed that in the New World the oppression and poverty that had so often been their lot elsewhere in the diaspora would disappear. While the more utopian of these expectations were naturally doomed to disappointment, the conviction that America represents the great hope of Jewry, a model for how Jews should be treated all over the world, has remained over the years basically unshaken. Some have looked to America as the anvil upon which a Jewish homeland in Zion should be forged. Others have insisted enthusiastically that America actually is Zion, sharing a common destiny with Jews, and cherishing values that are for all intents and purposes "Judaic."

Faith in pluralism. Cultural pluralism, a model of American society that promotes ethnic diversity as a positive good and rejects calls for Anglo-conformity or "the melting pot" as incompatible with America's democratic ethos, has been widely embraced by American Jews. America's chief exponent of cultural pluralism, Horace Kallen, was himself a conscious Jew, and his experiences as an American Jew helped give rise to his theory. By then, pluralism within the American Jewish community had already been achieved by default; there was no other way that Jews of so many different backgrounds and beliefs could coexist. The realities of American Jewish life—inner diversity on the one hand, minority status on the other—and the community's consistent ideological commitment to pluralism have thus happily reinforced one another. The result has seen this sociological model, born of necessity, transvalued into one of the central axioms of American Jewish life.

Quest for success. Based on a study of Jewish immigrant memoirs, Professor Moses Kligsberg has pointed to the importance of *takhlis*, an orientation toward final outcomes, ends rather than just means, as an important cultural attribute of East European Jewish immigrants. In fact, this orientation, akin to what Max Weber called "The Spirit of Capitalism," is part of a broader success-oriented mentality that has characterized the American Jewish experience as a whole. The quest for success motivated not only Jewish immigrants of every generation, but also their children who struggled to achieve what their parents did not. This goes far to explain American Jews' high rate of geographic and social mobility, their concentration in commercial and financial centers, particularly large, rapidly developing urban areas, and their willingness to venture into new frontiers, whether as peddlers in the West, as scientists in new fields of research, or as entrepreneurs venturing into newly emerging industries. Not that vaulting ambition was ever a Jewish monopoly in America; the "Horatio Alger" mentality extends far more widely. The characteristic, however, has in Jewish circles been particularly pronounced—with results that by any standard of measurement have been utterly remarkable.

takhlis

Commitment to Jewish survival. As a small minority, never reaching even four percent of the total population, Jews in America have always had to work at survival: losses through conversion, assimilation and intermarriage have been an ever-present threat. Spurred by this challenge, and motivated also by traditional religious values, American Jews from the colonial period onward have labored to create for themselves a self-supporting Jewish community: a network of individuals and institutions working together as a unit for the sake of Jewish fellowship, to provide for Jewish education and culture, to care for Jews in need, and to fulfill other functions as required in an effort to ensure the well-being of its members and the continuity of American Jewish life from one generation to the next. Looking beyond their own community, American Jews have also concerned themselves with world Jewry. Anti-Jewish outbreaks overseas, natural disasters affecting Jews, calls to relieve Jewish communities in need, and most especially appeals from Jews in the Holy Land have traditionally met with sympathetic American Jewish responses, based on the principle that "all Israel is responsible for one another." As Jews have done throughout their long history in the diaspora, American Jews have linked their own survival as a Jewish community to the survival of Jews elsewhere, and particularly (since 1948) to the State of Israel. This commitment, maintained through the generations, is summed up in a three word slogan popularized by the United Jewish Appeal—"We Are One!"

If these characteristic features of American Jewish life suggest a certain unwavering continuity over three centuries, the five challenges that have faced American Jews are of a different order. They have been a source of ongoing tension, for they pit basic values against one another, and sometimes demand that excruciatingly difficult choices be made. Fundamentally, all of these challenges are irresolvable, for they spring from dilemmas inherent in the very nature of the American Jewish experience itself. Yet, the existence of these challenges has in the final analysis also proved salutary, for confronting them has enormously enriched the lives of American Jews, and has provided an important stimulus for individual and communal creativity.

1. **Assimilation–Identity** Probably the foremost challenge of American Jewish life, this tension pits the desire to become American and to conform to American norms against the fear that Jews by conforming too much will cease to be distinctive and soon disappear. The problem is not unique to Jews; themes such as "adaptation vs. retention" and "accomodation vs. resistance" characterize all minority group history in America. In the case of Jews, however, the dilemma has been compounded for they form at one and the same time both a minority ethnic group ("the Jewish people") and a minority religion ("Judaism")—a fact that explains why, among Jews, assimilation has so often been linked to apostasy. Jewish tradition and history have been trotted out to legitimate a whole range of positions on this issue—everything from massive concessions to American ways, justified by "the law of the land," the "needs of the hour," and the virtues of "peaceful neighborly relations," to utter resistance to any form of accomodation, even with regard to dress, for fear of "following in the ways of the Gentiles." Since American Jewish leaders have been as divided as their followers in deciding what concessions to the majority culture American Jews should and should not make, answers have spanned the spectrum. None has ever proved totally satisfactory.

2. **Tradition–Change** While related to the problem of assimilation and identity, this historical challenge has been solely confined to the realm of religion. The spectrum here ranges from those who have insisted that tradition unites world Jewry, and that *any* changes are thus divisive and potentially disastrous (where will they end?), to those who have considered changes ("reforms") of one sort or another essential to Jewish survival, particularly given the number of Jews estranged from their religious heritage. All involved in this debate have been able to legitimate their positions on the basis of what they see as best for American Judaism. But the question of where (if at all) the demands of tradition and change must compromise has always defied solution. The challenge has been confronted anew every time another religious reform has been suggested—beginning early on in the nineteenth century with proposals to introduce choral singing and vernacular discourses into the synagogue, and continuing all the way down to contemporary proposals designed to alter the traditional place of women in synagogue life.

3. **Unity–Diversity** Just as general American life has long been challenged by disputes that pit the interests of the national government against those of the individual states, so too American Jewish life has seen a pervasive tension between the interests of the Jewish community at large and those of various subcommunities, defined by region, socio-economic background, religious orientation, or political ideology. The problem of the "one" and the "many" has been addressed throughout recorded history by covenants and federative systems, and at an organizational level this has been the tendency in American Jewish life as well. But the basic problem persists. On the one hand, American Jews have appreciated the benefits that unity brings in its wake, and have pledged their firm allegiance to the traditional Jewish value of *ahavat yisrael*, the expression of solidarity with fellow Jews of every sort. On the other hand, the innate diversity of Jewish life, the fact that there are many kinds of Jews and many ways to be Jewish, has encouraged a healthy respect for multiformity.

4. **Majority rule–Minority rights.** Woven into the fabric of American life, this tension also lies at the heart of American Jewry's historic relationship to the secular polity. On a host of domestic policy questions, especially those affecting church-state relations, American Jews have been forced to choose: should they subordinate American Jewish concerns to the larger will of the Christian majority, or should they demand that the wishes of the majority be cast aside so as to protect the Constitutional rights of the minority? Translated into concrete terms, this issue has, over the years, involved Jews in debates over such things as Sunday blue laws, the place of religion in the nation's

schools, and the public observance of Christmas. Foreign policy questions have not generated the same degree of controversy, but have demanded an equally difficult choice: should Jews subordinate themselves to the majority's international affairs agenda, or should they create a minority agenda of their own, highlighting issues like the protection of persecuted Jews around the world, and support for the State of Israel? The challenge has always been to find some means of preserving Jewish rights and interests without unduly offending majority sensitivities—a goal which, historically speaking, has proved much easier said than done.

5. **Historical experience–American exceptionalism** Is America different? This is, perhaps, the most vexing challenge that American Jews have faced. It pits their faith that America is somehow an exception, not subject to the same turnabouts that have so afflicted Jews elsewhere, against their bitter historical experience everywhere in the diaspora, even in countries like Spain and Germany where they also felt fully at home—until disaster struck. Evidence can be adduced on both sides. One side points menacingly to instances of vicious anti-Semitism scattered throughout the course of American history, warns that dangerous demagogues stand for election in America and often garner unexpected support, and cautions that prophecy is a very inexact science, the past being by no means a reliable barometer of what the future holds. The other side counters that America nonetheless *is* different, especially when compared to the experience of Jews in Europe. In America, they note, Jews never needed to be emancipated, and have therefore never worried about having their emancipation revoked. The nation's central documents guarantee Jews religious freedom, and its first president conferred upon them his blessing. Jews are only one of many persecuted minorities in America; national hatreds have as a result been varied and diffused. There has been in America a long-standing liberal religious tradition ("the great tradition of the American churches") that includes Judaism among the nation's great faiths, and advocates, just as Jews do, religious freedom and diversity, church-state separation, denominationalism, and voluntarism. Finally, proponents of this view point out that the two-party system, with close elections the rule and power widely diffused, makes anti-Jewish laws difficult to effect. Politicians have learned from experience that broadly based appeals aimed at all major blocs of voters prove far more successful at the polls than appeals to narrow provincialism or bigotry.

Whatever the future course of American Jewry proves to be, whether it goes down as the "great exception" in Jewish history or not, this much at least seems certain: that the future will be fashioned from the remains of the past. The characteristic features and ongoing challenges that have for so long helped to define American Jewish life, the events that have shaped it, the two great historical traditions drawn together within it—all these and more form the collective memory of American Jews, a repository of past experience now more than three hundred years in the making. What will become of that memory? What will American Jews learn from it? What will others derive from it?

Prophecy, Jewish tradition warns, is in our day given over to fools.

THE
American Jewish Experience

PART ONE
THE AMERICAN JEWISH COMMUNITY TAKES SHAPE

In 1654, twenty-three Jews from Recife, Brazil, sailed into the port of
New Amsterdam, seeking refuge from the Portuguese. This flight to
freedom marks the traditional beginning of American Jewish history.
But it took many decades before a viable Jewish community began to
take shape. In New York (formerly New Amsterdam), and later in
other port cities where Jews congregated, synagogues were gradually
established to meet communal needs, particularly in the areas of
worship, education, and charity. Jews also fought their first battles for
civil and religious rights. For the most part, however, early American
Jews concerned themselves with the basics of making a living. As
merchants and traders, they played a small but important role in the
expanding American economy.

    The articles in this section show how the American Jewish com-
munity developed and changed during three distinct periods in
American history: the Colonial period, the era of the American Revolution, and the early national period. During these roughly 175 years
many of the basic dynamics of American Jewish life were set—shaped
by the conditions of American life. Three challenges faced by early
American Jews particularly stand out: first, how to meld utterly
diverse Jews, immigrants from different countries with different traditions, into a cohesive community supported on a voluntary basis
alone; second, how to establish and safeguard the right of Jews to
differ from the Christian majority without prejudice; third, how to
preserve Jewish distinctiveness in an open society where Jews and
non-Jews could mix freely. These challenges met with no easy solu-
tions. Instead, they revealed early some of the basic tensions underlying American Jewish life—tensions between unity and diversity,
majority rule and minority rights, and, most important of all, between identity preservation and the assimilation of alien ways.

1654 (handwritten margin note)

3 periods (handwritten margin note)

3 challenges (handwritten margin note)

 (handwritten margin notes: ①, ②, ③)

3

CHAPTER

1

Jews formed only a minute element in Colonial America, not more than one-tenth of 1 percent of the population. Nevertheless, they deserve attention, for as Jacob R. Marcus points out in this essay, a summary of his three-volume work on the same subject, Colonial American Jews established patterns that shaped and characterized the lives of those American Jews who came later. Concentrated in urban centers and in largely mercantile occupations, intensely mobile, eager to better themselves economically, intent on achieving social, political, and religious equality without having to sacrifice Jewish traditions, Colonial American Jews were, from the start, distinctive enough from other Americans to be noticeable, and yet at the same time similar enough to their neighbors to allow for free interaction. Jews did face some restrictions and intolerance in the colonies—hardly surprising in a world that still viewed religious nonconformity of all sorts as a threat to social order. But in retrospect, mistreatment of Jews during this period seems less important than the rights Jews won in law, and the privileges frequently extended to them in fact. Compared with the Jewish situation in most of Europe, or even with the restrictions faced by Catholics, not to speak of the plight of Blacks in the colonies, Jews in the New World had much to be thankful for. Unsurprisingly, their numbers steadily increased.

In explaining Colonial American Jewish History, Marcus, taking his cue from the great American historian Frederick Jackson Turner, stresses the impact of the frontier: "If to be a frontiersman is to be a man who dares to hazard, then the Jews as a whole are America's frontiersmen par excellence." According to this view, Western American pioneers and Colonial American Jews shared many of the same qualities and attributes—"that buoyancy and exuberance which comes with freedom"—for both faced similar conditions. Other historians have pointed to the economic basis of Colonial America as the prime determinant of Jewish life in the period. Since, under the mercantile system, the colonies were supposed primarily to enrich the mother country, it made good economic sense to treat Jews well and encourage them to prosper. Colonies that admitted Jews frequently did so explicitly on these grounds. Yet another factor affecting conditions of Jewish life was the social character of Colonial American cities. Urban centers, filled with heterogeneous immigrant populations—peoples of different backgrounds and different religions—had to encourage a tolerant live-and-let-live attitude to prevent civil strife. This situation proved beneficial indeed to Jews, not only in the Colonial era but later as well.

The American Colonial Jew:
A Study in Acculturation

Jacob R. Marcus

"Jews"—people of Jewish origin—had been settling in the Western hemisphere since at least the early 1500s. The very first Marranos came with Columbus, and in less than a century they had spread throughout the Caribbean and found their way into Mexico (New Spain) and South America, but the Inquisition made it impossible for them to establish viable communities. It was not until the mid-1600s that the first overt Jewish settlements sprang up in the New World—in Dutch Brazil and Surinam, on Curaçao, and on English Barbados and Jamaica. These were soon to become large and cultured metropolitan communities, for the Caribbean basin was at the time far more attractive and more populous than the mainland provinces to the north. The most important American Jewries of the eighteenth century were to develop in Surinam and in the Islands.

When the Portuguese recaptured Brazil, a handful of Dutch Jews, fleeing north, found refuge in the Dutch trading colony of New Amsterdam, soon to become English New York. Their arrival on the Hudson River in 1654 represents the beginning of North American Jewish life. These twenty-three Jewish "Pilgrim Fathers" were followed during the next hundred years by immigrants from the Islands and from Spain, Portugal, France, Holland, Germany, and England. By 1730, Jews of Central European origin outnumbered their Iberian coreligionists in North America. The first settlers in the 1600s were characteristically traders who had little desire to remain, but a permanent community had been established by the turn of the century. The Jewish businessmen married, settled down, and began to raise families. Throughout the Colonial period, however, American Jewry would remain an essentially immigrant group. Up to the Revolution, some 70 percent of the presidents of the New York synagogue were foreign-born, and the men who assumed leadership of Colonial American Jewish life were, with one notable exception, all immigrants. Many of the émigrés were competent merchan-

by
1730

6

disers. Some of them had distinguished rabbinical ancestors; a few were unassorted misfits. The community's growth is reflected in the fact that there were about 250 Jews on the continent by the year 1700, whereas, by 1776, there were about 2,500. Jews never formed more than one-tenth of 1 percent of the Colonial population.

What prompted Jewish newcomers to set sail across the Atlantic? Was it a quest for religious freedom? The fact is that even the Dutch exiles from Brazil and the Spanish-Portuguese émigrés of converso ancestry who fled the Iberian Peninsula were not drawn to North American shores primarily for the sake of conscience; all of them could have found a haven in other lands, and if they came here, it was more often than not to better themselves economically. Nearly all of them sought, in addition, a measure of anonymity, an avoidance of public notice, for without exception they came from lands which still imposed disabilities on Jews and still enforced anti-Jewish laws of a medieval character. It is understood, of course, that these men would not have come to these shores if they had not been allowed to practice their faith. The immigrants took it for granted that they would be permitted to establish a community of their own.

Where did they settle? Some, to be sure, were found in the hinterland, but even they had trickled into the backcountry through the seacoast towns. Most Jews stayed well below the piedmont, in the tidewater areas. New Amsterdam–New York was the first and chief Jewish center, but only a short generation after the Brazilians arrived, a small settlement took shape at Newport, in the 1680s at the latest. That Rhode Island community did not last even a decade, however, and it was not until the 1740s that the New Yorkers, fanning out once again, reestablished Jewish life in Newport. Jewish newcomers, moving north, rarely bypassed the Rhode Island city; they tended to ignore Boston; apparently one center in New England sufficed them. That same decade of the 1740s saw the New Yorkers, in their southward trek, lay the foundations for a community at Philadelphia. Independently of New York, Charleston Jewry also established itself in the 1740s. Savannah, which had sheltered a substantial number of Jewish colonists in the 1730s, had already lost her first Jewish group by 1740, but, like Newport, would ultimately rebuild a durable Jewish settlement on the dead hopes of earlier émigrés. After the French and Indian War, New Yorkers moved up the Hudson and Lake Champlain to found a new congregation in Montreal.

It is obvious that nowhere in the fourteen provinces were Jews qua Jews ever openly denied the right to strike roots. By 1740, they were allowed the exercise of virtually every economic immunity and privilege. Not that such rights were obtained without a struggle! The Dutch in New Amsterdam, under the medieval-minded Stuyvesant, sought to deny them nearly all rights; yet it took no more than three years for them to wrest from the governor and his superiors in the Dutch West India Company the right to remain, to trade, to own land, and to hold worship services in private. These rights were extended under English rule, so that, even before the coming of the new century, England had, however reluctantly, accorded her American Jewish subjects full civil equality. In 1740, an imperial naturalization law confirmed the status of the Jew and offered him almost unlimited economic opportunity in the Empire as a whole as well as in the American provinces themselves.

Civil equality was not, of course, political equality. Jews in some colonies were certainly allowed the vote on a provincial and a local level, but they were nowhere permitted to hold honorific office. Such office was limited to Protestant Christians, especially those associated with the dominant or established church in each colony. On the whole, prior to the 1760s, the American Jew eschewed politics. Fourteen hundred years of Christian-imposed disabilities had taught him that political plums like lucrative offices were not within his reach, but this disability does not appear to have disturbed him before 1765. After all, the constant wars, the country's expanding economy, and the penetration of the West enabled the Jewish businessman to make a good living; he was simply too busy building an estate for himself and his family to concern himself with the fact that political appointments were denied him.

Still, when he was offered important communal committee assignments, he would seem to have gladly accepted them. Almost every town had some Jewish merchants of substance and wealth, and in the English world of mercantilism, the Jewish businessman, even if he could not sit in the Assembly, on the bench, or in the provincial council, was undeniably a part of the power structure. In Continental Europe, he could not have aspired to authority in the general community, for Jewry as an ethnic corporation was segregated by tradition and by the terms of separatist and divisive *privilegia*. The Colonial Jew, however, followed the developing pattern of English Jewry; he aspired to enter the general society within the ambit of a common unitary political system. He was not averse to office, to its opportunities and its responsibilities, nor was he indifferent to the improvement of his status. Ultimately the Jew here hoped to become one, politically at least, with the emerging American people and to be accepted as a full fellow citizen, but he was willing to bide his time. And his hopes achieved fulfillment, if as yet mainly on the federal level, in 1789.

The Jew of eighteenth-century America found his greatest opportunity in the world of commerce. Here, much more so than on the Continent, or even in England, he was almost exclusively a shopkeeper. To be sure, there were occasional dirt farmers in the northern provinces, and even an aristocratic planter on the South Carolina frontier, but farming was not the métier of these immigrants. Georgia Jewish merchants might hold good-sized ranches in the backcountry, and craftsmen, especially silversmiths, might be found in nearly every province, but the typical Jew was a businessman who owned a small shop. There he doled out credit to the customers who came to him for hardware, hard liquor, and dry goods. The successful shopkeeper became a merchant, and large-scale Jewish storekeepers were established even in the villages of Canada and as far west as Lancaster, Pennsylvania. The Montreal businessmen were primarily fur entrepreneurs, and Lancaster's outstanding merchant was well known as a supplier for the traders on the Ohio.

The important Jews in commerce were the tidewater merchant-shippers of Newport, New York, and Philadelphia. They exchanged American foods and forest products in Europe and the West Indies for consumer goods and for Caribbean staples like molasses, rum, sugar, and dyewoods. Sometimes, like the Jew who was Newport's commercial tycoon, they would participate in the African slave trade. Jewish merchant-shippers of that day were also industrialists, arranging through the put-out system for the manufacture of ships and barrels, the distillation of rum, the catching and processing of fish and whales, and the production of kosher and unkosher victuals for export. Above all, they were in the candle business. Indeed, it is no exaggeration to say that they constituted an important national factor in the manufacture of candles. Jews, however, were notably absent from the iron and tobacco industries, and though they included in their ranks substantial merchant-shippers, the total volume of their business, while it far exceeded their proportion to the population, was hardly determining in any field. The one exception, it might be said, was army supply: The most powerful Jewish commercial clan of the third quarter of the century was an Anglo-American family of army purveyors which reached its zenith during the French and Indian War. Like its Jewish counterparts in Europe, this clan carried on business operations reaching, at the very least, into the hundreds of thousands, if not millions, of pounds.

It may be fairly maintained that all but an infinitesimal number of North American Jews were to be included in a broadly conceived middle class. Some Jewish merchants were even wealthy by contemporary standards; practically none of the Jews were paupers, very few were proletarians, and a substantial number were lower-middle-class petit bourgeois shopkeepers and middle-class storekeepers and merchants. There were very few Jews who did not enjoy a degree of comfort; most of them made a "good living" and survived economically, though severe business reverses were by no means uncommon among them at some time or other.

The Colonial American Jewish community could be accurately described as a socioreligious group—or even a religiosocial group—whose members had grown up, for the most part, in the small towns of preindustrial Europe. Though they stopped to make no sharp distinctions between the religious and the secular, their orientation was definitely religious, and they were typically synagoguegoers. On their arrival here, they had immediately undertaken to set up de facto communities whose hub was, in every case, the house of worship. It was in a literal sense a meetinghouse. All newcomers were expected to join, to become paying members, or at least to attend the important services. Local Jewry was granted no state authority to compel membership, but social pressure generally saw to it that affiliation would be practically compulsory.

Even though religious devotions were undoubtedly held in every Jewish settlement as soon as the requisite quorum of ten adult males thirteen years of age or older could be mustered, the synagogue was not actually the first institution to be established. The first formal act was usually the acquisition of a plot of ground for a cemetery. Then came the synagogue. First the worshippers would rent a room, then a house; then they would purchase a building, and finally, they would erect a synagogue of their own. The synagogue-communal organization was of the simplest type, featuring a president, a small board, and at times a treasurer. Frequently the overburdened chief executive served also as secretary and treasurer; the major administrative duties were his. No rabbis—that is, no ordained, learned, professional officiants—were employed in North America prior to the second quarter of the nineteenth century. Colonial Jewry had no need for the services of experts to teach rabbinic lore to advanced students, or to sit as judges to adjudicate complex commercial disputes and matters touching on marriage, divorce, and estates. The chief salaried—or volunteer—officiant in every house of worship was the cantor, who chanted the liturgy. His ministrations were complemented by those of the shohet, who slaughtered food animals ritually, and the beadle, who served as the omnibus factotum for the board. These functionaries were certainly not overpaid, and all of them engaged in some form of gainful enterprise, on the side, to augment their incomes.

The liturgy employed by all the Colonial conventicles was the Sephardic or Spanish-Portuguese. Despite the fact that prerevolutionary American Jewry was overwhelmingly Ashkenazic (German-Polish) in ethnic origin, the Sephardic style had become the traditional American rite. Services were almost always held on the Sabbath and on all the holidays, though the difficulty of assembling ten busy adults often made it impossible to organize daily services. Ceremonial and ritual observance was expected of all Jews, even of those who lived in the backcountry, and the communal leaders attempted to exact conformity by threatening ecclesiastical punishments. The board was—or at least attempted to be—an authoritative body exercising discipline in religious matters over every confessing Jew in the region, but, unlike some of the Protestant sects, there was no effort to exercise surveillance in business concerns or even in the area of personal morals.

In the extant budgets of the country's chief synagogue, the largest items were salaries, pensions, and relief for the poor. It is true that congregants squabbled among themselves, often bitterly and vindictively, but generous provision was nearly always made for the needy and the impoverished. The

Jews took care of their own. Itinerants from the distant islands were "dispatched" back home at communal expense; Palestinian visitors were generously entertained and given gifts; and aspiring petitioners were granted modest loans to set them up in business. The sick received medical care, nursing, and hospitalization; the old were pensioned, and all the dead were buried at the expense of the community or for a purely nominal fee. Most Protestant groups also attempted to take care of their poor. Whether the Jews did more for their people than, for instance, Protestant sectarians like the Quakers, is difficult to determine, though a comparative study of budgets might answer this question.

Only to a limited degree was education associated with charity. Since the local community always included members who lacked the means to educate their children, the synagogal authorities never failed to provide a subsidized teacher for the children of the poor. Actually, however, the responsibility for providing instruction was the obligation of the head of the household; it was not a communal responsibility. Beyond question there had been private Hebrew instructors in New York City ever since the seventeenth century, and a communal Hebrew school was organized during the 1730s, at the latest, with all who had means paying tuition. Not all the children in the community had resort to the congregational school. Even in New York City—and this was certainly true of all the other Jewish communites as well—secular education was also acquired in private schools or through tutors.

The curriculum of the congregational school probably included the reading and translation of the prayer book and the Pentateuch, and at most some familiarity with the classical biblical commentaries. By the 1750s, this Hebrew school had become an all-day "publick school" teaching Spanish and the three "R's"—what we might call a "parochial" school. The language of instruction was English. The quality of the teaching in Hebrew was probably not too bad, for the first American-trained cantor is known to have had the capacity to consult the more elementary Hebrew codes. We have no way to gauge the quality of the instruction in "English reading, writing, and cyphering," but, since all Jewish children, even the humblest among them, were prepared for some form of business life, it may be assumed that the training the young natives acquired was adequate. Male immigrants with very few exceptions were literate. They could read English, write it phonetically at least, and keep a set of books. All were bilingual, for they knew English and Yiddish or German, or English and Spanish or Portuguese. A few had a third language at their command—Dutch, for instance—and some, if not many, were multilingual.

Exceedingly few young people were tempted to attend the country's colleges, although secondary schools were open to them in Rhode Island, New York, and Pennsylvania. Most Colonial Jews were not interested in the liberal arts as such, and professional training in law and medicine was not sought. The practice of medicine was not particularly lucrative, while lawyers were in bad repute throughout much of this period, and, if English precedent was determining, Jews would not have been permitted to practice in the courts. Prior to 1776, the American Jew wrote nothing in English worth preserving as a literary monument. The typical Colonial synagoguegoer, an immigrant, was too busy learning the language and making a living to achieve any facility or distinction in English letters; he could make no contribution even to the Jewish, let alone American, literary arts.

no controls to arts

What did their neighbors think of the Jews? Every Christian who came to these shores brought with him "invisible baggage": his European and pagan traditions going back for millennia. The West India Company in New Amsterdam never hid its distaste for Jews; the New York rabble, headed by a "gentleman," attacked a Jewish funeral cortege on one occasion, and the desecration of cemeteries was not uncommon. "Jew" was still a dirty word, and it was hardly rare to see the Jews denigrated as such in the press. A distinguished lawyer speaking in the New York General Assembly did not find it too difficult to rouse his fellow-members against the Jews as a people guilty of the great crime of the Crucifixion.

NB

Rejection does not tell the whole story, however, and one always does well to bear in mind that, if the Jewish businessman prospered in this land, it was because the Gentiles patronized him. Jews did not make a living by taking in each other's washing. There can be no question that the Jews here found more acceptance than in any other land in the world. Old-World traditions of Judeophobia were attenuated here. The Christian drama of salvation—a drama in which the Jew played the villain—was not dominant in molding public opinion in the colonies, for America offered everyone opportunity enough; there was no need to envy the Jew. In a society of Dunkers, Congregationalists, Moravian Brethren, Baptists, Christian Sabbatarians, Catholics, Methodists, Anglicans, Presbyterians (Old Side and New Side), Lutherans, Dutch Reformed, German Reformed, Mennonites, Schwenkfelders, a society of English, Scottish, Irish, German, Dutch, Welsh, Swiss, and Swedish settlers—not to mention Negroes and Indians—the Jew did not stand out too conspicuously. Christians in the villages and towns of the country discovered, sometimes to their dismay, that the Jews did not wear horns and that, if they had devil's tails and cloven feet, these were certainly not visible. The Christian who learned to know Mr. Judah, or Mr. Josephson, or Mr. Hays, or Mr. Gratz found that, after all, he was not so different, and the Jew was accepted. If he became a son-in-law, he was welcomed; he was a fine fellow.

pluralism

The Jew was accepted, but did he accept America? What was this man like? What was happening to him on this side of the Atlantic? Was he different here? What had he gained for himself? What did he do for others, for this country that generously gave him a haven and a new home?

Apparently he was still the same "eternal" Jew, still the European traditionalist, equally untouched by deism and by Protestant religiosity, whether of the decorous Anglican kind or of the less conventional emotionalism of the Great Awakening. Yet he was different, if only because he found himself in a different milieu, and this was bound to influence and change him. It was not simply that, instead of speaking Yiddish or a bad German, he now spoke fractured English and dressed like any middle-class Englishman. This young American Jewish community of which he was a loyal and exuberant member shaped itself on a "frontier" far removed from the European *Judengasse* and its age-old classical traditions. The New World challenged his Old World. In order to survive here, the Jew found it expedient to extemporize, to compromise, and all this, in the final analysis, spelt a form of emancipation. Europe had never offered him more than a second-class citizenship; here in America, however, he encountered less paternalism and a more sympathetic government. Here, after 1700, he had full civil liberties and even a degree of civic recognition. By 1775, he had come very close to achieving first-class citizenship.

America connoted economic opportunity, and this was of paramount importance: "Bread to eat and a garment to wear." He was no longer a peddler, a petty trader, a cattle dealer; he was now a shopkeeper, even a merchant. If only because of the "wealth" he was often enough enabled to accumulate in America, he became something of a community figure. Here he could rise on the social ladder; he could improve his status and even enter into the world of Anglo-Saxon education and culture. Here the Jewish heritage reached out to absorb a new language and new ideals: "democracy," "natural freedom," "dictates of humanity," "constitutional trial by jury," "to live free or not at all," "rights, liberties and immunities." He had acquired a new vocabulary.

When the Jew left Europe, he left behind him there—physically at least—the all-pervasive authority of the Jewish community. Ultimately, his departure from the European home was to effect a measure of spiritual distance as well. If Jewish orthodoxy in its most classical form was to be found then in Poland, the Jews of these colonies were as remote from it physically as a sailing vessel could carry them. America signified the ultimate frontier of Jewish life. Religious controls were inevitably relaxed here. There was much less concern about observance and ritual. The individual was far freer to do as he pleased. He could if he wished—and most commonly he did wish—pay much less attention to the rabbinic learning which, for a thousand years, had been the leitmotif of European Jewish life. The new American Jew, who was beginning to emerge on the Colonial scene, much preferred to be a successful merchant than a talmudic scholar. Yet this very Jew was not estranged from his faith, and the communities that studded the North American coast from Montreal to Savannah are eloquent testimony to his determination not to abandon his heritage.

The typical Colonial Jew was true to his heritage because he was not pressed to be untrue to it. There was no overwhelming, monochromatic culture here to force itself upon him. There was no national ethos to exact conformity of him. If he acculturated, it was by his own choice. Free here to express his religious loyalties, since the outside world imposed no religious limitations upon him and extorted no price of emancipation, he assimilated almost unwittingly and without hesitation. Slowly but surely he sloughed off Europe. He felt completely at home here. The Jewish immigrant—and this was very probably not characteristic of him alone—manifested an aptitude for acculturation and even for total integration. Bear in mind that he had come originally from a Portuguese city, a German *Dorf*, or a Polish hamlet; yet, when he appeared as an urban businessman, he was already an urbane American. He had speedily become acquainted with English amenities and often had even acquired an Anglo-Saxon name. If he finally settled in a Colonial village, it was usually only a matter of time before he married a Christian and permitted his wife to rear his children as she thought fit. But conversion to Judaism, formal or informal on the part of the woman, might also occur, though with much less frequency. In a way, it is astounding how easy it was for many an observant European Jew to forswear in a few years nearly twenty-seven centuries of hallowed tradition—seemingly without a struggle.

The Jew *was* different here. He had left the "ghetto" to become a pioneer on the American "frontier," a frontier which according to Frederick Jackson Turner gave its people

> coarseness and strength combined with acuteness and inquisitiveness; that practical, inventive turn of mind, quick to find expedients; that masterful grasp of material things, lacking in the artistic but powerful to effect great ends; that restless, nervous energy; that dominant individualism, working for good and for evil, and withal that buoyancy and exuberance which comes with freedom.

For Turner, the frontier that effected these changes in the American psyche was the "Great West." Yet a moment's reflection will remind the student that these enumerated characteristics bespeak the successful American businessman, Jew or Christian. Think of Thomas Hancock! Certainly for the professing Jew—who was never to become a backwoods hunter or an Indian fighter—all of America was a frontier. If to be a frontiersman is to be a man who dares to hazard, then the Jews as a whole are America's urban frontiersmen par excellence. As a group, they are, more than others, a "nation of shopkeepers," gambling with their future. (Actually, of course, the Diaspora Jew had always lived as a marginal man on the "cutting edge," where he had to struggle for survival juridically, commercially, and spiritually.) The Western frontier is in no sense important for the development of the American Jew; the Atlantic frontier is all important. It was determinative in changing him. It gave him his greatest opportunity in centuries to give free play to those traits that he had already brought with him and which had long been characteristic of him.

For the Jew, the style of life was different here. He learned to dispense with Slavic obsequiousness and Germanic servility. There was no need for him here to be submissive. Here he could be assertive—if that was his nature. If he possessed physical courage, America offered him ample opportunity to manifest it. He learned not to be easily cowed. Is there any doubt that it required moral courage to cross the broad ocean and to traverse the lofty mountains and the dark forests to distant Michilimackinac or the Forks of the Ohio? For the first time in centuries, the Jew felt free. He was no longer faced with the problem of treading softly in the presence of a virulent Judeophobia. It may have been hard for him, but he began to trust his Christian neighbors; he became less suspicious of them. They were his customers; often enough they were his partners in business ventures, and he learned to believe in them, for there is no intimacy greater than that of two men who are prepared to share profits and losses.

The Jew of the European village who could only dream of a great future had the chance here to prove his mettle. He could be venturesome, daring, and enterprising. Here there was an open road for the man of ambition. It was not ludicrous here to project gargantuan schemes. No one looked askance at the Christian-Jewish consortium which proposed to establish a western colony of millions upon millions of acres. America was one land where, more than any other, the Jew could fulfill his inmost self by attempting whatever career he wished. Here he could be an individual. With opportunity and achievement and the regard of others came self-respect and dignity. The Jewish merchant was conscious of his own works; he knew what he was doing for the land and the people—and it was good in his eyes. He was giving and getting. He had the pride of a merchant, and he expected recognition, not only socially, but in rights and privileges.

It is undeniable: The American Jewish businessman *was* more than a European who dressed and spoke like an Anglo-Saxon. His children, too, were different. The father may have been a Spaniard or a Pole or a native Briton, but the children through intramarriage with Jews of other backgrounds were something new. This was a Jewish melting pot that fused together the Jews of half of Europe's lands to produce a new ethnic type—an "American" Jew. This American Jew "in becoming" struck a balance between his European religiocultural loyalties and his emotional identification with the spirit of this land. In Europe, he had been an outsider; in this land, he blended with the others. Here there were a dozen different breeds and stocks pouring into one another to become one in a common environment with common interests. This man was among that dozen, and though he would never have admitted it, he was becoming less of a Jew and more of an American.

In 1711, a number of New York's Jewish businessmen generously contributed to the building of an Anglican church; some fifty years later, the Jews of Savannah were active in a nondenominational charitable society. Such participation by Jews in American philanthropy can take on meaning only if we remember that in most European lands at that time the Jew was still held in disdain and that in some countries he was even outlawed and in danger of massacre. But here in the colonies, he believed, he knew, that he was part of the body politic. It is true that he had his own way of life, but, unlike others, particularly some of the Germans, he never locked himself behind the walls of a cultural enclave. Of course, he was fully conscious of the fact that he was not yet a first-class citizen. He realized it only too well, but his resentment never impelled him to withdraw into himself. He was very much moved by the political unrest of his neighbors and shared their hopes. Like all dissenters and all who labored under legal disabilities, he was not satisfied with the status quo; he sought more rights and more opportunities. A large measure of freedom had already been accorded him, but the Revolutionary spirit of the 1760s unleashed in him the desire for an even larger measure. It was this hope that prompted Jews to throw in their lot with the Whigs. By 1775, even many of the most recent newcomers thought of themselves as Americans, and "as a man thinketh in his heart, so is he."

By 1776, the typical Jew in this land was an urban shopkeeper of German provenance in the process of blotting out his German ethnic past. Yet he was firmly, proudly, and nostalgically rooted in his European religious traditions. He spoke English by preference, had regard for Anglo-Saxon culture, and enjoyed the same civil rights as did his Christian neighbors. Socially, he was a cut above the masses, the farmers and the mechanics, for he was a shopkeeper or merchant. As such, he expected—and he received—a measure of deference.

What did this man achieve for himself? He moved Europe across the Atlantic, no mean achievement. Synagogues, schools, charities, a "community" were transferred here, nailed down and fastened, firm and viable and visible enough to attract hundreds and thousands of others who never would have come to a "waste howling wilderness" where there were no Jewish institutions. A dozen families in seventeenth-century New York laid the foundations for a twentieth-century community of nearly six million Jews. Colonial Jewry wrote the pattern of acculturation that made it possible for the Jew to remain a Jew and to become an American. The pioneers of the eighteenth century succeeded in making an exemplary transition from a still medieval European Jewish life to the new American world of modernism and personal freedom.

What did this man achieve for the land? Not that this Jew was conscious of it, but together with all dissenters—and every American denomination suffered disabilities in one or another of the provinces—he helped teach his neighbor religious tolerance. The fruit of this tolerance was respect for the personality of the individual. The prerevolutionary Jew made no contribution to the literature of the colonies; he cleared no forests and ploughed no furrow—yet he, too, built the land. He, as much as any other, made American life more comfortable through the necessities and luxuries which he provided. It is true that the trader needed his customers, but it is equally true that neither city craftsmen nor toiling rustics could exist without him. It is true, too, that in a literal numerical sense the Jew was one man in a thousand, but, in an economy where an overwhelming majority of all who labored made their living on the soil, it is difficult to overstress the importance of the shopkeeper and the merchant.

CHAPTER

2 An earlier generation of American Jewish historians studied the Revolutionary era in order to find Jewish heroes. They worked assiduously to locate the name of every Jew who fought for the patriotic cause, and stressed the contributions to American freedom made by such men as Haym Salomon, whose activities as a broker brought much-needed funds into the new nation's treasury. Today, American Jewish historians have other concerns. What is most important to them, as the title of the essay here demonstrates, is the impact of the American Revolution, how it affected the whole future shape of American Jewish life.

As we now know, the American Revolution marked a turning point not only in American Jewish history, but in modern Jewish history generally. Never before had a major nation committed itself so definitively to the principles of democracy and freedom in general and to religious freedom in particular. The Constitution's twin assurances—that "no religious test shall ever be required as a qualification to any office or public trust under the United States (Article VI)," and that "Congress shall make no law respecting an establishment of religion, or prohibiting the free exercise thereof (Amendment 1)"—meant for Jews that they could claim true equality in America, not mere toleration as was accorded them in even the most liberal of European countries. Religious pluralism had become a reality in America. Jews and members of other minority religions could dissent from the religious views of the majority without fear of persecution.

Momentous as this guarantee of legal equality was, it did not immediately translate for Jews into full social equality. As the following article demonstrates, Jews still had to fight for their rights on the state level, and they continued to face various forms of prejudice nationwide. Yet at the same time, as the article also shows, many Jews benefited materially from the Revolution and interacted freely with their non-Jewish neighbors. Having shed blood for their country side by side with their Christian fellows, Jews as a group felt far more secure than they had in Colonial days. They asserted their rights openly, and if challenged, defended themselves both vigorously and self-confidently.

The changes wrought by the Constitution, the effort to weave Jews into the fabric of the nation's social and religious life, and the early struggles to *maintain a Jewish life-style in the midst of a non-Jewish environment all serve as background to themes that appear over and over in the annals of American Jewish history. The number of Jews residing in America during this period may have been small, but the problems they faced were similar to those that Jews would always face in America's free environment. For this reason, the impact that the American Revolution had on American Jews is critical. It set in motion many of the forces that helped to shape the American Jewish community forever after.*

The Impact of the American Revolution on American Jews

Jonathan D. Sarna

2500

The American Jewish population in the late eighteenth century numbered about 2500, scarcely one-tenth of 1 percent of the national population. Jews' influence loomed far larger. Concentrated as they were in developing areas, Jews naturally became intimate with leading politicians and businessmen. Jewish merchants and non-Jewish merchants traded freely. Discriminatory legislation, though it existed in the colonies, rarely limited Jews' right to work and worship in peace. Indeed, Jews enjoyed far better conditions in the American colonies than in most other corners of the Diaspora.

Treatment of Jews did not, therefore, become the major factor determining Jewish loyalties in the struggle against Britain. Individuals based their decisions largely on business, national, and personal considerations. Many Jews vacillated, and pledged allegiance to both sides in the dispute for as long as they could. But when finally forced to choose, only a small minority sided wholeheartedly with the Crown. Most Jews came down on the side of the Whigs, and cast their lot for independence. They contributed what they could to the national struggle, shed blood on the field of battle, and, after the victory, joined their countrymen in jubilant celebration.

The Revolution had an enormous impact on Jewish life in America. Most immediately, wartime conditions caused massive human dislocations. Several families—among them the Gomezes, Frankses, Hayses, and Harts—divided into two hostile camps: Whig and Tory. A few British sympathizers, notably Isaac Touro, chazan of the synagogue in Newport, left the country altogether. Isaac Hart, a Jewish loyalist shipper who fled only as far as Long Island, was killed by patriotic Whigs. Some loyalists came in the other direction, from Europe to America. These were the Jewish Hessians, German soldiers employed by England's King George III (himself a German) to fight the rebellious colonists. Alexander Zuntz, the most famous Jewish Hessian, is credited with preserving Congregation Shearith Israel of New York's synagogue sanctuary during the period when the city was under British military control. Other Jewish Hessians settled farther south: in Charleston, South Carolina, and Richmond, Virginia. They seem to have met with mixed receptions from the Jews who preceded them there.

Supporters of the Revolution were no less mobile than their Tory opponents. A large contingent from Shearith Israel fled to Stratford, Connecticut, when the British moved on New York. Later, Philadelphia became the chief haven for patriotic refugees. Shearith Israel's minister, Gershom Seixas, moved there from Stratford in 1780. For Jews, as for non-Jews, war meant "fly[ing] with such things as were of the first necessity" when the British approached. Possessions that were left behind were usually lost forever.

wartime migrations

These wartime migrations had lasting effects. People who never had met Jews discovered them for the first time, and learned how similar they were to everyone else. Jews from different parts of the country encountered one another, and cemented lasting unions. A succession of Jewish marriages took place, as Jewish children made new friends. Finally, the distribution of Jews in the colonies changed. Newport, Rhode Island, formerly one of the four largest Jewish communities in America, had its port destroyed in the war. Its Jews scattered. The Savannah Jewish community also suffered greatly from the war's decimating effects. On the other hand, two cities that were spared destruction, Philadelphia and Charleston, emerged from the war with larger and better organized Jewish communities than they had ever known before.

In addition to geographical mobility, the Revolution fostered economic mobility among American Jews. Trade disruptions and wartime hazards took their toll, especially on traditional, old-stock Jewish merchants like the Gomezes and Frankses. Their fortunes declined enormously. On the other hand, adventurous entrepreneurs—young, fearless and innovative upstarts—emerged from the war wealthy men. Haym Salomon bounded up the economic ladder by making the best both of his formidable linguistic talents and of his newly learned advertising and marketing techniques. He and his heirs seem not to have adapted so well to the inflationary postwar economy, for when he died his family became impoverished. Uriah Hendricks, and Hessian immigrants like Alexander Zuntz, Jacob and Philip Marc, and Joseph Darmstadt rose to the top more slowly. But by the early nineteenth century all were established and prospering. Generally speaking, the postwar decades were years of progress in the United States. Opportunities were available, and Jews, like their non-Jewish neighbors, made the most of them.

new mobility

In order to take advantage of postwar economic opportunities, Jews sometimes compromised their ritual observances. They violated the Sabbath; they ate forbidden foods; and they ignored laws regarding family purity. War conditions had encouraged such laxities: The few Jews who struggled to observe the commandments while under arms are remembered precisely because they were so unique. Postwar America also encouraged such laxities.

violated mitzvot

While religious denominations scrambled to adapt to independence, many parishioners abandoned their churches for other activities. "Pious men complained that the war had been a great demoralizer. Instead of awakening the community to a lively sense of the goodness of God, the license of war made men weary of religious restraint," John B. McMaster observed. He likely exaggerated. Historians no longer believe that the postwar religious depression was quite so severe. Still, McMaster's comment demonstrates that Jews did not simply leave Shearith Israel empty on Saturday morning for business reasons. They also were caught up in the lackadaisical religious spirit of the age.

No matter how lax Jews may have become in their observances, they did not abandon them altogether. To the contrary, they remained proud Jews; more than ever, they expected recognition as such from their non-Jewish neighbors. Jews viewed the War for Independence (and later the War of 1812) as an initiation rite, an ordeal through battle. Having passed the test—having shed blood for God and country—they considered themselves due full equality. They felt that America owed them a debt, and they demanded payment. Jonas Phillips made this clear in his 1787 appeal for rights directed to the Federal Constitutional Convention meeting in Philadelphia:

> . . . the Jews have been true and faithful whigs, and during the late contest with England they have been foremost in aiding and assisting the states with their lifes and fortunes, they have supported the cause, have bravely fought and bled for liberty which they can not Enjoy.

Gershom Seixas, Haym Salomon, Mordecai Noah, and a host of other Jews employed precisely the same arguments in their battles for equal rights. In Maryland, where the debate over Jewish rights was particularly prolonged, even non-Jews appealed to the "Jews bled for liberty" plea. Thomas Kennedy reminded his fellow citizens that

> during the late war [1812], when Maryland was invaded, they were found in the ranks by the side of their Christian brethren fighting for those who have hitherto denied them the rights and privileges enjoyed by the veriest wretches.

Jews and sympathetic non-Jews thus appealed to their countrymen's patriotic piety. They demanded that the Jewish contribution to America's "sacred drama" be both recognized and rewarded.

It took time before these demands met with full compliance. Many Americans apparently felt that Jews' pre-Revolutionary gains sufficed. They wanted the old Colonial status quo in religion to remain in effect. Under the British, Jews had eventually won the rights—sometimes in law, sometimes in fact—to be naturalized, to participate in business and commerce, and to worship. They suffered from disabling Sunday closing laws, church taxes, and special oaths, and they were denied political liberties. But devout Protestants considered this only appropriate. In their eyes, God's chosen people still labored under a Divine curse.

Protestant Dissenters—Baptists, Methodists, Presbyterians, and smaller sects—were not content with the old status quo. Their interest in Jews was minimal; the reason that they opposed the Colonial system of religion was because it permitted church establishments. Since most established churches relegated Dissenters to an inferior status, or refused to recognize them at all, Dissenting Protestants insisted that church and state should be completely separate, and church contributions purely voluntary. They defended these positions by appealing to the arguments of British dissenters and Enlightenment philosophers.

Dissenters couched their rhetoric in the language of freedom. They endeavored to convince traditional forces that liberty of conscience and diversity of belief would not open the door to licentiousness and immorality. The question, as they saw it, was merely one of liberty—the very question that had been decided in the Revolution. "Every argument for civil liberty," Virginia Dissenters insisted, "gains additional strength when applied to liberty in the concerns of religion."

"Liberty in the concerns of religion," to these men, undoubtedly meant liberty in the concerns of the Protestant religion. With the exception of Roger Williams, whom succeeding Colonial generations viewed as a dangerous extremist, prominent Dissenters generally failed to fight for the rights of Catholics, non-Christians, or nonbelievers. They feared that admitting them to equality would threaten the safety and moral fiber of society. Logically, however, Dissentist arguments on behalf of liberty of conscience and church-state separation should have applied equally to non-Protestants. There was simply a disjunction between the radical ideas that Dissenters espoused, and the social realities which they were prepared to accept. The Baptist leader, Isaac Backus, for example, argued nobly that "every person has an unalienable right to act in all religious affairs according to the full persuasion of his own mind, where others are not injured thereby." Yet, he lauded Massachusetts lawmakers for decreeing that "no man can take a seat in our legislature till he solemnly declares, 'I believe the Christian religion and have a firm persuasion of its truth.' "

The development of complete church-state separation in America—the post-Revolutionary development that was of greatest significance to Jews—can thus not be credited to Protestant Dissenters. Though they spread the idea of religious liberty, and so helped all minority religions, their battle on behalf of this principle ended with the victory of Protestant pluralism over church establishment. Jewish rights rather came about through the work of a second group of Revolutionary-era thinkers: those inspired by the ideas of Enlightenment rationalism. Classic Enlightenment texts—among them the works of Locke, Rousseau, Grotius, Montesquieu, Harrington, and Voltaire—found many readers in America. Leading patriots like Franklin, Jefferson, Adams, and Paine openly avowed deistic or Unitarian principles. For these men, a utilitarian belief in the value of "all sound religion" was enough. Some argued that government should go so far as to encourage religion—though not any one particular religion—as a force for social good. Others, more radical advocates of church-state separation, felt sure that reason alone would guarantee society's moral order. Both agreed that Protestantism, for all its benefits, was *not* a prerequisite for good citizenship.

The Enlightenment view of religious liberty, in one of its two forms, eventually gained the upper hand in America, though Protestant pluralists continued to struggle—with various degrees of success—for many years. In 1777, New York became the first state to extend liberty of conscience to all native born, regardless of religion. An anti-Catholic test oath was required only of those born abroad. Virginia's justly famous "Act for Religious Freedom (1785)," written by Thomas Jefferson, was both more comprehensive and more influential. It carefully distinguished civil rights from religious opinions, and decreed that "all men shall be free to profess and by argument to maintain their opinions in matters of religion, and that the same shall in no wise diminish, enlarge or affect their civil capacities." Once the national Constitution, in Article Six and Amendment One, wrote Virginia's version of religious liberty into federal law, the claims of Revolutionary-era American Jews to equal rights were finally conceded. At least at the national level, an epochal change in Jews' legal status had come about.

Constitutional guarantees were not binding on the states; they could legislate as they pleased. As a result, some legislatures—notably those in New England, New Jersey, Maryland, and North Carolina—enacted into law only the principles of Protestant pluralism. Jews who refused to avow their faith in the Protestant religion were denied equality in state government. The implications of this were absurd: Theoretically, a Jew could be President of the United States, but ineligible to hold even the lowliest political office in Maryland. Realizing this, a majority of states granted Jews full rights by 1830 (though New Hampshire held out until 1877). Full rights, however, had only limited effects on social equality. Many Americans still viewed Jews with the greatest of suspicion.

Jews realized that they could win equality in popular eyes only by demonstrating that being Jewish in no way conflicted with being American. They had to prove that non-Christians could still be loyal and devoted citizens. As we have seen, they had taken major steps in this direction simply by fighting in America's great war. This justified their being granted legal equality in the first place. The fact that America's great orators associated the mission of the United States with that of the ancient Hebrews (King George was Pharaoh; America was the Holy Land; Americans were God's chosen people) may also have redounded to Jews' benefit. But no single action and no single speech could break down centuries of popular prejudice. Jews had continually to prove their patriotism. The battle against anti-Jewish stereotypes was a never-ending one.

Even before the Revolution, Jews had taken scrupulous care to display their loyalty through energetic participation in government-ordained religious ceremonies, both fast days and days of thanksgiving. New York's Congregation Shearith Israel, for example, held lengthy special services in 1760 on "the Day Appointed by Proclamation for a General Thanksgiving to Almighty God for the reducing of Canada in His Majesty's Dominions." In subsequent years, it, along with other congregations, celebrated or mourned at times of battle, times of victory, times of pestilence, and times of achievement. After the Revolution, the identical pattern prevailed. In 1784, 1789, and then almost annually, Jews gathered in their synagogues whenever governments ordained special days of prayer. They only demurred when insensitive politicians issued proclamations directed only at American Christians.

The two most famous early American Jewish displays of patriotism occurred outside the synagogue. They were the 1788 celebrations connected with the Grand Federal Procession in honor of the newly ratified Constitution, and the 1790 congregational letters to President George Washington. The former, held in Philadelphia, symbolized in remarkable fashion the tension between the Jewish desire to belong and the Jewish need to be separate. Jews participated fully in the celebrations, and their "rabbi"—probably Jacob R. Cohen—walked "arm in arm" with "the clergy of the different christian denominations." Yet, at the conclusion of the ceremony, Jews ate apart—at a special kosher table set aside for them at the end of the parade route. This was appropriate: In the eyes of the Constitution all religions were equal, yet each enjoyed the right to remain distinctive and unique.

Jews made the same point in their letters to the President. These letters, by their very nature, were sectarian expressions of support; they dealt largely with matters of Jewish concern. Yet, Jews did not wish to be considered a people apart. The Newport Congregation therefore assured Washington that its members intended to "join with our fellow-citizens" in welcoming him to the city. But they still wrote their own separate letter. The President understood. He hoped that Jews would "continue to merit and enjoy the good will of the other inhabitants," even as each Jew individually sat "in safety under his own vine and fig tree."

Besides these displays of loyalty, Jews sought to "merit and enjoy the good will of the other inhabitants" by organizing their synagogues on democratic principles. They may have done so unconsciously, following the example of those around them. They certainly knew, however, that Catholics and others resisted the temper of the times and in many cases continued to organize their churches on an autocratic model. By choosing to imitate patriotic Protestants, rather than the more traditionally oriented religious groups, Jews sided with the native-born majority; in so doing, of course, they subtly courted its favor.

Formerly, American Jews had imitated the example of the Anglican Church, the church that was officially established in many of the colonies. Synagogues modeled themselves on the Bevis Marks Synagogue in England, and looked to the Mother Country for guidance and assistance. After the Revolution, congregations prudently changed their constitutions (actually, they wrote "constitutions" for the first time; before 1776 they called the laws they were governed by "Hascamoth"). They became more independent and discarded as unfashionable leadership forms that looked undemocratic. At Shearith Israel, in 1790, the franchise was widened (though not as far as it would be in other synagogues), a new constitution was promulgated, and a "bill of rights" was drawn up. The new set of laws began with a ringing affirmation of popular sovereignty reminiscent of the American Constitution: "We the members of K. K. Shearith Israel." Another paragraph explicitly linked Shearith Israel with the "state happily constituted upon the principles of equal liberty, civil and religious." Still a third paragraph, the introduction to the new "bill of rights" (which may have been written at a different time) justified synagogue laws in terms that Americans would immediately have understood:

> Whereas in free states all power originates and is derived from the people, who always retain every right necessary for their well being individually, and, for the better ascertaining those rights with more precision and explicitly, from [form?] a declaration or bill of those rights. In a like manner the individuals of every society in such state are entitled to and retain their several rights, which ought to be preserved inviolate.
>
> Therefore we, the profession [professors] of the Divine Laws, members of this holy congregation of Shearith Israel, in the city of New York, conceive it our duty to make this declaration of our rights and privileges.

Congregation Beth Shalome of Richmond followed this same rhetorical practice. It began its 1789 constitution with the words "We the subscribers of the Israelite religion resident in this place desirous of promoting divine worship," and contined in awkward, seemingly immigrant English to justify synagogue laws in American terms:

> It is necessary that in all societies that certain rules and regulations be made for the government for the same as tend well to the proper decorum in a place dedicated to the worship of the Almighty God, peace and friendship among the same.

It then offered membership and voting privileges to "every free man residing in this city for the term of three months of the age of 21 years . . . who congregates with us."

By inviting, rather than obligating, all Jews to become members, Beth Shalome signaled its acceptance of the "voluntary principle" in religion. Like Protestant churches it began to depend on persuasion rather than coercion. This change did not come about without resistance. In 1805, Shearith Israel actually attempted to collect a tax of ten dollars from all New York Jews "that do not commune with us." But the trend was clear. The next few decades would see the slow transition from a coercive "synagogue-community" to a more voluntaristic "community of synagogues." As early as 1795, Philadelphia became the first city in America with two different synagogues. By 1850, the number of synagogues in New York alone numbered fifteen.

The voluntary principle and synagogue democracy naturally resulted in synagogues that paid greater heed to members' needs and desires. Congregational officers knew that dissatisfied Jews could abandon a synagogue or weaken it through competition. In response to congregant demands, some synagogues thus began to perform conversions, something they had previously hesitated to do for historical and halachic reasons. Other synagogues showed new leniency toward Jews who intermarried or violated the Sabbath. Leaders took their cue from congregants: they worried less about Jewish law, and more about "being ashamed for the Goyim . . . hav[ing] a stigma cast upon us and be[ing] derided."

The twin desires of post-Revolutionary American Jews—to conform and to gain acceptance—made decorum and Americanization central synagogue concerns. In the ensuing decades, mainstream Protestant customs, defined by Jews as respectable, exercised an ever greater influence on American Jewish congregational life. Not all changes, of course, reflect conscious imitation. When Christian dates replaced Jewish dates in some congregational minutes, for example, the shift probably reveals nothing more than the appointment of a new secretary—a more Americanized one. When Jewish leaders consulted "with different members of Religious Incorporated Societies in this city," and followed their standards, they also in all likelihood acted innocently, without giving a thought to how far social intercourse had evolved from the days when Jews only observed non-Jews in order to learn what *not* to do. Some, however, were fully conscious that Jews' accepted point of reference had become respectable Protestantism, and they turned this knowledge to their own advantage. When Gershom Seixas haggled with congregational officers about a raise, for example, he offered to submit his dispute to "three or five citizens of any religious society" for arbitration. He knew that an appeal to Christian practice was the easiest way to obtain redress from his fellow Jews.

In the heady atmosphere of post-Revolutionary America, it was easy for Jews to believe that they were witnessing the birth of a new age, one in which they would be accepted as perfect equals if only they proved themselves worthy and eager to conform. Jews had shed blood on the field of battle. The Constitution had promised them more than they had ever before been promised by any Diaspora nation. President Washington himself had assured them of "liberty of conscience and immunities of citizenship." All that America seemed to demand in return was loyalty, devotion, and obedience to law.

Jews kept their side of the bargain. They displayed their patriotism conspicuously, and diligently copied prevailing Protestant standards of behavior. In return, they won many new rights and opportunities. Yet, they failed to receive hoped-for equality. Instead, popular anti-Jewish suspicions lived on, and reaction set in. Missionaries arose to convert Jews, and succeeded in rekindling old hatreds. Many Americans, especially those affected by religious revivals ("the Second Great Awakening") and anti-Enlightenment romantic currents, insisted anew that America was a "Christian country."

Social, cultural, and political changes had taken place, of course, and Jews benefited from them. The Revolution did have a permanent impact— one that distinguished post-Revolutionary American Jewish life from its pre-Revolutionary counterpart. But, viewed retrospectively, the Revolution was no more than a single important step in a much longer evolutionary process. Many more steps would be needed in order to transform American Judaism from a barely tolerated Colonial religion into one of the twentieth century's three great American faiths.

CHAPTER

3
According to Malcolm Stern, American Jewry's leading genealogist, the 1820s were a time in American Jewish history somewhat akin to our own. In the 1820s, as in recent years, American Jews were native speakers of English, in most cases second-generation Americans or more. Sharing as they did in the culture and prosperity of the new nation, they sought to conform to its mores and trappings. The dilemma they faced—one that runs through all American Jewish history—was how properly to conform while still maintaining intact some measure of Jewish identity.

For many the dilemma was easily solved. They married non-Jews, raised their children to be Christians, and disappeared from the pages of Jewish history. Given the enormous difficulties many Jews had both in finding Jewish mates and in living Jewish lives—according to one researcher Jews formed less than 0.03 percent of the population—the greater wonder may be that more did not follow this route. This may be a tribute to tradition, identity, and Jews' stubborn insistence that they must somehow survive as a people. Whatever the case, it is clear that the survival strategies of these early Jews—their search for a viable American Jewish identity—anticipated much that would come later.

The leading American Jew of this period was Mordecai Noah, a man who at one time or another was a diplomat, journalist, politician, sheriff, playwright, and judge. While holding these lofty positions, he not only identified himself openly as a Jew, he also became a spokesman for the Jewish community. He worked to educate Christians about Jews, he sought to encourage increased Jewish immigration, and he defended Jews against those who sought to convert them. He once even tried to set up a Jewish colony—Ararat—on Grand Island, New York. But although Noah defended Jews, he also talked about the need for them to change some of their ways. He served as a living symbol of the fact that Jews could rise in American society without having to forfeit their faith, even as he implied that compromises with tradition could not be avoided.

This tension between tradition and change, between the lure of American life and the requirements of Jewish law, appeared simultaneously on many fronts in the 1820s. Stern cites demands for religious reform, particularly in

M. NOAH

29

Charleston, remembered today as the place where American Reform Judaism was born. He also offers examples of traditional Jews whose religion had fallen into disuse. Yet at the same time, he presents striking expressions of Jewish pride of heritage, especially in response to those who attempted to deny Jews equal rights, or sought to convert them. The picture, in short, is a mixed one. Many native-born Jews found themselves torn by conflicting emotions, pulled simultaneously in different directions, and uncertain as to what the future would hold.

The 1820s: American Jewry Comes of Age

Malcolm H. Stern

The decade of the 1820s saw the development of a truly American Jewry. For the first and last time until our own generation, the majority of American Jews were English-speaking, many of them second- and even third-generation (or more) Americans. Some of them had the time and the means to advance themselves culturally and educationally. Their interests extended beyond making a livelihood. They were busy exploring ways of adjusting to their environment, concerned with their identity as Jews, and anxious to help their less fortunate Jewish brethren overseas.

Between 1790 and 1820 the general population of the United States grew from 3.9 million to 9.6 million, while the Jewish population—according to a conservative survey—grew only from 1,500 to 2,700. That period coincided in Europe with the French Revolution and Napoleon, with their promises of liberty, equality, and fraternity. The upheaval of war and the promise of civil betterment made emigration from Europe less appealing to the Jews of France and Germany. The flow of Jewish immigrants to America slowed to a bare trickle. The defeat of Napoleon and the subsequent Congress of Vienna brought the return of anti-Jewish legislation in many German states, but the postwar economy on both sides of the Atlantic was not conducive to emigration from Europe. Despite the revival of "Hep! Hep!" riots in South German towns in 1819 and increasingly burdensome restrictions against them, it was not until the 1830s that German Jews emigrated in any appreciable numbers. The Jewish immigrants who began coming in ever larger numbers in the 1820s were chiefly of Dutch and British origin. These had lived long enough in lands of emancipation to have thrown off ghetto traditions and, therefore, blended easily into the American scene.

Meanwhile, in the American communities, the children and grand-children of the Colonial Jews were growing up as American Jews. The majority of those who resided in the cities where congregations existed were identified with the congregation, even when a mixed marriage occurred. Those in the more isolated communities found it more difficult to retain Jewish identification, but a number succeeded. Girls as well as boys were given classical education in academies or through private tutors. The arts were avidly pursued. One example of these trends is the Moses Myers family of Norfolk. Until he was impoverished by the impossibility of commercial shipping during the War of 1812, Moses Myers had been a prosperous merchant. In the first decade of the nineteenth century, he sent his oldest son, John, on a grand tour of Europe; his second son, Samuel, was the first Jewish matriculate at the College of William and Mary and became a lawyer; all his sons attended the Norfolk Academy; his daughters, tutored at home, could play the spinet and sing. Gilbert Stuart painted portraits of Moses and his wife; Thomas Sully painted one of John. Their Federal period home in Norfolk, Virginia, preserved with many of its furnishings, is a model of tastefulness. Their library, with volumes in French as well as English, and the nearly eight thousand letters that have survived, attest to the family's literate interests and abilities.

Perhaps the prototype of the evolving American Jew was Mordecai Manuel Noah, whose father and grandfather served in the Revolution. On his mother's side, he was a fifth-generation American. He grew up in his grandfather's Philadelphia home, taking advantage of Benjamin Franklin's Library Company of Philadelphia, the local theater, and "Poor Richard's" advice on manners and morals for a young man of character, while acquiring a passion for politics, journalism, and playwriting which became his joint career. With mixed success, Noah had already been by 1820 U.S. Consul at Tunis, editor of his uncle's pro-Tammany newspaper, and favorite orator of the New York Jewish community. The same environment that allowed Jews like Noah to feel truly American and to try any endeavor produced a growth of Protestant evangelism and conversionist activity among Jews in Europe and America. Jews invariably overreact to attempts at conversion of Jews, and Noah's reaction was to propose the creation of his proto-Zionist colony on an island in the Niagara River, Ararat. Although, in his lifetime, Noah was to achieve far greater prominence for his journalistic and political activities, it is for Ararat that he is best remembered. The experiment, and his dedication of it, as well as its failure, have been frequently noted and analyzed as idealistic, utopian, ridiculous, impractical, and the like. Suffice it to say here that it represents one of the flowerings of American Jewry's "coming of age." The dedicatory ceremony, so flamboyant and dramatic, is an early American public-relations scheme, the product of a fertile mind accustomed to journalism and drama.

Noah's Ararat is only the best known of a number of activities that evolved in the 1820s on the American Jewish scene. Another attempt at colonization and resettlement was carried on by Moses Elias Levy, a native of Morocco, who developed a successful lumber business in St. Thomas before becoming a purchasing agent for the Cuban government in 1816. Attracted by the potentialities of northern Florida, then under Cuban administration, Levy purchased a tract of land which he later traded for a more accessible plot. The latter carried with it the stipulation that at least two hundred colonists had to be settled on it within three years. This sent Levy traveling to Europe and the United States. He arrived in Philadelphia on June 28, 1818, and began to seek out leading Jews in the eastern seaboard communities, proposing the establishment of Jewish agricultural communities and a school for the education of Jewish children. He found enthusiasm for his project among the above-mentioned Moses Myers family of Norfolk, especially with Samuel Myers, the father of two infant sons. Levy carried on a lively correspondence with Samuel Myers, suggesting that the religion in their proposed community be reformed in consonance with the efforts of Israel Jacobson in Prussia. Through the Myers family, Levy obtained an introduction to Rebecca Gratz of Philadelphia, but made an unfortunate impression on that lady by arriving a day late and failing to remember that it was Sukkot! The opening of government lands in Illinois led Israel Kursheedt of Richmond and Moses Myers of Norfolk to purchase thirty-four patents, consisting of 5,440 acres, with Levy holding a quarter interest in Kursheedt's twenty-one patents and a one-third share in Myers's thirteen patents. Unfortunately, Moses Myers and Son went into bankruptcy and the land was lost. Undaunted by this and by his own financial reverses, Levy succeeded in interesting the Reverend Moses Levy Maduro Peixotto, Mordecai Manuel Noah, and Judah Zuntz, of New York's Congregation Shearith Israel, in joining him in the call to establish at least the boarding school for Jewish children, and a circular to this effect, dated May 9, 1821, was sent to Moses and John Myers, and their son- and brother-in-law, Philip I. Cohen, in Norfolk. Nothing came of the project, due probably to the inability of those involved to raise funds and to the fact that Levy, the guiding spirit, had left for Florida, whose entrance into the United States had just been ratified. Levy's energies were subsequently devoted to the development of his Florida properties. Like Noah, he was unsuccessful in persuading European Jews to settle on his lands. He did, however, go to Europe for three years, 1825–1828, and engaged in active polemics in England against con-versionist activities.

These conversionist activities instigated the creation of America's first Jewish periodical, *The Jew; being a Defense of Judaism against all Adversaries and Particularly against the Insidious Attacks of "Israel's Advocate."* In twelve issues, published between March 1823 and February 1825, editor Solomon Henry Jackson denounced and derided the leadership of the American Society for Ameliorating the Conditions of the Jews, founded 1820, and its publication,

Israel's Advocate. When that society's project of a Christian-Jewish community fell through because of lack of converts, Jackson felt that he had achieved his major purpose and stopped publishing.

To be as openly denunciatory of Christians in print as Jackson was testifies further to the security of the American Jew. So does the freedom with which Jews wrote directly to the President of the United States. On April 17, 1818, Mordecai Noah participated in the dedication of the second Mill Street Synagogue in New York. His discourse, a paean of praise for America and the Jewish religion, urged the Jew to take advantage of the opportunity America afforded for the development of the best in his faith and as a temporary Zion. When the address was printed, Noah sent copies to former Presidents Adams, Jefferson, and Madison, and received replies from all three. Noah's example was followed by Dr. Jacob De La Motta when he dedicated Savannah's first synagogue building on July 21, 1820. When his address, extolling the liberty enjoyed by the Jews in America, was printed, De La Motta sent copies to Jefferson and Madison and received complimentary replies. Joseph Marx of Richmond sent Jefferson a copy of the proceedings of the French Sanhedrin, convened by Napoleon to draft civil law for the Jews of his empire; this too was acknowledged with an expression of compassion for the Jews.

Jews were not hesitant about soliciting federal appointments. When bankruptcy hit in 1818, John Myers of Norfolk sought from President Monroe an appointment as commissioner of claims, citing his service in the War of 1812 as aide-de-camp to General Winfield Scott. This appointment was not forthcoming, but nine years later, John's father was recommended by John Quincy Adams to the Senate for appointment as collector of customs of the Port of Norfolk. The appointment was ratified on January 15, 1828, naming him also superintendent of lights and agent for the Marine Hospital, which Moses held until his resignation on March 28, 1830.

A reflection of the growing liberal spirit in American public life is the battle for ratification of the "Jew Bill" in Maryland. As early as 1797, Solomon Etting and his father-in-law, Barnard Gratz, prevailed upon Assemblyman William Pinkney to introduce a bill to abolish Maryland's requirement that anyone dealing with the law was required to declare his belief in the Christian religion. The bill, reintroduced annually, was defeated. In 1818, a Jeffersonian Democrat, Thomas Kennedy, took up the cause, but it was 1826 when a compromise version of the bill finally franchised the Jews of Maryland. Solomon Etting and Jacob I. Cohen were promptly elected members of the Baltimore City Council.

As indicated above in Moses Elias Levy's correspondence with Samuel Myers, the Jews were feeling a need to Americanize their religious practices. At a time when Christians were experimenting with new approaches to religion, Canadian-born Moses Hart, in 1815, published *General Universal*

Religion (republished in New York in 1818 as *Modern Religion*), in which he proposed a universal religion with special prayers, rites, theology, commandments, and nature festivals, all derived from the rationalism of the eighteenth-century Deists and the French Revolution. The book ran to a third printing and aroused interest, if not followers, at least as far south as Norfolk, for a copy of the 1818 edition was in the Myers family library.

A more serious attempt to remain within a Jewish traditional framework was the effort of forty-seven Jews of Charleston, South Carolina, to reform the worship in Congregation Beth Elohim. When the Adjunta (Board) rejected their request, the Reformed Society of Israelites was born on January 16, 1825, under the leadership of Isaac Harby. Their reforms were those which were to dominate Reform Judaism for more than a century and a quarter: sermons and prayers in the vernacular, abbreviating the service, the abolition of freewill offerings at worship to be replaced by dues, the abolition of auctioning *mitzvot*, dignity and decorum in the conduct of worship. As might be expected, the majority of this group were English-speaking, with at least thirteen native Charlestonians among them. The group grew to the point of raising funds for a synagogue, but economic problems in Charleston led to the migration of Harby and other leaders to New York, and the panic of 1837 brought the coup de grâce to the society.

Meanwhile, in 1825, rebellion against synagogue traditions began to appear in New York. So many members were abandoning the wearing of the *tallit* (prayer shawl) in Congregation Shearith Israel that the board voted to deny calling to the Torah anyone who failed to wear a tallit. It is significant that the punishment for infringement was so mild, an evidence of the breaking down of the authority of the synagogue. In another instance, Barrow E. Cohen, a comparative newcomer to the congregation from England, either willfully or from ignorance failed to make a charity pledge when called to the Torah. He was called on the carpet by the board. Partially as a result of the somewhat high-handed treatment of Cohen, a group calling itself *Chevra Chinuch Nearim* petitioned the Board for the right to hold services apart from the regular worship of Shearith Israel. Since the majority of the group were younger, recent arrivals from Europe, lacking the leisure to attend worship during working hours, they wanted pre-breakfast services. They also sought greater democracy in rotation of officers. This was a strictly Orthodox group; their one reform demand was for a person to preach weekly in English. Once again vested authority denied the right to change, so a new congregation was born, Ashkenazic B'nai Jeshurun, New York's second congregation. Such was the influence of America that the twenty-two-year-old Isaac Leeser, only four years out of Germany, could publish a series of six articles in defense of the Jew in the *Richmond* (Va.) *Whig*. These won for him a call, the following year, to serve as minister of Philadelphia's Congregation Mikveh Israel. A year later—in 1830—he began regular preaching in English, an innovation that was to earn him the epithet of "reformer" from his congregants, although to the later evolving Reform Judaism he was the champion of Orthodoxy.

The 1820s saw the movement of Jews away from the East Coast into the hinterland. A tiny group of English Jews met for High Holy Day worship in Cincinnati in 1819, but it was not until January 4, 1824, that they formed Bene Israel Congregation, now Rockdale Temple. Jews, chiefly from Charleston, moved into the South Carolina state capital at Columbia during the 1820s. In 1822 a burial society was organized, subsequently constituted as the Hebrew Benevolent Society. Presumably the Jews met also for worship, and Congregation Tree of Life dates itself from 1822. A pious Jew, Jacob S. Solis, came to New Orleans late in 1827 and was shocked to discover that although the community had at least twenty-five adult Jewish males, no congregation had been formed. Late that year or early in 1828, Solis succeeded in organizing "The Israelite Congregation of Shangarai-Chasset." As in New Orleans, Jews had been living in Baltimore since the last decades of the eighteenth century. The 1820s saw major growth of the Jewish community, but it was not until 1829, with the arrival of Zalma Rehiné from Richmond, that a minyan was formed—it convened in his home. The following year the Baltimore Hebrew Congregation was chartered.

The emergence of the Jew in the Christian communities in Europe and America, combined with the desire to convert him, led to a romanticization of the Jew. The thesis that the American Indian was a descendant of Israel's Ten Lost Tribes had long fascinated Protestants, producing such works as Elias Boudinot's *Star in the West* (Trenton, 1816). William Brown's two-volume *Antiquities of the Jews* (Philadelphia, 1823) paved the way for numerous editions of William Whiston's *The Genuine Works of Flavius Josephus*, which had been printed in America as far back as 1794. But no Jewish figure captured the popular imagination more than Rebecca of Walter Scott's *Ivanhoe*, published in American editions simultaneously in New York and Philadelphia in 1823.

Thus the 1820s can be seen as a productive, creative period for the tiny American Jewish community. Certainly word of Jewish freedom and self-assuredness must have reached abroad, for the following decade saw a new outpouring of immigrants from Europe.

What lasting results did the events of the 1820s have? Noah's dream of Ararat and Levy's colony for Jews in Florida, as well as the latter's Jewish boarding school, were too visionary. However, Levy did bring non-Jewish colonists to Florida at his own expense and developed some areas of that state. His son, from whom he became estranged, changed his name to Yulee and was elected Florida's first U.S. Senator. Levy Lake is named for the father, Levy County and the town of Yulee for the son. As the general and Jewish population of the United States grew, the relationships to the President became more formal, and fewer Jews sought and secured presidential appointments. The Maryland "Jew Bill," although not the last civil-rights stumbling block for Jews (it was 1877 before Jews and Catholics could hold office in New Hampshire), was undoubtedly the last in a state that had a sizable Jewish community. Jackson's periodical, *The Jew,* served its purpose and died; it was 1843 before its successor, Leeser's *Occident,* was born. Hart's *Modern Religion* was too radical and visionary to have an effect. The Reformed Society of Israelites was ahead of its time, but its goals penetrated into Beth Elohim, the Charleston congregation which had rejected them, and found fruition in Baltimore's Har Sinai (1843), New York's Emanu-El (1845), and Philadelphia's Keneseth Israel (1847)—although these groups were more influenced by ideas imported from Germany than by those planted in Charleston. New York's first Ashkenazic congregation, B'nai Jeshurun, was to spawn a whole series of landsmannschaften. Isaac Leeser, a product of 1820s thinking, became the most influential Jewish religious leader of his generation. The new congregations in Columbia, Cincinnati, New Orleans, and Baltimore were to provide manpower and inspiration for the creation of other congregations in the hinterland. The romantic image of the Jew was dissipated in the nativist Protestant-Catholic struggles of the 1840s and 1850s and in a growing anti-Semitic sentiment from which America has never been totally free. As for the American Jews of the 1820s in the succeeding decades, they found themselves inundated by German-born, German-speaking immigrant Jews with whom they had little in common. Consequently, the native-born Jews became more rapidly assimilated, often intermarried, and in many cases disappeared from the Jewish scene.

FOR FURTHER READING

The most comprehensive study of Jews in Colonial America is Jacob R. Marcus's three-volume opus, *The Colonial American Jew* (1970), summing up his lifetime of research in the field. Marcus's earlier two-volume work, *Early American Jewry* (1951, 1953) and his *American Jewry, Documents, Eighteenth Century* (1959) contain some of the source material upon which his later synthesis is based. Other documents are reprinted in Morris U. Schappes's invaluable *A Documentary History of the Jews in the United States, 1654–1875* (3rd. ed. 1971), which contains primary sources relating to all the subjects dealt with here in parts one and two.

Arnold Wiznitzer, "The Exodus from Brazil and Arrival in New Amsterdam of the Jewish Pilgrim Fathers," *Publications of the American Jewish Historical Society* 44 (1954), pp. 80–97, recounts the story of the twenty-three Jews who arrived in New Amsterdam in 1654. Asser Levy, the most famous of the twenty-three, is the subject of Malcolm H. Stern's "Asser Levy—A New Look at Our Jewish Founding Father," *American Jewish Archives* 26 (April 1974), pp. 66–77. Doris G. Daniels, "Colonial Jewry: Religion, Domestic and Social Relations," *American Jewish Historical Quarterly* 66 (March 1977), pp. 375–400, and Leo Hershkowitz, "Some Aspects of the New York Jewish Merchant and Community, 1654–1820," *American Jewish Historical Quarterly* 66 (September 1976), pp. 10–34, survey other social, economic, and religious aspects of Colonial American Jewry based on wide-ranging source materials.

The basic survey of Jews in the Revolutionary era is Samuel Rezneck's *Unrecognized Patriots: The Jews in the American Revolution* (1975). Richard B. Morris, "The Role of the Jew in the American Revolution," in Gladys Rosen (ed.), *Jewish Life in America* (1978) is a thoughtful, well-researched assessment by a leading American historian. For key documents, see Jacob R. Marcus (ed.), *The Jew and the American Revolution: A Bicentennial Documentary* (1975), and Jonathan D. Sarna, Benny Kraut, and Samuel K. Joseph (eds.), *Jews and the Founding of the Republic* (1985).

The complex question of Jewish rights in early America has been studied colony by colony and state by state in Abraham V. Goodman, *American Overture: Jewish Rights in Colonial Times* (1947) and in Stanley Chyet's "The Political Rights of the Jews in the United States: 1776–

1840," *American Jewish Archives* 10 (April 1958), pp. 14–75. Oscar and Mary Handlin surveyed the subject from a broader perspective in their "The Acquisition of Political and Social Rights by the Jews in the United States," *American Jewish Year Book* 56 (1955), pp. 43–98. The battle for Jewish Rights in Maryland, a unique case, is carefully detailed in Edward Eitches, "Maryland's 'Jew Bill,' " *American Jewish Historical Quarterly* 60 (March 1971), pp. 258–280.

The most comprehensive survey of Jewish life in America in the decades immediately following the American Revolution remains the massive three-volume documentary edited by Joseph Blau and Salo W. Baron, *The Jews of the United States 1790–1840: A Documentary History* (1963). Jonathan D. Sarna's *Jacksonian Jew: The Two Worlds of Mordecai Noah* (1981) details the life of the period's foremost Jewish leader in the context of his times. Sarna's "The American Jewish Response to Nineteenth Century Christian Missions," *Journal of American History* 68 (June 1981), pp. 35–51, sheds light on the subject of Jewish-Christian relations during this period, and Lou H. Silberman, "American Impact: Judaism in the United States in the Early Nineteenth Century," in A. Leland Jamison (ed.), *Tradition and Change in Jewish Experience* (1978) puts Jewish religious reforms of the day into proper perspective.

PART TWO

THE "GERMAN PERIOD" IN AMERICAN JEWISH HISTORY

German Jews began to immigrate to American shores in substantial numbers in the 1840s. Their origins were humble, and many began life in America trudging wearily over back roads, heavily laden with peddlers' packs. But with the American economy growing at a rapid pace, opportunities soon knocked, and German Jews took advantage of them. Over the next eighty years they prospered, established Jewish settlements throughout the country, created new social, religious, and cultural institutions, assumed positions of communal leadership, and effectively reshaped the American Jewish community along new lines. So pronounced was German Jewry's influence on American Jewish life that the entire period of their hegemony is commonly referred to as American Jewish history's "German period." This is somewhat of a misnomer since Jews from German-speaking lands formed only a fraction of those immigrating. Other Jews came from Poland, elsewhere in Europe, and outside Europe too, and for the same reasons: economic distress, outrageous persecutions, restrictive laws, and the failure of movements aimed at revolution and reform. It was, however, largely German Jews writing in the German language who gave this period its distinctive character. In not a few cases, Jews born elsewhere passed themselves off as Germans—that was one way of achieving status.

The articles in this section trace the influence of German Jews in such widely diverse areas as religion, culture, politics, and business. They portray a community flushed with economic success, actively involved in the world around it, intensely proud of its German-Jewish heritage, and fiercely determined to gain acceptance into the American mainstream—but not at the cost of abandoning Judaism itself. In time, America's German Jews stopped being German; some also stopped being Jewish. But German Jewry's overall impact on American Jewish life continues to be felt. Reform Judaism, B'nai B'rith, the American Jewish Committee, the National Council of Jewish Women, Hebrew Union College, and a host of other movements, institutions, and organizations—religious, social, cultural, and philanthropic—testify to the rich inheritance that German Jews bequeathed to those who came later.

CHAPTER

4

Germany stood at the center of western Jewish life during the nineteenth century. Its rabbis, scholars, and lay leaders were the leading Jewish luminaries of the day, renowned throughout much of the Jewish world. They labored tirelessly to bring Jewish life and culture into line with the demands of the modern age. By comparison, the American Jewish community was culturally underdeveloped. German-trained Jews who arrived in America frequently expressed shock both at how little American Jews knew of their faith and at how few resources existed for those who wanted to learn more.

The obvious solution to this problem was to make German-Jewish works available in America, either in their original or, better yet, in translation. Gradually this was accomplished. As time went on, however, many American Jews pressed for cultural independence. They felt, as Americans generally did, that their country's distinctive character and growing importance on the international scene made continued dependence on imports of any sort both inappropriate and undesirable. They came to believe that American Jews needed an American Judaism—one that was uniquely their own.

In the article that follows, Michael A. Meyer, a leading historian of German Jewry, examines this fascinating chapter in American Jewish history in careful detail. He concerns himself with the "discernible tension between forces making for preservation of the German Jewish heritage . . . and those which pressed in the direction of greater spiritual independence." He shows how German Judaism, at first venerated in America and held up as a model to be emulated, eventually came under severe attack—"even by those German Jews in America who owed it the most."

Meyer refers to two American Jewish religious leaders who merit particular notice. The first is Rabbi Isaac Leeser (1806–1868), an Ashkenazi Jew   Leeser
born in Neuenkirchen, Prussia, who immigrated to America at age eighteen and became spiritual leader (chazan) of the Sephardic congregation Mikveh Israel in Philadelphia. Single-handedly, Leeser undertook to create the major Jewish books and institutions—everything from English translations of the Bible and the prayerbooks, to Jewish textbooks, to the first significant Jewish periodical in America, and much more—that to his mind American Jewry

43

needed to have in order to survive as a Jewish community. He became the chief exponent of what would later become known as <u>enlightened Orthodoxy,</u> and was, in Meyer's words, "one of the principal Americanizers of German Jewry in the United States."

The second great American Jewish religious leader of this period was Leeser's main adversary in America, <u>Rabbi Isaac Mayer Wise (1819–1900).</u> Wise immigrated to America from Bohemia in 1846, and soon became the country's leading exponent of Reform Judaism. His contributions were as notable as Leeser's: books, periodicals, religious organizations, and the establishment of Hebrew Union College. He too was an Americanizer, convinced that American Jews needed a ritual (Minhag America) and a rabbinate distinct to itself. But where Leeser stressed the importance of tradition and confined his modifications largely to aesthetic areas of the service and the sermon, Wise sanctioned religious reforms of a considerably more radical nature, including changes in the form, language, and content of prayers, and the abandonment of many hallowed rituals. Each man thought that his strategy was best suited to preserve Judaism from the challenges it faced in its new American setting.

Differences between these two men reflected broader ideological and religious conflicts raging through American Jewish life during this period, conflicts that divided both the rabbinate and the laity. But ultimately these conflicts paved the way for the creation of an American Judaism that exhibited a full spectrum of beliefs and practices: everything from thoroughgoing traditionalism to the most far-reaching of innovations. This spectrum, allowing for limitless diversity in Jewish life, still adheres. It is one of the German period's most lasting and important legacies to later generations.

German-Jewish Identity in Nineteenth-Century America

Michael A. Meyer

Between 1825 and 1875 the Jewish population of the United States grew from about 15,000 to about 250,000. The vast majority of the immigrants in this period came from Germany, initially from the villages and small towns in Bavaria and other southern states, later also from northern Germany. They came on account of legislative restrictions limiting Jewish marriages and choice of occupation, but especially to better themselves economically. Few at any time came solely because of the attraction of American political ideals. Those who could stay usually remained. Particularly in the first half of the century the German-Jewish immigrants were mostly young, male, and poor, ill-educated Jewishly, and with little if any secular culture. Modernized German Jews began to come to America only in the 1850s and then again after the Civil War. All but a few intellectuals spurned emigration at any time. Many of the early migrants moved to small towns in the American South and Midwest, peddling inexpensive items and maintaining in America the rural patterns of life with which they were familiar in Germany. The rapid urbanization of Jews in Germany only after mid-century was paralleled by the German-Jewish experience in America.

Most of the early German immigrants had little time for matters either Jewish or German. They struggled to make a living and, if possible, to improve their economic lot. Their occupational situation required gaining a basic knowledge of the English language, considerable freedom from ritual constraints, and full devotion to the great American enterprise of "making money." But if Americanization was the key to economic success, it was also engaged in out of a sense of gratitude for what the new land offered. To be sure, supporting oneself in America was not easy, and some succumbed to the hardship, but there were no artificial barriers to advancement for those who combined skill or intelligence with hard work. In their initial drive to establish themselves economically, the early emigrants rarely looked back

45

46   *Michael A. Meyer*

upon Germany with any nostalgia. They had never really identified as Germans either politically or culturally. Most spoke and wrote only Judeo-German, not the German of Moses Mendelssohn; they were unacquainted with the classics of German literature. Germany represented for them predominantly the restrictiveness that they had been pressed to flee; positively, the old country meant little more than the landscape of their childhood.

Leaving Bavaria or Württemberg also meant leaving behind the pervasive religious atmosphere of its Jewish communities. Judaism in America was represented by the well-established Sephardim whose congregations those German Jews interested in religion initially joined rather than transplanting their own rite. Although there were considerable numbers of German Jews in America in the eighteenth century, the first successful Ashkenazi congregations were not established until the 1820s. And even after the creation of German synagogues, the trend to association with the more Americanized, prestigious, and dignified Sephardi congregations continued in some German-Jewish circles well into the nineteenth century. It is noteworthy that one of the principal Americanizers of German Jewry in the United States, Isaac Leeser, though himself born in Westphalia, served a Sephardi congregation, Mikveh Israel, in Philadelphia. Yet the Ashkenazi members were often treated as pariahs by the Sephardim and regarded with some contempt by more German-conscious Jews. Rabbi David Einhorn used to call them "Portugiesen aus Schnotzebach." As long as the German Jews were neither themselves Americanized nor brought with them any significant modern cultural baggage from Germany, the Sephardi elite presented the best exemplar of what a modern American Jewry should be like. But as German Jews appeared in the United States in ever greater numbers, as those who came had increasingly undergone modernization in Germany, and as the earlier immigrants from Germany found more time for culture and religion, a specific German-Jewish identity in America began to emerge.

As early as 1807, a member of the Bleichröder family, then resident in New York, had written that Jewish immigrants to America were considerably more cultured than those who were born in the country. Although this purported correlation between newness to the American scene and higher cultural level may not have held in the succeeding decades, it was generally true half a century later. As larger numbers of acculturated German Jews came to the United States, the process of Americanization slowed considerably. Germany ceased to be merely a land of origins and its Judaism no longer seemed inappropriate to the American context. For more than a generation after mid-century, American Jews of German origin looked across the ocean for direction and inspiration.

The more favorable attitude of American Jews to things German was

Gen'l
Germ.
immigr.

influenced by the rising respect accorded German culture in the United States. Jews constituted only a small portion of the five and a half million Germans in America, according to the census of 1850. By the 1860s it was widely felt that Germany had much to offer America and even that the mission of its emigrants was to conquer the New World for German values. While not all cities became as Germanized as Milwaukee, Cincinnati, or Saint Louis, the German immigrants sought minimally to preserve certain elements of their old life in the New World. The most obvious attribute of their cultural origins was the German language. Immigrant churches in America fostered the mother tongue, as did a variety of social, fraternal, and philanthropic societies. German-language newspapers flourished. Thus, while earlier Judeo-German-speaking Jews had no support in the American context for retaining their language—and as a result Americanized very rapidly—German-speaking Jews were part of a larger language group that encouraged their endeavors to preserve the German heritage.

Still in the 1840s Jewish parents usually did not attempt to teach their children German. When Rabbi Max Lilienthal served in New York during that period, he was forced against his will to give confirmation instruction in English. In the next two decades, however, a considerable proportion of the Jewish immigrants made determined efforts to pass the German language—and hence German culture—on to their children. In 1856, on a visit to Easton, Pennsylvania, Isaac Leeser complained that there, as elsewhere, parents in the Jewish school insisted on having German as the vehicle of instruction. Three years later Rabbi Bernhard Felsenthal of Chicago estimated that 90 percent of the present Jewish generation in America either knew only German or knew it better than English. Despite assimilatory pressures, German Jewry in America had considerable success in maintaining the German tongue. Still in 1874 the *Deutschamerikanisches Conversationslexicon* pointed out that in the majority of some four hundred Jewish communities in the United States the German language predominated. And even a decade after that, Rabbi Isaac Mayer Wise noted that in a number of congregations English-speaking children were still having to learn their catechism in German while the German language was taught in the Sabbath schools "as if it were a part of Judaism."

While English usually had to be used in business, the German tongue was retained in the sanctuary of the home, as the language of the family. Women immigrants especially continued to read and speak mostly German. To a high degree it became the language of the synagogue. Congregational records were kept in German, in one case—Rodeph Shalom of Philadelphia—after they had been written in English for a number of years. More important, and for a longer period of time, German served as the language of sermons and portions of the liturgy. Orthodox congregations no less than Reform ones wanted preachers who could deliver religious discourses of the type familiar to them from Germany. But for some Reform leaders the use of German in the synagogue was not merely a concession to familiar structures and expressions, not simply a passing phase in the process of Americanization. Felsenthal noted that the younger generation should learn German because the German people were still the leading cultural influence in the world "and we bow our heads in reverence before its spirit . . . we American-German Jews." The German tongue, it seems, was thought essential for modern spirituality even in America. Germany, said Rabbi David Einhorn, was the "land of thinkers, presently the foremost land of culture and, above all, the land of Mendelssohn, the birthplace of Jewish Reform. . . . Now if you remove the German spirit or—what amounts to the same thing, the German language—you have torn away the native soil and the lovely flower must wither." Without the German language, Einhorn believed, the Reform movement was nothing but a shiny veneer. It was a manikin without heart or soul; neither proud temples nor magnificent chorales could breathe any life into it. Hanns Reissner was right when he claimed that for the first generation of Jewish immigrants to America and beyond, German became nothing less than a "sacred language."

NB

The retention of the German language was strengthened by the usually favorable relations between Jewish and gentile immigrants. The Christians who took the initiative to leave Germany were less likely to have been under the influence of anti-Jewish prejudices than those who remained, and once they arrived most of them readily accepted the American value of social equality. When Jews reached America with German professional training, having fled German discrimination, they were—ironically—hailed as representatives of superior German university training. With few exceptions, Gentiles welcomed Jews into German cultural societies whose counterparts in Germany would likely have excluded them. German Jews could feel like insiders in these groups while they still remained outsiders in America.

Educated Americans gave considerable attention to German-Jewish writers, encouraging Jews to take pride in their former compatriots. Emerson, a great fancier of German literature, had also read Moses Mendelssohn; Heine was repeatedly translated into English by Americans, his poetry and essays frequently discussed. American periodicals mentioned the popular German-Jewish novelist Berthold Auerbach more often than any German author except Goethe; and for a time Auerbach was possibly more widely known in America than any other German writer. Jews and non-Jews came together in celebration of their common cultural heritage. Thus it occurred that German Jews in America continued the modernization process begun in Germany within an imported German context, thereby paradoxically slowing down their assimilation to modern America.

Even Jews who had not attained a formal education while still in the old country sought to make up for it once they had established themselves economically in America. They created their own literary societies and listened to lectures in German on diverse topics. In Philadelphia, a Gabriel Riesser Society was in existence for many years. Religious leaders established German-language Jewish newspapers and German sections for those published in English. Isaac Mayer Wise's popular *Die Deborah* went on for nearly half a century, from 1855 to 1902. A new Jewish intellectual journal, *Der Zeitgeist,* was established in Milwaukee as late as 1880.

German Jews in America broadened the framework of organized Jewish life, which for the Sephardim had been centered strictly upon the synagogue. They formed a panoply of independent fraternal and charitable associations perhaps patterned in part upon such long-standing German-Jewish models as the *Gesellschaft der Freunde* and the *hevrot* of the German communities. Yet the manner of raising funds—dinners, charity balls, lotteries, and the like—was strictly American. The most significant early association founded by German Jews in America was the B'nai B'rith, which originated in New York in 1843 and was apparently modeled upon Freemasonry. By 1851 there were eleven lodges, all but two conducting their transactions in German. Unlike the synagogue, which in the 1850s was already dividing traditionalists from reformers—and which left out those German Jews who had become wholly indifferent to religion—B'nai B'rith could include all German Jews within a framework that was secular without being secularist. Indeed, it has recently been suggested that B'nai B'rith in America initially served the function of a "secular synagogue." As such, it enshrined and exercised the culture and mores of German Jewry. Like the German-language synagogue, B'nai B'rith thus served as a brake upon assimilation by creating a unique amalgam of peculiar Jewish symbolism and transplanted German values.

One of the reasons that German Jews looked to their old homeland for inspiration was that they had not yet produced in America the equivalent of a Heine or a Riesser. In the nineteenth century American Jewry remained outside the cultural establishment to a greater degree than was true in Germany. Despite discrimination, a number of Jews in the old country had gained professorial chairs by the 1880s. There were notable Jewish philosophers, writers, poets, artists. But here in America, lamented an anonymous writer in a German-Jewish periodical, Jews "have contributed nothing either in art or in science." They had failed to produce men of the political stature of an Eduard Lasker or the literary merit of a Berthold Auerbach because the German spirit had insufficiently penetrated American Jewry, which—alas—was too much concerned with outer show and too little with inner content. For this writer—and for others—Germany meant the life of the spirit while America meant chasing after the almighty dollar.

As American Jews admired their German brethren for contributing so richly to general culture, so too they estimated highly their work as modern scholars of Judaism and bearers of Jewish religion and culture. Abraham

Geiger's *Jüdische Zeitschrift für Wissenschaft und Leben* had its readers and contributors in America, as did Ludwig Philippson's *Allgemeine Zeitung des Judentums*, the more traditional *Israelitische Wochenschrift*, and Samson Raphael Hirsch's neo-Orthodox *Jeschurun*. American rabbis praised and depended upon the work of Leopold Zunz and his fellow workers in the vineyard of *Wissenschaft des Judentums*. By comparison, American Jewish culture remained weak and immature. Still in 1878, Bernhard Felsenthal protested that American Jewry could not yet be expected to produce significant scholarship on its own. A few years earlier, in 1866, he wrote that American rabbis could only be trained in Germany, preferably in Berlin where they could study with Zunz, Steinschneider, and other teachers at the Ephraim'sche Lehranstalt. In the 1870s the Hochschule Für die Wissenschaft des Judentums drew students from America, including Felix Adler, who soon thereafter left the Jewish fold to found the Ethical Culture movement, and Emil G. Hirsch, who became a prominent Reform rabbi in Chicago. A decade later, Bernard Drachman, afterward a teacher at the Jewish Theological Seminary in New York, and Morris Jastrow, who became a professor of Semitics at the University of Pennsylvania, were the first American-born Jews to study at the Breslau Jüdisch-Theologisches Seminar.

In order to provide for the younger generation, which was not fully at home in the German language, American Jews began translating into English major works of German-Jewish thought and scholarship. Among the most active translators were the most Americanizing of the Jewish leaders in the United States, Isaac Leeser and Isaac Mayer Wise. Leeser, who also did English translations of the Hebrew Bible and prayerbook, produced an English version of Mendelssohn's *Jerusalem* in 1852. In rapid succession, Wise contributed to the *Asmonean* English excerpts from the writings of Zunz, Geiger, Frankel, Rapoport, Luzzatto, Krochmal, Holdheim, Jost, and Graetz. Others produced similar gleanings for English-language Jewish periodicals. In 1865, Geiger's *Judaism and Its History* appeared in New York, and all three works published by the predecessor to the present Jewish Publication Society during its three-year existence from 1872 to 1875 were translations from the German. The first major project of the society's later successor in name and task was a slightly abridged translation of Graetz's multivolumed history, which appeared between 1891 and 1898. In terms of Jewish culture and scholarship, Jews in America up to the last decades of the century appreciatively accepted the hegemony of German Jewry.

What was true for the realm of culture was true almost to the same degree in the area of religion. Here too German Judaism became the model. American Jewish leadership was not closed to specifically American influences, but

Germ. Juda - model in religion

until it gathered strength, until it recognized that American Jewry was destined to overshadow its nineteenth-century German source, it ascribed religious authority to the German thinkers who had tried to create post-ghetto Jewish ideologies and to the innovations that had modernized the German synagogue. Especially was this true for the Reformers, but not for them alone. The traditionalist, Isaac Leeser, for example, greatly admired the Berlin rabbi Michael Sachs, whose position on the religious spectrum he represented in America, and both he and those who shared his religious views have been regarded as American exponents of Zacharias Frankel's positive-historical Judaism. When American Jews sought to adapt their religious institutions to the modern world, they looked to the German example as a guide. The extent to which their religious leaders minimized or maximized the German connection seems to have depended largely on how deep their own German experience had been. Neither Leeser nor Wise had German university training or much direct acquaintance with the intellectual ferment in German Jewry during the first half of the century. Most of those who were especially tied to Germany—like Rabbis David Einhorn, Samuel Adler, and Samuel Hirsch—had both. Upon arrival, they set out to make American Judaism a true copy of the German original. Only gradually did they begin to claim that it possessed a lovelier form and a rosier future than the model upon which it was fashioned.

Much has been written about the first efforts at religious reform in the United States, which took place in Charleston, South Carolina, beginning in 1824. It seems evident that those members of Beth Elohim, a Sephardi congregation, who sought to introduce decorum, an English sermon, a few prayers in the English language, and somewhat later an organ, were motivated by specifically American influences, especially by Protestantism in the city. Yet even at the beginning they expressed awareness of religious reform in Holland and Germany. And when Gustav Poznanski, who had lived in Bremen and Hamburg, became preacher and reader of the congregation in 1836, he brought with him the spirit of the Hamburg Reform Temple—which, it must be remembered, had embodied Sephardi elements in its pronunciation of Hebrew, in the melodies used for the liturgy, and in the formulation of certain prayers. Some of the English hymns, published by the congregation in 1842, were adapted from the Hamburg Temple's *Gesangbuch*, and the memorial service on the Day of Atonement was taken from its prayerbook. A little later Beth Elohim introduced the confirmation ceremony, based on the ritual formulated by Rabbi Leopold Stein of Frankfurt.

For modernizing Ashkenazi Jewish congregations in America the Hamburg Temple ritual served as the chief model. A native of Hamburg living in Baltimore helped to found the first specifically Reform congregation in America, Har Sinai, in 1842. He was commissioned to present to the members a description of the Temple's prayerbook, which amidst great controversy had just appeared in a revised edition. It was thereupon adopted and apparently used until David Einhorn introduced his own prayerbook in 1856.

Temple Emanu-El of New York, which held its first service in 1845, did not begin a process of rapid reform until more than a decade later. But from the beginning its choir sang chorales from Munich and Vienna while members listened to sermons in German, at first by Ludwig Merzbacher of Fürth and later by Samuel Adler. Not until 1868 did the congregation elect a second professional preacher whose task it was to address the congregation in English. Without doubt the introduction of reforms did reflect—as Leon Jick has argued—the upward mobility of the congregation. But it is worth noting that David Einhorn attributed the slow progress of reform at Temple Emanu-El to the disproportionate influence of the small "aristocratic Portuguese element" in the congregation—just that element that was the most established in American society. Moreover, it must be stressed that the reforms which were eventually introduced were nearly all precedented in Germany, that the leadership was well aware of German examples, and that despite increasing wealth, the ambience of Temple Emanu-El and similar congregations in New York and elsewhere remained for decades more German than American. If Reform was motivated solely by the desire for rapid Americanization, its Germanic character remains inexplicable.

Increasingly the German congregations in America were populated by men who had been influenced by the modern rabbinate in Germany. In Baltimore and Cincinnati, there were former students of Leopold Stein; in New York, men who had been instructed as children by Samuel Adler and David Einhorn. Not surprisingly, the wealthier German synagogues in America soon sought to obtain as their rabbis leading figures from Germany. Abraham Geiger twice refused offers; Leopold Zunz, a contributor to the first German-language American Jewish periodical, *Israels Herold*, was considering a possibility in New York as early as 1833. Others did come, at first mostly lesser-known individuals (except Max Lilienthal) and then more prominent names after mid-century. German speakers continued to dominate the American rabbinate as late as 1872, when an editorial in *The New York Herald* took note of how few men were capable of giving sermons in English.

The outstanding Germanizer among nineteenth-century rabbis in America was David Einhorn who, beginning in 1855, successively occupied pulpits in Baltimore, Philadelphia, and New York. His influence, through his prayerbook, *Olat Tamid*, his intellectual journal, *Sinai*, and through the perpetuation of his ideas by his similarly inclined sons-in-law Emil G. Hirsch and Kaufmann Kohler, was ultimately more decisive for Reform Judaism in America than the less radical ideas of Isaac Mayer Wise. While Wise, the proponent of Americanization, was by far the more popular and practically effective leader, it was Einhorn's philosophy that dominated the Reform movement in Amer-

right to claim that it possessed a history at all. For Jewish history in its proper sense, Frankel held in common with his colleague, Heinrich Graetz, consists of endurance in the face of suffering on the one hand and of spiritual creativity on the other. But American Jewry had never had to struggle for its survival and it had not—at least as yet—produced a significant religious or scientific literature. Thus American Jews would simply have to recognize that they had yet to enter Jewish history. Not surprisingly, when Graetz published Volume Eleven of his *Geschichte der Juden* in 1870, he devoted only a solitary sentence and a half to the Jews of America. Even in the later English edition, Graetz included no more than a single paragraph on the subject.

One of the most positively inclined to American Judaism within the German-Jewish religious leadership was Abraham Geiger. Especially was this true at the end of his life after he had taught American students at the *Hochschule* in Berlin. Geiger encouraged his friend, David Einhorn, in the difficult task of transplanting the German spirit to the tumultuous environment of America, submitted material to his periodical *Sinai*, and pointed Kaufmann Kohler to the United States as the land of promise for progressive Judaism. While he believed that American Jewry still lacked maturity, he could appreciate its hopeful freshness and even admit that perhaps the German Jews were like the biblical Reubenites who reached their patrimony first, aided their brethren, but did not themselves settle in the promised land. It was only when the American rabbis dared to challenge his wisdom that Geiger became defensive—or rather, a bit aggressive.

In preparation for the Leipzig synod, held in the summer of 1869, Geiger had composed a list of theses on liturgy and marriage laws which he wanted that assembly to consider. Later the same year, eleven American Reform rabbis gathered in Philadelphia in order to deal collectively with religious issues and especially with questions of marriage law. The participants included all the major American Reformers, ranging from the most radical to relative moderates, like Wise and Moses Mielziner. One of them, Kaufmann Kohler, had just arrived from Germany and been present at the Leipzig synod. Of course, the Philadelphia deliberations were conducted in German and references were made to Leipzig and to Geiger's theses. A series of resolutions, ranging from the theological to the practical, was adopted and speedily became known in America and in Europe. On a number of points the resolutions deviated from Geiger's theses—to his very great displeasure. In the tone of a father castigating his wayward sons, the veteran German Reformer now chastised the Philadelphia gathering for straying from the proper path. The conference "must give up all petty jealousy toward the old homeland," he wrote in his *Zeitschrift*. "It should rather recognize spiritual depth as it is nurtured in Germany and participate in it, utilizing without conceit the greater freedom in practical matters given them by their circumstances." With all his sympathy for American Jewry, Geiger could not yet reconcile himself to German Jewry's being on the periphery rather than at the center of religious modernization—or to his views being ignored or contradicted by his colleagues in America. Perhaps he also recognized that, for all its German character, the Philadelphia Conference was an assertion of intellectual independence.

Even more striking than Geiger's parental expression of rejection is the overreaction to it by his spiritual son, David Einhorn. In an article in the *Jewish Times*, Einhorn accused Geiger of believing the Torah was only to be found *me'ever layam*, of taking the position *im aini kan mi kan*, and in effect holding the Philadelphia rabbis to account for not declaring *"in Geiger Alles, ausser ihm Nichts!"* Aside from the psychodynamic tension of the situation, there were of course general and specific points of significant difference between the two men. Einhorn leveled the most substantive general charge against Geiger when in the same article he called him—not favorably—a *ba'al teshuvah*. Geiger, as well as others of the early Reform leaders in Germany, had made their peace with the exigencies of united Jewish communities embracing liberal as well as conservative elements. Unlike Samuel Holdheim who, as Jakob Petuchowski has shown, was in some respects more of an antecedent for Einhorn than was Geiger, other Reformers in Germany had not stuck by their principles; the movement as a whole had succumbed to concession and compromise. Hence, it could no longer claim to be on the leading edge of religious development. In America, with its religious voluntarism and lack of communal constraints, religious reform was freer to take its destined course. And, in fact, just as the Reform movement in Germany was becoming more conservative, its offspring in America was becoming ever more radical in theory and practice. Ironically, Wise was now closer in spirit to German Reform than was Einhorn.

The most significant specific difference between Geiger and the American Reform rabbis concerned the position of women, an issue determined by the disparity of cultural values between the two countries. The Philadelphia Conference had voted to allow a bride to respond to the wedding formula recited by her husband by uttering the same words with only a change of gender. This institution of reciprocal vows, combined with an exchange of rings, did not find favor in Geiger's eyes. While he was willing to recognize the wife's equality with her husband, he insisted that the two would always occupy a different position in society, that the husband would "always remain master of the house" and he would have the determinative say. The husband should, therefore, speak for both while "the chaste bride, who has already more whispered than audibly spoken her 'yes,' should not have to speak and act publicly, but rather attend the words of her husband with a soulful look as she eagerly stretches out her finger so that the ring can be placed upon it. For the future as well," Geiger concludes, "the husband will be the one who gives, the wife the one who receives." For all his Germanism, Einhorn was by now sufficiently Americanized to brand such talk the worst romanticism. Though he claimed that woman's equality was a prophetic, and hence not originally an American notion, Einhorn lived in an environment where women—for all the disabilities they still suffered—were treated more as equals than in Germany. The Jewish traveler, I. J. Benjamin, had been struck and offended by the women's rights movement that he encountered in the United States in 1860. Whereas in nineteenth-century Germany even Liberal congregations seated men and women separately, in America the "family pew" had spread to nearly all the larger synagogues, including very conservative ones; and one looks in vain in nineteenth-century Germany for an equivalent of the American Rebecca Gratz, founder of the modern Jewish Sunday school.

During the seventies and eighties, even in those circles that had heretofore been most worshipful of their German antecedents, there now arose a chorus of criticism for Germany and German Jewry together with praise for America and its Jews. The case of Rabbi Bernhard Felsenthal of Chicago is illustrative. No one except perhaps Einhorn had been more fervent a devotee of German culture and more attached to German Jewry than Felsenthal. Still in 1866 he had written:

> With regard to the assertion that we should emancipate ourselves from German Jewry and proclaim our independence, we say: Alas, for us if we were now to free ourselves from German Judaism and its influences! As in the Middle Ages the sun of Jewish scholarship shone loftily and marvellously in Spain . . . that sun now stands in the German heavens and from there sends its beneficent light to all Jews and Jewish communities among the modern cultured nations. Germany has replaced Sefarad.

Felsenthal argued that without the influence of German Jewry, American Judaism would "either sink into an ossified orthodoxy or into nihilistic, raw and presumptuous bar-room wisdom." Both would be of a strictly American variety. The orthodoxy would more likely be a kind of hysterical Methodism, a benightedly strict Calvinistic Puritanism, or an ostentatious high-church display than a Torah-true Judaism in accord with Talmud and *Poskim*. For the nihilists, Thomas Paine would serve as the model. In short, Felsenthal believed that American Jewry—across the religious spectrum—still required a subservient relationship to German Judaism lest it assimilate the worst characteristics of American religion and philosophy.

In succeeding decades, however, Felsenthal's views changed almost completely. He came to believe that America had as much idealism as Germany— and without the attendant sickly romanticism. He even went so far as to claim that the American environment had been a blessing for Judaism, especially because, with the separation of church and state, it had not had to suffer governmental interference; it had been able to develop freely on its own. In fact, Americanization represented the real test of Jewish modernity. Could it survive in an open cultural context without state authority for community taxation as was the case in Germany? It was a challenge that American Jewry had met very well. In "idealistic" Germany, Felsenthal now writes with sarcasm, Jews did not make the same sacrifices to establish Jewish institutions that were being made in America. Moreover, American Judaism was more tolerant of diverse religious expressions. Unlike Germany, there were no elections of a centralized *Gemeinde* to factionalize the communities. Each of the three branches recognized the right of the others to practice Judaism differently. Perhaps it is no mere coincidence that as Felsenthal was becoming more of an American, he was also—paradoxically, one might say—becoming a fervent Zionist. Although Zionism during the 1890s was just as much a minority viewpoint in the United States as it was in Germany, the pluralistic American milieu must have seemed to Felsenthal more capable of tolerating a Jewish national movement than the more conformist political atmosphere of Germany.

During the 1880s, it became much more difficult for American Jews to speak favorably of the German state. While some had welcomed Prussia's liberalism in the 1860s and celebrated its victory over France in 1871, Germany was now seen as a land whose purported spirituality had failed to curb a vicious outbreak of anti-Semitism. Rabbi Jacob Voorsanger of San Francisco protested that the language of the German anti-Semite Adolf Stocker had no place in the American synagogue. As for the Jews of Germany, by American Jewish lights, they had not risen sufficiently to the occasion. The rabbi of Mobile, Alabama, Adolf Moses, severely castigated the philosopher Hermann Cohen when, in response to the anti-Semitism of Heinrich von Treitschke, he expressed the hope that Judaism would eventually dissolve into German Protestantism and that the Jews would one day lose the physical characteristics that set them apart. However profound Cohen's philosophy, his supine response showed that an attack on his Jewishness could turn an otherwise clear mind to confusion. American Jews, said this radical Reformer, were proud of their racial characteristics and did not intend to give up their separate religious identity for the sake of national unity.

From the perspective of German Jews in America, the lessons to be learned from the Jews of Germany were now mostly negative ones. For the radical Reformers, German Judaism had settled into stagnation—into a "murky swamp," as Kaufmann Kohler put it. The living spirit of Judaism had fled Germany, he believed, the "prophetic spirit that once called forth Reform has been exhausted." Although the founding fathers had failed in their own land, what they had sought to build could be created in America. While some of the Germanizing American rabbis continued to look askance at Isaac Mayer Wise's organizational efforts, sooner or later they had to recognize his accomplishments: a Union of American Hebrew Congregations in 1873 and the first successful American seminary, the Hebrew Union College, which he founded in 1875. Eleven years later Conservative Jews in America also established their own theological seminary. It remained now only to assert the new hegemony. Adolf Moses put it with typical American hyperbole in 1882: "From America salvation will go forth, in this land [and not in Germany] will the religion of Israel celebrate its greatest triumphs." Or, as Kaufmann Kohler believed, Judaism in the new world would reinvigorate it in the old. American Jewry had learned from Germany; now it was ready to teach.

If the Philadelphia Conference in 1869 symbolized the rabbinic turn toward independence in religious matters, the successful completion of the *Jewish Encyclopedia* in 1906 marked the coming of age of American Jewish scholarship. German Jewry had failed to produce a collective monument of equivalent stature. Now its best scholars contributed to an American project, whose editorial board was entirely composed of Jews resident in the United States. Although almost all the American writers—who wrote many of the most significant articles—had been trained in *Wissenschaft des Judentums* abroad, they were pursuing their discipline in America.

It is ironic that just as the mantle of modern Jewish religious and intellectual leadership was passing from Germany to America the German Jews in the United States should find themselves inundated by an influx of their brethren from Eastern Europe. It is equally ironic that the East European Jews should be largely responsible for sustaining the remnants of a separate German-Jewish identity in America for another generation and more. Still not a part of the American establishment, but for the most part ever more peripherally Jewish, the wealthier New York families now stressed their German ancestry far more than their Oriental heritage. Eager to remain separate from the newcomers, even as they sought to promote their welfare, the *Yahudim* segregated themselves both socially and religiously on the basis of their German origins, thus braking somewhat an otherwise accelerating pace of Americanization. For their part, East European Jews in America— whether devoutly Orthodox or secular Yiddishists—possessed their own Old World loyalties. Thus, it was not until after the Holocaust that hegemony within the Jewish people would finally pass incontrovertibly to American Jewry—and to the state of Israel.

CHAPTER

5 The Civil War divided Jews much as it did the nation as a whole. There were Jews in the North and Jews in the South, Jews who supported slavery and Jews who condemned it, Jews who fought for the Union and Jews who fought for the Confederacy. One well-known rabbi of the day, Morris J. Raphall, preached a sermon on the eve of the war intending to prove that the Bible sanctioned slavery. Another well-known Jew, Michael Heilprin, a leading lay intellectual, immediately penned a rejoinder, seeking to prove just the opposite. While few Jews joined the ranks of the radical abolitionists—their Evangelical Christian rhetoric was distasteful to Jews and sometimes downright anti-Jewish—some did echo their views. At the same time, others, notably Judah P. Benjamin and David Yulee, assumed prominent positions in the Confederacy, and defended slavery as a "positive good."

If in many respects the Civil War affected Jews much as it did other Americans, there were nevertheless three features of the struggle that affected Jews uniquely. _First_, wartime tensions led to an upsurge of racial and religious prejudice in America, and Jews, both in the North and in the South, proved to be convenient scapegoats. Even famous Americans slipped into anti-Semitic stereotypes when they meant to condemn one Jew alone. _Second_, Jews in the North (not in this case in the South) had to fight for their right to have a Jewish army chaplain—no easy task, since by law a military chaplain had to be a "regularly ordained minister of some Christian denomination." Although President Lincoln himself urged that this law be amended, it took heavy Jewish lobbying and over a year of hard work until the amendment was passed. _Third_, and most shocking of all to Jews, they had to face what was without doubt the most sweeping anti-Jewish official order in all of American history: General Grant's "General Orders No. 11," published on December 17, 1862.

This order, demanding the expulsion within twenty-four hours of all Jews in Grant's military department, was, as Joakim Isaacs explains below, an irate and highly prejudiced response to wartime smuggling and speculating—crimes engaged in by Jews and non-Jews alike. When Jews protested the order, President Lincoln personally intervened and, just eighteen days later, had it revoked. But the matter did not end there. Instead, it became a campaign issue

60

when Grant ran for president in 1868. <u>Never before had a Jewish issue carried</u> <u>so much weight in national politics.</u>

Isaacs's treatment of this episode is important for what it reveals about broader aspects of Jews on the American political scene. His picture of Grant's opponents using the issue of anti-Semitism to manipulate the Jewish vote, even as the Jewish community itself agonized, torn between political and religious loyalties, sheds light on dilemmas Jews have faced repeatedly in America. Whether or not a "Jewish vote" exists in fact, politicians have frequently assumed that it does and acted accordingly. This poses a problem that remains open for debate: To what extent should religious and ethnic considerations affect Jewish political behavior?

Ulysses S. Grant and the Jews

Joakim Isaacs

A Convenient Scapegoat

The great rebellion that rocked the nation in the years 1860 to 1865 brought to the surface much of the latent anti-Semitism which had lain dormant since the founding of the United States. Many Jews who had come to these shores seeking religious asylum and liberty felt secure in the knowledge that the scourge of anti-Semitism would never follow them here. The Civil War and its aftermath provided a rude awakening and caused many Jews to reassess both their Judaism and their Americanism.

Jews, like the rest of their fellow Americans, were at the time divided on the issue of whether one owed primary allegiance to one's state or to the nation as a whole. Many families were divided in their loyalties during the war. Jews, also, like the rest of their fellow countrymen, were involved in military and political affairs, and many, too, followed the economic pursuits stimulated by the war situation. Fortunes are always made in wartime through equipping armies and through other related financial transactions. A large number of Jews who had come to the United States since the 1600s had been merchants, and they were naturally attracted, as were many Gentiles, to the profits that could be made. The way to fortune seemed to lie in buying cotton in the South and selling it in return for Northern gold. The South was short of money, the North was short of cotton, and all that was needed was the trader to bring the parties together. Such trade, however, was frowned upon by the government, which was trying to starve the South physically and financially. The trader, therefore, had to be prepared to share a quarter of the profits illicitly with army officials in order to get the necessary permit and military assistance required for the operation.

While subordinate army officers might be bribed, the commanding officers were under constant pressure from the government in Washington to eliminate this trade. Official documents are filled with reports of the activities of cotton speculators. It seems that, in almost every combat area, both civilians and military personnel were involved in the trade. A Union army gunboat crew was alleged to have netted $100,000,000 during the war, and President Abraham Lincoln expressed concern that the army was so busy with cotton speculating that, as a consequence, the war effort was suffering. In such wide-scale operations, the Jews obviously played but a small role, and yet the Jewish trader provided a convenient scapegoat for commanding officers. Because the Jews were a recognizable group and their successes had aroused the envy of the other traders, what better way was there to satisfy the government at Washington, and at the same time to placate the powerful interests involved in the smuggling, than to outlaw the Jewish traders?

The Land of Canaan

Of the many military orders that were aimed at Jewish traders, one gained greater notoriety than all the rest. This was Ulysses S. Grant's Order No. 11, issued at Holly Springs, Mississippi, in 1862. The order declared:

> The Jews, as a class violating every regulation of trade established by the Treasury Department and also department orders, are hereby expelled from the [military] department within twenty-four hours from the receipt of this order.
>
> Post commanders will see that all of this class of people be furnished passes and required to leave, and any one returning after such notification will be arrested and held in confinement until an opportunity occurs of sending them out as prisoners, unless furnished with permit from headquarters.
>
> No passes will be given these people to visit headquarters for the purpose of making personal application for trade permits.
>
> By order of Maj.-Gen. U. S. Grant.
>
> Jno. A. Rawlins,
> Assistant Adjutant-General

This order was one of several on the subject issued by General Grant; it followed Order No. 2 of Colonel John V. Dubois, which had been written a week before and countermanded by Grant. Dubois' order had stated:

> On account of the scarcity of provisions, all cotton-speculators, Jews, and other vagrants having no honest means of support, except trading upon the miseries of their country, and in general all persons from the North, not connected with the Army, who have no permission from the General Commanding to remain in this town, will leave in twenty-four hours or they will be sent to duty in the trenches.

This order went comparatively unnoticed by the Jewish community. In response to Grant's Order No. 11, however, there was an immediate outcry from the Jewish community in the war zone. A Kentuckian, Ceasar Kaskel, one of the signers of a letter of protest to President Lincoln, personally went to Washington to speak with the President. Lincoln listened to Kaskel's plea, and replied, "And so the Children of Israel were driven from the happy land of Canaan." Kaskel failed to understand, or adroitly pretended not to grasp, the sarcasm implicit in Lincoln's reference to the cotton-rich territory beyond the Union lines as "the land of Canaan." Kaskel replied, "Yes, and that is why we have come unto Father Abraham's bosom asking protection." Lincoln promised to grant the protection, and carried out his pledge by having General Henry W. Halleck telegraph General Grant. Halleck told Grant: "The President has no objection to your expelling traitors and Jew Peddlers, which, I suppose, was the object of your order, but, as it is in terms [which] proscribed an entire religious class, some of whom are fighting in our ranks, the President deemed it necessary to revoke it." A Saint Louis delegation went to the President to thank him for ordering the revocation and reportedly was shown a letter written by General Grant to Lincoln which the President found amusing. In the alleged letter, Grant said:

> Mr. President, As you have directed me, I will rescind the order; but I wish you to understand that these people are the descendants of those who crucified the Saviour and from the specimens I have here, the race has not improved.

Except for a censure move in Congress against Order No. 11, which failed to pass, and scattered remarks in the press, this ended the controversy over Order No. 11 for the duration of the war.

General Grant and "The Hebrew Race"

The whole issue was revived in 1868, when the Republican party nominated General Grant for President. Now, for the first time since the founding of the United States, the idea of a Jewish vote and the question of a presidential candidate's alleged anti-Semitism became a central political issue. The Jewish community at the time was not organized as it is today. The age of the Anti-Defamation League was in the future, and the B'nai B'rith, the only large Jewish organization, busied itself with internecine quarrels over whether meetings should be opened with a prayer and whether Gentiles should be admitted to membership. The B'nai B'rith kept completely aloof from the political question.

In fact, the stimulus for arousing Jewish protest did not come primarily from Jewish groups, but rather from the Democratic press. The Democrats, badly shaken by the loss of the Southern wing of the party during the war and stung by Republican accusations that they had opposed the war effort and were traitors to their country, now faced an uphill struggle that pitted the most popular Union general against New York Governor Horatio Seymour. In seeking all the support they could get and searching for issues to employ in the campaign, the Democrats naturally looked to Grant's Order No. 11 and the 300,000 Jewish votes. The *New York Herald*, a leading Democratic journal, pointed out that attracting Jewish support might help the campaign in two ways. "This thing is at least certain, that against General Grant every influence of money and votes that can be controlled by the Hebrew race in the United States will be put forth with acrimonious activity; and their power is by no means to be despised." The *Herald* felt that the "Hebrews" would not forgive General Grant, especially since he had singled them out and had used the word "Jew," which the paper felt had offensive connotations, instead of the more genteel appellation of "Hebrew" or "Israelite."

The *Herald* was only one of many Democratic papers that sought to arouse the "Jewish vote." The *Atlanta Constitution* pointed to the great pertinacity with which the Jews clung to their "nationality," and the paper was sure that Grant would get few Jewish votes. At the same time as the Democratic papers sought to inflame the Jewish vote by appeals to their religious loyalty, they attempted to explain just why Grant was an anti-Semite. The *New York World* spoke of Grant's order "as the brutal order which expelled hundreds of inoffensive Jewish citizens who were peacefully attending to their own affairs miles away from the scene of conflict," and called upon Jews and all Americans to countermand Grant, just as Lincoln has countermanded Order No. 11.

The *La Crosse* (Wisconsin) *Daily Democrat*, in a front-page article, alleged that a cotton speculator, seeking from General Grant a permit to trade behind the Union lines, had offered Grant one-quarter of the profits. Grant had refused, insisting that he wanted a greater share of the profits. The Jew then offered Grant a one-eighth share, which Grant accepted. When Grant got his share, an adjutant expressed surprise that the amount was so small and, when told about the deal that Grant had made, he explained to Grant that one-eighth was less than one-quarter. As the story continues, it was then that Grant became a confirmed anti-Semite. This story in varying detail was given wide circulation in the Democratic press.

Who Drove the Hebrews from His Camp?

Not content with this jocular explanation alone, the Democrats revived the case of *Grant v. Mack Brothers* in attempting to give Grant's anti-Semitism a more substantial base and to link the general with the illegal cotton trade. The story of this lawsuit began in December 1862. Jesse Grant, the general's father, like his Jewish fellow citizens, saw opportunity knocking on his door in the form of cotton trading. While Jesse Grant lacked what many Jews had in the way of capital, he did have a son in a position to be of great help to him; so he began a two-pronged attack. First, he wrote his son soliciting his aid, and at the same time he negotiated a deal with the Mack Brothers, a firm of Cincinnati Jews. According to the terms, Jesse Grant was to receive a quarter of the profits for using his influence with his son to secure cotton permits.

Jesse Grant's plan was foiled because of total lack of cooperation from his son. Letters to Jesse's son, as well as a personal trip to the front, all failed to budge General Grant from his uncooperative position. Jesse Grant then turned around and attempted to place the blame for the failure of the enterprise on the Mack Brothers, who had since withdrawn from the agreement. Jesse sued the Mack Brothers in the Cincinnati Superior Court for breach of contract. The case was argued before Judges George Hoadly and Bellamy Storer, who dismissed the case on the grounds that, if Jesse Grant had used his privileged position with his son to get a permit, then such an agreement was illegal and could not be enforced in the court; on the other hand, if Jesse Grant had asked for a permit legally, then the contract was void, for Jesse's role would not have sufficed to warrant payments. Either way the court refused to enforce the contract.

While the case attracted little press attention when it was decided, it was revived and "played up" in the Democratic press in 1868. The Democratic press sought to prove that, since order No. 11 had followed closely on the heels of the Grant-Mack Brothers disagreement, the order's real aim had been to bar Jewish traders like the Mack Brothers from trading directly, without barring their capital from being employed in the trade by Gentiles like Jesse Grant. Despite protests from the Macks, who were all leading Republicans and argued that the facts were entirely different, the press continued its attack. The following poem is typical:

> Who drove the Hebrews from his Camp,
> Into the Alligator swamp
> Where everything was dark and damp?
>> Ulysses
> Who wrothy at those faithless Jews
> Who kept "pa's" share of Cotton dues,
> All further permits did refuse?
>> Ulysses
> Who licensed chaps that would divide
> With father Jesse, Argus-eyed,
> Who claimed the hair and eke the hide?
>> Ulysses.

The attempt by the Democratic press to arouse Jewish voters deeply concerned at least one Republican journalist, Joseph Medill, who said in a letter to Elihu Benjamin Washburne, one of Grant's campaign managers in Washington:

> I want to write to you on several subjects, and will put them all in one letter. First, what can be done in regard to that general order of General Grant issued in 1862 expelling "all Jews as a class" from his department? We have in this city [Chicago] at least six hundred Republican Jews headed by General Edward S. Solomon [Salomon]. . . . The General has written to Grant but has received no answer.
>
> It would only be necessary for General Grant to write a letter to Solomon or some other influential Jew saying that he has no prejudice against Jews, that he is in favor of full toleration of all religious opinions; that his subsequent experience in the army convinced him that other classes of men were just as likely to violate army regulations in relation to trading with the enemy, as Jews.
>
> Something to this effect would mollify the Jews and give us a good many thousand votes. The Jews of Cincinnati and St. Louis are numerous enough to defeat our ticket in both cities, and they are strong enough to hurt us in Chicago also, as they include many of our most active Republicans. That they are deeply grieved by [the] General's order is undoubted. The Copperheads [The Northern Democrats] are making a handle of the matter in all parts of the country and we shall lose large numbers of Jew votes among them besides converting them into very active bitter opponents. . . .

The majority of the Republican press, however, remained silent, secure in the knowledge that Grant's popularity would bring him victory despite Democratic attacks. An Indiana newspaper, however, angry at all the appeals to the Jewish vote in the Democratic press, editorialized as follows:

> The Jews are all Democrats anyhow. We never heard of a Jewish soldier, during the War, on either side. They did not care an itinerant tinker's cuss how the War terminated. Their object was to make money out of it. They formed mainly the myriad of army vultures that preyed constantly and mercilessly on the poor, half-naked, hungry soldiers. For every Republican Jew that, by the sort of reasoning of the *Courier* (Democratic) and other similar journals, are to be induced to vote against Grant, a dozen decent, honest Christian White men will vote for him.

Jews or Citizens

Editorials in the Democratic press and attacks like the above in Republican papers all combined to place the Jews in a dilemma. How were they to treat Grant's candidacy? Should they declare that a person's religion and his Americanism were separate and vote for Grant, if they were Republicans, or should they react, and vote, as Jews? The Jewish community was divided as to the best method to approach the situation.

Isaac M. Wise, a Reform Jewish leader and the editor of *The Israelite*, felt that a Jew always had to react as a Jew. Wise began his attacks on Grant months before Grant received the nomination. As early as February 1868, he declared:

> Worse than General Grant none in this nineteenth century in civilized countries has abused and outraged the Jew. . . . If there are any among us who lick the feet that kick them about and like dogs, run after him who has whipped them, if there are persons small enough to receive indecencies and outrages without resentment . . . we hope their number is small!

When Grant was nominated, Wise accelerated his attacks. He could not understand the argument that one could be an American in politics and a Jew in religion and never mix the two.

> We have been trying quite seriously to make of our humble self two Isaac M. Wises. The one who is a citizen of the State of Ohio, and the other who is a Jew, but we failed and we failed decidedly. . . . The duties and wishes of the Jew as such being in no wise in conflict with those of the citizen, we being both the Jew and the citizen to the public forum and to the synagogue, before our God and our Country.

Other Jews disagreed with Wise. A letter, signed "Julius" and published in *The Cincinnati Commercial*, declared:

> What does Dr. Wise care what becomes of the country? Whether we are making a living or not? He has a salary fixed during his life. . . . But how can we as Israelites seek to place in power a set of men who have been trying with all their might to destroy the Government our only refuge? . . . I think when we go to the polls next November our religious feeling ought to be entirely banished from our mind.

Samuel M. Isaacs, in his paper *The Jewish Messenger*, also attacked the Wise position and argued that Jews should refrain from forming Jewish protest groups. He favored action through existing political organizations. In an indirect reference to Wise, Isaacs declared that "Israelites are too intelligent and too self-asserting to be driven, or led by their ministers, especially in matters that have no connection with religion." Isaacs feared the consequences of political parties using the Jewish religion for their own purposes and questioned strongly the sincerity of the sudden solicitude for Jewish rights exhibited by the Democratic press.

The Jewish voters were thus faced with conflicting advice, and the letters that filled the columns of the Jewish press and the regular press reflected this anxiety. One group agreed with Wise and insisted that Jews could not vote for Grant. They felt that Grant's order had given an insight into his mind and showed that the nineteenth-century spirit of liberalism had totally escaped him. Therefore, as a man of the past he was unfit to rule a great and liberal nation. Others favored excusing Grant because of the difficult circumstances facing him at the time the order was given; they called for the "Yom Kippur" spirit of forgiveness to permeate the air. Still another group took the position that, regardless of what Grant had done against the Jews, the Republicans should be supported as the party of Lincoln and human freedom. Perhaps the most extreme statement of this position was a letter written by a Jew to the *Illinois Staatszeitung* and reprinted on the front page of the *Missouri Democrat:*

> I am a Jew, when Saturday, the seventh day, comes; I am one on my holidays; in the selection and treatment of my food; it was always written on my doorposts; it is always to be spoken in my prayers; and it always is to be seen in my reverence for my Bible, that I am a Jew. . . . But it is different when I . . . take a ballot in order to exercise my rights as a citizen. Then I am not a Jew, but I feel and vote as a citizen of the republic, I do not ask what pleases the Israelites. I consult the welfare of the country. If that party in whose hands I believe the welfare of the country, so far as the advancement of human rights was concerned, was the safest, were to place a Haman at the helm of state, and if the opposite party, whose nonexistence I believe would be better for humanity and my country, were to place Messiah at their head, make Moses the Chief Justice, and call the Patriarchs to the Cabinet, I should say, "Prosper under Haman, my fatherland, and here you have my vote, even if all the Jew in me mourns."

I Do Not Sustain That Order

Some Jews felt that the situation called for action, not words. Mass meetings were held by Jewish groups in many states. The one given the most publicity in the press was held in Memphis, Tennessee. Speeches were given urging that the only position Grant deserved to be elevated to was the one occupied by Haman in the last moments of his career. Naturally, these mass meetings were denounced by the Republican press as well as by those Jewish newspapers which felt that direct political action was not in the best interest of the Jewish people. Commenting on the Memphis meeting, one Republican paper declared:

> We have had a big meeting of Jews here, to denounce General Grant for the order issued in his absence by his Adjutant excluding Jew traders from the army lines. Nearly every Jew that figured in this meeting was, it is notorious here, a contraband dealer, who grew rich during the war by trading to both sides. The

order was wrong because it was aimed at a whole sect, but a more unmitigated set of scoundrels than the Jew traders who were engaged in running goods through the army lines, it would be hard to find anywhere. The idea of such men, whose lives were disgraceful to their religion and race, meeting to denounce General Grant because his subordinate issued an order [so the paper claimed] which reflected on all Jews, and which General Grant almost immediately annulled, is absurd.

Throughout the campaign a group of leading Republican Jews hoped that the whole issue could be avoided by a strong statement on the part of General Grant. One of the most active Jews in the campaign, Simon Wolf, interceded through one of Grant's advisors, Adam Badeau, to get a statement from the general. Grant answered through Badeau that he felt no animosity toward Jews, but had merely been trying to eliminate the evils of speculation. This statement satisfied Simon Wolf, but did not quiet the agitation in the press. Finally, Grant, probably stung by the invectives in the press, answered with a forthright statement a letter of Adolph Moses forwarded by Grant's friend, I. N. Morris. Grant declared that he had received hundreds of letters about Order No. 11 and, although he had followed his usual practice of not answering them, in deference to Mr. Morris, he was replying to Mr. Moses:

I do not pretend to sustain the order.

At the time of its publication, I was incensed by a reprimand received from Washington for permitting acts which Jews within my lines were engaged in. There were many other persons within my lines equally bad with the worst of them, but the difference was that the Jews could pass with impunity from one army to the other, and gold, in violation of orders, was being smuggled through the lines, at least so it was reported. The order was issued and sent without any reflection and without thinking of the Jews as a sect or race to themselves, but simply as persons who had successfully (I say successfully instead of persistently, because there were plenty of others within my lines who envied their success) violated an order, which greatly inured to the help of the rebels.

Give Mr. Moses assurance that I have no prejudice against sect or race, but want each individual to be judged by his own merit. Order No. 11 does not sustain this statement, I admit, but then I do not sustain that order. It never would have been issued if it had not been telegraphed the moment it were penned, and without reflection.

Grant's statement as to his motives in issuing Order No. 11 accords with the explanation he gave the War Department the day after the order was issued. This explanation, however, was not known, and the letter to Moses, written in mid-September, came too late to influence the campaign in any way.

While it is impossible to know how many Jews voted against Grant because of Order No. 11, the evidence from letters to the press is that most Jews supported the candidate of the party of their choice and rationalized their choice accordingly, although undoubtedly Grant did lose some Jewish votes as the result of Order No. 11.

Without Further Comment

Isaac M. Wise and those who followed his lead found themselves in an awkward position when Grant was elected. They feared that they had created animosity toward the Jews in the heart of the man who was now the Chief Executive. Wise, through an editorial in *The Israelite*, beat an ignominious retreat and, seizing on the Grant-Moses correspondence, declared it now clear that Grant was not an anti-Semite and had merely been misled by the sinister cotton speculators' lobby.

Grant himself, once he became President, proved a friend of the Jews and appointed many to posts at home and abroad. He sided with the Jews in the controversy raised by Harry Bergh of the A.S.P.C.A. over the alleged cruelty practiced by Jews in the slaughtering of animals. Grant refused in his later career to discuss Order No. 11 and failed to mention it in his memoirs. An inquiry made to Grant's son, Frederick D. Grant, about the omission elicited the reply that his father had wanted to let the controversy die without further comment.

CHAPTER

6

"Our Crowd"—a term that Stephen Birmingham made famous—was, in fact, only a small crowd composed of the leading German-Jewish families in New York. By the end of the nineteenth century, it had coalesced into a homogeneous elite, at once part of and distinct from general upper-class life in the city. Members were wealthy and heavily involved in finance and commerce, belonged to the same temples and the same clubs, took part in the same philanthropic and communal activities, and with some notable exceptions chose their friends and spouses from within the same limited sphere. They all lived in the golden age of German Jewry in America, an age when Jewish notables used their minds, money, and power to make their influence felt.

In the path-breaking article that follows, business historian Barry E. Supple explores the social and economic forces that shaped the members of this unified elite. He explains their rise in America in terms of their origins, early activities, ideologies, and habits, and shows how their similarities became more and more evident once they settled down in New York. For those outside New York, many of Supple's conclusions apply equally well. Sharing as they did common interests, common backgrounds, and a common faith, leading Jewish businessmen in numerous cities banded together into fraternal networks, depending upon one another for information, credit, and mutual aid. In some cases, acting according to the tradition of noblesse oblige, leading Jews assumed the burdens of "stewardship," involving themselves in Jewish charitable, educational, and community relations work. Members of the Jewish elite also played active roles in general community affairs, especially in cities such as San Francisco, where they faced relatively little prejudice. Some even rose to prominent positions in local and national politics, the prime example being Oscar Straus, who served as Secretary of Commerce and Labor under President Theodore Roosevelt.

Yet, the contributions of the German-Jewish elite were soon overshadowed. Assimilationist tendencies, the passing of the immigrant generation, World War I, and the new situation engendered by the mass migration from Eastern Europe weakened "our crowd." While individual German-Jewish families continued to wield influence, the community that once existed in New York fragmented. Power passed to a new elite, a less colorful and more heterogeneous one.

72

A Business Elite:
German-Jewish Financiers in
Nineteenth-Century New York

Our Crowd

Barry E. Supple

Although the German-Jewish immigrant of the mid-nineteenth century was rarely very wealthy, he usually had some small capital. The journey alone, in the years before steam revolutionized the cost of transport, demanded some money. To live during the passage was in itself a drain on resources: Joseph Seligman (the first of eight brothers to come) set out from Baiersdorf, Bavaria, in July 1837, at the age of seventeen, with about one-hundred dollars. Traveling with a small group and camping at the roadside, he took eighteen days to reach Bremen. From there he sailed steerage at a cost of forty dollars (which included only one meal a day), and took sixty-six days to cross the Atlantic—landing on September 24, 1837, and proceeding immediately to Pennsylvania.

Once in the United States, with his capital steadily dwindling, the immigrant who typically made a success of his economic activities usually had sufficient means or friends to find his way to one of many scattered regions throughout the land—unlike later generations of East European Jews, whose destitute immobility kept them concentrated in New York. In fact, the mid-century Jewish immigration as a whole produced a rapid growth of small communities from the East to the West Coast and from Chicago to New Orleans—although, naturally enough, there was a higher concentration in the East. By 1820 there was already a small community in Cincinnati, and the 1820s and 1830s saw a further penetration of the Midwest, while a few immigrants reached Louisville, Kentucky. In 1826 a congregation had been founded in New Orleans, and in the 1840s Texas and in the 1850s California were reached by Jewish settlers. The thirty-seven reported synagogues of 1850 increased to sixty-seven in 1860—and they were found for the first time in California, Alabama, Georgia, Illinois, Indiana, Maryland, New Jersey, Wisconsin, and the District of Columbia.

One reason for this distribution was that the contemporary Jewish immigrant often followed the frontier of peddling and petty retailing. The original

73

occupation structure of the German Jew had led him, unlike the peasant, to appreciate the significance of income as capital—as the potential source of further income; he, "even in the old country, had learned to reckon, to direct earnings toward a purpose." This grasp of a central proposition of entrepreneurship meant that he was less likely than the erstwhile peasant to feel economically rootless in the new environment. Once in America, then, he cast around energetically for a means of livelihood and capital accumulation. Peddling (if the immigrant had little capital) and settled retailing or wholesaling (which would, in any case, follow upon peddling as quickly as possible) naturally attracted a great number—and it seems possible that by 1860 a majority of the peddlers in the United States were Jewish.

Peddling

An itinerant life was something which, historically, was not too strange a mode of existence for the Jews. Initial difficulties with the language might militate against many other occupations. Historical social pressures and attitudes made Jews reluctant to enter unskilled manual occupations or go onto the land. Where the desire to keep their Sabbath free for worship was so strong, independence was a goal well worth striving for. And where family life and solidarity played such an important social role, any occupation in which the family as a whole might participate was the more welcome. In addition, since Jews were accustomed to being a persecuted minority group they had no compulsion to look outside their own community for social approval. The criteria against which actions were significantly measured lay within the circle of coreligionists; social snobbery from outside was the norm—and was therefore not a meaningful variant that conditioned their lives. If peddling was a menial task in the eyes of the majority, it was not so to the poor Jewish immigrant—in fact it might be a convenient means of escaping from the *real* degradation of working for others.

As everywhere in the West "the rapid march of settlement outdistanced the ability of the towns to supply the rural districts with needed goods," as the development of markets outpaced the rise of sophisticated and institutionalized retail distribution, so Jews were attracted into the field, selling notions, trinkets, dry goods, and old clothes, opening stores if they could, buying a pack (or even a wagon) if they could not. Most of the group under discussion here participated in this development, and as a consequence became well distributed geographically—although each peddler needed a base for his operations and each storekeeper wished to tap the richest market. Hence the rise of Jewish communities in strategic regional urban centers, usually near water routes. Especially remarkable in this sense were the Ohio Valley region (centering on Cincinnati), the Chicago area, the Pennsylvania mining towns and Philadelphia, the West Coast, and some southern areas.

The father of the founders of J. S. Bache & Co., Semon Bache, worked in a Mississippi store (owned by his uncle) after his landing in New Orleans. Marcus Goldman, who ultimately started Goldman, Sachs & Co., proceeded

DISTRIBUTED IN STRATEGIC REGIONAL URBAN CENTERS

to Philadelphia in 1848 and there peddled for two years before opening a men's clothing store which prospered greatly until his temporary retirement in 1867. Meyer Guggenheim, after his landing in New York in 1848, also peddled in Pennsylvania (in the mining areas), selling shoestrings, lace, stove and furniture polish, safety pins, needles, spices, and so forth; he then turned to the sale of home-manufactured stove polish, traveling with samples by train and horsecar; and about 1852 opened, in Philadelphia, a wholesale store for household products, ultimately importing goods from Europe. Philip Heidelbach peddled in Ohio and then went into the clothing trade (probably as a manufacturer) in Cincinnati; from a venture in local banking he ultimately graduated, in 1876, to a banking house in New York. Abraham Kuhn and Solomon Loeb, the founders of Kuhn, Loeb & Co., commenced with a commercial partnership in Lafayette, Indiana, about 1850, before moving to Cincinnati with a general merchandising store, which lasted until their temporary retirement in 1865. Henry Lehman immigrated in 1844, peddled in Alabama for a year and then opened a general store in Montgomery; he was joined by his brothers Emanuel and Mayer Lehman within five or six years and the firm expanded through the years into cotton brokerage with a New York branch; after the war the firm extended its commodity dealings to include coffee and petroleum, being joined by the second generation in the 1880s. Samuel Rosenwald, father of the future president of Sears, Roebuck, peddled in the South, on foot and then with the help of a horse and wagon, until the outbreak of the Civil War, when he moved North to Springfield, Illinois, and established what was to be one of the town's leading stores. Lazarus Straus landed in Philadelphia in 1852 and went to Oglethorpe, Georgia; after peddling for some months he settled in a general store in Talbotton. His family joined him in 1854 and in 1863 he moved to Columbus— returning North after the war to establish a wholesale crockery business. William Scholle, who arrived with little means in 1841, eventually came to deal on a large scale in clothing and woolens, opened a branch in San Francisco, and in 1850 moved there himself; at which point the firm developed a banking business—presumably under the influence of the gold discoveries. California after the gold discoveries also attracted the Seligman brothers and they, in fact, provide us with an archetype of geographical dispersion.

Joseph Seligman, the eldest of the eight, immigrated in 1837 and worked for a year as an assistant in Asa Packer's store in Mauch Chunk, Pennsylvania. Then he resigned and occupied himself with peddling in the locality. By spring 1839 he had amassed five hundred dollars and was joined by his brothers William and James, who also became peddlers. Next, Joseph and William opened a small store in Lancaster and James went South as an itinerant merchant, centering his peddling in Alabama. His success stimulated the others (together with Jesse who had, meanwhile, left Bavaria for

America) to accompany him back, and in 1841 the four brothers opened a store in Selma, Alabama—which, with one brother left in charge, they used as a base for peddling. By 1843 they had extended their activities to include four stores—in Selma, Greensboro, Eutaw, and Clinton—each managed by one brother who left his store in charge of an employee in order to peddle. After 1846, feeling restricted in Alabama, they opened a drygoods importing house in New York. Soon William went to St. Louis to establish a clothing business with his brother-in-law Max Stettheimer, and Jesse and Henry (who had come over in 1843) opened a branch of the New York house in Watertown, New York. In 1850 Jesse and Leopold were bitten by the gold bug—or at least by the prospect of commercial profit in California—and in the fall they moved to San Francisco with twenty thousand dollars' worth of merchandise. The fifties were to see some movement of Seligman personnel between branches, but up to the Civil War the framework remained essentially unchanged: The Seligmans had succeeded in establishing a network which placed them— even if fortuitously—in a preeminent position so far as the realities of distribution were concerned.

Thus, by the late 1850s, the initial phase of economic integration was largely completed. Twenty years had witnessed the arrival of a generation of German Jews with little capital. Among them were men who, seeing their opportunity in the field of distribution, launched forth inland yet more hundreds of miles. Some stayed out in the West and the South and their children established permanent communities, but another cluster also emerged: men who, back in New York with capital and commercial experience, would ultimately participate to no small extent in the critical development of the American capital market in the decades after the Civil War.

Within a relatively few years of their arrival in the United States, most of our men were firmly established in one aspect or another of the distribution system—retail or wholesale or overseas trade.

For most of them the Civil War brought prosperity—at least to some degree. Even where, as in the case of Straus and the Lehman brothers, operating within the southern economy, they had to bear the brunt of commercial dislocation and general insecurity, there might be some counterbalancing benefits. Thus, Lazarus Straus's son Isidor was in Europe for the last two years of the war with a commission to buy supplies for the Confederacy and, it appears, made a profit of several thousand dollars on the sale of Confederate bonds. But for most, the period was one of relatively uncomplicated prosperity. A boom in textiles helped those whose business was in clothing, and the general war inflation naturally aided those whose principal economic activity lay in buying and selling. The Seligmans, as always, could not go wrong. In the early years of the war, partly owing to their influence in government circles and their prominence in the Republican party, they obtained lucrative clothing contracts; and from 1 August 1861 to 30 July 1862, the government paid them, on this account, almost $1½ million. Later on in the war they were large-scale participants in the flotation of federal loans—principally in Europe. As early as April 1862, the brothers had a capital of just under $1 million; by March 1864, this had been augmented by over $250,000.

In general, then, the postwar position of these men was buoyant—and in two instances (Kuhn and Loeb in 1865 and Marcus Goldman in 1867) there was even a retirement from economic activity. But when Kuhn and Loeb, in 1867, and Goldman, in 1869, reentered business, it was in a way that typified the general movement: to New York and into finance. For most of the group who immigrated before the war with little money and no financial experience, the postwar decade was seminal. Private banking, commercial paper discounting, exchange transactions, stock dealings, all exerted a strong pull on men with agile minds and the requisite capital. Kuhn and Loeb, it has been estimated, had a capital of half a million dollars and some experience in extending credits, and we have seen how wealthy the Seligmans were—while their financial experience was extensive. It seems that Marcus Goldman's wife played a not unimportant role in persuading him to make the move. But his entry into the commercial paper field was made possible only by the attraction of New York as a financial center and by the capital which he had accumulated in Philadelphia. The Seligmans, of course, had long had their base in the metropolis, but as conditions changed it is possible to witness the long and purposeful thought which went into their decision to leave the importing of dry goods and to enter wholeheartedly into international investment banking.

It was at this stage of their development that the path of the originally unqualified men crossed that of the group who immigrated qualified, either with capital or experience, for the banking field. They, too, were consciously gravitating to a young and flourishing field, and they provide even more obvious examples of the mobility of factors of production. The two Speyer brothers (Philip and Gustav) had come in 1837 and 1845 respectively and established Philip Speyer & Co. They, like the Seligmans, sold federal bonds in Europe during the Civil War. In 1878 the firm name was changed to Speyer & Co., and it was by no means an insignificant factor in the American underwriting world. Ladenburg, Thalmann was established in 1880—as the successor of Limburger & Thalmann (1873)—Ernst Thalmann having been in banking since his immigration in 1868. Jacob Schiff had entered in 1865, already had a brokerage partnership in 1866, went back to Frankfort in 1872, and in 1875 returned, for good, to join Kuhn, Loeb & Co.

Once established in New York, both types of firm—all houses stemming from German-Jewish families—experienced a development parallel to that of the New York money and capital markets. Leopold Cahn & Co. (1879), which Semon Bache's son Jules S. joined in 1880, became J. S. Bache & Co. in 1892 and developed into a prosperous stockbroking business which is still on Wall

Street, operated by Jules's nephew Harold L. Bache. Goldman, Sachs and Co. (originally, in 1869, M. Goldman, Banker & Broker) dealt for many years in note-discounting, branched out into the handling of letters of credit and bills of exchange, started to buy railroad bonds, and under the leadership of Marcus's son Henry Goldman, and with the help of Samuel Sachs and his three sons, went into investment banking in the first decade of this century. In the latter venture Lehman Brothers joined Goldman, Sachs. The Lehmans had started with commodity transactions, and in the 1880s had commenced stock and bond dealings, railroad investment, and industrial banking—by which time the second generation was in control. Kuhn, Loeb's private banking house (established 1867), especially under the invigorating leadership of Jacob Schiff, gradually gave more attention to securities and helped establish a market for American government obligations and railroad bonds—until at the end of the century it was numbered among the six leading investment banking houses in the land. Hallgarten, Speyer, and Ladenburg, Thalmann were also outstanding in the financing of railroads, utilities, and industry.

Why this particular group should have been as successful as it was in this particular field is not a question that permits of a satisfying answer. Clearly they were not concerned in a conspiracy to monopolize the money market. To some extent, as will be seen, the common background facilitated their dealings with each other and with some clients; but this was not a continuous process, and it could not explain their success in financial transactions involving non-Jews. Neither can it be proved that personal experience in European finance counted for something in every case: the backgrounds of most of these men, before they went into finance, were not such as to provide them with a mastery of European techniques. However, it is more interesting that, besides the few who came to America with abilities based on years of family banking, many of the group were fully alive to the lessons to be learned from European experience. Schiff was undoubtedly aided by his early work in Frankfort banking and by his stay in Europe in 1872–1875, while Kuhn, Loeb in later years *continued* to call on European talent in the shape of Otto Kahn and the Warburgs. More than this, there were frequent visits to Europe for further education in finance even when the American firm was well established: Ernst Thalmann, Goldman, Sachs personnel, the Seligmans, all learned valuable lessons there. Of course, as J. P. Morgan's early history demonstrates, this interplay of ideas was by no means confined to German-Jewish houses. But, with their strong orientation to German culture and their continuous attachment to Europe, there can be no doubt that this particular group was in an especially favorable position to benefit from the advanced practices across the Atlantic. As will be seen in the final section, this cosmopolitan frame of mind enabled them to profit from the contemporary need to import capital from Europe, by establishing trans-Atlantic connections. In general, this particular result of their cultural background is not something to be underestimated, and therefore the fact of their having been *German* Jews was clearly significant.

To some extent, of course, the "open mind" had been important from the early days of their settlement in America. An ability to grasp the concept of productive capital which exceeded that of their fellow immigrants, a willingness to risk even more of the unknown in order to achieve economic and social independence, an historical aversion to unskilled manual labor or agricultural pursuits: all these factors go toward explaining their ultimate position in the interstices of trade organization. As America after 1865 came to provide for men of capital in the field of finance the opportunity and promise for which a host of other immigrants had looked, and were to look, in vain, these families easily made the transition into the new world, confident that it would fulfill its promises. The road that had led from the dusty lane to Main Street now pointed toward Wall Street and even more security. Scattered over much of America, these families could not but have felt socially isolated. Back in New York they set about building their own in-group. To the bases of this structure the next section is devoted.

Once in New York, the families who had originally arrived poor coalesced with those who had arrived with capital to form an elite differentiated in background, in culture, in religious observance, in social outlook and activities, from other groups around it. That Henry R. Ickelheimer, Jules S. Bache, three Seligman brothers, and James Speyer were all present at the marriage of Jacob Schiff's son, Mortimer, was more than evidence of business good manners: it demonstrated a strong social solidarity. That Mortimer, in fact, married the daughter of a Hallgarten partner, or that Henry R. Ickelheimer, four years later, married Pauline Lehman, were more than coincidences, for these young people went to the same clubs, worshipped at the same temple, and continually gathered at each other's houses. The elements which, at bottom, drew them all together were principally three: their business interests, their German background, their Judaism.

In some respects, the group adopted habits common to families of equivalent income. But much of its social life was basically insular, oriented around each other's homes or such clubs as the Harmonie. Founded in 1852, the *Harmonie Gesellschaft* was patronized almost exclusively by German Jews: Not until 1893 did German cease to be its official language. Interesting in this respect, and as reflecting the economic interests of club members, is the following quotation from one of Henry Seligman's letters, after Pacific Mail stock had tumbled 15 points in March 1885: "The Jews in particular have been badly nipped. . . . They are down on Ed Lauterbach who is on the board and at the Harmonie the members are going about singing *On Lauterbach hab ich mein gelt verloren.*"

The social solidarity of the German-Jewish banking community was in no

Intermarriage in the elite

way better exemplified, and furthered, than by the tendency—common to all unified elites—to intermarriage. Chart I represents the genealogies and marital ties of the families under consideration. As can be seen, one result was that the business *was* the family—in its economic aspect. To some extent the added strength which partnerships derived from marriage vows antedated the final rise to social and business success. Thus, Solomon Loeb's first wife was Abraham Kuhn's sister Fannie, and the marriage took place well before the move to New York and the establishment, by the brothers-in-law, of the famous investment banking house. On other occasions a new partner's entry into the established firm would follow on or be coincident with his marriage to an older partner's daughter, as in the case of Jacob Schiff's partnership in Kuhn, Loeb. Indeed, this firm was so interwoven by marriage relationships that from 1869 through 1911 it had no partners who were not related to Solomon Loeb or Abraham Wolff, and as late as 1931 this rule held good of three new partners: John M. Schiff (grandson of Jacob and therefore great-grandson of Solomon Loeb), Frederick M. Warburg (son of Felix and therefore, again, grandson of Solomon Loeb), and Gilbert W. Kahn (grandson of Abraham Wolff). In Goldman, Sachs & Co. it was not until 1915 that a person outside the two families was brought into the firm and the family histories show an early intertwining—two Sachs boys (who had been orphans under the care of their future father-in-law) marrying two of Goldman's daughters. Similar intrafirm unifications occurred in the Seligman enterprises and Heidelbach, Ickelheimer & Co., which was founded in 1876 after the marriage of Isaac Ickelheimer to Philip Heidelbach's daughter. Four of Hallgarten's partners, Bernard Mainzer (1864), Charles Hallgarten (1872), Sigmund Neustadt (1872), and Casimer Stralem, were also tightly knit—Mainzer's sister married Charles Hallgarten, and Neustadt's daughter married Stralem. Sometimes a business did not even need marriages to secure family continuity in partnership: Until 1924 all the eleven partners in Lehman Brothers bore the family surname!

The broken lines on Chart I also demonstrate that the marriage ties connecting both families *and* banking houses were of no less importance. In the resulting interlocking structure, the fecund Seligmans occupied an "anchoring" position, having connections with the Lewisohns, the Lehmans, Kuhn, Loeb, and the Guggenheims—the marriage of Benjamin Guggenheim and Florette Seligman in 1894 uniting the two most important families in American Jewry. Jacob Schiff, so closely tied by marriage to his own firm and the brother-in-law of a Hallgarten partner, who was the son-in-law of another partner, who, in his turn, was the father-in-law of an Ickelheimer!

Clearly, the marriages were not entirely consciously arranged with an eye to business solidarity. The formation of the group was the initial step. With the consequent participation in an insular social world—with a constant meeting in the same homes, the same clubs, and the same restaurants—it was inevitable that the younger generations should choose their spouses as they did. These ties, in any case, were only the framework upon which was built a towering structure of mutual friendships. Descendants of the families today, who were then conscious of such things, can remember from their childhood a period when most of these people were intimate acquaintances—when Jacob Wertheim, for instance, was a close friend of Daniel Guggenheim, the Hallgartens, Julius Rosenwald, the Seligmans, the Ickelheimers, the Loebs, Jacob Schiff, the Strauses, the Lehmans, Felix Warburg, and Henry Goldman. The firmness of the group's social position cannot be doubted. Springing from religion, nationality, occupation, and wealth, it was strengthened by education, culture, club membership, and religious observance. It was, perhaps, almost as much a matter of defense as of spontaneity. This cluster of families had a background and cultural acquisitions pushing them toward the conventional social graces; but they carried an ethnic stigma which, at least in the first generations, prevented their moving into the graceful echelons of New York society for which they no doubt considered themselves fitted. For only a small minority was assimilation an acceptable solution to the problem. In rare instances an individual might participate in two communities. But for the great majority the answer was a society within a society, an elite perhaps equal but certainly separate, forced into being by prejudice and buttressed by participation in a specialized culture.

[margin note: a separate elite]

Nevertheless, it would be wrong to claim that the German-Jewish group had been completely divorced from some aspects of American society. Most of their friendships and much of their social activity *was* insular. But the Seligmans knew Lincoln and loved him well, they helped arrange a pension for his widow, and they were extremely close to President Grant; Oscar S. Straus is best known as someone who made his mark in government circles— as Ambassador to Turkey and the first Jewish member of the Cabinet; Jacob Schiff was ultimately considered the equal of the Yankee financial aristocracy, and was very close to Edward H. Harriman, and Nathan Straus was on the best of terms with President Cleveland. Equally, too, and as a corollary of their devotion to Reform Judaism, these men fought hard against any tendency to "separatism" in American Jewry. Schiff's opinion was that "we are all Americans," and Oscar Straus, although he felt his ethnic background very keenly, was no less devoted to America: Jews, he said, "are not less patriotic Americans because they are Jews, nor any less loyal Jews because they are primarily patriotic Americans." For this reason too, because they saw the clash with Americanism, most of these men were opposed to the Zionist movement, which they viewed as dangerous in so far as it established a prior lien on citizenship.

[margin note: But were patriotic]

In spite of these early trends to Americanization and in spite of the ultimate crumblings of social demarcations, it is possible to see at the end of the nineteenth century a social elite based primarily on ethnic factors: strong

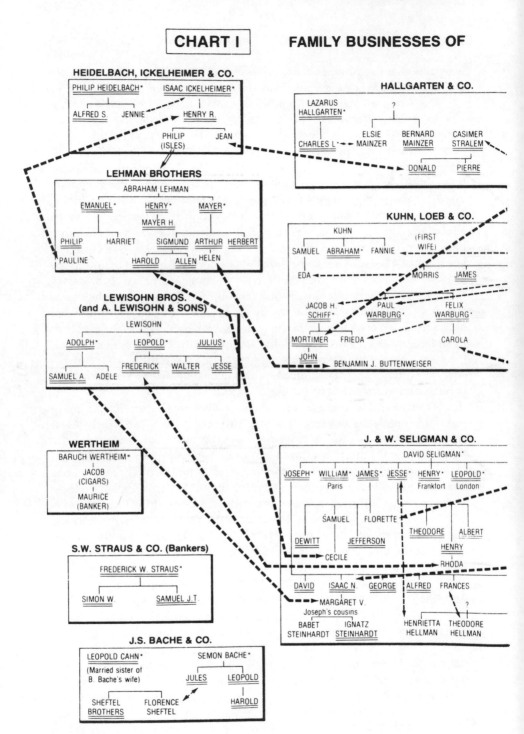

CHART I   FAMILY BUSINESSES OF

HEIDELBACH, ICKELHEIMER & CO.
PHILIP HEIDELBACH*   ISAAC ICKELHEIMER*

ALFRED S.   JENNIE   HENRY R.

PHILIP (ISLES)   JEAN

HALLGARTEN & CO.
LAZARUS HALLGARTEN*   ?

ELSIE MAINZER   BERNARD MAINZER   CASIMER STRALEM

CHARLES L.

DONALD   PIERRE

LEHMAN BROTHERS
ABRAHAM LEHMAN

EMANUEL*   HENRY*   MAYER*

MAYER H.

PHILIP   HARRIET   SIGMUND   ARTHUR   HERBERT

PAULINE   HAROLD   ALLEN   HELEN

KUHN, LOEB & CO.
KUHN

SAMUEL   ABRAHAM*   FANNIE   (FIRST WIFE)

EDA   MORRIS   JAMES

JACOB H. SCHIFF*   PAUL WARBURG*   FELIX WARBURG*

MORTIMER   FRIEDA   CAROLA

JOHN   BENJAMIN J. BUTTENWEISER

LEWISOHN BROS.
(and A. LEWISOHN & SONS)
LEWISOHN

ADOLPH*   LEOPOLD*   JULIUS*

FREDERICK   WALTER   JESSE

SAMUEL A.   ADELE

WERTHEIM
BARUCH WERTHEIM*

JACOB (CIGARS)

MAURICE (BANKER)

J. & W. SELIGMAN & CO.
DAVID SELIGMAN*

JOSEPH*   WILLIAM*   JAMES*   JESSE*   HENRY*   LEOPOLD*
   Paris   Frankfort   London

SAMUEL   FLORETTE   THEODORE   ALBERT

DEWITT   JEFFERSON   HENRY

CECILE   RHODA

S.W. STRAUS & CO. (Bankers)
FREDERICK W. STRAUS*

SIMON W.   SAMUEL J.T.

DAVID   ISAAC N.   GEORGE   ALFRED   FRANCES

MARGARET V.
Joseph's cousins

BABET STEINHARDT   IGNATZ STEINHARDT   HENRIETTA HELLMAN   THEODORE HELLMAN
                                               ?

J.S. BACHE & CO.
LEOPOLD CAHN*
(Married sister of B. Bache's wife)   SEMON BACHE*

JULES   LEOPOLD

SHEFTEL BROTHERS   FLORENCE SHEFTEL   HAROLD

GERMAN–JEWISH ORIGIN

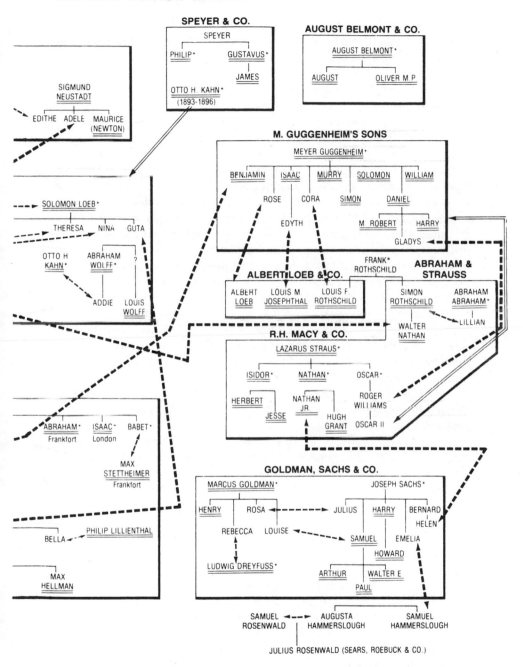

SPEYER & CO.

SPEYER

PHILIP*   GUSTAVUS*

JAMES

OTTO H. KAHN*
(1893-1896)

AUGUST BELMONT & CO.

AUGUST BELMONT*

AUGUST   OLIVER M.P.

SIGMUND
NEUSTADT

EDITHE ADELE MAURICE
(NEWTON)

M. GUGGENHEIM'S SONS

MEYER GUGGENHEIM*

BENJAMIN ISAAC MURRY SOLOMON WILLIAM

ROSE   CORA   SIMON   DANIEL

EDYTH   M ROBERT   HARRY

GLADYS

SOLOMON LOEB*

THERESA NINA GUTA

OTTO H   ABRAHAM   ?
KAHN*   WOLFF*

ADDIE   LOUIS
WOLFF

ALBERT LOEB & CO.

FRANK*
ROTHSCHILD

**ABRAHAM &
STRAUSS**

ALBERT   LOUIS M   LOUIS F
LOEB   JOSEPHTHAL ROTHSCHILD

SIMON   ABRAHAM
ROTHSCHILD   ABRAHAM*

WALTER   LILLIAN
NATHAN

R.H. MACY & CO.

LAZARUS STRAUS*

ISIDOR*   NATHAN*   OSCAR*

HERBERT   NATHAN   ROGER
          JR   WILLIAMS

JESSE   HUGH   OSCAR II
         GRANT

ABRAHAM*   ISAAC*   BABET*
Frankfort   London

MAX
STETTHEIMER
Frankfort

GOLDMAN, SACHS & CO.

MARCUS GOLDMAN*   JOSEPH SACHS*

HENRY   ROSA   JULIUS HARRY BERNARD

                              HELEN

REBECCA LOUISE   SAMUEL EMELIA

BELLA   PHILIP LILLIENTHAL

          HOWARD

LUDWIG DREYFUSS*   ARTHUR WALTER E

MAX   PAUL
HELLMAN

SAMUEL   AUGUSTA   SAMUEL
ROSENWALD HAMMERSLOUGH   HAMMERSLOUGH

JULIUS ROSENWALD (SEARS, ROEBUCK & CO.)

NOTES: BROKEN LINES INDICATE MARRIAGES. DOUBLE UNBROKEN LINES INDICATE MEMBERS OF A FIRM.
ASTERISKS INDICATE ACTUAL IMMIGRANTS, IF KNOWN. NOT ALL MEMBERS OF FAMILIES ARE SHOWN.

[handwritten margin notes: "NB – primary social unit of premodern business was family" and "NB //"]

and united, a series of interlocking kinship groups revolving around the New York financial scene. Yet the important question for business history remains unanswered. How did the foregoing arrangements and attitudes impinge on business activity? This can best be considered from two points of view: the internal strength and structure of the firm, and the relationship between the individual business and the financial world outside it.

It is, perhaps, possible to argue that historically the primary social unit for business organization before the recent development of impersonal bureaucracies was the family. In medieval Italy the Bardi or the Medici, in sixteenth-century Germany the Fuggers or the Hochstetters, in colonial America the Browns of Providence and many other mercantile enterprises, in the early nineteenth century the Lowells and Cabots in textiles, all substantiate the proposition that men sought in marriage or blood relationships the ties that strengthened and gave security to the structure of their business enterprises. German-Jewish investment banking in the late nineteenth century, as has been seen, was also based upon the proliferation of kinship groups. In place of a set of partners united only by their common economic aspirations and, perhaps, by their regard for business unity, there was created a firm skein of common universal aspirations and interests—an identification of the family and the firm which in the early days of the Seligmans had led to a continuous pooling of capital for both private and business use, and which, at the least, would produce a heightened regard for the business and a continuity of entrepreneurial skill.

Most significant in this respect was an attitude imported from the Old World: that of family solidarity and unity. For the Seligmans, the Guggenheims, and Schiff, Friday night was family night—a time when children and grandchildren gathered in the patriarch's house. "I have made it a rule," wrote Schiff in 1890, "to spend Friday evening exclusively with my family, and I can under no circumstances vary from this." All members were concerned with the affairs and well-being of their respective families, and this orientation, which is noticeable in nearly all the firms, sprang directly from the structure of everyday life—nothing was more natural than to find a place for a relative. For example, Joseph Seligman for a period was plagued by the necessity of creating a position in the Seligman enterprises for Max Stettheimer, who had married Joseph's sister Babet. Thus in 1863 he reported that Stettheimer was anxious to go into importing, "and if we do not enter into it as largely as of old he will try to get other partners. . . . Nothing would please me more, were it not for dear Babet; who says as soon as Max ceases business connections with us, she will face a life more insupportable than hitherto, and begs of me, to try to keep him in. If only for her sake I deem it my duty, provided I cannot place him in Paris or Frankfort as I would prefer, to commence importing again."

The repercussions of this attitude were complicated. On the one hand there can be little doubt that it served to provide a powerful, although intangible, motivation to accept entrepreneurial training; and for business activity the identity of kinship group and firm meant an added strength and unity of purpose. This coincidence, in fact, as was clearly demonstrated in the case of the Seligmans, produced a dedication, almost a compulsion, to commercial activity, which might otherwise not have been present. "I think it is our duty toward our children," wrote Joseph Seligman, "to have a decent business for them." Although not every descendant came into the business, for many years it was considered normal for son to follow father, nephew to cooperate with uncle, son-in-law to participate in this particular field of economic endeavor. And this was applicable, to some extent, to the whole of American business, as well as to other types of investment banking houses, an outstanding example being the Boston firm of Lee, Higginson & Co., which, from 1848 to 1918 drew twelve of its twenty-two partners from the two Yankee families who gave the house its name. In an activity so dependent upon confidence and trust as finance, it was to be expected that family participation should have been considered an economic advantage.

On the other hand, there were distinct disadvantages. Primary among these was the fact that the facilitation of the entry of relatives into a business might mean assuming the burden of a poor businessman. This most often must have happened unknowingly, but (as in the case of the Seligman brother-in-law) there might be little to be done even if the fact were realized. However, this drawback need not have been disastrous. Businesses and families were organized along patriarchal lines: As long as decision-making could be concentrated, as long as the number of sellers and purchasers of securities was small, the personality of the head of the firm—his ability, contacts, and reputation—was all-important. Underneath him there might be (within reason) any number of poor businessmen who could do little lasting harm to the business because they were not near the center of decision-making. In the long run, too, there was no hesitation about bringing in outside talent when it was needed—which was often tantamount to going outside the circle of blood relatives and choosing or creating relatives by marriage in order to bolster the business. Finally, it is most probable that it was only the existence of unified German-Jewish houses which enabled men to enter the realm of high finance who might otherwise have been prevented from so doing on the basis of their race and background, for it is a remarkable feature of the rest of the financial world that other prominent firms never had Jewish partners.

On the whole in the late nineteenth century there were two basic groups of investment bankers: the New Englanders and the German Jews. It is to be hoped that one day the former will be analyzed and compared with the latter. But initially it seems possible to say that the German-Jewish groups had a strategic role to play in the provision of capital from Germany for America's industrial development. While the Yankee bankers were able to tap the capital resources of old England, it was the Germans who were able, through cultural, social, and linguistic affinities, to draw German capital across the Atlantic. As early as the Civil War the Speyers and the Seligmans had played a major role—overcoming Rhineland reluctance to subscribe to federal loans. Indeed, a remarkable feature of the bankers' operations was their cosmopolitan outlook. Goldman, Sachs created intimate relationships with houses in London, Amsterdam, Berlin, and Zurich. The Speyers, of course, were from the beginning closely tied to Speyer-Ellison in Frankfort and, later on, to Speyer Brothers in London. Kuhn, Loeb & Co. had close connections with Europe—one with *Disconto Gesellschaft*, and another very strong one with Sir Ernest Cassel, which was well buttressed by a personal friendship between him and Schiff, and which also led to Cologne and Frankfort. Hallgarten & Co. was allied with the Darmstaedter Bank. The Seligmans constructed the strongest network of all—not even relying on existing firms abroad. Once the decision to enter international banking had been made in the 1860s, the eight brothers, under Joseph's patriarchal guidance, set up houses in London, Paris, and Frankfort, each house controlled by one or more brothers. With J. & W. Seligman & Co. in New York (1864), J. Seligman & Co. in San Francisco (which became a fully fledged banking house in 1867), Seligman, Hellman & Co. in New Orleans (1865), Seligman Brothers in London (1864), Seligman & Stettheimer in Frankfort (1864), and *Seligman Frères et Cie* in Paris (1868), the family was unrivaled in its international framework. Throughout the last decades of the century houses such as Kuhn, Loeb or Hallgarten demonstrated a supreme ability to establish contact with sources of supply of German capital.

From this point of view, the rise of an investment market, with all that that meant in terms of economic growth, might have been very different without the influence of these men, and without the solidarity and progress of this particular financial and social grouping.

CHAPTER

7

The German period in American Jewish history witnessed the rapid growth of Reform Judaism at the expense of traditional Orthodoxy. In 1890, according to the census, Reform commanded almost 55 percent of the total reported Jewish congregational memberships, and close to 60 percent of all synagogue buildings—astonishing statistics when one keeps in mind the fact that the first Reform rabbis only arrived in America in the 1840s. Calling itself "a progressive religion, ever striving to be in accord with the postulates of reason," Reform linked its ideology with that of the country as a whole. Considering the high regard Americans paid to reason, it is no wonder that many viewed Reform as the wave of the future, and awaited with lively anticipation its ultimate triumph over Orthodox Judaism.

Yet Reform Judaism was not nearly so secure as it seemed to be in the late nineteenth century. It was bitterly divided between adherents of Radical Reform, associated with Rabbi Emil G. Hirsch (son-in-law of the pioneering Radical Reform rabbi, David Einhorn), and more moderate figures, like Rabbi Benjamin Szold. It faced challenges both from new immigrants, many from Eastern Europe, who promised to revive Orthodox forms, and from those who called themselves Conservative Jews and favored a middle way between tradition and change. Most serious of all, its very integrity as a separate movement was being challenged by its closest liberal religious ally, Unitarianism.

Benny Kraut, who has specialized in the relationship between American Jews and nineteenth-century liberal religious groups, examines this last challenge in the selection that follows. "Reform Judaism and Unitarianism," he points out, "shared much in common." They "affirmed unequivocally their commitment to religious universalism," "preached the coming of a 'Religion of Humanity' whose central ideals were the 'Fatherhood of God and the Brotherhood of Man,'" denied the divinity of Jesus, abandoned many beliefs and rituals deemed inconsistent with human reason, and opened the way for their adherents to interact together socially. Some predicted merger, but Reform rabbis wanted no part of it. Their task was to distinguish Reform Judaism from Unitarianism to keep Jews from slipping away.

As Kraut realizes, Reform's dilemma was, in microcosm, the dilemma of the modern Jew, eager to be accepted but unwilling to apostatize. He goes further, however, in showing that despite outward similarities, liberal Jews

and liberal Christians remained far apart on key issues, notably their rela-
tionship to Jewish history, to Jesus of Nazareth, and to Jewish feelings of
peoplehood. By the end of the nineteenth century, as these differences became
more apparent, liberal Jews and liberal Christians actually appeared far more
distinctive than they had two decades earlier. Both sides had come to realize a
painful and irresolvable dilemma: On the one hand, as religious minorities,
they needed to forge coalitions with like-minded adherents of other faiths; on
the other hand, they needed just as much to keep their own religious identities
firmly fixed in place.

Reform Judaism and the Unitarian Challenge

Benny Kraut

In the wake of the Pittsburgh Platform of November 1885, Rabbi Solomon H. Sonneschein of Saint Louis received a letter from Lewis Godlove, former treasurer of his Jewish weekly the *Jewish Tribune* and a member of his temple, which posed the following question:

> If the mission of Judaism is to bring about the common Brotherhood of Man, if the doctrines of Judaism are the three named: Unity of God, Immortality of the soul and the binding force of the Mosaic moral code, why not take a heroic step and become Unitarians?

Implicit in Godlove's query is the notion that the eight-point rabbinic platform that crystallized the fundamental theological, religious, and moral affirmations of contemporary American Reform Judaism was essentially identical to the accepted beliefs common to Unitarians; hence Reform Jews could, and perhaps should, readily merge with their liberal Christian counterparts. Furthermore, Godlove observed, this union would ease the social assimilation of American Jews since "we would then become part of the majority (represented by Christianity) instead of remaining a powerless minority growing weaker." A similar, much publicized call for Reformers to unite with Unitarians also came from Felix Adler, founder of the New York Society for Ethical Culture, only a few days after the Pittsburgh Conference.

These two suggestions that Reformers join Unitarianism were not isolated phenomena precipitated by a rather unique rabbinic conference. From time to time during the last third of the nineteenth century, one finds dozens of other references to similar proposals made by both Jews and non-Jews. The actual number of these published suggestions, however, is less significant than the public perception which they reflected, that Reform Judaism and Unitarianism were synonymous. To be sure, such calls for a merger were sometimes motivated by polemical purposes. At other times, they betrayed a lack of complete understanding of either Unitarianism and/or Reform Judaism and their significantly distinctive religious and emotional commitments. Moreover, such calls often projected flattened images of a monolithic Reform Judaism and a monolithic Unitarianism which ignored the subtle nuances of internal theological debate, the vital internal differences in religious practice and custom, and the deep personality conflicts within each religious group which, interestingly enough, led to some extent to the rise of East-West factions in both liberal religions. Nevertheless, the impression of a blurred distinction between Reform Judaism and Unitarianism and the anticipation of their imminent unification which was periodically mentioned in the press was neither totally ill founded nor altogether unreasonable.

As the major liberal, institutional expressions of Judaism and Christianity, Reform Judaism and Unitarianism shared much in common. The religious and intellectual leaders of each religion confronted and sought to creatively assimilate the modern scholarship of the natural sciences, comparative religion, and Bible criticism. They affirmed unequivocally their commitment to religious universalism, and with equal intensity preached the coming of a "Religion of Humanity" whose central ideals were the "Fatherhood of God and the Brotherhood of Man." With such fervent agreement in basic intellectual orientation and eschatological goals, it is hardly to be wondered that, as Reform Judaism streamlined its demands for ritual observance, repudiated Jewish national identity, and dismissed belief in supernatural concepts such as the personal messiah and resurrection, it should be regarded as identical to Unitarianism, which had dropped all Christian dogmas, humanized Jesus, and disclaimed biblical infallibility and religious finality.

This impression that the two faiths were indistinguishable was certainly deepened as Reform Jews and Unitarians acknowledged each other's thinking and activities and came together in various forms of religious and social interaction. While generally restricted to clergy, scholars of religion, and the more educated laymen, this rapprochement between Jewish and Christian religious liberals was nevertheless seen and felt by the general public. The last third of the nineteenth century witnessed the innovation of pulpit exchanges between Reform rabbis and Christian ministers, newspaper subscription exchanges between editors of Reform and Unitarian papers, and the participation of Jewish religious leaders in the Free Religious Association—the first American Jewish-Christian interfaith organization—as well as in various congresses of liberal religious societies. More than two dozen of the most prominent Reform rabbis across the country, not to mention scores of Jewish laymen, participated in some of these activities with an even greater number of their liberal Christian counterparts. Invited to speak at Unitarian churches, Reform rabbis, to their delight, sometimes drew many liberal Christians to their own temple services which were oftentimes patterned after those of Unitarian services. On a sociopolitical level, Reform Jews joined forces with Unitarians, religious liberals, and religious radicals in the fight for religious liberty and equality and for a politically secular democratic America against the forces of sectarianism and evangelical Christianity.

Rabbinic sermons in temples and churches also helped foster the atmosphere in which a union of Reform Judaism and Unitarianism could be expected. They gushed with somewhat platitudinous sentiments avowing the common belief in brotherhood and the imminent appearance of a universal religion. On occasion, some proclaimed that concern for America takes precedence over religious affiliation, that all religions preach the same ideal of love of God and humanity, though in different forms, and that all religions agree on moral fundamentals. Moreover, Reform rabbis regularly lauded William E. Channing and Theodore Parker, patron saints of Unitarianism, and appropriated them as fellow workers in the cause of Judaism. The statement of the Unitarian Reverend Robert Collyer that the best of Reform Jews claim Channing and Parker as "members of true Israel" was as true in 1890 as it was in 1870 when it was originally made.

While these various forms of interaction and sentiments of common religious ideals lent credence to the belief that Reform Judaism and Unitarianism were converging at the same religious point, public comments to this effect deeply troubled some Reform rabbis. They were aware that the identification of Reform Judaism with Unitarianism could imply Reform Judaism's redundance and irrelevance and render continued Jewish existence in America problematic. Rabbi Bernhard Felsenthal of Chicago highlighted Reform fears when he perceptively asked a B'nai B'rith audience in 1875 what the consequences for American Judaism would be if people conclude that "it is just as good to have Unitarian theologians or at least Aryan Unitarians as teachers of religion as to have Israelites as such," if American Unitarian heroes such as Channing, Parker, and Moncure D. Conway were regarded as equivalent to Moses and their writings equal to the Bible, and if people felt "it would be money-saving or paying policy to merge Jewish congregations into non-Jewish congregations?" The answer to his rhetorical question was clear. No less clear was the challenge that Unitarianism represented to Reform Judaism. As the favored, liberal religious expression of the American social majority and intellectual elite, Unitarianism was the religious and intellectual "significant other" for Reform Judaism, and Unitarians served as the "significant other" in taste, manners, and culture for socially aspiring Jews. Therefore, if Unitarianism and Reform Judaism also shared common theological and eschatological convictions, why indeed should Jews not join Unitarian ranks as Godlove had asked? Of what value was American Reform Judaism, and what need of a separate Jewish community?

Reform rabbis confronted the challenge directly. Already in the 1870s and especially in the 1880s and 1890s, one finds published sermons and essays as well as *en passant* remarks by some of them reflecting on the relationship between Reform Judaism and Unitarianism. Some of them have suggestive titles such as "Why I Am a Jew," in which the spectre of Unitarianism lurks in the background, while others, with such titles as "Judaism and Unitarianism," are far more obvious. The rabbis took great pains to delineate what they felt to be the surface similarities yet fundamental distinctions between the two faiths. In the process, they articulated and refined a synthetic American Jewish identity that melded the affirmations of religious universalism, liberalism, and Americanism with Jewish separateness and chosenness. To a considerable degree, therefore, Unitarianism stimulated Reform introspection to seek an intellectual justification for ongoing Jewish existence. To be sure, rabbinic affirmations of the need for continued Jewish existence were also prompted by Jewish behavior and beliefs that reflected a diminished will to remain Jewish—religious laxity, laziness, or ignorance as well as intellectually rooted atheism and agnosticism. Still, the impact of liberal Christianity on the Reform Jewish mind should not be underestimated.

A perusal of the reactions of five of the rabbis—Isaac M. Wise (Cincinnati), Solomon H. Sonneschein (Saint Louis), Emil Hirsch (Chicago), Bernhard Felsenthal (Chicago), and Solomon Schindler (Boston)—to the equating of Reform Judaism with Unitarianism and to calls for their merger reveals an interesting, though perhaps not unexpected, fact. Despite the significant differences of the rabbis in personality and temperament, in their preaching and writing styles, in their places of residence and personal circumstances, and in their theological conceptualizations, these men formulated remarkably similar points of view on the issue, so much so that one may meaningfully subsume their reactions into broad categories.

The rabbis underscored three major areas of dispute or mitigating factors which made the two religions of Reform Judaism and Unitarianism distinct and merger inconceivable despite their espousal of an identical monotheistic faith. The first of these—and I list them in order of convenience for this presentation without suggesting their priority—relates to the category of history. Fervid loyalty to their respective historical religious origins as well as an antithetical understanding of the history of religious development profoundly divided Reformers and Unitarians. Both Reform Jews and Unitarians cherished their own historical continuities, a feeling perhaps best expressed by Unitarian Reverend John W. Chadwick: "We are creatures of association and affection, and we love the familiar places, the familiar names and things." Unlike the contemporary situation, the vast majority of Unitarians sought to retain the name "Christian" for themselves, despite having been rejected as Christians by the Christian right wing. As Charles W. Wendte, a Cincinnati Unitarian and later president of the Free Religious Association asserted in a public polemic with Isaac M. Wise, "Why should I not claim to be a Christian? I was born one." Moreover, the intellectual leaders of Unitarianism perceived themselves to be in the vanguard of creating a scientifically acceptable form of liberal Christianity; not infrequently, they referred to their task or "mission" within Christendom to purify Christianity of centuries of accumulated dogmas.

For the Jews' part, one need but read any of the writings of the rabbis under consideration, especially those of Wise and Hirsch, to discover their passionate allegiance to the history of the Jews and Judaism and to the Jews and Judaism of past history. They praised past Jewish religious achievements, empathized with and even justified medieval Jewish religious insularity, and constantly reminded everybody of Jewish suffering at the hands of Christians. This Jewish allegiance to the Jewish past also took an ideological expression with the concept of a historically mandated Jewish mission to disseminate ethical monotheism to the world. The past, present, and future existence of Jews was given glory and meaning by the felt Jewish need to fulfill a historic religious calling.

Emotionally attached to their respective religious histories that endowed each faith community with a contemporary sense of purpose and religious mission, Reform Jews and Unitarians perforce differed markedly in their evaluation of *each other's* religious past and future. To Unitarians, no less than to more conservative Christians, Judaism ceased to have any further meaning or function with the coming of Jesus; with his arrival Judaism had been superseded. Though articulated by the anti-Christian religious radical Francis E. Abbot, the following observation reflects the broad consensus on the Jews of virtually all Christians, liberal and conservative: "Christianity is the natural development of Judaism, Judaism is germinal Christianity; Christianity is fructified Judaism." Reformers vigorously repudiated this axiomatic interpretation of religious history so prevalent in the Christian world, and they forwarded an entirely different schema. They argued that Judaism had not been superseded. On the contrary, as the mother of all theistic religions, Judaism had bequeathed to the world the cardinal spiritual ideal of pure monotheism and, through the prophets, had presented the most sublime and unsurpassed vision of social ethics and hope for human brotherhood.

To paraphrase Isaac Mayer Wise, anything true in Christianity is borrowed from Judaism; anything in Christianity not of Jewish origin is not true. The rabbis suggested that over time, the Christian church had added to Judaism's ethical monotheism certain superstitious dogmas and doctrines that now, spurred by science and reason, were gradually being dropped. Therefore, those forms of liberal Christianity, like Unitarianism, which hastened the removal of the collected dross and excrescences of Christianity were, in reality, returning to pristine Judaism. Wise, Hirsch, Felsenthal, Sonneschein, and Schindler all suggested at one time or another and in one way or another that Unitarianism *was* Judaism, if only Jesus was properly understood and if Unitarians would properly label their faith. To their understanding, Unitarians were Judaizing. With this interpretation of the history of religion, Reformers identified the future religion of humanity as Judaism, and asserted that any calls for a merger between the two liberal faiths should request that the daughter, that is, Unitarianism, unite with the mother, and not vice versa. As bearers of the religion of the future, the Reform rabbis upheld American Jewry as the paradigmatic American socioreligious community that would usher in the era of achieved universalism, and they gave an important rationale for perpetuating distinctive Jewish religious life.

To support these historical self-perceptions, the rabbis drew on the popular doctrines of contemporary science. Consistent with the doctrine of evolution which stressed linear, progressive development through time, Judaism was portrayed as the most historical—and thus most authentic—of all religions; it was a three-thousand-year-old phenomenon, organically unfolding its truth over time. It had a past, present, and future and was not the product of a few speculative minds, as was Unitarianism, at least according to Wise. Or, as Hirsch noted, "The past produces the future; without constant interchange, exhaustion will ensue. This being the case, all healthy liberalism must be grounded on a historical basis." And, to him, the best case for a historical religious liberalism could be made for Judaism. Moreover, Jewish religious chosenness to preach a religious ideal, far from being "socially narrow" and "tribal" as Unitarians and others often charged, corresponded well with the insights of the developing field of ethnopsychology, which attributed a national soul or character to each group. Each group had special talents, and in that sense, was "chosen." That of the Jews lay in their religious sensitivity, which produced and reaffirmed the universal religion of humanity, ethical monotheism.

Their respective loyalties to and interpretations of religious history clearly separated Reform Jews from Unitarians. As long as the latter sought to preserve the name "Christian" and maintained the veracity of their historical religious story, the rabbis had ample grounds to depict Judaism as religiously distinct, and from their point of view, more authentic.

The second factor that the rabbis asserted separated Reform Judaism from Unitarianism and which militated against their union was the Unitarian adherence to Jesus as a model for emulation. By and large, Unitarians clung to a humanized Jesus as a paradigm for pristine religiosity and human perfection. This was one outcome of their grappling to salvage both their liberalism and their Christianity. But this conception carried with it the belief that Jesus—his personality, moral teachings, and religious thought—represented a departure from Judaism and contributed ideals and a religious view superior to that of Judaism. The rabbis would have none of this. For Wise and

Hirsch, Jesus contributed no novel ideas; all his teachings were of Jewish origin. Schindler challenged that no proof existed that Jesus was the greatest prophet; moreover, he asserted, to view Jesus as perfection was a form of idolatry. Sonneschein observed that "the Nazarene was *one* of the *Great* and sainted saviors of the race, but he is not *The Savior!*" The figure of Jesus clearly functioned as a symbol of Unitarian-Jewish separation; it was a visible last outpost beyond which no American Jew could trespass without controverting his Judaism and Jewish affiliation. Though Jewish himself, Jesus could not be incorporated into the pantheon of American Jewish heroes as could Washington, Jefferson, Lincoln, Channing, and Parker.

The third issue that divided Jews and Unitarians was Jewish "ethnic" or "national" group loyalty. While few of the rabbis used these terms, still choosing to refer to Jews as a religious community and stoutly denying kinship based on nationality, their reactions to anti-Semitism made clear that Reform Jews—even those committed to religious universalism—felt deep responsibility for their fellow Jews. Persistent anti-Semitism abroad in the form of pogroms or intellectual racism reinforced the will of Jews to remain apart. Any possible social and theological centrifugal force leading Reform Jews to Unitarianism was countered by the far more powerful centripetal force of anti-Semitism that aided Jewish group survival. In a forum of liberal religious societies, Emil Hirsch, for example, dramatically cited anti-Semitism as a reason for his staying Jewish. As long as the world did not accept Jews as human beings, he would not leave his birthright; to do otherwise, he suggested, would smack of contemptible religious cowardice. Of the five rabbis under consideration, Felsenthal alone translated his emotional kinship for fellow Jews into the new ideology of Zionism; but the other rabbis also felt the powerful emotional tug of Jewish group solidarity.

In the Reform rabbinic response to a perceived Unitarian threat, one is struck by the deep ambivalence of Reformers with regard to Unitarianism in the last third of the nineteenth century. On the one hand, Reformers wanted to align themselves and their Judaism with Unitarianism to attain recognition of Reform Judaism as a legitimate expression of American religious liberalism. Indeed, not a few rabbis found their own standing as leaders in the Jewish community enhanced by their acceptance in liberal Christian circles. On the other hand, the rabbis simultaneously reaffirmed Jewish religious distinctiveness and the validity of continued Jewish existence. Out of this ambivalence, the rabbis shaped the basic contours of an American Jewish religious identity that attempted to reconcile Jewish particularism with American religious liberalism, and which provided a reason for separate Jewish existence. A Jew ought to remain a Jew because of loyalty to the Jewish past and because of a historic religious mission that still awaited fulfillment, because of his opposition to Jesus as a central religious hero, and because of a sense of group fellowship to other Jews largely shaped by his exposure to the hostility of anti-Semitic forces. He nonetheless could claim to be an American religious liberal because America's truest liberal religious expression—Unitarianism—was essentially defined as Judaism. This Jewish religious ambivalence reflects the fundamental dynamic of the American Jewish experience as a whole, which sees Jews attempting to integrate themselves fully into American society, to blend in, and yet to remain apart.

FOR FURTHER READING

Rudolf Glanz authored some of the most important studies dealing with the German period in American Jewish history. He collected the bulk of them in his *Studies in Judaica Americana* (1970), but two more recent ones also merit close attention: "The German Jewish Mass Emigration: 1820–1880," *American Jewish Archives* 20 (April 1970), pp. 49–66, and "Vanguard to the Russians: The Poseners in America," *Yivo Annual of Jewish Social Science* 18 (1983), pp. 1–38. Glanz's 2,500-item bibliography, *The German Jew in America* (1969), lists a wealth of primary materials in this area, most of them, of course, in German.

Naomi W. Cohen's *Encounter with Emancipation: The German Jews in the United States, 1830–1914* (1984) is the first book-length study dealing with this period, and contains a great deal of new information. Eric E. Hirshler (ed.), *Jews from Germany in the United States* (1955) is one of the best collections of its kind and contains several fine articles. Briefer surveys include H. G. Reissner's comprehensive study of "The German-American Jews (1800–1850)" in the *Leo Baeck Institute Year Book* 19 (1965), pp. 57–116, which includes a valuable bibliography; and Bertram W. Korn's more loosely focused "German-Jewish Intellectual Influences on American Jewish Life, 1824–1972" in A. Leland Jamison (ed.), *Tradition and Change in Jewish Experience* (1977). Some of Korn's other articles dealing with this period are collected in his *Eventful Years and Experiences* (1954). Robert Ernst's book on *Immigrant Life in New York City 1825–1863* (1949) puts Jewish life into broader perspective, but does not duplicate Hyman B. Grinstein's *The Rise of the Jewish Community of New York 1654–1860* (1945).

The Civil War forms the subject of one of the best books ever written in American Jewish history, Bertram W. Korn's *American Jewry and the Civil War* (1951; rev.ed., 1971). The new edition includes a valuable chapter on "Jews and Negro Slavery in the Old South," which should be read in conjunction with Maxwell Whiteman's "Jews in the Antislavery Movement," published as an introduction to the reprint edition of Peter Still's *The Kidnapped and the Ransomed* (1970) and Louis Ruchames's "The Abolitionists and the Jews: Some Further Thoughts," in Bertram W. Korn (ed.), *A Bicentennial Festschrift for Jacob Rader Marcus* (1976). Sefton D. Temkin, "Isaac Mayer Wise and the Civil War," *American Jewish Archives* 15 (November 1963), pp. 120–142, puts into perspective one leading rabbi's obvious ambivalence toward the war effort; and F. S. Frank, "Nashville Jewry During the Civil War," *Tennessee Historical Quarterly 39* (Fall 1980), pp. 310–322, examines the war's impact on one Jewish community. Stephen V. Ash, "Civil War Exodus: The Jews and Grant's General Order No. 11," *The Historian* 44 (August 1982), pp. 505–523, is the finest single study of Grant's anti-Jewish order, and brings to light much new information. Louis Schmier, "Notes and Documents on the 1862 Expulsion of Jews from Thomasville, Georgia," *American Jewish Archives 32* (April 1980), pp. 9–22, makes clear that such incidents were by no means limited to the North alone.

A serious economic history of American Jewish life during this period has still to be written. Stephen Birmingham's *Our Crowd* (1967) and Leon Harris's *Merchant Princes* (1979) offer popular accounts of financiers and department store magnates; and Allan Tarshish has surveyed "The Economic Life of the American Jew in the Middle Nineteenth Century" in *Essays in American Jewish History* (1958). Other, more narrowly focused monographs appear in two special issues of *American Jewish History:* vol. 66 (September 1976), devoted to American Jewish business enterprise and vol. 72 (March 1983), devoted to quantification (with a bibliography).

American Judaism in the German period has formed the subject of two important books: Moshe Davis, *The Emergence of Conservative Judaism* (1965), which is much broader than its name implies, and Leon A. Jick's *The Americanization of the Synagogue* (1976). The related theme of Jewish-Christian relations has been broadly surveyed by Allan Tarshish in "Jew and Christian in a New Society: Some Aspects of Jewish-Christian Relationships in the United States, 1848–1881" in B. W. Korn (ed.), *A Bicentennial Festschrift for Jacob Rader Marcus* (1976). More focused essays include Naomi W. Cohen, "Pioneers of American Jewish Defense," *American Jewish Archives 29* (November 1977), pp. 116–150, which discusses anti-Semitism; Jonathan D. Sarna, "The American Jewish Response to Nineteenth-Century Christian Missions," *Journal of American History 68* (June 1981), pp. 35–51, which deals with conversionism; and Benny Kraut, "Judaism Triumphant: Isaac Mayer Wise on Unitarianism and Liberal Christianity," *AJS Review 7–8* (1982–1983), pp. 179–230, which expands on themes briefly examined in his essay here.

PART THREE

THE ERA OF EAST EUROPEAN IMMIGRATION

East European Jewish immigration to America dates all the way back to Colonial times. Thereafter, every decade saw some *Ostjuden* (Eastern Jews) trickle into the country, but their numbers down to the Civil War remained far too small to be noticeable. In the 1860s and 1870s East European Jews arrived in greater numbers, particularly in the wake of persecutions, and they soon set up their own synagogues and fraternal organizations. They remained, however, no threat at all to German-Jewish hegemony. Then, in 1881, came the assassination of Russia's Tsar Alexander II, and the resulting government-inspired anti-Jewish pogroms. Suddenly, the trickle of East European Jewish immigrants turned into a flood.

  If anti-Jewish violence sparked many a decision to risk life and fortune in the New World, the root causes of the mass immigration lay deeper—in overpopulation, oppressive legislation, economic dislocation, wretched poverty, and crushing despair, coupled with tales of wondrous opportunity in America and offers of cut-rate tickets from steamship companies plying the Atlantic. By the time restrictive immigration quotas took effect, in 1924, well over two million Jews from Russia, Austria-Hungary, and Rumania had journied to America's shores. The nation's German-Jewish community was effectively overwhelmed.

  The articles in this section focus on the inner world of East European Jewish immigrants: how they lived, how they worked, how they interacted with other American Jews, how they struggled to overcome the many hurdles that stood between them and the American dream of success. The East European Jews seen here were doing far more than just passively Americanizing. To a considerable degree they were also actively transforming the American Jewish community: changing its composition and geographical distribution, realigning its politics and priorities, injecting new elements of tradition, nationalism, and socialism into its religious life, and seasoning its culture with liberal dashes of Yiddish civilization and East European

Jewish folkways. One generation later, when the new American Jewish community emerged, it retained elements of the German and Sephardic pasts and was as heterogeneous as ever, but it looked altogether different. It was this refashioned community—large, wealthy, and influential—that became the foremost Jewish community in the world.

CHAPTER

8

The saga of the East European Jewish immigrant has been recounted many times, most recently in Irving Howe's best-seller, The World of Our Fathers. *Here, historian Deborah Dwork surveys immigrant Jewish life from a unique perspective, that of a medical historian. After noting three features that distinguished Jewish immigrants from their non-Jewish counterparts—a larger percentage of Jews immigrated with the intention of staying, brought their families with them, and came equipped with marketable skills—she concentrates on conditions that affected the immigrants' life and health. "Living conditions," she rightly warns, "must not be romanticized. . . . Poverty, as it existed on the Lower East Side of New York, was noisy, foul smelling, diseased, hungry." Dwork's later research—not reproduced in these pages—demonstrates that living conditions formed only part of the story. The psychic toll exacted by immigration was even heavier:*

> *Despite the foul housing and work conditions, Jews on the whole were physically healthier than their neighbors, both immigrant and Yankee. . . . However, they were not spared the emotional illnesses and conditions which stemmed from the rupture with tradition and the pain of dislocation. Depression, suicide, gonorrhea, and nervous disorders were more common among European Jews in America than in the old country. Neurasthenia, hysteria, and mental alienation were more common among Jews than among their non-Jewish neighbors.*

Swept into a new and alien culture, cut off from loved ones left behind, and, in many cases, forced to violate religious tenets once held dear, immigrants frequently spent lifetimes trying to reconcile what they had left behind with what they had gained. Many cursed Columbus and wondered aloud if the travail they had put themselves to was justified. A few returned to Europe. But in the wake of the infamous Kishinev pogrom of 1903 and subsequent persecutions in Russia and elsewhere, the promise of American life shined ever brighter. Most Jewish immigrants struggled on, hoping for a better life for their children.

Handwritten margin note (top):
- 2 million in 33 years
- ⅓ of Jew. popul. of E. Europe

Immigrant Jews On the Lower East Side of New York: 1880–1914

Deborah Dwork

The mass immigration of Eastern European Jews to the United States oc-curred between 1880 and 1914. From 1881 to 1900, 675,000 Jews entered the United States; from 1901 to 1914 the number doubled to approximately 1,346,000. The dates 1881–1914 are related to specific historical events: the assassination of Tsar Alexander II with its subsequent pogroms, and the beginning of World War I. In the thirty-three years between these two events, over two million Jews, or one-third of the Jewish population of Eastern Europe, came to the United States. Prior to 1881, Jews emigrated in search of a less oppressive society. Then, as a result of three events, the character of Jewish emigration changed. First, the assassination of Tsar Alexander II unleashed a fury of pogroms, which continued intermittently at least until World War I. A mass exodus of Russian Jews occurred following the 1881 pogroms, the 1903 Kishinev massacre, and pogroms following the unsuc-cessful revolution of 1905. Second, the increased legal restrictions on Jews, such as the so-called May Laws of the 1880s, forced Jews to abandon their previous employments and way of life and to migrate to urban centres. Prohibited from owning or renting land outside towns and cities, indus-trialization encroaching rapidly on their occupations as artisans and crafts-men, Jews turned to the industrial labour force. The population of Jews in Lodz soared from eleven in 1793 to 98,677 in 1897 and 166,628 in 1910. Similarly, Warsaw had 3,532 Jewish inhabitants in 1781 and 219,141 in 1891. These migrations within Russia and Poland were often only temporary solu-tions to the problem of survival, especially for young skilled Jews who saw no future in the cities. Finally, the decline of Central European emigration to America encouraged the German transatlantic passage companies to seek out Eastern Europeans as new passengers.

There were also more private reasons for leaving: to escape military service; lack of a dowry; hunger. They left because the others were dead, or

Handwritten margin notes (left):
① pogroms
② legal ↓ over-populat.
③ cheap boats

102

had left already. They left because "the struggle for living was too great and hard. . . . The persecution of the Jews became unbearable." "People who got it good in the old country don't hunger for the new."

The Jewish immigration was a movement of families. Between 1886 and 1896, an average of 41.6 percent of Jewish immigrants entering the port of New York were women, and 33.8 percent were children under sixteen years of age. This continued after the turn of the century. From 1899 to 1910, women accounted for 43.4 percent of the Jewish immigrant population, and children under fourteen years of age for 24.9 percent. Nearly 70 percent of Jewish immigrants were between the ages of fourteen and forty-four.

For most, it was a permanent move. A smaller percentage of Jews returned to the Old World than of any other immigrant group. Between 1908 and 1924, 94.8 percent of the Jewish immigrants, as contrasted with two-thirds of the total immigrant population, remained in the United States.

The occupational training of Jewish immigrants changed considerably before and after 1900. Prior to 1900, there were fewer industrial workers and more artisans and people engaged in middleman occupations. The years between 1880 and 1900, however, saw great industrial and urban development in both Eastern Europe and the United States. Thus, later immigrants had the opportunity to learn industrial skills in Europe. Immigrants wrote to their family and friends still in Europe, extolling the virtues and necessity of industrial skills. For example, due to the geometric growth of the U.S. garment industry, young people began to take sewing lessons in preparation for emigration. "By 1900 even the daughters of respectable householders had turned their energies and talents to it." The hero of Abraham Cahan's novel, *The Rise of David Levinsky*, recounts his arrival in New York:

> "You're a tailor, aren't you?" [the contractor] questioned him.
> My steerage companion nodded. "I'm a ladies' tailor, but I have worked on men's clothing, too," he said.
> "A ladies' tailor?" the well-dressed stranger echoed, with ill-concealed delight. "Very well; come along. I have work for you."
> . . . "And what was your occupation? You have no trade, have you?"
> "I read Talmud," I said confusedly.
> "I see, but that's no business in America." . . .

The immigration statistics verify this emphasis on skilled labour. Although Jews constituted only 10.3 percent of the total immigrant population between 1900 and 1925, they accounted for one-quarter of the skilled industrial workers entering the United States—nearly one-half of the clothing workers, jewellers, and watchmakers; one-third of the printers; 41.4 percent of the leather workers; and one-fifth of the shopkeepers and merchants. From 1899 to 1914, "Jews ranked first in 26 out of 47 trades tabulated by the Immigration Commission, comprising an absolute majority in eight."

Immigrants often encountered great difficulties arranging passage to America. Often the male members of the family would leave first, sometimes one at a time, and live depriving themselves of all but bare necessities until they had enough money to "bring over" their wives, mothers, sisters, and children. In Anzia Yezierska's short story, *Brothers*, the hero Moisheh tries to save money for ship tickets for his mother and two brothers:

> . . . Moisheh the Schnorrer they call him. He washes himself his own shirts and sews together the holes from his socks to save a penny. Think only! He cooks himself his own meat once a week for Sabbath and the rest of the time it's cabbage and potatoes or bread and herring. And the herring what he buys are the squashed and smashed ones from the bottom of the barrel. And the bread he gets is so old and hard he's got to break it with a hammer.

Even if a ticket were sent, money was needed for travel from the village or town to a port of embarkation. People simply sold all their possessions and left for America by cart, train, or on foot, with packs on their backs held in feather bedding—if that hadn't already been sold as well. If the immigrant was male and of conscription age, he had to be smuggled out of the country, and often left with no passport or identifying papers. Steerage from Hamburg, Bremen, or Antwerp cost $34; from Liverpool, $25. Bribing various officials was another major expense.

At the port the immigrants were examined by a physician. This was not done for their health, but rather with an eye to the ship company's profit: upon arrival at Castle Garden, and after 1892 Ellis Island, immigrants with incurable or contagious diseases or conditions had to return to Europe at the ship company's expense. The medical examination is the subject of the short story *Off for the Golden Land* by the great Yiddish author Sholem Aleichem:

> The time comes to go on board the ship. People tell them that they should take a walk to the doctor. So they go to the doctor. The doctor examines them and finds they are all hale and hearty and can go to America, but she, that is Goldele, cannot go, because she has trachomas on her eyes. At first her family did not understand. Only later did they realize it. That meant that they could all go to America but she, Goldele, would have to remain here in Antwerp. So there began a wailing, a weeping, a moaning. Three times her mamma fainted. Her papa wanted to stay here, but he couldn't. All the ship tickets would be lost. So they had to go off to America and leave her, Goldele, here until the trachomas would go away from her eyes. . . .

The vast majority of immigrants travelled steerage class. They were crammed into the bowels of the ship; some companies even locked them in to prevent them from going on the upper decks and mingling with the second-class passengers. For many the food was inedible since it was not kosher. The nonobservant found it equally inedible because it was so disgusting and decayed. Many people subsisted on a diet of black bread, herring, and tea. Some were fortunate enough to have cheese and butter. Sanitation was terrible, with a few saltwater basins used as dishpans, laundry tubs, and for personal hygiene. The condition of the toilets was worse—open troughs that were rarely flushed and even more rarely cleaned. Throughout their memoirs and oral histories, people recounted tales of terrible seasickness, explaining that the filth and foul smell of their surroundings alone caused nausea.

The voyage lasted anywhere from ten days to three weeks; usually it was a two week trip. They arrived dazed, confused, weak from hunger and seasickness, at "The Island of Tears," Ellis Island. From all reports—those of the immigrants, officials, and the Hebrew Immigrant Aid Society—Ellis Island was a bewildering experience, full of the pain of displacement. During the late nineteenth century, a few thousand immigrants had arrived at Castle Garden each week; throughout the early years of the twentieth century, tens of thousands arrived at Ellis Island each week.

Each immigrant was given a medical and cursory mental examination. People with suspected problems were marked with symbols drawn in chalk on their outer garments. One immigrant recalled that day with horror:

> It was so crowded and noisy. I was a small child then and held fast to my mother's hand. A man in uniform leaned down and drew a letter on my coat. I was frightened. My mother made as if it was hot and opened her cloak wide, doubling it back over her shoulders. Then, after we passed that man, she did the same to me. There were so many people, no one noticed. That's how I got into America.

Trachoma was the cause of more than half the medical detentions, and according to a contemporary article in Scribner's magazine, "most of those detained by the physicians for trachoma are Jews."

Some immigrants were met by relatives, others, sometimes unexpectedly, by landsmen, or fellow-villagers. One immigrant writes that his rabbi in Russia had written to the _landsmanshaften_ (a fraternal organization or lodge composed of fellow townspeople) in New York on his behalf. Thus, to his surprise, he was met at the pier by an old neighbour. Still others were met by contractors on the watch for "greenhorns" (newcomers) experienced at their trade but not in American ways. And finally there were those, like David Levinsky, Abraham Cahan's fictional protagonist, who were simply pointed in the direction of the Lower East Side, and walked until they were greeted with recognizable signs and understandable speech.

Between 70 percent and 90 percent of the Jewish immigrants remained in

70 - 90% stayed in NYC

New York, for a number of reasons. Social ties were very important. Family, friends, or neighbours might have already established themselves there. The desire to settle in a Jewish community was also of great importance. Despite a decrease in strict religious observance, certain essentials were necessary: kosher meat, a rabbi, a minyan (the mandatory minimum of ten men necessary to hold religious services). Many immigrants recalled the great uprooting and intense loneliness mitigated by homely companionship and customs. And, finally, New York was attractive because industrial work was more readily available there than in other parts of the country.

The Jewish immigrant population concentrated in the seventh, tenth, eleventh, and thirteenth wards of lower Manhattan. By 1900, Jews comprised an average of 79 percent of the population of these wards, or an estimated 252,821 individuals. Thus, these can be considered "Jewish" wards.

The living conditions in these wards must not be romanticized. There is a common notion that poor today is not like poor then; old-time poverty was clean, honest, and upright. This is utter nonsense. Poverty, as it existed on the Lower East Side of New York, was noisy, foul-smelling, diseased, hungry:

> The squalid humans that swarmed about . . . the raucous orchestra of voices, the metallic bedlam of elevated trains, the pounding of horses . . . the teeming ghetto . . . haggling pushcart peddlars . . . the dirt and din of screaming hucksters. . . . The slattern yentehs lounging on the stoops, their dirty babies at their breasts. . . . Wedged in, jumbled shops and dwellings, pawn shops and herring-stalls, strained together. . . . Broken stoves, beds, three-legged chairs sprawled upon the sidewalk.

The congestion was overwhelming. The *New York Times* reported on 18 January 1895 that sections of the Lower East Side were more densely populated than the most crowded areas of Bombay or Prague, and immigration had not yet reached its peak. The tenth ward was more densely populated than any European city, with 626.25 persons per acre as compared with 485.4 in Prague and 125.2 in Paris.

In 1905, there were 115 blocks on the Lower East Side with an average density of 750 or more persons per acre, and 39 with a density of 1,000 or more per acre. In Manhattan in the early years of this century, 70 percent of all workers engaged in manufacturing, 67 percent of the factories, and 28 percent of the city's inhabitants were located below 14th Street on one one-hundredth of the city's land area. Furthermore, the Lower East Side had only 29.8 acres of park space, or 2 percent of the city's total park area.

There was an astounding variety of activity in the Lower East Side. The University Settlement Report of 1896 included a social census of the tenth ward. There were 989 tenement houses; eight public schools; three theatres, with a total seating capacity of 9,500; sixteen stables, with a capacity of 210;

thirteen pawnshops; seventy-two restaurants; forty-one churches, of which thirty-one were synagogues; sixty-five factories; 172 garment makers' shops; 236 saloons, of which 108 were Raines Law Hotels, a combination saloon and brothel of the seediest type; and eighteen "disorderly places." There were thirty-four bathtubs; four in private houses, twelve in barber shops, and eighteen in lodging houses. In 1904 David Blaustein, superintendent of the Educational Alliance, took a private census of approximately thirty-two streets south of Houston Street and east of the Bowery. He found 5,007 tenements housing 64,268 families engaged in eighty-four different occupations. There were 306 synagogues, and so few public schools in comparison to need that the children could only attend half-day sessions.

prostitut.

The Lower East Side also had a burgeoning red-light district centred on Allen Street. As the neighbourhood became increasingly Jewish in character, the saloons moved out; Jews were temperate, and business became slack. The red-light district, by contrast, became more prominent. Allen Street was not simply a spectacle in the ghetto. It was part of the way of life of the poor. Michael Gold, an active Communist, remembers the neighbourhood in which he grew up:

> The East Side of New York was then the city's red light district, a vast 606 playground under the business management of Tammany Hall. . . .There were hundreds of prostitutes on my street. They occupied vacant stores, they crowded into flats and apartments in all the tenements. . . .On sun-shiny days the whores sat on chairs along the sidewalks. They sprawled indolently, their legs taking up half the pavements. People stumbled over a gauntlet of whores' meaty legs. . . .Earth's trees, grass, flowers could not grow on my street; but the rose of syphilis bloomed by night and by day.

tenements

Living conditions for the families of the Lower East Side were dictated largely by the conditions of their homes. The tenements, in turn, were fundamental to the health conditions of Lower East Side inhabitants. Legally, "tenement house" was defined in 1867 as, "any house, building . . . occupied as the home or residence of more than three families living independently of one another, and doing their own cooking on the premises, or by more than two families upon a floor, so living and cooking and having a common right in the halls, stairways, yards, water-closets, or privies, or some of them. . . ."This definition could also suit flats and apartment houses, which were not then or now known as tenements. Jacob Riis, an ardent reformer and pioneer photographer-journalist, described the tenement:

defined

> It is generally a brick building from four to six storeys high on the street, frequently with a store on the first floor which, when used for the sale of liquor, has a side opening for the benefit of the inmates and to evade the Sunday law;

four families occupy each floor, and a set of rooms consists of one or two dark closets, used as bedrooms, with a living room twelve feet by ten. The staircase is too often a dark well in the centre of the house, and no direct ventilation is possible. . . .

The immigrants' descriptions were more pithy, if less precise. "Our tenement was nothing but a junk-heap of rotten lumber and brick. . . .The plaster was always falling down, the stairs broken and dirty. . . .There was no drinking water in the tenement for days." "The bedbugs lived and bred in the rotten walls of the tenement, with the rats, fleas, roaches. . . ." "In America were rooms without sunlight."

The number of houses without light, ventilation, hot running water, baths, or water closets was overwhelming. In 1900, the Tenement House Committee of the Charity Organization Society illustrated this problem by exhibiting a cardboard model of an entire block. The chosen block, bounded by Chrystie, Forsyth, Canal, and Bayard streets, was in the tenth ward. The 80,000 square foot area boasted thirty-nine tenement houses (nearly all six storeys high) with 605 apartments. These buildings housed 2,781 people, 2,315 over five years of age and 466 under five. There were 264 water closets; only forty apartments had hot water. The one bathtub on the block, wedged in an air shaft, was obviously unusable. Of the total 1,588 rooms, 441 or 27.7 percent were completely dark, with no access to outer air; 635 rooms or 40 percent were ventilated only by dark, narrow air shafts. The rent roll was high, at $113,964 a year. The disease toll was also high. During the preceding year (1899), thirteen cases of diptheria had been reported to the health department; during the past five years (1895–1900), thirty-two cases of tuberculosis had been reported. It was estimated that "not over two-thirds of the cases are actually reported to the department." Startling as they may seem, these conditions were by no means unique. The block was typical.

The tenement house was not a new invention at the turn of the century, manufactured to accommodate the late mass immigrations. Tenement houses had been a social, political, and health problem in New York City since the early 1800s. Public action, however, was not taken until the middle of the century. In 1842, Dr. John H. Griscom, a city inspector of the State Board of Health, drew attention to tenement house conditions and urged that legislative action be taken to ameliorate the situation. Although this was not done, in 1846 the New York Association for Improving the Condition of the Poor (AICP) began investigating slum conditions. An 1854 report disclosed the startling extent of poverty and disease which the AICP had found, and prodded the public conscience by stressing the great need for reform. As a result of this report, the State Legislature appointed a commission to study the tenement situation and to propose ameliorative legislation. However, in 1857, the legislature turned down the commission's reform bill.

Public interest waned until the draft riots of 1863 and high death rates stimulated a group of prominent New Yorkers to form a Citizens' Association. A sub-committee on sanitary conditions, the Council of Hygiene and Public Health, included eminent physicians. Despite the council's reports on the loathsome sanitary conditions of New York City, the State Legislature still did not act. Finally, in 1865, after cholera appeared in Europe, fear of an epidemic in New York convinced the legislature to establish a Metropolitan Board of Health for New York City (1866), and a Tenement House Law (1867).

The fact that these measures were passed at all was highly significant. It demonstrated the development of a legal consciousness of the importance of the public health. With the Tenement House Law, society recognized the right to limit the entrepreneurial freedom of builders in the interest of public health. However, the law itself was vague, and standards were low. Most requirements could be altered at the discretion of the Board of Health; and the requirements themselves were not sufficient to protect the inhabitants. Among the major provisions: tenements had to have fire escapes or some other means of egress; a water tap had to be furnished either indoors or outside. Only one water closet or privy had to be provided for each twenty inhabitants, and it could be located outdoors (usually in the rear yard). Water closets and privies had to connect with sewers, but only if such existed. Cesspools were forbidden, except where necessary. There was no limit on the percentage of the lot which the building might cover.

In 1879, the history of the tenements took a sharp turn. During December of the previous year, editor Charles F. Wingate held a $500 competition in Henry C. Mayer's new trade journal, the *Plumber and Sanitary Engineer.* The competition, entitled "Improved Homes for Workingmen" or "The Model Home Competition," called for erection on a standard city lot (25 × 100 feet) of a brick building which provided "security against conflagration (including fireproof staircases open to the air), distribution of light, ventilation, drainage and other sanitary appointments . . . inexpensiveness."

James E. Ware won first prize; his construction, commonly known as the "dumbbell" or "double-decker" tenement, was published in March 1879. Despite the magazine's exhortations that "it is irrational to suppose that a commodious and healthful house for a large number of families can be built upon an ordinary lot 25 × 100" and that "the present competition has demonstrated that stringent restrictions should be made upon the erection of houses of this class," the dumbbell tenement was mass-produced for the working class in New York between 1879 and 1901.

The competition stimulated public interest in tenement house reform. On Tenement House Sunday (23 February 1879), concerned New York clergy preached on the subject. On 28 February, at Cooper's Union, Mayor Cooper presided over a large public meeting, again dealing with tenement house reform. Within days, the Mayor's Committee of Nine was formed with a mandate to devise reform measures. Approximately one month later, it introduced a successful bill amending the Tenement House Law of 1867. While the bill modified various regulations of the preceding law and provided for thirty sanitary police to enforce the housing code, it still subjected all requirements to the discretionary power of the Board of Health. It did, however, limit the percentage of space a new building could occupy to 65 percent of the lot, and required a window measuring a minimum of twelve square feet in rooms used for sleeping.

There was no new legislation or important public agitation until 1884, when Professor Felix Adler, founder of the Society for Ethical Culture, again roused public interest and energy with a series of lectures decrying the tenement blight. This renewed public concern forced the legislature to appoint a second legislative commission, whose recommendations stimulated the passage of further amendments to the Tenement House Law in 1887. The number of sanitary police was increased to forty-five. Running water on every floor and one water closet per fifteen inhabitants were now required. The board also took responsibility for inspecting every tenement semiannually.

The mayoral Tenement House Commissions of 1894 and 1900 produced further landmarks of tenement house reform. The 1894 commission was created due to public anger caused by a series of exposés published by a newspaper, the *Press*. The resulting Tenement House Law of 1895 provided for two small parks on the Lower East Side and five recreation piers to be built along the river.

The commission of 1900 grew out of interest stimulated by the Charity Organization Society's (COS) Tenement House Committee exhibit. Lawrence Veiller, who directed this committee, was appointed secretary of the commission. Its recommendations, adopted in their entirety in 1901, prohibited the future erection of dumbbell-type tenements. In new construction, the space between buildings was to be enlarged from an air shaft to a court. A separate water closet had to be installed in each apartment. Although baths were not required, an inspection of 311 new tenement houses revealed that 125 of them, or 40 percent, had a private bath for each apartment. Veiller also reported that many landlords voluntarily improved the plumbing on their property. Clearly, the tenement population desired toilets, sinks with running water, and baths, and were willing to repay the landlord for his investment through increased rent.

Unfortunately, at least initially, the majority of Jewish immigrants were not in a position to take advantage of the major innovations of the 1901 law. For example, the tenth ward had been built up during the last decades of the nineteenth century, and by 1901 little land was left for new construction. The few new apartments built after 1901 were in great demand, especially by those immigrants who had been in New York for a number of years and could afford the luxury. Often, the apartments were rented even before they were completed.

In existing tenements, landlords were required by the 1901 law to install a window in any room which had none. School sinks (sewer-connected privies) and privy vaults had to be replaced with individual water closets. The commission also detailed specifications for fireproofing, fire escapes, and the lighting of public hallways of existing and future tenements. These measures to safeguard the public health were influenced by contemporary medical knowledge. The bacteriological origins of disease set forth by Koch and Pasteur in the 1870s were by this time becoming popularly understood and accepted. The importance of sunlight and ventilation in destroying the tubercle bacillus was stressed in the commission's report.

Within the Jewish wards the dumbbell tenement was the predominant housing structure, and there were a significant number of rear buildings as well. The latter were built prior to 1879 and, without direct access to the street, were less well ventilated and sunlit, and more of a fire hazard than the dumbbell tenement. The dumbbell structure, built between 1879 and 1901, was characterized by an air shaft which was supposed to provide light and air to the rear rooms. In fact, the air shaft was as much a hazard as a convenience. It conveyed noise and odours, and acted like a huge flue in a fire. According to Jacob Riis, "more than half of all fires in New York occur in tenement houses," and the air shaft, functioning like a chimney, "added enormously to the fireman's work and risk." The air shaft also served as a garbage dump, and, consequently, was even more infested with rats and vermin than the other parts of the tenement structure. Statistics prove that landlords were slow to comply with the 1901 window requirements, designed to succeed where the air shaft had failed in providing light and air. There were 350,000 dark interior rooms in Manhattan in 1902. In 1908, there were still 300,000 south of Houston Street alone.

Tenement houses were not just inadequate, unsanitary homes, they were also inadequate, unsanitary work sites. It was not possible to separate "workshop" from "living quarters" among immigrant Jews.

> Let us follow one [immigrant man] to his home and see how Sunday passes in a Ludlow Street tenement.
> Up two flights of stairs, three, four, with new smells of cabbage, of onions, of frying fish, on every landing, whirring sewing machines behind closed doors betraying what goes on within, to the door that opens to admit the bundle [of unfinished garments] and the man. A sweater, this, in a small way. Five men and a woman, two young girls, not fifteen, and a boy who says unasked that he is fifteen and lies in saying it, are at the machines sewing knickerbockers, "knee-pants" in the Ludlow Street dialect. The floor is littered ankle-deep with half-sewn garments. In the alcove, on a couch of many dozens of "pants" ready for

the finisher, a bare legged baby with pinched face is asleep. A fence of piled-up clothing keeps him from rolling off on the floor. The faces, hands, and arms to the elbows of everyone in the room are black with the colour of the cloth on which they are working. . . .

They are "learners," all of them, say the woman . . . and have "come over" only a few weeks ago.

The immigrants arriving in New York found employment wherever they could. "Everyone grabbed the type of job he could get, and changed it very often. . . . Today, one can be a shoemaker; tomorrow, a tailor, and the day after tomorrow he is forced to become a farmer; later a bookkeeper and so on ad infinitum," wrote George Price. Price himself worked in six different types of factories, taught, did manual labour, worked in ditches and on trains, and finally became a prominent physician in the trade union movement.

#1:
NEEDLE
TRADES

The majority of immigrant Jews found work in the needle trades shortly after arrival. Tailoring was easy to learn and was not physically demanding— an excellent combination for the immigrants. Some were snatched up by a contractor at Castle Garden or Ellis Island. Many others entered the needle trades following the example of family or friends who had preceded them. By and large they sought employment among other Jews. This enabled them to observe religious law and eliminated a formidable language barrier. An 1890 survey by the Baron de Hirsch Fund found that 14,316 or 55 percent of the employed permanent residents of wards 7, 10, and 13 worked as tailors, cloakmakers, and labourers in white goods and other branches of the needle trades. There were also 452 furriers and 309 dealers in clothing. Peddling, the

#2:
PEDDLING

second most common occupation, employed another 9.3 percent or 2,440 people. The survey found 1,382 clerks, 976 cigarmakers, 633 shoemakers, and 500 who owned tailor stores. By 1897, according to the 12th Annual Report of the Factory Inspector of New York, 75 percent of the 66,500 workers in the clothing industry in Manhattan and 80 percent of the 15,000 cloakmakers were Jewish. Manhattan was rapidly becoming the hub of the industry; by 1905, half of the clothing manufactured in the United States was produced in New York. The predominance of Jews in the needle trades continued well into the closing years of our study. The fur trade in 1910 was 75 percent Jewish. In 1911, the Joint Board of Sanitary Control in the Cloak, Suit, and Skirt Industry reported that 85 to 90 percent of its workers were Jewish. The dress and waist industry reported in 1913 that 77.7 percent of its workers were female, and that 56.16 of these women were Jewish.

By the late nineteenth century, the needle industry in New York was also overwhelmingly owned and operated by Jews. Historically, Jews had always been involved in the clothing industry. Christians in the United States had allowed Jews to deal in secondhand clothing because this was considered a despicable occupation. This traditional foothold in the clothing industry enabled Jews to take advantage of its fantastic growth during the second half of the nineteenth century.

Three factors greatly stimulated this growth: the Civil War created an unprecedented demand for mass-produced uniforms, the invention of the sewing machine in 1846 provided a means of manufacture, and the large influx of Irish and, later, German immigrants during the mid-century provided the labour force. After the Civil War, the demand for uniforms decreased, but the industry created a consumer market by providing fashionable clothing at much lower cost than custom tailoring. Until the early 1880s skilled German tailors and Irish cutters controlled production. Then competition arrived in the form of Eastern European Jews who had spent time in London learning not only the tailor's craft but also English language and customs. These tailors broke into the production business and paved the way for future immigrants. The clothing industry thus became one of the few in which Jews were employers.

Within the American needle industry, there were three systems and three sites of production. Most antiquated was the so-called "family system," which had become the dominant system of production under German immigrant influence in the mid-nineteenth century. Irish tailors worked in shops, but the Germans worked at home, dividing the labour among family members. Usually the husband was the most skilled worker, the master tailor. He operated the sewing machine while his wife and children did the basting, buttonholes, and finishing touches. This "homework" was done in the family's tenement apartment.

The contracting or "sweatshop" system grew out of the family system. As competition and the volume of work increased, much time had to be spent obtaining work to do; picking up the cloth or, more commonly, pre-cut, unsewn garments; and then delivering the completed product to the warehouse. Enter the contractor. He knew English and had lived in America at least longer than the greenhorns. He contracted with the manufacturer to do X work for Y price by Z date, and was then free to conduct his business as he chose. This seemed ideal to newly arrived immigrants; they could communicate in their own language, observe the Sabbath on Saturday, and maintain other religious laws.

There were a few variants to the contracting system. The contractor could act as a middleman between the working family and the manufacturer, or hire labourers of his own (who would also work in the tenement, either in the contractor's own apartment, or one rented for work purposes), or he could sell the job to a sub-contractor who performed the same function as the contractor himself. Until the last decade of the nineteenth century, the cloak, suit, and skirt trade was primarily controlled by these petty manufacturers. One estimate ascribed 90 percent of all ladies' coats and suits produced in

New York City in 1890 to the contractor. Dr. George Price, by then chairman of the investigative committee of the Joint Board of Sanitary Control in the Cloak, Suit, and Skirt Industry, explained the proliferation of contractors. "Very little capital was needed for the establishment of a shop, as the workers were compelled to furnish their own machines, which were run with foot power. The workers were also often compelled to pay deposits for the privilege of work. All the enterprising manufacturer had to invest was his ability to get work, and perhaps capital enough to pay for the rent of his 'factory.'" These factories were located in lofts, tenement house apartments "converted" for industrial use, or in the tenement home itself. A "cockroach sweater" was the lowest man on the contractor totem pole; his was a small business with few employees, usually run in his own tenement apartment.

The third production site was the inside shop, in which the manufacturer dealt directly with the store buyer, hired his own workers, and ran his own factory. The manufacturer usually worked with a designer, who created fashions or imitated famous designs. The manufacturer displayed these models to the store buyer, who ordered them for the season.

As was generally the case in industry, the physical conditions in which garment workers laboured ranged from poor to foul. The lack of light, space, ventilation, plumbing, and sanitation in tenements has been described already. This situation was exacerbated by the use of the tenements for manufacture. Jacob Riis described the filth and penury over and over again in prose and with photographs. The third annual report (1888) of the New York factory inspectors also discussed the problem of Jewish homework. "They usually eat and sleep in the same room where the work is carried on, and the dinginess, squalor and filth surrounding them is abominable." Annie S. Daniel (1858–1944), an eloquent physician interested in the welfare of the poor and particularly concerned about public health, perceived the problem in 1904–5 from another standpoint:

> These "homes" of working men and women consist of from two to four rooms. In one room, that which opens on the street or yard, is carried on all the domestic life. This room serves for parlor, dining-room, and kitchen; and in this room in addition is carried on the manufacturing. It is quite obvious that the word home was never intended to apply to such an apartment. . . . Every garment worn by a woman is found being manufactured in tenement rooms. . . . [Some] I have seen being made in the presence of small-pox, on the lounge with the patient. . . . Among the 150 families [I attended who did] manufacturing in the living rooms, 66 continued to work during the entire course of the contagious disease.

Conditions in the sweatshops and most factories were equally abominable. In his memoirs, Gregory Weinstein describes a printshop of the 1880s: "Dark shops in rickety buildings; climbing up four, five and six flights of wooden stairs; cases full of dust and rat dirt; working under gas-light from seven o'clock in the morning till six in the evening." Nearly twenty years later, in 1903, conditions in the needle trades were just as bad. Yetta, the heroine of Arthur Bullard's *roman á clef, Comrade Yetta*, views her surroundings: "She saw the broken door to the shamefully filthy toilet, saw the closed, unwashed windows, which meant vitiated, tuberculosis-laden air, saw the backs of the women bent into unhealthy attitudes, saw the strained look in their eyes."

By 1910, homework was in Italian immigrant hands: Jewish labour had moved into inside shops. Unfortunately, most workshops were not a great improvement. In 1910, inspection of 228 waist shops employing 11,000 workers showed that 62 percent used inadequate artificial light, and 60 percent provided no protection against the glare. Thirty percent had filthy water closets with no light or ventilation, and in 28 percent of the shops the general conditions were labelled "extremely dirty". Loft buildings housed 91 percent of the inspected establishments, and over one-half of the employees worked above the sixth floor. This was basically the case in all branches of the needle trades. Loft buildings had improved sanitary conditions in the industry; they were new edifices with large windows providing natural illumination and ventilation, and had up-to-date plumbing facilities. But they posed a much greater fire hazard than previous work sites. Building materials were flammable, fire escapes were either not provided or inadequate, and the loft buildings were simply too high—the Fire Department could not handle fires above the seventh floor. This dilemma was horribly illustrated by the famous fire at the Triangle Waist Company on 25 March 1911, which killed 146 employees.

A 1913 inspection of 700 dress and waist shops revealed that 97.3 percent were located in loft buildings, 2.7 percent in converted buildings, and none in tenements or cellars. The sanitary conditions of the loft buildings were considered very good with only 5 percent using artificial light and 3 percent having no protection from glare. Only 4.5 percent had dirty water closets. However, if anything, the danger from fire had increased, as there were now more people working at greater heights. A little over 50 percent of those in the industry, or 18,417 persons, worked on or above the sixth floor, and nearly 10 percent, or 3,530 persons, worked on or above the twelfth floor. The Fire Department was still incapable of handling fires at these heights, and only 7 percent of the shops practised fire drills. Fifteen shops had no fire escapes; forty-seven had obstructed access to the fire escape; and forty-six had no safe means to escape from the fire escape, which meant that workers could be trapped in an enclosed courtyard or alley—a tunnel of fire. A full 30 percent of the shops had doors which opened inward, making escape difficult and dangerous. Finally, as in the Triangle fire, a few employers still illegally locked their employees in the work room, making escape impossible.

Similar conditions prevailed in the predominantly male cloak, suit, and skirt industry. After the great cloakmakers' strike in 1910, a Joint Board of Sanitary Control was established to study and ameliorate shop conditions. In 1911, the committee of investigation published its report on 1,738 shops. Two-thirds were found deficient in fire protection and/or sanitary conditions. At a time when chewing tobacco was common and spitting was not considered impolite, over 99 percent of the shops had no cuspidors (in direct opposition to the law), thus increasing the risk of tubercular infection. The legal limit of one water closet for every twenty-five persons was also largely ignored—some shops had only one water closet for eighty-five workers. Hot water, towels, and rubbish bins were nearly unheard of, and 6.8 percent of the shops were poorly ventilated. Lunch was eaten in the shop room itself. As in the dress and waist industry, however, fire was by far a greater danger to the workers than were the poor sanitary conditions. Loft buildings housed 90 percent of workers, 50 percent between the sixth and twelfth floors. The interiors of the buildings were hazardous, and rapid escape difficult. The halls were narrow; there were only 1,951 stairways in 1,738 buildings. Thus, most shops had only one means of egress, built either of stone, which heated quickly and then crumbled when wetted, or of wood, which burned easily. The vast majority of shops (84 percent) had only one fire escape, often narrow, leading into an enclosed courtyard or alley.

In 1911, the Joint Board of Sanitary Control adopted sanitary standards which included fire precaution and prevention regulations. Certificates were given to worthy shops. In February 1912, shops employing 40 percent of the workers were so certified, and in September 1912, shops employing 61 percent of the workers were found sanitary. By September 1913, 79 percent of the workers were employed in certified shops. In May of the same year the Joint Board published an alphabetical list of approved establishments.

Thus far, we have primarily examined the physical and sanitary conditions of two branches of the ladies' garment industry. While the great majority of Jewish immigrants were industrial workers, not all were employed in the clothing industry. Industrial conditions in general were on a par with those of the needle trades prior to the 1910 cloakmakers' strike and subsequent formation of the Joint Board of Sanitary Control. George Price, reporting in 1912 for the Factory Investigating Commission (which had been established in response to the public's outcry after the Triangle fire), noted that 54 percent of the shops had no, or insufficient, washing facilities, and an even larger percentage had no hot water. Few had lunch rooms; the great majority of workers ate in the work room. Poor toilet accommodations were the rule. Very few shops had emergency rooms or first aid facilities in case of illness or accident. The worst offender was the food industry, with baking, nutpicking, and ice cream manufacture commonly done in the tenement.

Not only were the physical conditions of the workplace disgusting, degrading, and unhealthful, but the long hours and low wages increased the strain on the worker's constitution. Lillian Wald, founder of the Henry Street Settlement, wrote:

> From the windows of our tenement home we could look upon figures bent over the whirring footpower machines. One room in particular almost unnerved us. Never did we go to bed so late or rise so early that we saw the machines at rest, and the unpleasant conditions where manufacturing was carried on in the overcrowded rooms of the families we nursed disquieted us more than the disease we were trying to combat.

It is impossible to discern exactly how many hours per day or week people worked. Hours differed from industry to industry, from "outside" shop to "inside" factory, and from rush to slack seasons. In 1891, New York factory inspectors reported a sixty-six-to-seventy-two-hour minimum work week during the slack season in the clothing industry (if the worker was lucky enough to maintain his position), and sixteen to nineteen hours a day, seven days a week during the busy season. Dr. Annie Daniel reported women working at home nineteen hours a day, seven days a week during the busy season in 1904–5. Workers were hard put to decide which was worse: the anxiety and poverty of the slack season with little or no employment, or the hours and tension of the rush season with greater and greater work demands. Hours in the factories were slightly better. In 1894 the cloakmakers' union went on strike for—and won—a ten-hour day, reduced from the standard twelve to fifteen hours. In 1901, nearly all clothing union workers sought a fifty-nine-hour week.

Wages depended upon position, piecework, sex, and whether the worker was employed by a contractor or in a factory. In all cases, wages were low, the difference being between poverty and penury. In 1888, male cloak-makers in inside shops earned an average weekly wage of $12. Annie Daniel reported that female homeworker wages averaged $1.04 a week in 1904–5, and the average weekly income from the man's work was $3.81. Jacob Riis gives various piecework prices: there were knee pants "for which the manufacturer pays seventy cents a dozen," or another grade of kneepants at 42¢ a dozen. The finisher of the garment "gets ten and the ironer eight cents a dozen: button-holes are extra, at eight to ten cents a hundred." According to the United States Industrial Reports, between 1880 and 1901 the weekly wage of New York coatmakers in task shops fell nearly 17 percent. The work day increased by 20 percent and productivity increased by 66 percent. There were no significant technical advances during this period, nor any improvement in the division of labour. The workers simply worked harder and longer.

CHAPTER

9

The tension between the native and the newcomer is a perennial theme in immigration history. What makes the case of late nineteenth century American Jews different is the fact that the natives and the newcomers were kinfolk: German Jews and East Europeans. Enmity between them went back to Europe, where German Jews habitually viewed Ostjuden (Eastern Jews) as unenlightened medievals, and Ostjuden in turn viewed them as assimilated and godless. But such stereotypes did not prevent German Jews from being both sympathetic to the plight of the East Europeans and eager to help them.

The rift between the two groups—referred to as the split between "uptown" and "downtown," or between the "Yahudi" and the "immigrant"—developed in America early in the 1880s. German Jews feared that immigration would provoke anti-Semitism, saw newcomers as social inferiors, recognized that their own community was fast becoming outnumbered, and, at least in the early years, discouraged East European Jews from immigrating, doubting that they could succeed. East European Jews were naturally resentful, notwithstanding the material support that German Jews extended to them, and many bristled at being the objects of charity, much as they may have needed it. Some projected onto German Jews their frustrations about America as a whole, and sought as a matter of right the kind of social equality that time alone could create for them.

Yet, bad as feelings sometimes became, German-Jewish leaders continued to work long and hard on behalf of the East Europeans. The great "uptown" leader and lawyer, Louis Marshall, actually learned Yiddish—and he was not alone. As time went on, individuals in both camps grew to respect one another. When critical issues arose, such as immigration legislation and bills aimed at abrogating America's commercial treaty with Russia, German Jews and Eastern European Jews stood shoulder to shoulder; they planned strategy together. In the end, bonds of kinship proved far stronger than petty in-group squabbles.

Moses Rischin, in the essay that follows, traces these developments as they took place in New York. Moving beyond an earlier generation of historians concerned only to affix blame, Rischin sees the interplay between native Jews and immigrants in its full complexity: negative images as well as positive

118

actions, altruism as well as self-interest. He describes the manifold institutions created by Germans and by East Europeans, and shows how they functioned together to promote Jewish unity.

As Rischin realizes, a fascinating process was taking place in New York. Though scarcely recognized at the time, German Jews and East European Jews, by coming together, were paving the way for a new community. Leaving behind one riddled with inner divisions that fractured even immigrant enclaves, they were forging what would become known as an ethnic community. It divided along ideological and religious lines, and left old-world geographical ones behind.

German	E. Europ.
uptown	downtown
Yahudi	immigrant
yekkes	Hunkies
	Ostjuden
Western/ Occidental/ European	"Eastern/ Oriental/ Asiatic"
classes	masses
Americans	foreigners
mansion	tenement
employer	employee
cultured/refined	primitive/medieval

Germans versus Russians

Moses Rischin

At a time when established Jews were becoming acutely sensitive to the opinions of their fellow New Yorkers, they were faced with the prospect of a mass migration of coreligionists from Eastern Europe, whose coming seemed to threaten their hard-won respectability. German Jews had shed the tradesman's mien and were acquiring the higher mercantile manner. As they became Americanized, their ties with the German community in New York became less pronounced and they, along with Jews of American origin, were discovering a common identity as Jews that they had not known earlier.

Yet in the years of the great Jewish migration, to be identified as a Jew became more and more irksome. The hosts of uncouth strangers, shunned by respectable New Yorkers, seemed to cast a pall upon all Jews. Disturbed native and German Jews, heirs to the age of reason and science, condemned everything that emanated from the downtown quarter.

It had not been so earlier, when disparities had been less marked and less consequential. East Europeans, few and far between, blended into the immigrant city and created no problems. Place of origin, family pride, clan solidarity, and intellectual tastes loosely defined business and social relations, but differences were in degree rather than in kind and fleeting contacts minimized friction. Gruff-mannered East Europeans tended to hover on the edge of more elegant "German" society despite mutual animosities. The Russian-Polish Jew, assuming German airs, became the "Kavalier Datch." Selig became Sigmund, eager to dwell in the shadow of German respectability, at last to claim, "Mayn waib is gevoren ah datchke un ich bin gevoren ah datch" (My wife has become a lady and I a gentleman). As the East European colony took shape, the German model persisted; but it lost its primacy, for Russian pioneers could now turn to their own circles to satisfy their social needs.

Established New York Jews made every effort to become one with progress. In 1870 the *New York Times* saluted Temple Emanu-El in its new Moorish edifice as one of the globe's leading congregations, "the first to stand forward before the world and proclaim the dominion of reason over blind and bigoted faith." Clearly an age was dawning when all men, regardless of race or ancestral faith, would come together in universal communion. "In the erection and dedication of the Fifth Avenue Temple, it was not only the congregation that was triumphant, it was Judaism that triumphed, the Judaism of the heart, the Judaism which proclaims the spirit of religion as being of more importance than the letter." In 1873 German Emanu-El turned to Manchester, England, and called Gustav Gottheil to its pulpit to preach Judaism's universal message in impeccably English accents, comprehensible to all New Yorkers.

European events sustained in German Jews the conviction of the supreme merit and eventual acceptance of all things German—all, regrettably, but language. With the rise of a new Germany, New York Germans, even as they became more American, compensated for earlier rebuffs with a rising flamboyance. Jews shared in the elation and further celebrated the removal of lingering disabilities upon their kin in the new empire. They took new pride in their roots and vicariously partook of German imperial prestige, assured that the German Empire meant "peace, liberty, progress, and civilization." German Jews, insisted Rabbi Kaufmann Kohler, free of the "shackles of medievalism," their minds "impregnated with German sentiment . . . no longer Oriental," stood convinced of their superiority to East Europeans and regarded all vestiges of a segregated past with discomfort.

The fears of uptowners, colored with racist phraseology, smoldered in the Anglo-Jewish press. There anti-Russian sentiment assumed a withering metaphysical rationale as "a piece of Oriental antiquity in the midst of an ever-Progressive Occidental civilization" called forth the ghost of a happily forgotten past. Uptown Jews, sensitive to the reverberations of the new German anti-Semitism, were far more distressed by the "un-American" ways of the "wild Asiatics" than were non-Jews. "Are we waiting for the natural process of assimilation between Orientalism and Americanism? This will perhaps never take place," exclaimed the *American Hebrew*. The *Hebrew Standard* echoed these misgivings: "The thoroughly acclimated American Jew . . . has no religious, social or intellectual sympathies with them. He is closer to the Christian sentiment around him than to the Judaism of these miserable darkened Hebrews." Even Emma Lazarus in her sonnet inscribed to the Statue of Liberty, "Mother of Exiles," called the immigrants of the 1880s "the wretched refuse of your teeming shore."

Nothing in the newcomers seemed worthy of approval. Yiddish, or Judeo-German, "a language only understood by Polish and Russian Jews," though intelligible to non-Jewish Germans, was denounced as "piggish jargon." Immigrant dress, ceremonials, and rabbinical divorces were anathema.

"wretched refuse"

Yiddish theaters were barbarous, Yiddish newspapers, collectively stig-
matized as "socialistic," even worse. Furthermore, "dangerous principles"
were "innate in the Russian Jew." Mounting newspaper publicity proved
especially distasteful. "The condition of the Jewish quarter . . . has too often
been the subject of extravagant word-painting." Lincoln Steffens's reports of
East Side life in the *Evening Post* and *Commercial Advertiser* were resented
equally with Abraham Cahan's realist fictional essays.

> Our newspapers have daily records of misdemeanors, marital misery, and
> petty quarrels that may largely be attributed to the same source. The efforts of
> intelligent brethren to raise the standards of Judaism have been frustrated by the
> efforts of misguided people who regard all teaching and criticism, as an outrage
> on their suddenly acquired and misunderstood liberty.

Most intolerable of all was that "anomaly in America, 'Jewish' trades unions."
Germans, embarrassed by Russian business competition, dismissed their
rivals, whose names often ended with "ki," as "kikes." So Russians often were
forced to Germanize their names in order to escape the stigma among German credit men. "Uptown" and "downtown" separated employers from employees, desirable from undesirable, "classes" from "masses," "Americans"
from "foreigners," and icily confirmed the most categorical judgments.

Making New Americans

Yet, uptowners of means spared no effort to assist downtowners. "The
uptown mansion never forgets the downtown tenement in its distress."
Uptowners, taken unawares by the heavy immigration of terror-stricken
refugees in 1881 and fearful of a pauper problem, attempted to restrain further
immigration. But as the tide could not be stemmed, the Jewish charities of the
city, aided considerably by West European Jewry, chafingly accepted their
new responsibilities. The *American Hebrew* urged: "All of us should be sensible
of what we owe not only to these . . . coreligionists, but to ourselves, who will
be looked upon by our gentile neighbors as the natural sponsors for these,
our brethren."

The established Jewish charities proved unequal to the new demands.
The United Hebrew Charities, formed in 1874 during the economic crisis, had
efficiently administered extra-institutional relief, but so moderate had been
the claims made upon it, that in 1880 its treasury showed a balance of $14,000.
Mass migration transformed the scope of Jewish charity. The Hebrew Emigrant Aid Society, improvised for the crisis, raised $300,000 to succor the first
contingents of refugees. In a single year, the HEAS expended as much as had
the United Hebrew Charities in its seven-year existence. "Assistance was no

longer claimed as a fraternal right, nor extended as a kin-like obligation," recalled Professor Jacob H. Hollander two decades later at the Fifth Biennial Session of the National Conference of Jewish Charities.

It was the imperious demand of stricken humanity. But, as the situation lost its bitter novelty and the burden settled in onerous pressure, benevolence waned and something akin to patronage grew. The charitable association became no longer a semi-social device whereby the more prosperous members of the community relieved the misfortunes of neighbors and associates, but a tax-like charge for the indefinite relief of misery and dependence of a distinct class, different in speech, tradition and origin, unsought in arrival and unwelcome in presence, whose only claim was a tenuous tie of emotional appeal and an identical negation in religious belief.

Help continued nevertheless. Local groups and individuals, aided by the Independent Order of B'nai B'rith, the Baron de Hirsch Fund, and the Union of American Hebrew Congregations, ministered to the needs of immigrants. The Forty-Eighter Michael Heilprin of the *Nation* came to a premature end as a result of his exertions to settle immigrants on the land. When refugees overflowed Castle Garden and the lodging houses nearby, the State Commissioners of Emigration opened the Ward's Island buildings to the newcomers and Jacob H. Schiff contributed $10,000 for the erection of auxiliary barracks. The United Hebrew Charities provided free lodgings, meals, medical and midwife care, and, for countless unfortunates, free burial. The UHC's employment bureau did its best, even when "the market was overladen with the kind of work offered" and "applicants were nearly all without special trade or calling and . . . physically unable to comply with the conditions demanded in this country." In 1885, despite depressed trade conditions, the UHC's employment bureau turned away only 744 of 3036 applicants as unemployable.

German Jews devised comprehensive schemes to divest downtown brethren of the marks of oppression and to remodel them in the uptown image. Mrs. Minnie D. Louis's sixteen-verse poem outlining uptown's Americanizing mission, "What it is to be a Jew," opened with the image of the ghetto Jew,

> To wear the yellow badge, the locks,
> The caftan-long, the low-bent head,
> To pocket unprovoked knocks
> And shamble on in servile dread—
> 'Tis not this to be a Jew

and closed with a portrait of the American Jew, fully realized,

> Among the ranks of men to stand
> Full noble with the noblest there;

To aid the right in every land
With mind, with might, with heart, with prayer—
This is the eternal Jew!

Vocational training

First and foremost came vocational preparation, training not available to immigrants under other auspices, and tutelage in American customs. With these goals in mind, the United Hebrew Charities had organized special classes in the domestic and sewing arts for girls as early as 1875, and a few years later the Hebrew Free School Association had opened the Hebrew Technical School for girls. After 1890 the Baron de Hirsch Fund supervised and supported an array of educational facilities that included the Hebrew Technical Institute for boys, an evening technical school, and evening English classes, initiated by the YMHA to supplement the public evening schools. "Jargon journalists, Hebrew teachers, musicians" anxious to qualify for admission to professional schools, were given special instruction; in 1896, of a class of eighteen, eight were admitted to medical school, three to law school, and four to special technical schools. Earlier as later, insufficient classrooms postponed for many months admission to public education, and a preparatory school was organized to drill the fundamentals into children who waited to be admitted to the bulging city schools. Between 1905 and 1910 school buildings on the Lower East Side were so strained that the Camp Huddleston Hospital Ship at the foot of Corlears Hook was converted into a city school where ten thousand children received instruction.

The zeal to Americanize underlay all educational endeavor, from kindergartens first organized in 1882, on up through the grades. The Hebrew Free School Association, originally founded to discourage Christian missionizing among the children of the poor, recast the course of study of its afternoon schools. Training in the amenities, cleanliness, and the practical home and industrial arts crowded aside the curriculum of Jewish history, Jewish religion, and the Hebrew elements. The Reverend Clifton Harby Levy's advice to the trustees of the Baron de Hirsch classes that the addition of Hebrew to the curriculum would enlist parental support was ignored. The Federation of Temple Sisterhoods, originating in 1887 with the Emanu-El Sisterhood, sponsored classes of like pattern and maintained day nurseries as well. But in 1905 only one Jewish-sponsored crèche, the Brightside Nursery, served the entire Lower East Side.

Uptown reached the summit of its Americanization program in the Hebrew Institute. This Jewish-sponsored community house, hailed by its founders as a "center of sweetness and light, an oasis in the desert of degradation and despair," was organized jointly in 1889 by the Hebrew Free School Association, the Young Men's Hebrew Association, and the Aguilar Free Library Society. In 1891 it was housed in an impressive five-story structure at the northeast corner of Jefferson Street and East Broadway, and in 1893

Uptown : Americanizatn

Ed.
Alliance

it was renamed the Educational Alliance. From 9 A.M. to 10 P.M., class and meeting rooms, an auditorium seating seven hundred, library, gymnasium, shower baths, and a roof garden entertained a wide range of activities. While adults learned "the privileges and duties of American citizenship," youngsters received the benefits of its many advantages. Vocational courses, classes in English, civics, American history, and English literature, and Edward King's especially popular classes in Greek and Roman history were augmented by sermons, public lectures sponsored by the Board of Education, and flag-waving exercises on the national holidays.

CULTURE

Not until the first decade of the twentieth century was the Educational Alliance to bridge the gap between modern, urban New York and the psychological world of Torah and ghetto by conducting its courses in Yiddish. But its initial program remained an outstanding unifier. A host of clubs, each with patron author, poet, scientist, statesman, or philosopher—including the George Eliot Circle for girls—crowded the calendar and vied for the never-adequate meeting rooms. In a city growing more sensitive to the collective pleasures given by music, musical training especially was encouraged. Piano, violin, mandolin, and singing classes met regularly and the melodic din of rehearsing trios, quartets, orchestras, choral groups, and a children's symphony echoed through its halls. If drawing classes elicited a poor response, art exhibitions jointly sponsored with the University Settlement, assisted by the public schools, set unprecedented attendance records. A ten-cent admission charge to Saturday evening concerts and entertainments discouraged only the mischief makers from attending. The first English performances in the Jewish quarter, "As You Like It" and "The Tempest," added Shakespearean fare to Purim and Hanukkah plays. Physical exercise, slighted by serious youngsters, was promoted by a full and vigorous athletic program. Dr. Jane Robbins, a founder of the College Settlement, spoke to young women on personal health and feminine hygiene in 1898, and leading physicians lectured to young men on "The Marriage Question: Its Physical and Moral Sides." A few years later the Henry Street Settlement welcomed similar talks, presaging the introduction of such education into the public schools. In the first decade of the new century, a few hundred paid and voluntary workers descended upon the Alliance, its annex, and its two subbranches to direct and supervise a beehive of activity that weekly attracted some 37,000 adults and youngsters.

Deeply influencing the children, the Educational Alliance remained alien to the adult East Side, more so perhaps than the public schools and settlements, for these at least did not represent themselves as Jewish. At the Alliance, English was the official language and at the Alliance's People's Synagogue Dr. Adolph Radin conducted religious services in Hebrew and German. Yiddish, in immigrant eyes the touchstone of Jewishness, was taboo. Although the Alliance's successive Russian-born directors, Isaac Spec-

Yiddish taboo at Alliance

torsky and David Blaustein, could do little to affect the major lines of institutional policy, they were sensitive to the needs of their countrymen. The reading room, visited by a thousand persons daily, bulged with over one hundred Hebrew, Russian, and Yiddish journals. The Zionist Hebrew Literary Society, where youngsters sampled their first Hebrew idyl or renewed a romance with a reborn Hebrew literature, "is certainly in the line of moral culture," noted David Blaustein apologetically in the Alliance's annual report. The Russian-American Hebrew Association, founded in 1890 by Dr. Radin, its president and sole officer, "to exercise a civilizing and elevating influence upon the immigrants and to Americanize them," broke precedent to permit Zevi H. Masliansky, the East Side's magnetic Zionist preacher, to lecture in his native Yiddish. No less than Hebrew and Yiddish, Russian, the language of the intelligentsia, was unwelcome at the Alliance, although on occasion Russian-speaking societies met on the premises. Radin, a Posen Jew, felt moved to explain that "Russian" simply designated the place of origin of the immigrants, not the "half-barbarous civilization often signified by that name."

Philanthropy versus Self-Help

Despite their failings, German-Jewish charitable institutions aroused the admiration of all New Yorkers. Echoing Andrew Carnegie, Jacob H. Schiff, writing in the *Independent*, reaffirmed the stewardship of wealth with Jewish overtones. "Philanthropy as the aim and ideal of Judaism," succinctly described the path taken by the religious impulse.

Few human needs were overlooked. Old institutions were modernized and expanded and new ones were established to meet unanticipated requirements. Mount Sinai, formerly the Jews' Hospital, admitted more free clients than any other private institution in the city; nearly nine-tenths of its patients in the 1880s were treated without charge. The Hebrew Orphan Asylum Society and the Hebrew Sheltering and Guardian Society generously provided for orphans, while the Clara de Hirsch Home for Working Girls provided adolescents with recreational facilities. The Association for the Improved Instruction of Deaf Mutes—the oldest oral and only Jewish school for the deaf in the country—and societies for the blind and the crippled aided the handicapped. In 1893 a Jewish Prisoners' Aid Association was formed reluctantly to minister to the relatively small but growing number of Jewish prison inmates. Before the turn of the century offending Jewish lads had been sent to the state-maintained House of Refuge or to the Catholic Protectory, as Jews proved laggard in providing for their youthful transgressors. But a precipitous rise in juvenile delinquency led to the founding in 1907 of the Hawthorne School of the Jewish Protectory and Aid Society. The Lakeview Home for Jewish unmarried mothers followed; and a few years later, the

Jewish Big Brother and the Jewish Big Sister associations were formed to supervise youngsters on probation. Rounding out the major Jewish social agencies organized primarily to care for immigrant needs was the National Desertion Bureau, founded in 1911 to locate missing husbands.

Uptown institutions, however proficient and commendable, did not satisfy downtowners. East Europeans, treated as mendicants, were hardly grateful for the bounty bestowed. Efficient charity, with its documents and inquests, seemed incapable of performing the religious obligation of *Zedakah*—on its highest plane, pure loving-kindness. Prying strangers outraged the sense of decency of folk who in their home circles were often persons of consequence. As soon as it was possible, self-respecting immigrants made every effort to assist their own.

> In the philanthropic institutions of our aristocratic German Jews you see beautiful offices, desks, all decorated, but strict and angry faces. Every poor man is questioned like a criminal, is looked down upon; every unfortunate suffers self-degradation and shivers like a leaf, just as if he were standing before a Russian official. When the same Russian Jew is in an institution of Russian Jews, no matter how poor and small the building, it will seem to him big and comfortable. He feels at home among his own brethren who speak his tongue, understand his thoughts and feel his heart.

LANDSMANSCHAFT

From their earliest coming, immigrants in need instinctively turned to their fellow townsmen. "The amount of small charity given directly from the poor to the poorer will never be known." The many-sided *landsmanshafts*, uniting the features of the Old World burial, study, and visitors-of-the-sick societies, bound the immigrant to his *shtetl* and birthplace. At first these societies had been coextensive with synagogues. But with the onset of the *e g Tifereth* great migration each town and village asserted its individuality. As early as 1892 a contemporary directory listed 136 religious societies in the Lower East Side and doubtless there were more. Ninety-three were registered as Russian-Polish; the rest, classified as Austro-Hungarian, embraced Austrian, Hungarian, Rumanian, and some German congregations. The Beth Hamedrash Hagadol on Norfolk Street alone welcomed all Jews.

After 1880 *landsmanshafts* independent of synagogue ties began to supersede the religious societies. The better managed benevolent societies furnished insurance, sick benefits, and interest-free loans, as well as cherished cemetery rights. In time, women's auxiliary aid societies were founded, whose members were tutored in the parliamentary amenities by their male sponsors. In 1914, 534 benevolent societies, with from fifty to five-hundred members each, embraced virtually every immigrant household in New York City. When *landsmanshafts* affiliated with fraternal orders, they were transformed into familiar American lodges. Since the established German associations discouraged the entrance of newcomers, East Europeans formed their own. In 1887 Hungarians organized the Independent Order Brith Abraham, which conducted its business in German, but welcomed all comers; this organization soon became the largest of all Jewish fraternal orders. In 1900 the Workmen's Circle and in 1912 the Jewish National Workers' Alliance were founded by Jewish trade unionists dissatisfied with the quasi-religious ritual and tone of the existing orders.

By the late 1880s, East Europeans had already begun to organize their own communal charities. Russians and Austro-Hungarians founded their respective free burial societies. The cathedral Russian congregation established the Passover Relief Committee of the Beth Hamedrash Hagadol and prided itself on its catholicity: "In dispensing money and matzos to the poor, all are recognized as the children of one Father, and no lines are drawn between natives of different countries." The *Hevra Hachnosas Orchim* (the Hebrew Sheltering Society), formed in 1890, undertook to feed, lodge, and clothe friendless immigrants and to aid them in finding employment or in seeking out *landsleit*. In 1909 the Hebrew Sheltering Society was united with the Hebrew Immigrant Aid Society, founded in 1902 to ease the entrance of newcomers into the country. The expanded HIAS was to serve the needs of immigrants for over half a century.

The self-help principle took characteristic communal form in 1892 in the *Gemillat Hasodim* Association, the Hebrew Free Loan Society. The Society, relying solely on the endorsement of merchants of standing, made interest-free loans of from $10 to $200 to immigrants eager to set up independently in business. Within little more than a decade, the society's funds soared to over $100,000 as grateful borrowers, recalling the source of their success, contributed to its capital.

East Europeans also founded their own hospitals. Beth Israel, beginning in 1889 as a dispensary on Birmingham Alley, "the shortest and most dismal street in the whole city," grew to become the Lower East Side's leading hospital. Lebanon Hospital, Beth David, and the Hungarian People's Hospital followed, and in 1904 Galicians and Bukovinians undertook to found Har Moriah. Despite the opposition of the United Hebrew Charities, East Side physicians organized the Jewish Maternity Hospital in 1906 so that East Side mothers no longer had to depend on the New York Lying-In Hospital. These East Side institutions could be trusted to be kosher and to treat East European patients and physicians as equals. (Although 90 percent of Mount Sinai's patients were East Europeans, East European physicians were not admitted to that hospital's staff.) In 1897 institutional care for the aged poor also was inaugurated with the founding of the Home of the Daughters of Jacob.

Levantine Jews maintained an existence independent of Yiddish New York. As early as 1884 Gibraltans, culturally akin to the Levantines, founded Congregation Moses Montefiore in East Harlem. However, the number of true Levantines did not become significant until over two decades later when unrest within the Turkish empire brought a mixed multitude of ten thousand to the city. Dominantly Judeo-Spanish (Ladino) in speech, they included several hundred Greek-speaking Jews, and one thousand Arabic-speaking Jews from Aleppo in Syria. At first they were aided especially by the sisterhood of the city's oldest congregation, the Sephardic Shearith Israel, distant kin indeed to the newcomers. But in 1913 these latest immigrants organized a mutual benefit society and the Oriental Ozer Dalim Society to care for their own needy.

The religious urgency to provide a genuinely Jewish education for their sons drove downtowners to trust to their own resources. Half the Lower East Side children receiving a religious education in the 1890s attended the classes of the Hebrew Free School Association, but most of them were girls, for these classes did not answer the needs of East Europeans (many of whom even suspected that the cookie-laden Mrs. Minnie Louis of the Downtown Sabbath School was a Christian missionary). Parents gladly sacrificed to send their sons to the traditional Hebrew schools; the registration in 1903 at the Lower East Side's 307 *cheders* (religious elementary schools) was 8616 boys and only 361 girls. There the *rebbe* (religious teacher) linked the generations in intimacy of mood, ritual, and language, and slaked the consciences of parents who welcomed the opportunities thrown open to their children by the public schools, but who dreaded the impiety and the emptiness created between generations.

Late afternoon and early evening, pedagogues in basements or tenement flats, above saloons and dance halls, drove youngsters through the mechanics of prayer-book reading, rarely understood in the Old World, but in the New not even feared or respected. More ambitious and systematic were the Talmud Torahs which at first dispensed shoes and clothing along with a traditional religious education. In 1886 the Machzike Talmud Torah acquired its own building on East Broadway and soon shed its charitable aspect. In the same year the Yeshiva Etz Chaim was founded as an all-day school where a small number of youngsters pursued talmudical learning. In 1901 the Americanized Jacob Joseph Yeshiva was organized "to prepare Hebrew boys for life in this country." Finally, the Yeshiva Isaac Elchanan, organized in 1896 for the pursuit of advanced talmudical studies, completed the educational ladder for traditional Jewish learning. While most parents strained to pay the small fees, many were neglectful or unable to meet their obligations. The announcements in 1908 that three out of every four children received no religious education was doubtless exaggerated. Even so, it did reflect poverty, indifference, and weakened parental control. A dismal literal translation of the Talmud testified to the hopelessness of inspiring respect for traditional knowledge among the American-born.

A few enthusiasts, disgusted with formalistic Jewish studies, pioneered modern Jewish schools in an effort to link son to father, to breathe meaning into an ancient heritage in the modes of a new age. Zionists opened modern Hebrew schools in the 1890s while Jewish nationalists founded Yiddish folk schools around 1910, both groups searching for bridges over the chasm separating the generations that would unite the most advanced democratic ideals to a transvalued Jewish tradition. Random trials also were made with socialist Sunday schools, sponsored by the Socialist party, where lessons in "capitalist ethics" were replaced by lessons in "socialist ethics." At Emma Goldman and Alexander Berkman's Ferrer Center and School, two dozen youngsters were regaled with the lessons of anarcho-communism and listened to lectures by Clarence Darrow, Edwin Markham, and Lincoln Steffens that pointed to the free development of the individual. However humanitarian in intent, these experiments remained on the fringe of the immigrant community and acquired but a small and uncertain following.

The Larger Giving

Traditions of Jewish communal responsibility left little need for outside aid. Despite seasonal unemployment and acute poverty in the mid-nineties and during the 1907 and 1914 depressions, the resources of city, state, and non-Jewish private agencies were lightly taxed. In crisis years, aroused private citizens lent a hand, and examples of nonsectarian charity were many. In 1882 non-Jewish merchants and bankers contributed to the Hebrew Emigrant Aid Society, while in 1891, at a banquet honoring Jesse Seligman, non-Jews contributed to the Russian Transportation Fund for the Moscow refugees. In the depressed nineties Mrs. Josephine Shaw Lowell's East Side Relief Work "put our poor 'Hebrew Jews' at work to clothe the poor Negroes of the Sea Islands," and John B. Devins, pastor of Hope Chapel, transformed the East Side Relief Workers' Committee into the Federation of East Side Workers that included Protestants, Catholics, and Jews. In 1907 Mrs. Russell Sage and Warner Van Norden made substantial gifts to the United Hebrew Charities; Henry Phipps, too, proved a generous and steady supporter of the Legal Aid Bureau of the Educational Alliance.

Where municipal, state, and private institutions felt the pressure of the newcomers, they shared the burdens with the Jewish agencies. The City's Board of Estimate annually allotted a small sum to the United Hebrew Charities; and the state earmarked more subsantial amounts for the Hebrew Orphan Asylum Society, the Hebrew Sheltering and Guardian Society, the Aguilar Free Library Society, and the Jewish hospitals. The Charity Organization Society, the New York Association for Improving the Condition of the Poor, the Children's Aid Society, and the Society for the Prevention of Cruelty to Children cooperated with the United Hebrew Charities. The Sloane Maternity, the New York Lying-In, and the Mother and Babies' hospitals aided expectant mothers in out-patient departments. The *Tribune* Fresh Air Fund, the *Herald* Ice Fund, the spectacular fund-raising of the *World* and the *Journal*, and Nathan Straus's sterilized milk for the children of the tenements also contributed to the well-being of the immigrant East Side.

Two nonsectarian agencies proved especially useful. The Deutscher Rechts Schutz Verein, founded in 1876 by German immigrants, became the Legal Aid Society in 1894. By then most of its litigated cases were recorded on the East Side, and in 1899 an East Side branch was opened at the University Settlement. The society's panel of prominent attorneys, cooperating with the Legal Aid Council of the United Hebrew Charities and the Legal Aid Bureau of the Educational Alliance, arbitrated petty disputes without charge and kept thousands of cases from reaching the court dockets. The Provident Loan Society, authorized by a select committee of the Charity Organization Society, also performed a special service. Operating as a small loan association, it proposed to reduce the high interest rates of pawnbrokers, permitted to charge 3 percent per month, by charging 1 percent. By 1911 there were three Provident Loan Society branches on the Lower East Side and one each in the Bronx, Williamsburg, and Brownsville, the major foci of East European Jewish settlement.

Promise of Community

At the turn of the century all East Europeans, despite their diversity, were characterized as "Russians." Russian immigrants, with their numbers, variety, intellectual drive, and sense of historical exigency, defined and redefined the quarter's horizons of heart and mind. Despite their nostalgia for the scenes of their childhood and youth, having fled a despotic homeland to which there was no returning, they were quick to embrace America as their first true homeland. Galicians, however, harbored a genuine affection for the benevolent Austrian empire and could easily return. While idealistic Russians formed the Lermontoff Benevolent Society and a host of liberty-loving clubs, celebrating the Russia to be, wistful Galicians founded the Crown Prince Rudolph Verein, the Franz Joseph Kranken Unterstutzung Verein, and the Franz Ferdinand Benevolent Society, honoring the Hapsburg empire as it was. In 1884 Hungarians organized the Magyar Tarsulat (Society) and in the same year lonely Rumanians banded together in the Roumanisch-Amerikanischer Bruderbund. The huge Russian colony, agitated by the winds of the world to come rather than by monuments to attained liberties, overshadowed the lesser enclaves. In 1904 immigrants isolated from the main currents of the quarter formed the Federation of Galician and Bukovinian Jews to promote intercourse with culturally more energetic Russians.

The low intermarriage rate, even between individuals of the diverse East

European Jewries, reflected their group solidarity. After 1900 the equipoise between the sexes in each group and a clan-centered social life especially limited contacts. The barriers that separated East European Jews from non-Jewish New Yorkers militated against marriage outside the fold. After 1900, however, the association of Jewish women with Italians and non-Jewish Russians in the apparel trades led to some marriages. The highly publicized nuptials of Americanized "emancipated" Jewish women and social reformers were unusual. Yet, in these years, such alliances were only slightly less frequent than marriages between uptowners and downtowners.

In time bridges of communication formed between Germans and Russians. Yet only a complex transformation wrought on both groups by American and world experiences over more than half a century was to boil away the mutual incomprehension and intolerance that kept Jews apart. In these years, cooperation was rare and halfhearted in the lone area of social encounter between uptown and downtown—charitable endeavor. In 1901 the downtown Auxiliary Society of the United Hebrew Charities disbanded, no longer content with a subordinate, mere fund-collecting role. In the same year the Downtown Burial Society, *Chesed Shel Emes*, assumed full responsiblity for the Lower East Side, and the United Hebrew Charities dissolved its Free Burial branch. After 1904 requests for aid to the UHC declined; inadequate relief discouraged those in desperate need, while the galaxy of mutual aid societies provided for those less seriously distressed. Yet, even as Germans and Russians pulled apart, the rise of an American-trained generation of Russians spelled the onset of a new equilibrium. Indeed, as early as 1901 downtowners envisioned a United Hebrew Community, "to effect a union of Jewish societies and congregations in New York City."

In the early years of the twentieth century, the beginnings of accommodation between Germans and Russians were discernible, as the spirit of American reform penetrated both groups.

CHAPTER

10

The study of immigrant Jewish women has proceeded rapidly in recent years. No longer are they seen as mere passive extensions of their immigrant husbands. In fact, evidence now reveals that many women immigrated to America unmarried. What's more, immigrant Jewish women often assumed assertive roles: they educated themselves, obtained paying jobs, and in some cases played active roles in the labor movement and in community politics. Where other immigrant women found themselves barred from participation in what was considered to be the "male sphere," Jewish women faced far fewer restrictions. They could appear unescorted at evening lectures and classes and participate in public demonstrations without giving rise to scandal.

Once married, Jewish women did not so frequently leave home to enter the marketplace. But while a 1911 study from New York contends that only a paltry 1 percent of immigrant Jewish wives were employed "officially," many more were certainly working in fact, either at home or in so-called "Mom and Pop" businesses like groceries, delicatessens, or candy stores. Nor were married women necessarily inhibited from participating in community politics. To the contrary, Jewish housewives operating at the grass-roots level led various strikes and boycotts. As Paula E. Hyman, a modern Jewish historian who specializes in women's history, points out, they expressed their political concerns in their own neighborhoods, "where they pioneered in local community organizing."

Professor Hyman focuses here on a women-led kosher meat boycott. Kosher meat—meat slaughtered and prepared according to the dietary requirements set forth in Jewish law—gave rise to various scandals in the immigrant period (and later), as unscrupulous merchants sought to exploit an essentially captive market by price-fixing; some even passed non-kosher meat off as kosher and sold it at great profit. In the absence both of state consumer legislation and effective Jewish community controls, shoppers—women, in the main—had to fend for themselves. In May 1902, as the retail price of kosher meat soared, they did just that, and undertook to boycott kosher meat in an effort to force prices down.

As an incident, the meat boycott quickly faded; attention turned to other

133

problems. As a case study, however, the boycott has lingering significance for it portrays immigrant Jewish women in a new light. It shows, for example, that even those who were married with growing families and years of experience on American soil could if provoked assert themselves and organize effectively, using traditional friendship groups as their base. It also shows that women had developed considerable political savvy—a valuable asset in America, and one that Jewish women activists both in the labor movement and in Jewish women's organizations would later exploit with success.

Immigrant Women and Consumer Protest: The New York City Kosher Meat Boycott of 1902

Paula E. Hyman

Women have always participated in politics. Despite their eclipse in the conventional seats of political power, women in preindustrial societies frequently engaged in popular protest, particularly when the price, or availability, of basic foodstuffs was at issue. As one English historian of the working class and of popular culture has pointed out regarding eighteenth-century food riots, women were "those most involved in face-to-face marketing [and hence] most sensitive to price significancies. . . ." In fact, he adds, "it is probable that the women most frequently precipitated the spontaneous actions." In the popular ferment of the early days of the French Revolution, women were also conspicuous by their presence. The image of grim-faced market women on the march to Versailles to bring the royal family back to Paris has been sharply etched in the mind of every student of history or enthusiast of historical dramas. Even before the emergence of modern political movements committed to the recruitment of women into the political process, the "crowd" was an important means of expression for women's economic and political interests.

Immigrant Jewish women, too, took to the streets in spontaneous food riots on several occasions. Like their British and French forerunners more than a century before, they were reacting to the sharp rise in the price of food. Most noted and flamboyant of these incidents were the 1902 kosher meat riots in New York City. Erupting in mid-May, they precipitated political activity which continued for almost a month, attracting considerable attention within both the Jewish community and the larger urban society. Indeed, in a fierce and vitriolic editorial of May 24, 1902, the *New York Times* called for a speedy and determined police repression of this "dangerous class . . . especially the women [who] are very ignorant [and] . . mostly speak a foreign language. . . . It will not do," the editorial continued, "to have a swarm of ignorant and infuriated women going about any part of this city with pe-

135

troleum destroying goods and trying to set fire to the shops of those against whom they are angry."

What impelled immigrant Jewish housewives to take to the streets (of Williamsburg, in this case) with bottles of kerosene in their hands? Was this simply an act of spontaneous rage, a corroboration of the English writer Robert Southey's comment that "women are more disposed to be mutinous [than men]"? Are the kosher meat riots a late manifestation, as Herbert Gutman has suggested, of a preindustrial sensibility that focused upon the illegitimacy of violating a fair price for food? Finally, and most importantly, what can we learn of the self-perceptions, political consciousness, and sense of community of immigrant Jewish women by examining their role in this incident?

Despite their superficial similarity to earlier food riots, the kosher meat riots of 1902 give evidence of a modern and sophisticated political mentality emerging in a rapidly changing community. With this issue of the high price of food, immigrant housewives found a vehicle for political organization. They articulated a rudimentary grasp of their power as consumers and domestic managers. And, combining both traditional and modern tactics, they temporarily turned their status as housewives to good advantage, and used the neighborhood network to stage a successful three-week boycott of kosher meat shops throughout the Lower East Side, parts of upper Manhattan and the Bronx, and Brooklyn. The dynamics of the kosher meat boycott suggest that by focusing almost exclusively upon organized political activity in the labor movement and the socialist parties, historians have overlooked the role of women. Although for a great part of their life absent from the wage-earning market, immigrant Jewish women were not apolitical. They simply expressed their political concerns in a different, less historically accessible arena—the neighborhood—where they pioneered in local community organizing.

In early May, 1902, the retail price of kosher meat had soared from twelve cents to eighteen cents a pound. Small retail butchers, concerned that their customers would not be able to afford their produce, refused to sell meat for a week to pressure the wholesalers (commonly referred to as the Meat Trust) to lower their prices. When their May 14 settlement with the wholesalers brought no reduction in the retail price of meat, Lower East Side housewives, milling in the street, began to call for a strike against the butchers. As one activist, Mrs. Levy, the wife of a cloakmaker, shouted, "This is their strike? Look at the good it has brought! Now, if *we women* make a strike, then it will be a strike." Gathering support on the block—Monroe Street and Pike Street—Mrs. Levy and Sarah Edelson, owner of a small restaurant, called a mass meeting to spread the word of the planned boycott.

The next day, after a neighborhood canvas staged by the organizing committee, thousands of women streamed through the streets of the Lower East Side, breaking into butcher shops, flinging meat into the streets, and declaring a boycott. "Women were the ringleaders at all hours," noted the *New York Herald*. Customers who tried to carry their purchased meat from the butcher shops were forced to drop it. One woman emerging from a butcher store with meat for her sick husband was vociferously chided by an elderly woman wearing the traditional sheitel that "a sick man can eat tref meat." Within half an hour, the *Forward* reported, the strike had spread from one block through the entire area. Twenty thousand people were reported to have massed in front of the New Irving Hall. "Women were pushed and hustled about [by the police], thrown to the pavement . . . and trampled upon," wrote the *Herald*. One policeman, trying to rescue those buying meat, had "an unpleasant moist piece of liver slapped in his face." Patrol wagons filled the streets, hauling women, some bleeding from their encounters with the police, into court. About seventy women and fifteen men were arrested on charges of disorderly conduct.

After the first day of street rioting, a mass meeting to rally support and map strategy was held at the initiative of the women activists, who had formed a committee. Two of their number addressed the crowd, as did the popular figure Joseph Barondess and the Zionist leader Rabbi Zeft. The next day, May 16, Lower East Side women again went from house to house to strengthen the boycott. Individuals were urged not to enter butcher shops or purchase meat. Pickets were appointed to stand in front of each butcher shop. On each block funds were collected to pay the fines of those arrested and to reimburse those customers whose meat had been confiscated in the first day of rioting. The *Tribune* reported that "an excitable and aroused crowd roamed the streets. . . . As was the case on the previous day, the main disturbance was caused by the women. Armed with sticks, vocabularies and well sharpened nails, they made life miserable for the policemen." On the second day of rioting another hundred people were arrested. The boycott also spread, under local leadership, to the Bronx and to Harlem, where a mass meeting was held at Central Hall.

On Saturday, May 17, the women leaders of the boycott continued their efforts, going from synagogue to synagogue to agitate on behalf of the boycott. Using the traditional communal tactic of interrupting the Torah reading when a matter of justice was at stake, they called on the men in each congregation to encourage their wives not to buy meat and sought rabbinic endorsement of their efforts. For once, urged a boycott leader, citing a biblical passage, let the men use the power of "And he shall rule over her" to the good—by seeing to it that their wives refrain from purchasing meat.

By Sunday, May 18, most butcher shops on the Lower East Side bowed to reality and closed their doors. And the boycott had spread to Brooklyn, where the store windows of open butcher shops had been broken and meat burned. That night, the women held another meeting, attended by more than five hundred persons, to consolidate their organization, now named the Ladies' Anti-Beef Trust Association. Under the presidency of Mrs. Caroline Schatzburg, it proposed to continue house-to-house patrols, keep watch over butcher stores, and begin agitating for similar action among Christian women. Circulars bearing a skull and crossbones and the slogan "Eat no meat while the Trust is taking meat from the bones of your women and children" were distributed throughout the Jewish quarters of the city. The association established six similar committees to consolidate the boycott in Brownsville, East New York, and the Bronx. Other committees were set up to visit the labor and benevolent societies, labor union meetings, and lodges and to plan the establishment of cooperative stores. The association also sent a delegation to the mayor's office to seek permission for an open-air rally. Local groups of women continued to enforce the boycott in their neighborhoods. In Brooklyn four hundred women signed up to patrol neighborhood butcher stores. Buyers of meat continued to be assaulted and butcher shop windows smashed. In Harlem two women were arrested when they lay down on the elevated tracks to prevent a local butcher from heading downtown with meat for sale. Throughout the city's Jewish neighborhoods restaurants had ceased serving meat.

However, competition between Sarah Edelson, one of the founders of the boycott, and Caroline Schatzburg, the president of the Ladies' Anti-Beef Trust Association, erupted by May 18 into open quarrels between their followers at meetings. Taking advantage of this rivalry and winning the support of Edelson and her backers, on May 21 male communal leaders, with David Blaustein of the Educational Alliance presiding, held a conference of three hundred representatives of synagogues, *hevras*, landsmanshaften, and unions "to bring order to the great struggle for cheap meat." In his remarks at the conference meeting, Joseph Barondess made explicit that a new leadership was asserting itself. Urging the women to be quiet and leave the fighting to the men, he noted that otherwise the women would be held responsible in the event of the boycott's defeat. Calling themselves the Allied Conference for Cheap Kosher Meat, the male conference leaders appointed a ten-person steering committee, among whom were only three women. (Women continued, however, to engage in propaganda activities and sporadic rioting in their neighborhoods.) The Allied Conference published a circular in both Yiddish and English, noting that "brave and honest men [were] now aiding the women" and declaring that the conference had "decided to help those butchers who [would] sell cheap kosher meat under the supervision of the rabbis and the conference." "The people feel very justly," continued the statement, "that they are being ground down, not only by the Beef Trust of the country, but also by the Jewish Beef Trust of the City."

On May 22, the Retail Butchers Association succumbed and affiliated itself with the boycott against the Trust. On May 27, Orthodox leaders, who had hesitated to express formal endorsement of the boycott, joined the fray. By June 5 the strike was concluded. The wholesale price of kosher meat was rolled back to nine cents a pound so that the retail price would be pegged at fourteen cents a pound. Kosher meat cooperatives, which were established during the strike in both Brooklyn and Harlem, continued in existence. While meat prices began to rise inexorably again in the period following the conclusion of the boycott, the movement can still be considered a qualified success.

The leaders of the boycott were not typical of other women political activists of the period. Unlike the majority of women organized in the nascent garment unions, they were not young. Unlike the female union leaders, they were housewives with children. The mean age of those boycott leaders who could be traced in the 1905 New York state manuscript census was thirty-nine. They ranged from Mamie Ghilman, the thirty-two-year-old Russian-born wife of a tailor, to Mrs. L. Finkelstein, a fifty-four-year-old member of the Women's Committee. All but two were more than thirty-five years of age at the time of the boycott. These women were mothers of large families, averaging 4.3 children apiece living at home. Fannie Levy, who initiated the call for the strike, was the mother of six children, all below the age of thirteen. None had fewer than three children. While only two women were United States citizens, the strike leaders were not, for the most part, recent arrivals to America. They had been living in New York City from three to twenty-seven years, with a median residence of eleven years. Having had sufficient time to accommodate themselves to the American scene, they were not simply expressing traditional forms of cultural resistance to industrial society imported from the Old Country.

In socioeconomic terms, the women initiators of the boycott appear representative of the larger immigrant Jewish community of the Lower East Side. Their husbands were, by and large, employed as artisans in the garment industry, though three were self-employed small businessmen. The husband of Annie Block, a member of the Women's Committee, was a tailor, as were three other husbands. Fannie Levy's husband was a cloakmaker and Bessie Norkin's a carpenter, while J. Jaffe's husband, Meyer, and Annie Levine's husband, Morris, topped the occupational scale as a real estate agent and storekeeper respectively. With one exception, all of their children above the age of sixteen were working—two-thirds of them in artisan trades and the remainder as clerks or low-level business employees (e.g., salesladies). Only the eighteen-year-old son of the real estate agent was still in school (though his older brothers were employed as garment-industry operators). Thus, the women formed not an elite in their community, but a true grass-roots leadership.

It is clear from their statements and their activity that the women who led the boycott had a distinct economic objective in mind and a clear political strategy for achieving their goal. Unlike traditional food rioters, the Lower East Side housewives were not demanding the imposition of a just and popular price on retailers. Nor were they forcibly appropriating meat for purchase at a popularly determined fair price, though they did retain a traditional sense of a moral economy in which food should be available at prices which the working classes could afford. Rather, recognizing that prices were set by the operation of the laws of supply and demand, as modified, in this case, by the concentration of the wholesale meat industry, they hit upon a boycott of meat as the most effective way to dramatically curtail demand. They referred to themselves as strikers; those who did not comply with the boycott were called "scabs." When they were harassed in the street by police, they complained that denial by police of their right to assemble was an attack on their freedom of speech. Thus, Lower East Side women were familiar with the political rhetoric of their day, with the workings of the market economy, and with the potential of consumers to affect the market.

While the impulse for the boycott originated in spontaneous outrage of women consumers at the price of kosher meat and their sense that they had been manipulated (or swindled, as they put it) by the retail butchers, who had sold out their customers in their agreement with the wholesalers, this incident was not simply an explosion of rage. It was a sustained, though limited, movement whose success lay in its careful organization. As the *New York Herald* rightly commented, "These women were in earnest. For days they had been considering the situation, and when they decided on action, they perfected an organization, elected officers, . . . and even went so far as to take coins from their slender purses until there was an expense fund of eighty dollars with which to carry on the fight."

In fact, the neighborhood focus of the boycott organization proved to be its source of strength. The initial boycott committee, composed of nineteen women, numbered nine neighbors from Monroe Street, four from Cherry Street, and six from adjacent blocks. This was not the anonymous city so often portrayed by antiurban polemicists and historians but a neighborhood community whose residents maintained close ties. The first show of strength on May 15 was preceded by an early morning house-to-house canvas of housewives in the heart of the boycott area. A similar canvas occurred the next day in Harlem under the aegis of local women. Rooted in the neighborhood, where many activities were quasi-public rather than strictly private, housewives were able to exert moral (as well as physical) suasion upon the women whom they saw on a daily basis. They assumed the existence of collective goals and the right to demand shared sacrifices. Individual desires for the consumption of meat were to be subordinated to the larger public good. As one boycott enthusiast stated while grabbing meat from a girl leaving a butcher store, "If we can't eat meat, the customers can't eat meat."

Shouting similar sentiments in another incident, striking women attempted to remove the meat from cholent pots which their neighbors had brought to a local bakery on a Friday afternoon. Participants in the boycott picketed local butchers and also resolved not to speak to the "scabs" in their midst. The constant presence in the neighborhood of the housewife leaders of the boycott made it difficult for individuals to evade their surveillance. The neighborhood, a form of female network, thus provided the locus of community for the boycott: all were giving up meat together, celebrating dairy shabbosim together, and contributing together to the boycott fund.

The women who organized and led the boycott considered themselves the natural leaders of such an enterprise. As consumers and housewives, they saw their task as complementary to that of their wage-earning spouses: "Our husbands work hard," stated one of the leaders at the initial planning meeting. "They try their best to bring a few cents into the house. We must manage to spend as little as possible. We will not give away our last few cents to the butcher and let our children go barefoot." In response, the women shouted, "We will not be silent; we will overturn the world." Describing themselves as soldiers, they determined to circulate leaflets calling upon all women to "join the great women's war." An appeal to their "worthy sisters," published by the Ladies' Anti-Beef Trust in the *Forward*, expressed similar sentiments, calling for "help . . . in the name of humanity in this great struggle which we have undertaken out of need."

Sharper formulations of class resentment mingled with pride in their own talents in some of the women's shouts in the street demonstrations. One woman was heard lamenting to another, "Your children must go to work, and the millionaires snatch the last bit from our mouths." Another called out, "My husband brings me eight dollars a week. Should I give it away to the butcher? What would the landlord say?" Still another screamed, "They think women aren't people, that they can bluff us; we'll show them that we are more people than the fat millionaires who suck our blood." When the son of the Chief Rabbi, who supervised the kashrut of the meat, passed through the area, he was met with shouts of "Trust—Kosher *Korobke*," a reference to the kosher meat tax, much despised by the poor in Czarist Russia.

The ringleaders who were arrested and charged with disorderly conduct defined their behavior in political terms and considered it both just and appropriate to their status as housewives. "Did you throw meat on the street?" Rosa Peskin was asked. "Certainly," she replied. "I should have looked it in the teeth?" When the judge condescendingly commented, "What do you know of a trust? It's no business of yours," she responded, "Whose business is it, then, that our pockets are empty . . . ?" "What do you have against a woman who has bought meat," the judge persisted. "I have nothing against her," retorted Peskin. "It doesn't matter to me what others want to do. But it's because of others that we must suffer." Rebecca Ablowitz also presented the boycotters' rationale to the judge: "We're not rioting. Only see how thin our children are, our husbands have no more strength to work harder. . . . If we stay home and cry, what good will that do us?"

Of similar conviction and eloquence was Mrs. Silver, one of the most articulate spokeswomen of the boycott, who headed the campaign to interrupt services in the synagogues. When one irate opponent roared that her speaking thus from the bima was an effrontery *(chutzpa)* and a desecration of God's name *(chillul ha-Shem)*, Mrs. Silver coolly responded that the Torah would pardon her.

The climate of the immigrant Jewish community facilitated the resolute behavior of the women. While a few rabbis, particularly those with close ties to the meat industry, were hostile to the boycott enterprise, they were the exception. Support for the boycott was widespread within the community. Friendly crowds packed the courtroom to cheer the arrested women. In every one of the synagogues on the Lower East Side, it was reported, "the uprising of the Hebrew women was referred to by the rabbis." Most synagogue members warmly greeted the women who brought their cause to the congregation. When police were brought in to arrest Mrs. Silver after a disturbance erupted in one synagogue, a congregant rose to compare the woman to the prophet Zachariah, "who preached truly and whose blood demanded vengeance." So persuasive was he that Mrs. Silver was released. Feeling that they could count upon the support of the traditionally observant community, the Ladies' Anti-Beef Trust Association, in an appeal printed by the *Forward*, called for communal ostracism of the one prominent rabbi, Dr. Adolph N. Radin of the People's Synagogue, who had not only refused to approve the boycott but had treated representatives of the association rudely in his synagogue. He should be removed from his position as chaplain to Jewish prisoners, urged the women, for if this "half-German" could refer publicly to the boycotting women as "beasts" and receive them so coarsely in front of his congregation, how must he treat the unfortunate Jewish inmates he sees within the confines of the prison?

Both the socialist *Forward* and the Orthodox *Yiddishes Tageblat* portrayed the initial disturbances as well as the later movement in a sympathetic manner and were offended by the rough treatment meted out to the women and their families by the police as well as by the unsympathetic attitude of much of the English language press. Jewish socialists, in particular, stood squarely behind the protest. The *Forward* heralded the boycott with the banner headline, "Bravo, bravo, bravo, Jewish women!" To the *Forward*, the boycott provided an opportunity not only to support a grass-roots protest action but also to level an attack upon the collusion of the rabbis with the German-Jewish meat trust. There was little reason for the differential between kosher and non-kosher meat to stand at five to six cents a pound, proclaimed the newspaper's editorial. Those who raised the prices "are Yahudim with gilded beards, who never eat kosher. Why are they suddenly so *frum* (pious)? Since when is there a partnership between those who give rabbinic endorsements in the Chief Rabbi's name and those Yahudi meat handlers? . . . The Chief Rabbi's son is merely a salesman for the Trust," continued the editorial. "He goes about in carriages collecting money in the name of his unfortunate father's endorsement. . . . Whether the strike of the good Jewish women brings down the prices or not," concluded the *Forward*, "one thing remains certain, the bond between the Trust and the rabbis must end. If they are truly pious, let them serve their religion and not the Trust in whose pay they are in." In Russian Poland, noted the paper the next day, the meat tax was seven cents a pound, but at least there the *korobke* supported all kehilla (communal) activities. Here, on the other hand, it went only to the Trust.

While the *Forward* conducted its pro-boycott campaign, the labor movement as a whole extended monetary donations and aid to the boycott; two men active in the Ladies' Garment Workers' Union were appointed as vice president and secretary of the Ladies' Anti-Beef Trust Association, while the posts of president and treasurer remained in women's hands. In Harlem it was the Women's Branch No. Two of the Workmen's Circle, with the support of the parent organization, that coordinated local boycott activity.

Communal support was not, however, without its limits. Jewish communal leaders were clearly upset by the initiative assumed by the women activists. The sight of Jewish women engaged in picketing and in the physical coercion of butcher shop customers as well as their arrest at the hands of a none too gentle police force aroused concern. "Don't give the Trust and the police an opportunity to break heads," cautioned the *Forward*. "More can be accomplished lawfully than not. . . . Agitate quietly in your homes." Moreover, when the boycott was recognized as a force to be reckoned with, men tried to wrest control of the movement from its female leaders. However, the women were never entirely displaced, and the Yiddish language media continued, if somewhat ambivalently, to view the success of the boycott as a legitimate example of the "power of women." (On the other hand, the *American Hebrew*, the organ of the Uptown Jews, studiously ignored the kosher meat riots.)

In a larger sense, the immigrant Jewish community was quite supportive of women's political activity. East European Jewish immigrants were highly politicized; just how highly can be seen in the meat boycott, whose participants were sufficiently traditional to buy kosher meat and to use the synagogues and *hevras* as areas for potential recruitment. Indeed, the development of the boycott suggests that the compartmentalization of the immigrant community by historians into Orthodox, socialist and anarchist, and Zionist sectors does not do justice to the interplay among the groups. Boundary lines were fluid, and socialist rhetoric tripped easily from the tongues of women who still cared about kosher meat, could cite biblical

NB

IN FACT, FLUIDITY

passages in Hebrew, and felt at ease in the synagogue. Moreover, the boycotters consciously addressed themselves to several different constituencies—
synagogues, landsmanshaften, the labor movement, and socialist groups.

Even within the traditional community, women had never been banned
from the *secular* public sphere. In developing cadres of female activists, both
the Jewish labor and Zionist movements in Russia built upon the relative
freedom of public activity accorded women within the Jewish community. As
Mary Van Kleeck of the Russell Sage Foundation commented in her study of
one Lower East Side trade that employed Jewish women, "The Jewish girl . . .
has a distinct sense of her social responsibility and often displays an eager
zest for discussion of labor problems. . . . Her attitude is likely to be that of an
agitator. Nevertheless, she has the foundation of that admirable trait, 'public
spirit,' and a sense of relationship to a community larger than the family or
the personal group of which she happens to be a member." Sufficient toleration existed within the family circle to enable Jewish women to express their
"public spirit," to permit wives and mothers to attend evening meetings and
to demonstrate in the streets. As the *Yiddishes Tageblat* put it, somewhat
condescendingly, at the beginning of the boycott, "The women this time let
the men play at home with the children while they went to attend the
meeting." While this was clearly a situation worthy of comment, it was not a
violation of communal values.

If the immigrant Jewish community helped to sustain the meat boycott,
the English-language socialist press was far more ambivalent in its attitude to
this form of political activity. Indeed, it saw the only appropriate weapon for
workers in the struggle against capitalism in the organization of producers
rather than consumers. As *The Worker* commented,

> The Meat Trust does not care two-cents for such opposition as this, no matter
> how sincere the boycotters may be. . . . [A boycott] is so orderly and law-
> abiding, so free from all taint of socialism or confiscation or class hatred, so truly
> individualistic, and above all, so perfectly harmless—to all except the poor
> workingmen. . . . We cannot oppose the aggression of twentieth century cap-
> italism with weapons fitted to the petty conflicts of eighteenth century small
> producers.

Added the *Daily People*, organ of the Socialist Labor Party, "It does not make
the capitalist hungry if the workingman goes without food. . . ." Such an
attitude overlooked the potential of community organization outside the
workplace. It precluded reaching out to the neighborhood as a possible
secondary locus of political activism, and incidentally resulted in an inability
on the part of the socialists to tap the ranks of the politically conscious
housewife.

The difference in attitudes between the Yiddish-speaking and English-language socialists is also of broader interest. While the Jewish socialists were often seen as assimilationist, they remained closer to the shared value of their own immigrant community than to the perhaps ideologically purer stance of the American radicals.

The boycott movement enables us to look at the potential for political organization among Lower East Side women, the majority of whom were housewives unaffiliated in any formal sense with the trade-union movement. But it also raises questions for which there are no readily available answers.

Was there any precedent for this type of direct action among married women in Eastern Europe? One can find a tenuous connection to the Eastern European scene in reference to the *korobke*, the meat tax, which in the nineteenth century constituted as much as one-third of the budget of some Jewish communities and was passionately resented. Some Hasidic rebbes in the first half of the last century urged passive resistance against the tax, even including a boycott on the purchase of meat. Clearly, the ability to draw an analogy, as both the women activists and the *Forward* editorials did, between the *korobke* and the high price of kosher meat caused by collusion between the meat trust and rabbis selling their hechsher (certification of kashrut) was an appealing propaganda device. It linked the 1902 boycott to the long-standing disaffection of the poor with the authorities of the Eastern European kehilla. However, the boycott's leaders do not refer to earlier Eastern European examples of reaction against the *korobke*, nor is there any other evidence of direct influence from the Eastern European to the American scene.

As interesting as the boycott is as a vehicle for examining the political sensibilities and assessing the political potential of Jewish housewives on the Lower East Side, the fading away of the Ladies' Anti-Beef Trust Association is as significant as its sudden appearance. If the neighborhood network was so effective a means to reach women and mobilize them, why was it not sustained to deal with other social problems? True, the 1904 and 1907–8 rent strikes on the Lower East Side espoused similar tactics and hailed the meat boycott as their model. Beginning with a house-to-house canvas initiated by women, strike leaders promoted neighborhood solidarity by collecting written pledges of refusal to pay rent. In 1908 women also lent their support to retail butchers protesting the rising cost in wholesale meat prices. These further incidents of local activism confirm the growing consumer consciousness of Lower East Side women. However, there appears to be no overlap in leadership between these several expressions of female popular protest. Were women co-opted into already established fraternal and political organizations, or did the politics of crisis bring with it inertia once the crisis had passed?

Because its leaders faded into obscurity with the conclusion of the boycott, because of the very nature of a short-lived grass-roots movement, it is impossible to assess the impact of the movement upon its participants. However, it is likely that the political awareness expressed by the boycotters was no isolated phenomenon but was communicated effectively, if quietly and informally, to their younger sisters and daughters. The boycott alerted the immigrant community as a whole and the labor movement in particular to the political potential of women. Moreover, the communal support of the boycott could only have encouraged women themselves to further activity. As Alice Kessler-Harris notes of Jewish women in the garment trades, whose numbers in the unions exceeded their proportion in the industry as a whole, they "unionized at their own initiative" and were "responsible for at least one quarter of the increased number of unionized women [in America] in the second decade of the twentieth century." In that sense the kosher meat boycott should be seen not as an isolated incident but as a prelude to the explosion of women activists in the great garment industry strikes at the end of the decade.

CHAPTER

11

On September 1, 1908, New York City Jews read with shock and outrage the report by their police commissioner, Theodore A. Bingham, that the "Hebrew race" produced "perhaps half" of the city's criminals. Bingham's statistics were quickly disproved, and the man himself labeled an anti-Semite; sixteen days later he issued a retraction. Privately, however, many Jews knew that there was a certain amount of truth to Bingham's allegations. The existence of criminality, prostitution, truancy, and a host of other social ills within the immigrant Jewish community was too evident to be denied. In search of solutions to these problems and in an effort to unite the entire Jewish community in defense of Jewry's good name, three hundred delegates representing all segments of the Jewish community met together on February 27, 1909. They formed what became known as the <u>Kehillah—the organized Jewish community of New York</u>.

The Kehillah, as historian Arthur Goren points out in his definitive study of the organization, combined elements of traditional European-Jewish communal structures with American-style Progressive-era democracy. Sponsors "envisioned a democratically governed polity which would unite the city's multifarious Jewish population, harness the group's intellectual and material resources, and build a model ethnic community." Various "bureaus" of the Kehillah addressed specific community problems—education, crime, industrial relations, religious supervision, and the like. Yet for all this, the Kehillah scarcely lasted into its thirteenth year; by 1922 it was dead completely. In the excerpt that follows Goren explains why.

For one thing, he shows that the Kehillah coalition was unstable from the start. With so many conflicting aims among the organizers—so many unresolved differences between natives and immigrants, rich and poor, religious Jews and secular ones—the wonder may be that the Kehillah accomplished as much as it did. Exacerbating these tensions were ongoing problems regarding the Kehillah's relationship to the American Jewish Committee, problems that escalated into a full-scale battle for leadership between the "Old Guard" struggling to maintain control, and the "Young Turks" allied with the rising immigrant generation, who sought to replace them. The death knell sounded with World War I, which engendered a host of new difficulties, not the least of

KEHILLA

1909(b)

1922(d)

which was the uncompromising (some said disloyal) pacifism of the Kehillah's chairman, Rabbi Judah Magnes. His downfall brought the Kehillah down with it.

The significance of the Kehillah lies not so much in its immediate achievements, which were modest, as in its dream: to forge an organized and united New York Jewish community by wedding traditional Jewish forms to contemporary American ideals. Like so many similar dreams over the years, this one failed, punctured by sobering realities. But the quest for some happy medium, at once American and Jewish, promoting assimilation, identity, and unity at one and the same time, endures. It forms a continuing theme in American Jewish life.

AOR =
OD Moore "A New Amer Juta"
in Brinner/Rischin Like all the Nations :
41 : linked to rise of NYC

The Kehillah Vision and
the Limits of Community

Arthur A. Goren

In 1908, when the advocates of the Kehillah used the Bingham incident to raise the spectre of "communal anarchy," they sounded an alarm that stirred a troubled Jewish public. Striving for acceptance in the larger community yet committed to the preservation of its ethnic life, the Jewish group reacted in a variety of ways. Those who understood Police Commissioner Theodore A. Bingham's charge as a dangerous anti-Semitic attack—and they were primarily the immigrant Jews—accepted the argument that communal disunity had prevented an effective rebuttal and marred their image as an upstanding and industrious group. Since all Jews were vulnerable, the entire group had to support a body capable of defending the Jewish name. Others, mostly uptowners, admitted the existence of criminality. It was, they declared, a symptom of the social disorganization of the immigrant quarter, and it called for an extraordinary communal effort. But more than the efficient organization of the community was necessary, a group of young intellectuals added. Social amelioration to be meaningful and enduring had to go hand in hand with the promotion of a Jewish cultural revival and the bolstering of the traditional values of Judaism. Thus spokesmen of the Kehillah proposal plumbed the depths of the group's fears, touched its sensitive defense mechanism, and appealed to its idealism.

The Kehillah's sponsors also employed a progressive rhetoric that legitimized the venture in American terms. The project promised to activate wide circles of the Jewish quarter, coordinate and expand its services, foster self-help, and absorb immigrants into the life of the community. Here was a civic contribution of the first magnitude. Moreover, the give-and-take of the democratic process led to "intelligent social action," to a high order of "enlightened self-discipline," and to "social efficiency." Thus, democratic organization and "constructive social engineering," in philosopher John Dewey's terms, or a combination of the "democratic method and the scientific method," as Rabbi

Judah Magnes stated it, would enable New York Jewry to create an American kehillah. These general objectives, the movement's leaders hastened to add, carried a workaday, pragmatic importance for the host of small, independent associations to whom the majority of Jews owed their first allegiance. The officials and constituencies of such institutions would benefit from a central agency able to provide services of specialists, and plan a more rational use of existing resources.

The protagonists of the Kehillah used these disparate arguments to induce a significant cross section of the Jewish public to join the new venture. But their outstanding feat consisted of winning over the American Jewish Committee (AJC). Brilliantly, Magnes used downtown's tumultuous protests against the criminality charge to compel uptown to enter the Kehillah despite its fears that the organization would encourage self-segregation. Only if they affiliated, he warned the notables, might the volatility of the Jewish quarter be controlled and their own influence maintained. Without their wealth, prestige, and experience in public service no major communal undertaking could in fact have survived. Collaboration by Jacob Schiff, Felix M. Warburg, Louis Marshall, and Cyrus L. Sulzberger, then, immediately transformed the Kehillah from a visionary scheme to a major enterprise.

Their joining the Kehillah carried additional significance. Affiliation—indeed, sponsorship—changed their view of Jewish communal life. At the founding convention of the Kehillah, when AJC leaders united with moderate Russian-Jewish circles and champions of an American ethnic pluralism, they announced a long-range strategy that projected the establishment of a network of AJC-sponsored, democratically run kehillahs. For the AJC, such a program promised the popular base needed to establish itself as the coordinating body of American Jewry. But the process was to be gradual and organic, guided by the combined wisdom of the elders of both segments of the community and executed in strict accord with American practice. Conceptually, these old-stock worthies were abandoning, at least for a time and undoubtedly for tactical reasons, a Protestant-congregational model of communal polity for a broadly functional, pluralistic structure. Instead of employing a confessional definition of Jewish identity, they were reluctantly acknowledging that an operationally useful definition had to embrace a group splintered by dogma, culture, localism, and class. To reach and, they hoped, to control the radical, the Orthodox, the Zionist, and the *landsmanschaft* Jew demanded a conception of community coinciding with the bounds of a multifarious ethnicity.

For a time the strategy succeeded. The Kehillah's service bureaus were promising enough to win the approbation of the community. In regard to education, the Kehillah could indeed claim some remarkable achievements. In other instances—as in the case of the industrial bureau's mediation activities and the rabbinical board's kashruth supervision efforts—limited or fleeting success did not disprove the need for these agencies nor invalidate their conceptual basis. And the annual conventions gave every indication of evolving into a popular tribunal for reviewing the community's needs and policies. True, the Kehillah had failed to encompass the majority of societies which made up the immigrant community. Some important patrician-supported institutions like the Educational Alliance had also remained aloof. Nevertheless, even judged by level of participation the achievements were notable. Represented at the 1915 convention were approximately 10 to 15 percent of the Jewish organizations in the city. Kehillah leaders quite correctly claimed that member organizations embraced a high proportion of the larger institutions and that the delegates included the more influential leaders of the Jewish quarter. As the only body of its kind in the community, the Kehillah's weight exceeded the sum total of enrolled societies.

But the Kehillah did not fulfill its founders' goals. For the uptowners, it was to control the unruly ghetto. The "moneyed powers," Mordecai Kaplan wrote in his journal, were eager to maintain the status quo, and they were using the Kehillah, the Jewish Theological Seminary, and the Bureau of Education as "nothing but Jewish social pacifiers." By 1917, an alternative to the Kehillah existed, one which it had, in fact, been instrumental in creating. The wealthy contributors now turned to the Federation of Jewish Philanthropies as a more convenient means of "social pacification." Russian-Jewish leaders also lost interest in the Kehillah as the gap between commitments and performance widened. Beginning in 1917, the Kehillah stood, shorn of its bureaus, unable to claim a mass following, and overshadowed by the newly established Federation of Philanthropies. The grand design of the founders—the transformation of an amorphous public into an organic community—had not been realized.

First, the Kehillah was overwhelmed by the circumstances of the time. Its struggle for existence coincided with the high tide of Jewish immigration, the moment of New York Jewry's greatest fragmentation. In 1914, the midpoint of the Kehillah's life, probably the majority of Jews living in the city had been in the country fewer than ten years. Eager to prove the utility of the Kehillah, its leaders committed the organization to an unprecedented scale and range of activity, arousing expectations that all too often were disappointed. Orthodox rabbis, bewildered by the New World, supported the Kehillah, expecting to be invested once again with their traditional authority. Zionists battled at conventions to win majority votes for their policy proposals, only to be ruled out of order. And when scores of small, hard-pressed Talmud Torahs applied to the Kehillah's education bureau for relief, they were refused for lack of funds. Conceivably, had greater resources been available, the Kehillah might have provided the support and created the stable structure it promised—one sufficiently strong to contain even the dissenters. But though financial aid came from uptown, mass support from downtown failed to materialize. Yet at the same time, Russian Jews were devoting their resources to their local institutions and associations.

In part, the Kehillah's newness and its experimental quality explain downtown's reserve, for despite the immigrants' familiarity with the traditional "kehillah," the New York version was different. The size of the Jewish community and the complexity of the questions it faced made collaboration difficult. The American idiom of the Kehillah's spokemen, moreover, further strengthened downtown's ambivalence. But perhaps most important, synagogues and fraternal orders with their Old Country attachments and benefits, and trade unions and social movements offering economic amelioration and intellectual satisfaction, already crowded the communal world of the immigrant Jews. Ardent party men and competing functionaries polemicized, organized, and kept the quarter in turmoil. In this setting, critics attacked the Kehillah as either irrelevant, utopian, or an uptown intrusion.

Granted this catalog of encumbrances and failures, the fact remains that during its early years the Kehillah did make headway. It defined the problems facing the community and laid the groundwork for meeting them. So long as a modicum of goodwill and stability existed, the Kehillah registered gains. But by the end of 1914 new issues agitated the community, upsetting communal priorities and disturbing the power structure upon which the Kehillah depended. Time had run out.

The outbreak of war turned the attention of the Jewish public to the ordeal of European Jewry, and soon a call for extraordinary measures persuaded people, hitherto quiescent or disaffected, to come forward and challenge the established leadership. The new group, mostly of Russian-Jewish origin and of a Zionist persuasion, joined the Jewish congress movement to contest the hegemony of the AJC. In the name of popular control and activism, leaders like Louis Brandeis, Stephen Wise, and Louis Lipsky assailed the AJC for its "paternalism and timidity." They rejected its gradualism and mounted a bitter attack against the "tutelage of the grand moguls."

Could the Kehillah, the congress faction asked, maintain its democratic integrity while continuing to be tied to an oligarchic body? In 1915, when it moved its dispute with the AJC over the organization of Jewish communal life to the Kehillah convention, it recognized the fact that the Kehillah offered the one open forum where issues could be debated and a consensus of sorts recorded. For a triumphant moment it appeared as though the Kehillah had contained the quarrel and produced a compromise, only to have the agreement vetoed by the AJC. At the 1916 convention, when Magnes declared national issues out-of-bounds, he may have insulated the organization against an acrimonious debate (and saved the AJC from further embarrassment), but he also isolated the Kehillah from the critical issues of the time. He seemingly confirmed what critics were stressing, that the Kehillah was no more than an appendage of one party to the dispute. A key change had occurred in the

Jewish community and with startling speed: the AJC's hegemony had been challenged, upsetting existing arrangements; the Kehillah's patron was no longer the informal but nonetheless uncontested arbiter of Jewish communal life.

The Kehillah had been caught, observers at the time explained, in the crossfire of a struggle between a patrician Old Guard and a rising immigrant community. And in no small measure their view was accurate. But other elements also exacerbated the situation and took their toll of the Kehillah. Jewish radicals, for example, regularly denounced AJC as the class enemy and belittled the Kehillah as an uptown plot to dominate the Jewish quarter. In the controversy over the establishment of a Jewish congress these same radicals allied themselves with the AJC "plutocrats" (Nachman Syrkin called it "the unholy alliance between Hester Street and Wall Street"). The Congress party behaved no differently. It finally agreed to confine the Congress to the specific issue of formulating postwar demands for Jewish rights abroad and to disband once it fulfilled this function, a far cry from its declared purpose. In the first instance a common abhorrence for the Zionists who dominated the congress party had brought the Jewish socialists and the AJC magnates together. The "democratic" faction, the congress men, on the other hand, compromised their declared goals in order to reach an accommodation with the numerically insignificant but financially and politically powerful AJC. If Zionists justified their action as hardheaded compromising, obviously for them the Kehillah in 1916 was not worth a similar sacrifice of principle. The one institution dependent upon the collaboration of all parties could hardly survive this brand of Realpolitik.

The crowning blow for the Kehillah was Magnes's withdrawal from active leadership. He had been, until the congress issue forced him to choose sides, the mediator par excellence, the only public figure with an entree to all groups in the community. In the years prior to World War I, Magnes was, in all likelihood, the most popular figure in Jewish public life. To the Kehillah he had brought much goodwill, a considerable personal following, and a virtuosity of leadership that went far to lift the organization to the stand it reached. The Kehillah became his cause and remained inextricably bound up with him. His pacifism, therefore, dealt a double blow to the Kehillah, vitiating his effectiveness as chairman and casting a heavy pall upon the organization with which he was so closely identified.

The total impact of the congress controversy, the effect of the war on the community, and then Magnes's pacifism proved to be disastrous for a fragile institution. Yet though the Kehillah failed to achieve its primary objective of molding New York Jewry into a single, integrated community, it did leave behind a considerable legacy. Now a Federation of Philanthropies existed with a wider sense of communal responsibility. A Bureau of Jewish Education and a Jewish Education Association carried on the tradition of communal

MAGNES w/ draws

responsibility for education. Interest in community planning and research as well as in the training of professional communal workers had developed. And the Kehillah had raised disciples. The young college men who had been induced by Samson Benderly to make a career of Jewish education held key positions in the community. They were in turn raising up another generation of disciples. These products of the Kehillah idea continued to work for community collaboration despite the lack of a formal framework.

The Kehillah left its impression in other ways as well. It had provided a common meeting ground for the leaders of New York Jewry in all its ethnic, social, and ideological diversity. Cyrus Sulzberger described well the Kehillah's efforts to bring "some semblance of order" to the community. With just a touch of exaggeration, he wrote in 1915:

> See, now, what a few years have wrought. The conventions of the Kehillah bring together the most varied assemblage of Jews that can be imagined. Side by side with the extremest orthodox—men with long beards and side curls, men who not for a moment have their heads uncovered—are members of the most reformed temples. Rich men and men practically penniless; extreme socialists and extreme conservatives gather together and under parliamentary methods discuss the subjects they have in common.

The convention addesses of Louis Marshall, Magnes's state-of-the-community messages, the debates on the activities of the Kehillah's bureaus, the parliamentary maneuverings, and the elections to office—all gave the participants a broader view of the community and more tolerant understanding of one another. For the immigrant leaders, the Kehillah democracy also provided a prime education in American civics. It contributed to their quick assimilation of American ideology which included, significantly, learning the limits of ethnic community.

Magnes defined these limits in his remarks to the special convention of the Kehillah in January, 1918:

> The European notion of a uniform . . . all-controlling . . . kehillah cannot strike root in American soil . . . because it is not in consonance with the free and voluntary character of American religious, social, educational, and philanthropic enterprises. . . . The only power that the kehillah can exercise is moral and spiritual in its nature, the power of an enlightened public opinion, the power of a developed community sense.

One had to agitate for community, then, by persuading individuals to affiliate with the organized communal body; joining entailed an act of personal self-identification. In the early days of the Kehillah movement, the emphasis had been different. Magnes had assumed the existence of an ethnic solidarity which, grounded in the group's minority experience and the national-religious quality of Judaism, led to collective responses to outside threats. He had proposed channeling these group sentiments into the creation of an integrated community—the Kehillah. Its utility and reasonability, he believed, would bring the institution stability and recognition. This process fitted his understanding of the thrust of American society, which he saw as evolving into a "republic of nationalities." But in the declining period of the Kehillah, Magnes came to understand that under the free conditions of American life, ethnicity was but one of many attachments shared by group and individual. Only some leaders would continue the elusive pursuit of "organic community." Indeed Magnes's co-worker in the Kehillah, Mordecai Kaplan, would make this goal a central feature of his philosophy of Jewish life. But most Jews remained interested in the minimum of separation from the larger society necessary for maintaining their Jewish identity. They would be content with a more modest vision of community.

NB

cf the present efforts at Jew. Unity in Israel + USA :

→ "the elusive pursuit of "organic community"

CHAPTER

12

"Without question," writes Irving Howe, "the most important secular institutions created by the [Jewish] immigrants were the Jewish trade unions." All agree that there was some special Jewish flavor to these unions, traits that distinguished them from other labor-movement unions developing at the same time. Howe argues that these traits stemmed from the way Jewish unions served immigrants not only as bargaining agencies defending their rights as workers, but also as "homes away from home"—as "social centers, political forums, and training schools." Historian Lucy Dawidowicz, in her essay here, points to Jewish values and traditions as being what made Jewish unions different: "that welfare, education and philanthropy became union concerns in Jewish unions demonstrated the ways through which the Jewish workers transferred the social responsibilities of the East European Jewish community to the labor movement."

Dawidowicz stresses other characteristically Jewish features of the Jewish labor movement as well. In the first place, Jews formed a unique kind of working class. They concentrated in a few industries, particularly the garment trades, and were eager to advance or at least to see their children advance to a higher socioeconomic status—an aspiration that made class consciousness difficult to achieve. Second, Jews continually faced tensions between their class identities and their Jewish identities, especially on issues such as immigration restriction, where class interests and Jewish interests diverged. This problem became particularly acute whenever anti-Semitism reared up in labor's ranks. Finally, Jews came from a tradition that long emphasized arbitration and conciliation as means of resolving intragroup conflicts. While not alone in this, Jews, being an endangered minority group, did have a special interest in preserving communal solidarity and social stability. By accepting the principles of "industrial peace" as set forth in the so-called "Protocol of Peace" that ended the cloakmakers' strike of 1910, the Jewish labor movement set an example of how harmonious relations between employers and workers might be achieved in the future—without strikes.

The influence of the Protocol of Peace, as Dawidowicz points out, was lasting—especially in the garment industry, where Jews continued to play a central role. The social-welfare programs pioneered by Jewish labor unions

156

may have had even more impact, since the New Deal made many of them standard employee benefits, available nationwide, and sponsored in some cases by the government. Of course, the Jewish labor movement itself declined with the widespread entry of Jews into the middle class. But while it lasted it embodied something of American Jewry's ideals: offering a way for immigrant Jews to help themselves, their countrymen, and humanity, even as they remained rooted in a thoroughly Jewish environment, open to the wide world beyond.

The Jewishness of the Jewish Labor Movement in the United States

Lucy S. Dawidowicz

According to the findings of the National Jewish Population Study, nearly 90 percent of American Jews in the labor force in 1971 were white-collar workers, whereas fewer than 10 percent were blue-collar craftsmen and operatives. But half a century ago the proportions were different. Not only did Jewish blue-collar workers preponderate over Jewish white-collar workers, but in centers of Jewish immigrant concentration, Jewish workers were actually a plurality in the total industrial labor force.

Over 1,500,000 Jews were part of the great stream of immigrants that expanded and transformed the industrial and commercial structure of the United States. For the most part they came from the towns and villages of the Russian Pale of Settlement, from the Galician backwaters of the Hapsburg empire, and from the Moldavian heartland of Rumania. In the old country they had been artisans or merchants, but in America most of them became shopworkers, primarily in the clothing industry. (In the 1880s German Jews owned 234 of 241 clothing factories in New York City. The statistic facilitated the influx of the Russian Jews in tailoring.)

From 1881 to 1910 nearly eighteen million immigrants arrived in America. These were the "new" immigrants who came from Southern and Eastern Europe—the Italians, Slovaks, Croats, Poles, Ruthenians, Greeks, Hungarians, and Jews. The "old" immigrants who had come before the Civil War from Northwestern Europe—the English, Scotch, Welsh, Irish, Germans, and Scandinavians—had become assimilated into the native population.

The new immigrants began to replace the old immigrants and the native Americans in the coal fields and in the steel mills. They crowded America's great manufacturing and mining centers—New York, Detroit, Chicago, Pittsburgh, Buffalo, Cleveland, bringing their own ethnic flavor, linguistic variety, religious practices, and political traditions, which still linger, giving each urban community its unique character. Each wave of new immigrants fol-

lowed their compatriots into the same neighborhoods of the same cities and
the same industries, clinging together for comfort and aid in alien urban
America. Tensions multiplied between old immigrants and natives, on the
one hand, and the new immigrants, on the other. Old-timers resented newcomers, aliens speaking foreign tongues, who displaced them on the job,
underbid them in wages, worked longer hours, and were, to boot, full of
dangerous ideologies.

The early labor movement incorporated the prejudices of its members,
sharing their nativism, xenophobia, and even anti-Semitism. Narrowly con-
struing its interests, the organized labor movement vociferously opposed free
immigration. It was not unexpected, then, that the Jewish immigrants from
Eastern Europe, long habituated to exclusion from social institutions and to
the separatism of their own institutions, should set about forming their own
"Jewish" unions. The United Hebrew Trades, organized in 1888, was a natural
outgrowth of the inhospitality on the American labor scene to immigrant
Jewish workers. Even a quarter of a century later, the formation of the
Amalgamated Clothing Workers Union as a split-off from the United Garment Workers reflected the unabating tension between Jewish and non-
Jewish workers in the men's clothing industry. Among the hat workers, too,
the Jewish and non-Jewish unions had developed in mutual hostility for over
thirty years, until 1934 when they finally combined, the conflicts between the
"old" and "new" immigrants finally having subsided.

These Jewish unions in the garment trades, born in the struggles of the
Jewish immigrant workers to find their place in America's industrial society,
eventually helped to shape an enlightened trade unionism in America. In
addition, they served as a way station on the road to acculturation. Fortuitously these unions became the vehicle through which the Jewish immigrant workers expressed their values and transmitted their traditions.
Blending Russian radicalism with Jewish messianism, these unions sounded
an alien note on the American labor scene at the turn of the century. They
were too radical for the American Federation of Labor and its head, Samuel
Gompers—an English Jew—who feared that the Russian Jewish socialists
forever chanting about a better world were jeopardizing the here-and-now of
pure-and-simple trade unionism. But the ideological vocabulary of the Russian Jewish radical movement, with its thick overlay of German philosophy,
French political slogans, and English economic theories, obscured its emotional impulse and fundamental character.

The Jewish revolutionary passion—whether for socialism, anarchism,
and even, finally, communism—originated in the Jewish situation. Anti-
Semitism, pogroms, discrimination, had alienated the Jews from Russian
society. In the revolutionary movement, the Russian Jews protested against
Russia's tyranny, its denial of the common humanity of all men and particularly of Jews, and its refusal to grant the basic political rights already

[margin notes: begins w/ Jewish unions; Gompers + AFL]

Russian Jew. radicalism

commonplace in most of Western Europe—freedom of speech, press, and assembly, the right to vote and to elect representatives to a legislative assembly, and freedom from arbitrary arrest. The economic goals of the radicals were in fact modest: the right to organize, to work only a twelve-hour day, for a living wage to be paid each week. The Jewish radicals in Russia were not engaged in a class war against a ruthless industrial capitalism, for it did not exist there. They hoped for a revolution that would create a constitutional state and guarantee political equality. These Jewish radicals embraced a liberal-humanitarian utopianism, rational and this-worldly, in contradistinction to the chiliastic utopianism of the *hasidim,* who computed the coming of the messiah by the extent of Jewish suffering.

In America, where they found most of their political utopia already in existence, the Jewish immigrants directed their revolutionary energy toward economic utopia. They talked in class-war terms about redistributing the wealth and taking over the means of production, but in practice they fought on the barricades only for union recognition. That was the American equivalent of the struggle for the dignity of man, the dignity of the worker, and his parity with the boss as a human being. These Russian Jewish immigrants were not really as class-conscious as they sounded and did not perceive their position in the class structure in Marxist terms. Not content to remain proletarians, many "sweated" workers quickly became entrepreneurs—from worker to subcontractor, to contractor, to manufacturer, to jobber, to wholesaler. No group had a more fluid class structure than the immigrant Russian Jews. They soon outranked all other immigrant groups in attaining, in their own generation, a socioeconomic status as high as or higher than third-generation Americans.

fluid class structure

Not all Jewish immigrants succeeded in escaping from the sweatshop. Those who remained concentrated on educating their children for something better than the shop. They formed a one-generation working class, being "neither the sons nor the fathers of workers." For themselves they sought dignity and community in their unions and the institutions associated with Jewish labor. In Russia the Jewish community had been an organic whole, and most Jews, however alienated, found their place within it, whether as upholders of the tradition or as secularists. In America, however, Jewish communal life was atomized and the immigrant had to recreate a community of his own. The Jewish labor movement and its institutions became the secular substitute for the old community. In many ways, the Jewish immigrant workers looked upon the institutions of the Jewish labor movement—the unions; their fraternal order, the Workman's Circle; their Yiddish daily newspaper, the *Forverts*—as their contribution to Jewish continuity. They brought Yiddish into their unions and sustained a Yiddish labor press for many decades. They were the consumers of a "proletarian" literature in Yiddish (largely revolutionary didacticism tempered with self-pity). They established Yiddish schools with a labor orientation. The labor movement was their vehicle to preserve Jewish values and traditions as they understood them.

François Guizot once wrote that peoples with a long history are influenced by their past and their national traditions at the very moment when they are working to destroy them. In the midst of the most striking transformations, he said, they remain fundamentally what their history has made them, for no revolution, however powerful, can wipe out long-established national traditions. The Jewish revolutionaries who fled Tsarist prisons and Siberian exile were hostile to the Jewish religious tradition, which they rejected as clerical and superstitious. They sought desperately to break out of what to them was its constricting mold. Yet even they had been shaped by that Jewish mold. David Dubinsky, at the convention of the International Ladies Garment Workers' Union (ILGWU) in May, 1962, when he was re-elected president, conjured up his youthful dreams, in which Jewish messianism and the perfect society had appeared in a Jewish Labor Bundist guise. "I was sent to Siberia," Dubinsky said, "because I dreamt at that time of a better world. I dreamt of being free, of not being under the domination of a czar and dictatorship." He then recalled that his father, a religious man, used to read to him from the Bible on Saturday afternoons. In reading, his father used to stress that "a good name is better than precious oil." He had heard it so often, Dubinsky confessed, that it became part of him and of the movement with which he was identified: "When we saw the labor movement imperilled because of lack of ethics, I realized a good name is better than all the riches and all the offices to which one could aspire." Like many other Jewish labor leaders, Dubinsky had lived only briefly within the Jewish tradition he wistfully recalled, and had rebelled against it. Yet this Jewish tradition, discarded and unacknowledged, significantly affected the way the Jewish labor movement developed.

Innovations:

In America, shortly after World War I, the Jewish unions pioneered with their social welfare programs: medical care, housing, unemployment insurance, health insurance, vacations (and vacation resorts), and retirement benefits. They were the first to develop educational programs and the first to make philanthropy a union practice. Such activities became accepted in the general labor movement only after the New Deal. That welfare, education, and philanthropy became union concerns in Jewish unions demonstrated the ways through which the Jewish workers transferred the social responsibilities of the East European Jewish community to the labor movement. In the Jewish world of Eastern Europe, the community took care of its sick and its poor, its old and needy, and created the institutions to administer this care. This tradition the unions took over. It was only natural, then, that the ILGWU started the first union health center in 1916 and the Amalgamated started the first *gemilut-hesed* in 1923. The Amalgamated Bank was not the first labor bank; a few labor banks had been established a little earlier, in the hope that banking might yield large profits and make the unions independent. But the Amalgamated Bank was the first to offer union members low-interest loans, without collateral, which they could not get elsewhere. This was the sort of *tsedakah* which Maimonides might have designated as the highest degree.

In 1927 the Amalgamated built the first cooperative houses in New York to provide some of its members with housing that was not only decent but also attractive. Thirty years later other unions followed that example. Probably the most paradoxical episode in union housing occurred in 1957 when the ILGWU lent a corporation headed by Nelson A. Rockefeller $2.6 millions to help finance a workers' housing development in Puerto Rico.

The Russian immigrant passion for learning had been stilled partly by the revolutionary movement, which had been teacher as well as agitator, publishing popular science and philosophy along with political tracts. In America Jews had more educational opportunities. Hutchins Hapgood wrote in 1902 in *The Spirit of the Ghetto* that "the public schools are filled with little Jews; the night schools of the east side are practically used by no other race. City College, New York University, and Columbia University are graduating Russian Jews in numbers rapidly increasing." Despite classes, lectures, and debates at the settlement houses, at the Americanizing agencies like the Educational Alliance, at Cooper Union and the Rand School, the immigrant workers continued to look to the labor movement for learning, so the Amalgamated and the ILGWU gave courses in English and economics, history and philosophy. They were indeed labor colleges. It took a quarter of a century, during Roosevelt's New Deal, for other unions to sponsor labor education.

Philanthropy, too, as the Jewish unions practiced it, demonstrated the pervasiveness of Jewish tradition. For many decades, a small portion of union dues has been set aside for donations—to labor organizations, health and welfare agencies, educational and cultural institutions, civic and political causes, and finally to the ethnic beneficiaries—Jewish organizations, Italian, and later, as a consequence of ethnic succession, Negro and Puerto Rican. During the Nazi period and in the immediate postwar era, the unions distributed colossal sums of money for relief and rescue, mostly for Jews, but also for non-Jewish labor leaders and unionists. Jewish causes—the Jewish Labor Committee and the United Jewish Appeal being the top beneficiaries—enjoyed the support of the ILGWU. The Histadrut and many Israeli labor projects have been the richer for gifts from the Jewish labor movement.

The Jewish influence has perhaps been deepest in the realization of industrial peace in the garment industry, though industrial peace was not particularly a

Jewish idea. The National Civic Federation, founded at the turn of the century, had brought together representatives of labor, capital, and the public to head off strikes by mediation and to use conciliation to settle disputes. But the federation had limited success, being accepted, at best, on a temporary basis by some segments of capital and labor, because labor for the most part suspected that cooperation meant sellout, and capital thought conciliation meant surrender. But the situation was different with regard to Jewish labor and capital in the clothing industry.

In 1910 the Protocol of Peace settled the "Great Revolt," an eight-week strike of some sixty thousand cloakmakers in New York. The strike involved mostly Jewish workers (with a substantial minority of Italians) and nearly all Jewish manufacturers. The mediators were Jewish community leaders, many associated with the Ethical Culture Society. The most active in the settlement were Louis D. Brandeis, distinguished Jewish lawyer and political liberal; leading Boston merchant and Ethical Culturist A. Lincoln Filene, who was also a member of the National Civic Federation; pioneer Jewish social workers like Meyer Bloomfield in Boston and Henry Moskowitz in New York; and the most prominent of Jewish community leaders, Jacob Schiff and Louis Marshall, of the American Jewish Committee. The manufacturers and the union alike were torn between the militants and the compromisers. Yet a precedent-setting settlement was reached, which, besides increasing wages and decreasing hours, established a preferential union shop, a union-management joint board of sanitary control in the factories, a grievance committee, and a board of arbitration. The arbitration board was to consist of one representative of the union, one of the manufacturers, and one of the public. To be sure, the protocol broke down, was repaired, and broke down again after some years. But most scholars agree that its influence was lasting.

Several months thereafter, a four-month strike of some eight thousand workers at Hart, Schaffner and Marx, the world's largest men's clothing manufacturer, in Chicago, was settled by establishing a three-man arbitration board. As in New York, most of the workers were Jews and nearly all the manufacturers were Jewish. That settlement started a tradition of such harmonious labor-management relations between Hart, Schaffner and Marx and the Amalgamated that, in 1960, the late Meyer Kestenbaum, then president of the company, spoke at the Amalgamated's convention commemorating fifty years of collective bargaining.

Exceptional in this history of cooperation between labor and capital have been its liberal, humanitarian qualities. The unions did not "sell out" their workers nor did they "compromise" their ideals. On the contrary, they succeeded in enlisting the employers' support for economic and social programs once considered eccentric and visionary, turning these into commonplace realities.

Was Jewishness the determinant? The existential Jewish situation, Jewish workers and Jewish bosses in a gentile world, must have had an effect, entangling them in one community. They could not extricate themselves, even if they chose, from each other's fate. Nor could they divest themselves of the habits and outlooks of centuries-old traditions. This is not to minimize the specific conditions in the garment industry. Professor Selig Perlman has pointed to its special character—the multitude of small shops in an industry that had not quite reached the factory stage, the cutthroat competition of highly individualistic employers, the industry's seasonal character, in which a strike meant unemployment for the worker and financial calamity for the employer.

Garment industry

But the Jewish differential remains. Jews in a gentile world, despite class differences, workers and bosses felt responsible for one another. The wealthy Jews may have been more sensitive to the Jewish situation, feeling their position and prestige imperiled by the flow of immigration from Eastern Europe. They were ashamed of the appearance, the language, and the manners of the Russian Jews, aghast at their political ideologies, and terrified lest the world crumble by the mad act of a Jewish radical. (The fear was not entirely unfounded: a crazy Polish anarchist had assassinated President McKinley.) Unhappily and involuntarily identified with the immigrant community, the American Jews sought to restrain and tranquilize the revolutionary temper of the immigrant workers with Americanization programs and traditional Jewish education. Afraid to be accused of burdening the public charities with immigrant Jewish paupers, they contributed to Jewish relief societies and to welfare and educational institutions. But they knew that employment and labor peace were better guarantees against economic hardship than charity. In the long run, it may have been cheaper to pay higher wages than to make bigger donations. Besides, labor unrest was bad for the Jewish name and for the reputation of the Jewish employers. The dignity of man and the dignity of labor were as high in the system of values of the Jewish capitalist as the Jewish worker, for it was Judaism itself that endowed labor with divine attributes ("Israel was charged to do work on the six days, just as they were ordered to rest on the seventh day"). Louis Marshall, who had not much sympathy for radical ideologies, nonetheless had a deep sense of the dignity of labor and the working man. Some months after the Protocol of Peace had been signed, he chided a manufacturer whose workers had struck: "So long as the manufacturer considers his employees as mere serfs and chattels, so long as they are considered as unworthy of being brought into conference or consultation, so long as their feelings and aspirations as human beings are lost sight of, so long will labor troubles be rampant and a feeling of dislike, if not of hatred, will be engendered against the employer in the hearts of the employees."

The practice of Judaism, as well as its principles, helped bridge the gulf

Judaism
bridges class gulf

between worker and boss. Sholem Asch's Uncle Moses, who brought his whole *shtetl* over to work in his factory, prayed with his workers at the evening services, if only to encourage them to work overtime. Lillian Wald reported an incident about a Jewish union leader who met Jacob Schiff. At first the union man was uncomfortable about his shabby clothing, but this was forgotten when, arguing an issue, both he and Schiff began to quote Bible and Talmud, trying to outdo each other. This kind of familiarity reduced the workers' awe for the boss and made discussion between them not only possible but even likely.

The Jewish situation had made many wealthy American Jews receptive to liberal and humanitarian ideas. They befriended the pioneering social workers of their day and were willing to learn from them about the conditions of the industrial poor. Lillian Wald in New York City taught Jacob Schiff; Judge Julian W. Mack and Jane Addams educated Julius Rosenwald in Chicago. Little wonder, then, that Schiff used to contribute anonymously, through Lillian Wald, for the relief of striking workers and sometimes even to a union treasury. Back in 1897 during a garment workers' strike, he asked Lillian Wald, "Is it not possible that representatives of workers, contractors, and manufacturers meet to discuss ways and means in which a better condition of affairs could permanently be brought about?"

The question may have seemed novel or naive in those days of labor's unrest and capital's indifference. Yet in a short period radical Jewish unions, conservative Jewish community leaders, and profit-seeking Jewish manufacturers answered Schiff's question affirmatively. Perhaps the most curious milestone on this path was erected in 1929, when three great Jewish financiers and philanthropists—Julius Rosenwald, Herbert H. Lehman, and Felix Warburg—lent the ILGWU $100,000 to help the union's reconstruction after its locals had been rewon from Communist capture.

The Jewish tradition of arbitration and conciliation had cut a broad swath. Originating in talmudic times, incorporated in the *Shulchan Aruch*, practiced for centuries in all Jewish communities, these principles of compromise, arbitration, and settlement were familiar and venerable to worker and boss alike. The rabbi and *dayanim* decided in the *beth din*, the religious court, but disputants frequently took their case to communal leaders who acted as arbitrators, *borerim*. The procedure must have seemed commonplace to most Jewish workers, not long from the old country and the old culture. As for the manufacturers, they, too, were responsive to the teachings that peaceful compromise was preferable to the humiliation of a court and that Jews should settle their disputes within the Jewish community.

Jewish solidarity and the Jewish tradition, albeit secularized, bred innovations in the institutions of modern American labor. The Jewish situation itself—the Jew poised on the margins of gentile society, in an existential

Galut—created the energy and the impetus for those innovations. Whereas lower-class anti-Semitism had separated Jewish workers from the non-Jews, anxiety among upper-class Jews about anti-Semitism had more securely fixed their solidarity with the Jewish workers. The tension of Jews living in a gentile world has accounted for much of Jewish creativity in modern society. The Jewish labor movement, too, shared in that creativity.

FOR FURTHER READING

World of Our Fathers (1976), Irving Howe's epic history of East European Jewish immigration to America, is *the* book that anyone seriously interested in this subject should turn to first. For briefer surveys, see Salo Baron, "United States, 1880–1914," in Jeanette Baron (ed.), *Steeled by Adversity* (1971); Bernard D. Weinryb, "East European Immigration to the United States," *Jewish Quarterly Review* 45 (April 1955), pp. 497–528; and Oscar and Mary Handlin, "A Century of Jewish Immigration to the United States," *American Jewish Year Book* 50 (1948–1949). These may be supplemented by various documentary histories of the period: Irving Howe and Kenneth Libo, *How We Lived* (1979); Abraham J. Karp, *Golden Door to America* (1976); and Uri D. Herscher's collection of immigrant memoirs, *The East European Jewish Experience in America* (1983).

Moses Rischin's *The Promised City* (1962) is an essential volume that offers a panoramic portrait of East European Jewish immigrants in the city that almost all of them either lived in or passed through: New York. Indeed, New York has been the focus of a great many studies of Jewish immigration. Thomas Kessner, in *The Golden Door* (1977), demonstrates statistically the relatively rapid occupational mobility of New York Jews. Ronald Sanders's *The Downtown Jews* (1969), Hutchins Hapgood's classic *The Spirit of the Ghetto* (1902, reprinted 1965), and Allon Schoener's *Portal to America* (1967), a collection of photographs and newspaper articles, evoke the flavor of New York's old Lower East Side. Isaac Metzker (ed.), *A Bintel Brief* (1971) translates "help" letters to the *Jewish Daily Forward*, shedding light on the heartaches of Jewish newcomers. Jonathan D. Sarna (ed.), *People Walk on Their Heads* (1981) presents in translation an early critique of Jews and Judaism in New York by an Orthodox immigrant rabbi, while discussing in his introduction the transition from immigrant Judaism to American Judaism.

Literary portrayals of Jewish immigration to America abound. Abraham Cahan's *The Rise of David Levinsky* (1917, 1960) is certainly the best, and may be supplemented by Cahan's earlier efforts, notably *Yekl* (1896, 1970), the basis for the movie "Hester Street." Anzia Yezierska views immigration through a woman's eye, particularly in her fictionalized autobiography, *Bread Givers* (1925, 1975). Other literature from the period has been gathered by Milton Hindus in *The Old*

East Side: An Anthology (1969), and listed by Carole S. Kessner, "Jewish-American Immigrant Fiction Written in English Between 1867 and 1920," *Bulletin of Research in the Humanities* 81 (1978), pp. 406–430.

Focused studies on selective aspects of immigration are too numerous to list. For a recent review of some of them, see Eli M. Lederhendler, "Jewish Immigration to America and Revisionist Historiography: A Decade of New Perspectives," *Yivo Annual of Jewish Social Science* 18 (1983), pp. 391–410. Other valuable recent studies are found in a special issue of *American Jewish History* 71 (December 1981) and in David Berger, *The Legacy of Jewish Immigration: 1881 and Its Impact* (1983). One of the most important contributions in recent years is Simon Kuznets's statistical study, "Immigration of Russian Jews to the United States: Background and Structure," *Perspectives in American History* 9 (1975), pp. 35–124, which analyzes all available data.

The relationship between German Jews and Russian Jews in America is still a passionately debated subject in some circles. Ande Manners, in *Poor Cousins* (1972), offers a highly readable account. Zosa Szajkowski, "The Yahudi and the Immigrant: A Reappraisal," *American Jewish Historical Quarterly* 63 (September 1973), pp. 13–45, is a major revisionist statement that seeks to understand the conflict more objectively and in context. For Moses Rischin's most recent thoughts on this subject, see *American Jewish History* 73 (December 1983), pp. 194–198.

The world of Jewish immigrant women has now begun to be studied. Charlotte Baum, Paula Hyman, and Sonya Michel summed up much of what they uncovered in *The Jewish Woman in America* (1975). Jacob R. Marcus, *The American Jewish Woman: A Documentary History* (1981) makes available a bounty of new material. Paula Hyman's "Culture and Gender: Women in the Immigrant Jewish Community," in D. Berger's *The Legacy of Jewish Immigration* and Sydney Stahl Weinberg's "The World of Our Mothers: Family, Work, and Education in the Lives of Jewish Immigrant Women," *Frontiers* 7 (1983), pp. 71–79, pose new and more significant questions about what made the experience of Jewish women unique.

No definitive study of the Jewish labor movement in America exists. Special issues of *Yivo Annual* 16 (1976) and *American Jewish Historical Quarterly* 65 (March 1976) contain invaluable articles, including in the latter a fine historiographical review-essay by Irwin Yellowitz. These supplement Elias Tcherikower's pathbreaking *The Early Jewish Labor Movement in the United States* (1961), and Melech Epstein's *Jewish Labor in U.S.A.* (1969). Will Herberg's "The Jewish Labor Movement in the United States," *American Jewish Year Book* 53 (1952) is a penetrating survey, and Moses Rischin, "The Jewish Labor Movement in America: A Social Interpretation," *Labor History* 4 (1963) underscores the wider significance of the subject. Finally, Irwin Yellowitz, "Jewish Immigrants and the American Labor Movement, 1900–1920," *American Jewish History* 71 (December 1981), pp. 188–217, recounts the often stormy relationship between Jewish labor and the labor movement at large.

If one were to read but one book on the New York Kehillah it would have to be Arthur A. Goren, *New York Jews and the Quest for the Community: The Kehillah Experiment, 1908–1922* (1970), one of the best known and most influential books in American Jewish history in recent decades. Irving Howe in Berger's *The Legacy of Jewish Immigration*, pp. 152–155, however, makes some telling points in suggesting that the Kehillah's importance has often been exaggerated. For more on the Kehillah's impact, see Nathan H. Winter, *Jewish Education in a Pluralist Society* (1966), a biography of Samson Benderly, and Jenna Weissman Joselit, *Our Gang* (1983), a history of "Jewish crime and the New York Jewish community, 1900–1940."

PART FOUR

COMING TO TERMS WITH AMERICA

The era of mass Jewish immigration into the United States ended with World War I, as wartime conditions and then restrictive quotas stemmed the human tide. Soon, for the first time in many decades, the majority of American Jews would be native born. Where the central focus of American Jewish life had been concentrated on problems of immigration and absorption, American Jewry now entered a period of stable consolidation. The "second generation" moved up into the middle class and out to more fashionable neighborhoods, creating new institutions—synagogue-centers, progressive Hebrew schools, and the like—as they went. "Americanization" stopped being a serious community concern at this point; history had proved that East European Jews would become Americans with a vengeance. The question now was whether, as Americans, they would still remain Jews. Programs designed to ensure that they would do so became high community priorities.

With stability and the rise of a new generation came a growing commitment to communal unity. Germans and East Europeans in America had been drawing closer together even before World War I. After the war, given the growth of external threats directed against all Jews, and the increasing internal pressure for unity coming from young ones, the process of ethnicization speeded up. Leaving old world divisions behind, Jews began to coalesce into an avowedly *American* Jewish community—a community that could attempt, at least on some issues, to speak with a single voice.

Even as the community was uniting, however, it was being rent asunder in new ways. The three-part division among Orthodox, Conservative, and Reform Jews, firmly institutionalized in this period, gave expression to long-standing intracommunal conflicts over rituals, beliefs, and attitudes toward tradition and change. The issue of Zionism proved even more divisive, since it raised fundamental questions about the meaning of American Jewish life, the obligations of Jews to the country in which they lived, and the relationship of American Jews to the Jewish people as a whole.

By the eve of World War II, then, American Jewry presented a mixed picture: united in some respects, divided in others. It was a community at home in America and proud of its achievements, but still uncertain of its identity or its position vis-à-vis other Jewish communities in the world. Many anticipated a long period of transition, during which time Jews in America would organize and gradually assume new responsibilities for their brethren worldwide. But as Hitler's armies began to reduce European centers of Jewry to ashes, it became clear that that was not to be. Instead, given the crisis in Europe, the mantle of Jewish leadership fell to American Jewry at once.

CHAPTER

13

The passions engendered by World War I set off a period of intense social tension in America. The civil rights of many were violated, and innocent people fell prey to hysteria-driven mobs. At first, most hostility focused upon German-Americans and those deemed for one reason or another insufficiently patriotic. Before long, however, Catholics, "radicals," and Jews also felt the sting of popular animus. Anti-Semitism became an increasingly serious problem.

Anti-Jewish hatred was not a new phenomenon in America; it had waxed and waned periodically, and, as we have seen, rose to a particular peak during the Civil War. During the late nineteenth century, America witnessed an unprecedented increase in social anti-Semitism, mostly directed at upwardly mobile German Jews, who found themselves denied membership in certain clubs and refused admittance to certain resorts. Public and private expressions of anti-Semitism, particularly directed against immigrants, also increased during this period, as did the appearance of anti-Semitic images in print.

To be sure, anti-Semitism formed only one side—the dark side—of Jewish-Christian relations in America; on the bright side lay many examples of warm interreligious friendship coupled with severe condemnations of religious prejudice of every sort. Furthermore, the American strain of anti-Semitism proved less virulent than the European variety, given America's constitutional ideals and liberal traditions, its pluralism (pluralism also meant that Jews were far from the only group facing prejudice), its two-party system (that saw both parties vie for Jewish votes), and the fact that Jews could fight back freely against anti-Semitism, without fearing—as some did in countries where Jews had only recently been emancipated—that their rights would be taken away. Still, unpleasant anti-Semitic incidents did occur, and with increasing frequency. They caused Jews considerable anguish and raised disquieting fears about the future.

The first significant incident to arouse the Jewish community in the twentieth century was the Leo Frank case in Atlanta. Frank, a twenty-nine-year-old Jewish factory superintendent, was convicted in 1913 of murdering one of his employees, fourteen-year-old Mary Phagan, and dumping her body in the basement of the pencil factory where they both worked. The case attracted widespread publicity, and much attention centered on Frank's religion. Crowds outside the courthouse chanted "Hang the Jew!" The Jewish community's efforts to help Frank resulted in religious polarization. When Georgia governor John Slaton, unpersuaded that Frank was the murderer, commuted his sentence in 1915 from death to life in prison, a mob broke into the jail, kidnapped Frank, and lynched him: the first known lynching of a Jew in American history. Only recently, an eyewitness has confirmed what many for so long believed: Mary Phagan was murdered by the janitor of the pencil factory, the "star witness" against Frank. Frank himself was innocent.

The Frank case, in spite of its notoriety, was an isolated incident. Its effects were felt mainly in the South, and outside Atlanta the case was soon forgotten. By contrast, Henry Ford's virulent and well-financed anti-Semitic campaign, discussed in the article that follows, had a nationwide impact. It pitted Jews against a genuine American hero, the manufacturer of the Model T car, and lasted for seven long years, reaching millions of people worldwide before Ford retracted and apologized in 1927. Rooted in traditional European Christian thought and modern Progressive-era American fears, Ford's anti-Semitism, as Leo Ribuffo, a leading student of American extremism, demonstrates, was a complex phenomenon related to social, cultural, economic, and psychological aspects of Ford's life. Ford used "the international Jew" as an organizing principle; it "explained" whatever he found wrong with the modern world. Neither logic nor contrary facts fazed him.

Sigmund Freud once observed that "when a delusion cannot be dissipated by the facts of reality, it probably does not spring from reality," and such was certainly the case with Ford. Yet to view him and other anti-Semites of his day merely in narrow pathological terms is not enough. Ribuffo's broader perspective, set against a wide canvas, discloses much more—both about American anti-Semitism and about the culture that nourished it.

Henry Ford and
The International Jew

Leo P. Ribuffo

Although historians still disagree about the extent of anti-Semitism during the late nineteenth century, the dominant attitude among Christian Americans, as Leonard Dinnerstein rightly concludes, was an amalgam of "affection, curiosity, suspicion and rejection." Comparing Americans and Europeans, we can say that anti-Semitism in the United States was relatively less violent, less racist, and less central to the worldviews of those who accepted it.

The first two decades of the twentieth century witnessed a shift toward greater suspicion and rejection. The lynching of Leo Frank in 1915 was only the most dramatic incident in an era that marked, according to George Fredrickson, a peak of "formalized racism." After World War I, hostility toward Jews escalated, operating in three overlapping areas. First, "polite" anti-Semites, including President A. Lawrence Lowell of Harvard, restricted admissions to clubs, resorts, universities, and the professions. Second, supported by many leading psychologists, such popularizers as Lothrop Stoddard and Kenneth Roberts spread the Anglo-Saxon cult to a wide audience. Third, commentators and members of Congress increasingly associated Jews with radicalism in general and communism in particular. For example, Dr. George A. Simons, a former missionary in Russia, told a Senate committee that the "so-called Bolshevik movement" was "Yiddish." Simons's allegations, which particularly impressed Senator Knute Nelson, were largely endorsed by other witnesses, including a Northwestern University professor, a Commerce Department agent, two representatives of National City Bank, a YMCA official and vice counsel in Petrograd, and several Russian émigrés.

To Simons, "Yiddish" Bolshevism seemed to "dovetail" with the plot outlined in *The Protocols of the Learned Elders of Zion*. In this notorious forgery created by Russian royalists at the turn of the century, a leader of a secret Jewish world government allegedly explained the plot to destroy Christian civilization. For almost two thousand years, the Elders had been "splitting society by ideas" while manipulating economic and political power. Currently they popularized Darwinism, Marxism, "Nietzche-ism" and other anti-Christian doctrines, undermined clergy, corrupted governments, and arranged wars that would profit Jews while killing Gentiles. Above all, the conspirators controlled both the mechanisms of capitalism and the radical movements pretending to offer alternatives. The *Protocols'* generality left room for interpolations to fit local circumstances. Eventually, their basic charges were "Americanized" and disseminated under the imprimatur of a national hero, Henry Ford.

Along with the nation as a whole, Henry Ford faced a series of crises during the years 1915 to 1920. With the introduction of the Model T in 1908, he had begun to achieve his great goal, mass production of a reliable, inexpensive automobile. By the mid-1910s, his decision to freeze auto design and expand production instead of paying dividends alienated subordinates and minority stockholders. Undaunted, he fired employees who disagreed with him, bought out dissatisfied shareholders, and gained full control of the Ford Motor Company in 1920. Thereafter, except for his able son Edsel, he rarely encountered anyone who openly disagreed with him.

Ford became, in Keith Sward's words, "as inaccessible as the Grand Lama." He remained eager to offer wide-ranging advice, but now usually filtered opinions through Ernest G. Liebold, his secretary since 1911. An ambitious martinet, Liebold expanded his authority by exploiting Ford's quirks, such as his dislike of paperwork and refusal to read most correspondence. The secretary gladly managed public relations, issued statements or answered letters in Ford's name, and exercised power of attorney after 1918. Indeed, he substantially controlled Ford's access to the world outside Dearborn.

To promote the views that he developed in virtual seclusion, Ford in 1919 purchased a weekly newspaper. The *Dearborn Independent* was designed to disseminate practical "ideas and ideals" without distortion by the "world's channels of information." The Dearborn Publishing Company, moreover, looked like a family enterprise. Henry Ford, his wife Clara, and his son Edsel were respectively president, vice president, and treasurer. Editorship of the *Independent* was bestowed on E. G. Pipp, a friend of Ford who had edited the *Detroit News*. William J. Cameron, an intelligent but hard-drinking veteran of the *News*, listened to Ford's ruminations and then wrote "Mr. Ford's Page." Both men operated under the watchful eye of Liebold, who detested Pipp and barely tolerated Cameron.

Despite a promise on the masthead to chronicle "neglected truth," the *Independent* at first printed nothing extraordinary. It supported Prohibition, prison reform, the Versailles Treaty, and the League of Nations; yet, these serious issues often received less attention than light stories about prominent persons, cities, or colleges. For sixteen months, the newspaper did not mention an alleged Jewish conspiracy. The owner, however, had been contemplating the issue for several years, and had considered raising it during the 1918 senatorial campaign. After the election, Pipp recalled, Ford began to talk about Jews "frequently, almost continuously."

The source of Ford's animus remains obscure. Ford himself told Liebold and Fred Black, the *Independent* business manager, that Herman Bernstein, editor of the *Jewish Tribune,* and other passengers on Oscar II (the "peace ship" Ford charted in World War I) had blamed Jewish financiers for the war. Liebold, who said that unspecified behavior by Jewish journalists in Norway "confirmed" Ford's suspicions, obviously shared and encouraged the automaker's bias. Indeed, Ford's secretary suspected Jewish automobile dealers of thwarting company policy and, a generation later, still recalled *The International Jew* as a worthwhile enterprise. Closer to home, Clara Ford may have promoted her husband's bigotry. At least she opposed Jewish membership in the country club and urged Ford to fire an executive whose wife was half-Jewish.

Pipp acted briefly as a countervailing influence. Six months after buying the *Independent* in 1919, Ford wanted to run a series on Jewish subversion. The editor held out for almost a year. In April, 1920, he quit instead of sanctioning the articles. The imminent anti-Semitic campaign was probably not the only reason for Pipp's departure. Liebold had been undermining his authority and restricting access to Ford. When he resigned, Pipp joined a formidable list of former employees who had refused to be sycophants.

Because the office files of the *Dearborn Independent* were destroyed in 1963, and because other records for 1920 have disappeared, we must rely on scattered correspondence, self-serving reminiscences, and conjecture to trace the composition of *The International Jew.* Apparently research and writing began toward the end of Pipp's tenure. Investigators directed by Liebold forwarded anti-Semitic information to Dearborn where, Pipp recalled, Ford swallowed "all . . . that was dished out." William J. Cameron, who succeeded Pipp as editor, did most of the writing. Initially unaware of the *Protocols,* Cameron did little "preliminary work" for the first article. He read "whatever was around," including Werner Sombart's *The Jews and Modern Capitalism.* But Cameron's later protests that he considered the articles "useless" must not be taken at face value. Fred Black recalled that Cameron "walked the floor" for three months before agreeing to write *The International Jew.* Within a year or two, however, he came to believe most of what he wrote. In the meantime, along with other Ford employees, he followed orders.

The first article, "The International Jew: The World's Problem," appeared on May 20, 1920. Liebold had suggested the title and date of publication in order to coincide with an attack on "greedy" Jews by Leo Franklin, a prominent Detroit rabbi and Ford's former neighbor. Although the *Independent* promised further revelations, the staff seems not to have planned more than a month ahead. Indeed, Black thought that Ford himself did not anticipate a sustained campaign.

Yet several developments kept the series alive until January 14, 1922. Ford, Liebold, and—eventually—Cameron got wrapped up in their project. Ford visited the *Independent* almost every day, concerning himself only with "Mr. Ford's Page" and *The International Jew*. Despite their mutual hostility, Liebold and Cameron consulted often on the series, sometimes poring over articles together until three o'clock in the morning. Critics provided grist for the mill. When former President Taft or columnist Arthur Brisbane attacked *The International Jew*, they were denounced in subsequent articles as "gentile fronts." Moreover, Liebold's agents regularly supplied rumors, clippings, and forged documents.

The main detective operation, located on Broad Street in New York City, was managed by C. C. Daniels, a former lawyer for the Justice Department, whose aides, including several veterans of military intelligence, used secret identification numbers when contacting Dearborn. Norman Hapgood exaggerated only slightly when he said that the group "muckraked everybody who was a Jew or was suspected of being a Jew." It attracted "adventurers, detectives, and criminals" and gave credence to their stories. For example, though Daniels's brother Josephus, the secretary of the navy, might have told them otherwise, Ford investigators thought that President Wilson took orders from Justice Brandeis over a private telephone line. Daniels's special concerns included Eugene Meyer, Jr., of the Federal Reserve Board, whom he accused of blocking Ford's acquisition of the nitrate plants at Muscle Shoals, Alabama. "As you know," he wrote to Liebold in 1922, "locks and bars make no difference to that portion of God's chosen people seeking to displace the stars and stripes with the Jewish national flag and that calls Lenine [sic] the greatest Statesman alive."

Liebold recalled that he needed few European agents because "people came over here and revealed their stories to us." Russian émigrés ultimately provided a copy of the *Protocols*. Here, too, slight surviving evidence obscures the story. Sometime before the summer of 1920, Liebold apparently met Paquita de Shishmareff, a Russian émigré married to an American soldier. Liebold told Ford that Shishmareff, who is better known as Mrs. Leslie Fry, possessed "full and thorough knowledge of all Jewish operations in Europe." According to Liebold's reminiscences, she provided his "first knowledge" of the *Protocols* as well as a copy of the forgery. Whatever the original source, the *Independent* staff was studying the *Protocols* in the middle of June, 1920. On June 10, W. G. Enyon, a company employee in Delaware, dispatched several copies to Dearborn.

Starting with the July 24 article, the *Protocols* description of an international Jewish conspiracy provided the central thread of *The International Jew*.

For the next three years, Liebold expanded his contacts with Russian royalists and their dubious documents. In addition to Mrs. Fry, he consulted Boris Brasol, an erstwhile member of the Black Hundreds, and several of their friends. A Ford agent in Paris paid seven thousand francs for a report by former Russian Judge Nicholas Sokoloff purporting to show that Jewish conspirators had murdered the Romanovs. Liebold was impressed and invited Sokoloff to Dearborn. The émigrés soon discovered that they were treated as capriciously as other Ford employees. When Sokoloff fell ill, Liebold "hustled" him out of Michigan, and later refused to support his widow and orphans.

Although the *Dearborn Independent* was indebted to émigrés for the *Protocols*, *The International Jew* was not, as Norman Cohn contends, "far more a Russo-German than an American product." The alleged manifestations of the "world's foremost problem" coincided with issues that had unsettled the United States since the Civil War.

First, the *Independent* complained that both the monopolistic activities of large corporations and the countervailing actions of government had produced a "steady curtailment" of freedom.

Second, joining the search for moral order that intensified after World War I, the *Independent* condemned new styles in dress and music, changing sexual mores, Hollywood "lasciviousness," and the "filthy tide" sweeping over the theater. Sensitive to unraveling family bonds, the newspaper warned that children were drawn from "natural leaders in the home, church, and school to institutionalized 'centers' and scientific 'play spots.'"

Third, the *Independent* addressed the issue that had grown in importance since the "endless stream" of immigrants had begun to arrive in the 1880s: What was Americanism? These strangers, especially residents of the "unassimilated province" known as New York City, were responsible for the "mad confusion that passes in some quarters as a picture" of the United States.

Fourth, the *Independent* worried about the problem of determining truth in the modern world. Even before the anti-Semitic campaign, the newspaper had shared the prevailing fear of deception by propaganda. People were "born believers" who needed "deeply" to affirm something. But it was hard to know what to believe. *The International Jew* protested that man was ruled "by a whole company of ideas into whose authority he has not inquired at all." Not only did he live by the "say of others," but "terrific social pressures" on behalf of "broadmindedness" discouraged probes beneath conventional wisdom. Sounding like Walter Lippmann or Harold Lasswell, the newspaper warned that credulity was especially dangerous in the current "era of false labels."

The *Protocols* offered a "clue to the modern maze." Hedging on the question of authenticity, as Liebold did in correspondence, the *Independent* said that the documents themselves were "comparatively unimportant." They gave "meaning to certain previously observed facts." Whether or not an Elder of Zion actually gave these lectures, it was clear that Jews used ideas to "corrupt Collective Opinion," controlled finance, sponsored revolution, and were "everywhere" exercising power.

Following a "historical" survey, The International Jew purported to document the current activities of Hebrew capitalists, radicals, and propagandists. In the economic sphere, the Independent distinguished between Jewish "finance" and the "creative industry" dominated by Gentiles. From the Rothschild family on down, Jews were "essentially money-lenders" who rarely had a "permanent interest" in production. Rather, they seized a commodity "at just the point in its passage from producer to consumer where the heaviest profit can be extracted." Squeezing the "neck of the bottle" in this way, they dominated the grain, copper, fur, and cotton markets. The rising national debt was another "measure of our enslavement." Furthermore, in 1913, Paul Warburg, a German Jew who had emigrated "for the express purpose of changing our financial system," convinced Congress to pass the Federal Reserve Act. The Reserve Board helped the "banking aristocracy" to contact currency and centralize funds for speculation.

Through four volumes, Jewish vices appeared as the reverse of any "American view." The dichotomies between making and getting, morality and sensuality, fair trade and chicanery, "creative labor" and exploitation, heroism and cowardice, were only the beginning. Some of the most important differences impinged on politics. Anglo-Saxons had created the press to prevent secret domination by any minority, but Jews twisted news for their own advantage. Democratic procedures were another Anglo-Saxon inheritance; Jews "instinctively" favored autocracy. One of the "higher traits" of "our race" fostered obliviousness to Hebrew machinations. Eschewing conspiracies themselves, Anglo-Saxons neither expected them among other groups nor followed the available clues "through long and devious and darkened channels."

Above all, Gentiles advanced "by individual initiative," while Jews took advantage of unprecedented "racial loyalty and solidarity." Because success—a preeminent American and "Fordian" value—could "not be attacked nor condemned [sic]," the Independent hesitated to criticize Jews for doing "extraordinarily" well. Neither could it concede superiority to another "race." In essence, therefore, the newspaper cried foul. Because Jews took advantage of their position as an "international nation," it was "difficult to measure gentile and Jewish achievement by the same standard." Jews captured the "highest places" only because they began with an unfair advantage.

The Independent said that Jewish solidarity required "one rule for the Gentile and one for the Jews." In fact, the newspaper itself not surprisingly held to the double standard. It condemned acts by Jews which, if done by Christians, would have been considered innocuous, legitimate, or admirable. The wartime ban on German and the fundamentalist effort to drive Darwin from the classroom were acceptable; Jewish objections to *The Merchant of Venice* violated "American principles." George Creel's chairmanship of the Committee on Public Information did not prompt a discussion of Protestant traits; Carl Laemmle's production of *The Beast of Berlin* for the same committee was a "lurid" attempt to profit from war. Jacob Schiff's use of dollar diplomacy on behalf of Russian Jews seemed sinister; efforts by E. H. Harriman to squeeze concessions from the Czar passed without comment. Similarly, Irish-American agitation about the Versailles Treaty went unremarked; Jewish concern elicited complaints about the "kosher conference." The immigrant's willingness to change his name was seen as evidence of duplicity, not of a desire to assimilate.

In addition to assuming the worst, the *Independent* singled out Jewish participants in any endeavor and concluded that they were *acting as Jews*. But while Paul Warburg did play a major role in the passage of the Federal Reserve Act, he acted on behalf of major bankers of all faiths. Although the War Industries Board did create a "system of control such as the United States government never possessed," Chairman Baruch believed that the general welfare was synonymous with capitalism, not Judaism. Jews may have been represented disproportionately in the Soviet hierarchy, but they used their positions to further Marxist ends, including the secularization of Russian Jewry; almost none of the "Yiddish" Bolsheviks spoke Yiddish. In 1911 Jacob Schiff's objections to the Russian-American commercial treaty would have meant little if outrage among grass-roots and elite Gentiles had not moved three hundred Representatives to agree with him.

The disposition to single out Jews and to create a separate standard for them derived from three circumstances. First, as Irving Howe notes, Jewish immigrants from Eastern Europe were "radically different from the dominant Protestant culture." The *Independent* was incensed by this lack of "conformity" to the nation's "determining ideals and ideas"; the recent arrivals seemed to think that the United States was "not any definite thing yet." Second, as John Higham argues, Jews attracted special attention because they were relatively more successful—and more visible—than other groups in the "new immigration." Third, despite professed indifference to Jewish religious practices, the *Independent* supposed that acceptance of the nation's ideals meant acquiescence in its "predominant Christian character." Jews, however, were determined "to wipe out of public life" every Christian reference. Their "impertinent interferences" included contempt for Sunday blue laws and protests against Christmas celebrations and Bible reading in public schools. Louis Marshall, president of the American Jewish Committee, even said that the United States was "not a Christian country." Such actions by a race that had had "no hand" in building the nation naturally stirred a "whirlwind of resentment."

From this matter-of-fact amalgamation of Christianity and "100 percent Americanism," the *Independent* moved to theology. The transition was easy for

William J. Cameron, who had preached occasionally, without benefit of ordination, to a "people's church" in Brooklyn, Michigan. Accepting the man-
gled history and biblical exegesis of the Anglo-Israelite Federation, Cameron
believed that contemporary Anglo-Saxons had descended from the lost tribes
of Israel. Hence they were "chosen" to receive the blessings that God had
promised to Abraham's progeny. But this divine choice of Israel did not
extend to Judea, or to the Jewish offspring of the two southern tribes. On the
contrary, Anglo-Israelites were often hostile to contemporary Jews.

Fred Black speculated that Cameron's Anglo-Israelism had prepared him
to accept conspiratorial anti-Semitism. Certainly the editor's faith gave a
peculiar twist to the discussion of religion in *The International Jew*. Citing the
Protocols' injunction to undermine clergy, the *Independent* blamed Jews for
biblical criticism and "liberal" Protestantism, a typically mislabeled doctrine
that reduced Jesus to a "well-meaning but wholly mistaken Jewish prophet."
Discriminating between Israel and the rebellious Judeans, the weekly said
that Jesus was not Jewish in the modern sense of the word. Neither was
Moses nor any disciple—except Judas. Fundamentalists also read the Bible
through "Jewish spectacles" when they confused modern Hebrews with
God's chosen people. Not only did Jews reject Christ, but they abandoned the
Old Testament in favor of the Talmud's "rabbinical speculation." Instead of
fulfilling the prophetic promise of a return to Jerusalem, as many fundamentalists supposed, Zionism represented the "Bolshevist spirit all over again."

In the broadest sense, then, the *Independent* presented the "Jewish question" as a contest between two peoples, each supposing that God was on its
side. There was "no idea deeper in Judaism" than the belief in divine election.
But, the newspaper protested, the "Anglo-Saxon Celtic race" was the "Ruling
People, chosen throughout the centuries to Master the world." Beneath the
bragging, however, there lay a hint of the insecurity that fueled nativism in
the 1920s. On the one hand, Yankees could beat Jews "any time" in a fair fight.
Still the Kehillah's "extraordinary unity" was impressive. Unpatriotic American "mongrels" and "lick spittle Gentile Fronts who have no tribe . . . would
be better off if they had one-thousandth the racial sense which the Jew
possesses."

The *Independent* maintained that its pages contained "NO ATTACK . . .
ON THE JEWS AS JEWS" (though it was not always possible to "distinguish
the group" deserving censure). Occasionally the weekly made ostentatious
efforts to sound fair. It quoted admirable (meaning unobtrusive) Jews, admitted that Paul Warburg's Federal Reserve Act contained "important improvements," and recognized Bernard Baruch's intelligence and energy. On
January 17, 1922, a "candid address" to Jews urged them to recover Old
Testament morality and practice "social responsibility." If Jews stopped trying
"to twist Americanism into something else," they could participate without
objection in finance, entertainment, and government.

The newspaper's remedies for the "world's foremost problem" combined faith in expertise, national unity, and publicity. A "scientific study of the Jewish Question" would forestall prejudice by transforming gentile assailants and Jewish defenders "both into investigators." Research by "qualified persons" would yield "society's point of view" which, the *Independent* claimed, was the perspective taken in its pages. In the interim, to combat Jewish adulteration of products, a consumer movement should "educate people in the art of buying." Most important, "clear publicity" must be the "chief weapon" against the Hebrew cabal. Their program would then be "checked the moment it is perceived and identified." Russia, Germany, and England had failed to solve the "Jewish Question," but the United States would succeed—without violence.

While new installments of *The International Jew* continued to unroll in its pages, the *Independent* collected in book form articles that had already appeared; sometimes two hundred thousand copies were printed in a single edition. The staff sent complimentary volumes to locally influential citizens, especially clergymen, bankers, and stockbrokers.

To supplement *The International Jew,* the *Independent* ran "Jewish World Notes." This regular feature charged that Madame Curie was treated less well in New York than the spurious Jewish scientist Albert Einstein, chided Billy Sunday for ignorance of the Elders' conspiracy, derided Zionist immigration to Palestine, and feared that President-elect Harding, like his predecessors, was falling under Jewish influence. The *Independent* also kept up persistent attacks on alcohol, tobacco, movies, comic books, jazz, Wobblies, Soviets, and immigration. Simultaneously looking to Ford's financial interests, editor Cameron promoted highway construction, opposed federal aid to railroads, and looked greedily toward Muscle Shoals. In 1922, as Ford began to covet the presidency, his newspaper dutifully emphasized the inadequacy of other possible nominees.

If the *Independent* had offered only a perverse mixture of reform, eccentricity, internationalism, and nativism, it would have attracted relatively little attention. But *The International Jew* was extraordinary even for the "tribal twenties." Opponents mobilized quickly. The Federal Council of Churches condemned the articles in December, 1920. A month later, without specifically mentioning Ford, 119 prominent Christians, including William Howard Taft, Woodrow Wilson, and William Cardinal O'Connell, signed "The Perils of Racial Prejudice," a statement asking Gentiles to halt the "vicious propaganda" against Jews. Officials in several cities considered censoring the *Independent* or removed it from public libraries.

At first many Jews wondered, as Louis Marshall asked, if *The International Jew* had Ford's personal "sanction." Returning Ford's annual gift, a new sedan, his former neighbor Rabbi Leo Franklin warned Ford that he was inflicting harm on innocent people. Similarly, Herman Bernstein, a voyager on *Oscar II*, appealed to the automaker's "humanitarian" nature. Even after Jewish spokesmen recognized the depth of Ford's commitment to the anti-Semitic campaign, they disagreed on countermeasures. Following an initial protest, Marshall worked behind the scenes, sponsoring Bernstein's rebuttal, *The History of a Lie*, recruiting signers for "The Perils of Radical Prejudice," and in mid-1921 urging President Harding to intervene. Others preferred more militant tactics. The *American Hebrew* challenged Ford to abide by an impartial investigation, attorneys for the B'nai B'rith Anti-Defamation League advocated laws against the libel of groups, Yiddish newspapers rejected advertisements for Ford cars, and individual Jews refused to buy them.

The *International Jew* elicited support as well as opposition. Colonel Charles S. Bryan of the War Department appreciated particularly the attack on "East Side Scum." The journalist W. J. Abbot expressed "sympathy" with Ford's views and critic John J. Chapman hailed the "lucidity and good temper" of Volume II. C. Mobray White, an "authority" on revolution for the National Civic Federation, urged supplementary publication of the *Protocols*. According to Liebold, J. P. Morgan, Jr., liked the series. The number of *Independent* readers fluctuated widely over short periods because Ford dealers, who were ordered to sell the paper, showed little enthusiasm for the task. It appears, however, that *The International Jew* temporarily attracted new subscribers.

Liebold responded to protests and praise. Agreeing with the *Independent* that good Jews had "nothing to fear," he urged them to join Ford's crusade against the worldwide peril. But his supercilious tone was hardly reassuring. He accused Marshall of sounding like a "Bolshevik orator," lectured Rabbi Franklin on the importance of principles, and generally praised the newspaper's reliance on "actual facts." Conversely, he thanked friends of *The International Jew* and encouraged their efforts, telling C. Mobray White, for example, that there was "quite a field" for distribution of the *Protocols*. Occasionally he was forced to retreat. "Amazed" by the accusation that he had been Wilson's Jewish "mouthpiece," columnist David Lawrence wrote to Ford, whom he considered a friend. A testy exchange followed with Liebold, the perennial shield, who finally said that the automaker had had "no knowledge" of the articles relating to Lawrence.

Indeed, consistently distancing his employer from *The International Jew*, Liebold answered protests in his own name and testified in 1924 that Ford devoted his time to the company's "numerous and complex" operations. The *Independent* promoted the same fiction. Because Cameron explicitly attacked Jews on every page except "Mr. Ford's Page," devoted followers could believe that Ford was too busy making cars to supervise his own newspaper. The strategy was transparent, but it laid the groundwork for his face-saving retraction in 1927. The pause did not mean that Ford had begun to doubt the existence of a Jewish conspiracy. He still raised the matter in interviews. In addition, Liebold's agents collected fresh material which, Pipp warned, Ford would order into print "whenever the whim may strike him again." Apparently the whim struck within a year. In November, 1922, anti-Semitic references resurfaced in the *Independent*.

Starting in April, 1924, the *Independent* focused on "Jewish Exploitation of Farmers' Organizations," and on Aaron Sapiro, the alleged chief exploiter. After serving as counsel to the California marketing bureau, Sapiro began in 1919 to organize farm cooperatives in other states. Within four years, he created the National Council of Farmer's Cooperative Marketing Associations, whose constituent groups represented 700,000 farmers. Presidents Harding and Coolidge, Secretary of Commerce Herbert Hoover, former Governor Frank O. Lowden of Illinois, and Senator Arthur Capper, leader of the congressional farm bloc, encouraged Sapiro and sometimes provided substantial assistance. By 1923, however, many cooperative associations collapsed and enthusiasm began to ebb among farmers. In 1926 the National Council quietly disbanded.

Sapiro was a natural target. Cherishing the myth of the sturdy Christian farmer, the *Independent* and its publisher assumed that Jews entered agriculture only as greedy middlemen. Ford joked that he would pay one thousand dollars to anyone who brought in a Jewish farmer "dead or alive." Moreover, farm cooperatives fostered the "steady trend toward systematization" deplored in *The International Jew*. And Sapiro's financial backers included two of *The International Jew's* foremost villains, Bernard Baruch and Eugene Meyer, Jr.

Still, the *Independent's* assault had an ironic aspect because Ford and Sapiro shared more common ground that either realized. Like Ford, Sapiro cherished farming as a virtuous way of life untainted by radicalism or federal planning. Furthermore, he too was a proud man who resented attacks on his character. In January, 1925, therefore, Sapiro sent a thirty-one-page letter to Ford and his associates, demanding a retraction of "Jewish Exploitation." When the *Independent* refused to comply, Sapiro sued Ford and the Dearborn Publishing Company for a million dollars in order to vindicate "myself and my race."

Sapiro's was the third suit provoked by Ford's anti-Semitism. In January, 1921, Morris Gest had sought five million dollars in damages because the *Independent* accused him of producing lewd plays. Two years later Herman Bernstein had filed a complaint denying that he had told Ford of an international Jewish conspiracy. Neither case came to trial. Nor did they alter the newspaper's course.

The *Independent* repudiated *The International Jew* only after Sapiro pressed the issue. In March, 1927, his suit alleging 141 libels by Ford and the Dearborn Publishing Company began in Federal District Court in Detroit. Opening for the plaintiff, attorney William Henry Gallagher called the *Independent* Ford's "mouthpiece" and held him responsible for malicious attacks on "Sapiro and his race." The defense, led by Senator James A. Reed (Democrat, Missouri), responded that the weekly had had a "moral duty" to expose Sapiro as a "grafter, faker, fraud, and cheat." The *Independent*'s discussion of Jews was irrelevant, Reed added, because the law did not recognize libel of a "race"; Sapiro raised the religious issue merely to "capitalize" on sympathy. Finally, making the familiar distinction between Ford and his newspaper, Reed said that the automaker had not read the series on Sapiro "to this blessed day."

The rival attorneys were skilled and well matched. Gallagher raised doubts about Cameron's sobriety and Ford's intelligence. On the other hand, defense objections excluded from evidence letters to Ford protesting inaccuracies in "Jewish Exploitation of Farmers' Organizations." Gallagher called James Martin Miller, a former *Independent* employee, to testify that Ford personally had charged Sapiro with manipulating agriculture for a "bunch of Jews." Asking one question to reveal that Miller had sued for back pay, Reed dismissed him, *"That's* all." The two sides persistently clashed over Gallagher's effort to broaden the discussion of anti-Semitism. Poking fun at the defense's "extraordinary sensitiveness" to the word "Jew," Gallagher said that comparable "apprehension" three years earlier would have prevented the suit.

The most famous figure in the case avoided an appearance. At first, Ford planned to take the stand. Then he changed his mind and walled himself off from process servers. Company officials claimed that a subpoena intended for Ford was mistakenly presented to his brother. After Gallagher threatened to begin contempt proceedings, Ford's lawyers said that he would speak voluntarily. On March 31, however, he was the victim of a strange accident. A Studebaker sedan forced Ford's car off the road and down a fifteen-foot embankment. The automaker was taken to Henry Ford Hospital where he was treated and shielded by friendly physicians.

Sapiro suggested that Ford "faked" the accident, which has never been fully explained, because his "vanity was punctured at the collapse of his case." Indeed, sensing the jury's skepticism, defense lawyers did fear the verdict. On April 11, using reports from some of the fifty Ford service agents who prowled through the courthouse, they told Judge Raymond that a juror, Mrs. Cora Hoffman, had lied during the venire and later was offered a bribe by a Jew who wanted to convict Ford. Because Mrs. Hoffman's vehement denials appeared in the press, Raymond granted a defense motion of mistrial on April 21. The Court scheduled a retrial for September 12 as lawyers continued to spar. Valuing Raymond's restrictions on discussion of the "Jewish Question," Reed blocked Gallagher's attempt to change judges.

Judge Raymond adhered to the legal fiction that the *Independent*'s attack on Jews was largely irrelevant to the suit, but Ford knew better. By repudiating *The International Jew,* he could open the way to an out-of-court settlement and avoid testifying. During a May 11 meeting with Arthur Brisbane, who remained friendly even though the *Independent* labeled him a "gentile front," Ford mentioned his decision to close the newspaper. At roughly the same time, he told Joseph Palma, head of the United States Secret Service field office in New York City, that he had underestimated the impact of the Jewish series; he wanted the "wrong righted." Serving as Ford's emissaries, Palma and Earl J. David, a former assistant attorney general, met secretly with Louis Marshall of the American Jewish Committee. On July 9, Ford announced through Brisbane that "articles reflecting upon Jews" would "never again" appear in the *Independent*. Liebold, Cameron, and Edsel Ford had known nothing of the negotiations.

The retraction, written by Marshall, allowed Ford to slip through the loophole held open since 1920 by Liebold, Cameron, and a formidable array of lawyers. Ford said that he had failed to "keep informed" about the actions of his newspaper. Thus he was "deeply mortified" to learn that the *Independent* had reprinted a series based on the "gross forgeries," the *Protocols of Zion*. "Fully aware of the virtues of the Jewish people," he begged their forgiveness, promised to withdraw *The International Jew* from circulation, and pledged "future friendship and good will." Marshall considered the statement "humiliating" and was surprised that Ford accepted it.

Sapiro and Bernstein quickly dropped their suits in return for apologies and reimbursement of legal expenses. On July 30, the charge that Sapiro had belonged to an international conspiracy was formally "withdrawn" by the *Independent*. Sapiro pronounced himself "entirely satisfied," embraced the illusion that Ford had been "misled," and claimed credit for helping a "great man get right."

Unfortunately the apologies of 1927, like the remission of 1922, did not mean that Ford had "got right." He closed the *Independent* on December 30, 1927 but—contrary to his lawyers' promise to Marshal—kept Liebold and Cameron, both unrepentant, in his employ. He ordered destruction of thousands of copies of *The International Jew*; yet, despite entreaties by Marshall and Bernstein, barely publicized his retraction in Europe. His subordinates intervened to halt circulation abroad only when pressed by Jewish leaders. Furthermore, Ford informed the *Manchester Guardian* in 1940 that "international Jewish bankers" caused World War II. At roughly the same time, he told the nativist Gerald L. K. Smith that he had allowed Bennett to forge his signature on the retraction, hoped to someday reissue *The International Jew* and urged Smith to do so if he could not.

Partly due to Ford's laxity, the series continued to circulate among the "rabid Jew-baiters" whom the *Independent* professed to disdain. Norman Cohn estimates that *The International Jew* "probably did more than any other work to make the *Protocols* world-famous." The Nazi youth leader Baldur von Schirach recalled the "great influence" of the books on young Germans of his generation. In *Mein Kampf,* Hitler applauded Ford's efforts. Within the United States,

The International Jew provided a "usable past" for anti-Semites like Smith, who ultimately published an abridgement. As early as 1922, Norman Hapgood angrily held Ford responsible for letting "loose a malicious force that added fury to similar forces already in existence."

Detached analysis of *The International Jew* and its supplements illuminates attitudes toward Jews as well as broader aspects of our culture. First, the text undermines the assumption that Christian belief and practice hardly influenced anti-Semitism in the United States. *The International Jew* was imbued with Ford's faith that the national "genius" was "Christian in the broadest sense" and destined to remain so. The series portrayed a clash between two "chosen" peoples, and William J. Cameron, the chief compiler, sometimes cast the conflict in terms of Anglo-Israelite theology. Although we cannot infer the attitudes of a complex society from motifs in a single literary source, there is warrant for paying closer attention to the Christian roots of American anti-Semitism.

Second, a reading of *The International Jew* prompts yet another consideration of the relationship between "populism," "progressivism," and anti-Semitism. While Ford and *Independent* editor Cameron remained aloof from populism, their weekly explicitly endorsed "sane progressivism." The adjective may seem inappropriate, but the general identification makes sense. Ford contributed $36,000 to Woodrow Wilson's campaign in 1916 and was convinced by the president to run for senator two years later. Throughout the 1920s he was hailed as the preeminent business statesman whose commitment to efficiency, social service, and paternal labor relations promised industrial peace. Certainly *The International Jew* contained characteristic progressive themes. For example, adapting a growing consumer movement to its anti-Semitic ends, the *Independent* urged a boycott of Jewish merchants. Furthermore, the "Jewish question" must be subjected to "scientific study" by experts.

The most striking progressive legacy was *The International Jew*'s assertion that "clear publicity" was an American alternative to Jewish disfranchisement or pogroms. Richard Hofstadter observed that progressive intellectuals, scholars, and journalists alike "confirmed, if they did not create a fresh mode of criticism" that purported to uncover "reality." They believed that "reality" was "hidden, neglected, and offstage," something to be dug out from under superficial explanations. Norman Hapgood shrewdly saw that Ford's detectives "muckraked" Jews and suspected Jews. Ford apparently shared the *Independent*'s faith in publicity. In *My Life and Work*, he maintained that the Jewish threat could be "controlled by mere exposure."

Third, an interpretation of *The International Jew* helps to sort out "crucial differences in the variety of things called anti-Semitism." The *Independent* distinguished its answers to the "Jewish Question"—consumer protection, scientific study, and publicity—from violent European solutions. Ford himself claimed only to oppose "false ideas," called hatred of individuals "neither American nor Christian," and remained personally fond of several Jews, including the architect Albert Kahn, baseball player Hank Greenberg, and Rabbi Leo Franklin; he was perplexed by Franklin's refusal of a sedan in 1920 to protest *The International Jew.* These actions by Ford and his newspaper, though eccentric or self-serving, nevertheless point to complexities within nativism during the "tribal twenties."

A venerable nativist position, presented eloquently in Josiah Strong's 1885 polemic, *Our Country,* held that the "new immigration," including Jews, was *culturally* regressive and therefore must be taught superior Anglo-Saxon ways. The racial theorists who gained prominence after 1900 held that the "new immigration," including those whom Kenneth Roberts called "mongoloid" Jews, was *innately* inferior and therefore incapable of learning Anglo-Saxon ways. Whereas Strong suggested that "our country" might benefit from a blend of "races" under Anglo-Saxon guidance, Madison Grant, the premier "Nordic" ideologue in 1915, insisted that assimilation would backfire, producing a "mongrel" nation. Although the doctrine of inherent racial inferiority never fully superseded the earlier tradition, by the 1920s most nativists mixed the two attitudes in varying proportions. For example, Ford and the *Independent* sometimes ascribed behavior by Eastern European immigrants to "nasty Orientalism" or "Tartar" origins. More often, however, they complained that these Jews refused to be like Anglo-Saxons. In the final analysis, *The International Jew,* the major nativist tract of the 1920s, was closer to Strong's assimilationist ethnocentrism than to Grant's biological determinism.

The distinction may provide little comfort to victims of discrimination (though in the long run they gain from it), but it does suggest that the nation's liberal tradition even affects our nativists. Hence, they are more likely than counterparts in Germany or France to judge ethnic targets, in this case Jews, on the basis of individual behavior instead of putative genetic traits. Significantly, the *Independent* did not concur in the basic premise of *Mein Kampf,* that all Jews betrayed "definite racial characteristics."

Fourth, we must ask how thousands, perhaps hundreds of thousands of readers could believe *The International Jew*'s farfetched thesis that a worldwide Jewish network threatened their way of life. Richard Hofstadter maintains that adherents to such conspiracy theories betray a "paranoid style," a frame of mind qualitatively different from normal thinking. Indeed, the notion that bigots make up a psychologically abnormal fringe is popular. It is nonetheless misleading. Much as they exaggerate the tolerance of the dominant culture, leading scholars also mistakenly assume that it was imbued with their own version of liberal rationalism. During the 1920s, however, following a government-sponsored war scare and Red Scare, belief in some sort of conspiracy theory may have been the norm instead of an aberration. In this context, *The*

International Jew's perverse accomplishment was to combine the inchoate anti-Semitism of the Progressive era with the postwar fear of hidden forces.

To be sure, belief in a cabal of Zionist Elders (as opposed to conspiracies by Huns and Bolsheviks) was not endorsed by the government or by a majority of the population. Still we cannot assume that conspiratorial anti-Semites were pathological. The sociologists Peter Berger and Thomas Luckmann recently stressed an old insight, that our knowledge rests on the authority of others and remains plausible only as long as they confirm it. But these significant "others" need not represent the whole society. In the United States, semiautonomous cultures have often nurtured unconventional world-views in the face of sensible objections by outsiders.

Finally, what disposed Ford to agree with Liebold that there was a Jewish conspiracy instead of accepting counterarguments? As we have seen, Ford's animosity toward Jews grew during the personal crisis after 1915. Seeking to make restitution to the farmer, he was drawn to the convention that Jews were, as Edward Ross wrote, "slovenly" agriculturalists. Moreover, whether or not the process is called projection, Ford attributed to Jews traits that he refused to recognize in himself. For example, in 1920–1921, shortly after Ford had tricked stockholders and exploited his dealers to gain full control of the company, his newspaper accused Jews of violating business ethics. Ford thought that Sapiro inflicted "systematization" on the farmer, but his own machines did more to alter rural mores.

In 1923, more than one-third of 260,000 voters polled by *Collier's* favored Ford for president. They overlooked, if they did not endorse, his personal peculiarities, repression of labor, and sponsorship of anti-Semitism. Ford's reputation thrived partly because it was protected by Liebold and the public-relations experts who followed. But they built on a popular craving to esteem an unspoiled country mechanic whose ingenuity and effort made a contribution to the general welfare as well as a fortune. Samuel Marquis reported that many workers on the assembly line denied that Ford knew of their misery. Similarly, Jews initially doubted that he sanctioned the *Independent*'s attack; their praise of Ford in 1927 moved Louis Marshall to warn against excess. Like their gentile neighbors, Jews wanted to believe in self-made men, benevolent capitalists, and a just system that produced them. In ways that Ford failed to comprehend, these immigrants and their children were embracing American dreams and illusions.

CHAPTER

14

Even before mass Jewish immigration to America ended, American Jewish leaders began to turn their attention to the children of immigrants, "the second generation." Being American born, these children had no difficulty Americanizing; the problem was how to prevent them from Americanizing so much that they left their Judaism behind. Several prominent second-generation Jews spurned Judaism entirely; others intermarried. Fears for the future were widespread.

The Young Men's and Young Women's Hebrew Associations—forerunners of today's Jewish Community Centers—suggested one alternative. They offered social and cultural activities in a secular Jewish setting, and welcomed those who sought to be Jewish without being religious. Many, however, doubted that secular Judaism—whether this kind or that preached by the Jewish labor movement—would actually be strong enough to counteract fierce outside pressures to assimilate and intermarry. The synagogue, they warned, offered the only guarantee that Judaism would survive at all.

The synagogue, however, had to change. Young Jewish religious leaders, trained in America, talked of transforming it into a bustling, full-time "synagogue center," a hub of Jewish religious, educational, cultural, and social activities. They also advocated a new Americanized version of Judaism—not Reform Judaism, but a modern, decorous, and aesthetically pleasing traditional ritual, far removed from the "old fashioned" norm.

As early as 1886, advocates of an Americanized traditional Judaism established the Jewish Theological Seminary of America in New York. Reorganized in 1902 along somewhat more liberal lines, it became the training ground for Conservative rabbis committed to an historically evolving religious faith. Those with a more Orthodox bent often studied at Rabbi Isaac Elchanan Theological Seminary, founded in 1897. It merged in 1915 into what would later be known as Yeshiva University, and became the training ground for Modern Orthodox rabbis seeking to synthesize tradition with secular culture. Graduates of these two schools, much as they may have differed over theology and ritual, resembled one another in their determination to shape a distinctively American Judaism. Both sought to win second-generation Jews back to the synagogue.

Jeffrey Gurock, a leading student of Orthodox Judaism, traces these *developments from where they began, in the Jewish community of Harlem in New York. He shows how the first synagogue centers—the work of young, American-trained rabbis, many of whom went on to distinguished careers— succeeded, and how synagogue centers spread, particularly through the Conservative movement. Within one generation, synagogues crowded with activities all through the week—sometimes more then than at Sabbath services— became common. The American synagogue had emerged.*

The Emergence of
the American Synagogue

Jeffrey S. Gurock

The earliest adumbrations of the Jewish center movement date back to the turn of the century and to a group of Harlem synagogues expressedly constituted to serve the needs of American-born Jewish young adults. The first, Beth Ha-Knesset Ha-Gadol, was organized in December 1896 by fifty men, all of whom, according to newspaper reports, were thirty-seven or younger, who had been born in New York City and had recently migrated from the Lower East Side. They held their first meeting at the Harlem Lyceum (107th Street and Third Avenue), soon purchasing a church at the corner of 109th Street and Madison Avenue, which they converted to a synagogue.

Six years later, responding to what was perceived to be a need for a "large well constructed Orthodox synagogue," Rabbi H. P. Mendes of the Spanish and Portuguese Synagogue and Rabbi Bernard Drachman of Congregation Zichron Ephraim joined with local Harlemites in establishing Congregation Shomre Emunah at 121st Street and Madison Avenue. The organizers of this synagogue promised services conducted according to "Orthodox ritual in an impressive decorous manner." They pledged to their prospective Americanized constituency that the unsightly noise, commotion, and blatant commercialism that attended the immigrant landsmanshaft congregation would find no place in the up-to-date Orthodox synagogue. In 1904 a second modern congregation, Congregation Mount Sinai, was established in central Harlem at 118th Street and Lenox Avenue. This congregation was organized along lines similar to the German Conservative-Orthodox synagogues of the late nineteenth century, offering to its members Orthodox ritual, mixed seating, and a weekly "sermon in the vernacular." These two congregations hoped to attract acculturated, English-speaking East European Jews who wanted to retain a modified traditional form of prayer, while eliminating some of the obvious immigrant trappings of worship.

The first Harlem congregation specifically organized to attract what its leadership called "the rising generation in Israel" was Congregation Mikveh Israel, founded in 1905. This synagogue offered uptown young people decorous Orthodox Sabbath and Holiday services conducted by two English-speaking, university-trained ministers. Both Henry S. Morais and his assistant, Jacob Dolgenas, emphasized the importance of active congregational participation in the prayers and encouraged congregational singing. Recognizing that many young people were uncomfortable in synagogues where cantors droned on in solo recitations of the prayers, Morais instructed his cantor to be a true "servant of the community" by singing simple melodious prayers which could be easily followed by worshippers. Lay people were encouraged to join in singing the prayers, thereby making traditional forms of prayers more meaningful for all those drawn into the synagogue. Congregational singing also helped synagogue leaders to maintain decorum during services; lay people actively participating in the services had little time for idle gossip.

Congregation Mikveh Israel was also ahead of its time in the admission of two women to its original twelve-member congregational board of directors. Most congregations barred women from synagogue office, relegating them to the leadership of a women's auxiliary or sisterhood. Although services were conducted according to Orthodox ritual, which precluded females from leadership in prayer, Mikveh Israel's women had an important voice in all other synagogue affairs. Contemporary observers applauded Morais's efforts both here and as head of the Young Folks' League of the Uptown Talmud Torah. One writer declared him to be the "only Rabbi in Harlem who stands for principle" and his young supporters to be "Harlem's only hope for the future."

Despite this enthusiastic endorsement, Morais and his followers failed in their ambitious undertaking. Morais's synagogue, like all these early youth-oriented congregations, was plagued by persistent financial woes arising from having overestimated the numerical and economic strength of that "rising generation of Israel" which it hoped to influence. The majority of Harlem's second-generation Jews had yet to reach young adulthood, leaving Morais's group with a constituency too narrow from which to draw financial support. Congregation Mikveh Israel was consequently never able to raise sufficient funds to move out of rented quarters. Congregation Shomre Emunah likewise saw its dream of erecting a synagogue shattered when a temporary financial recession in 1908 caused its few financial supporters to withdraw their promised monetary assistance from the institution. The uptown youth-synagogue movement first appeared in Harlem about half a generation too early. None of these early forward-looking congregations lasted more than a very few years.

Several of the community's largest congregations more effectively serviced the spiritual needs of Harlem's small but ever-expanding group of

American-born young. By 1910, at least four Harlem congregations had appointed American-born university-educated and Jewish Theological Seminary–trained rabbis to uptown pulpits and charged them with inspiring the new generation. These young rabbis served either as associates of or as replacements for incumbent German or Yiddish speaking rabbis. Jacob Kohn became rabbi of Congregation Ansche Chesed in May 1910, replacing German-born Gustav Hausman who was dismissed for "not possessing the spiritual uplift which a spiritual leader and religious teacher must have" to lead his laity successfully. The new dynamic rabbi soon inspired "a new religious awakening" in the synagogue. He popularized the study of Hebrew by children and adults alike. Kohn's classmate, Benjamin A. Tintner, son of Moritz Tintner, one of Harlem's earliest German reform rabbis, became rabbi of neighboring Temple Mount Zion in 1911. Tintner came to this prestigious uptown pulpit after a three-year tenure as assistant rabbi of the West Side Congregation B'nai Jeshurun. His appointment sparked an immediate upsurge in synagogue membership as many of Tintner's former young West Side congregants followed their spiritual leader and began attending services in Harlem. Bernard Drachman attracted a similar youthful following when he became English-speaking rabbi of uptown Congregation Ohab Zedek in 1909. Drachman worked in close partnership with Rabbi Philip Klein, whose own sermons were most meaningful to the less-Americanized segment of the congregation.

Congregation Anshe Emeth of West Harlem hired on a part-time basis an English-speaking graduate of the Jewish Theological Seminary, Rabbi Julius J. Price. He was given the primary responsibility of preaching to the American-born children of immigrants on the High Holidays, when these young people would be most likely to join their parents in attending services. These several well-conceived personnel moves, which were designed primarily to attract children of immigrants to services, undoubtedly also helped these congregations retain the continued allegiance of their Americanized immigrant members to synagogue life.

The opportunities to minister to the spiritual needs of American Jewish young adults marked a turning point in the fortunes of the American-born, Conservative-Orthodox rabbi. Earlier, few Jews residing in America identified with the spiritual messages preached by native-born, English-speaking traditional rabbis. Most German Jews had supported the Reform rabbinate, which was certainly American and English-speaking but decidedly not traditional. Their late-arriving German immigrant brethren of both the traditional and Reform persuasions preferred their own imported European-born spiritual leadership. Immigrant East European Jews were similarly content with their own "landsmanshaft synagogue" Orthodoxy and were suspicious of an "Orthodoxy" preached by clean-shaven, university-educated American rabbis. They looked to their transplanted East European rabbinic leadership to serve their religious needs. American Conservative-Orthodox rabbis of the late nineteenth and early twentieth centuries found that they had almost no one to preach to. One such rabbi recalled his frustrations when "it seemed for a time that I had mistaken my vocation, that there was no room, no demand in America for an American-born, English-speaking rabbi who insisted on maintaining the laws and usages of traditional Judaism. . . . There were considerable groups of East European, Polish, and Russian Jews in the East Side or Ghetto districts of the great cities, who adhered to the Orthodox traditions of their native lands, but they were Yiddish-speaking and wanted rabbis of that type. They were strange to me and I was stranger to them." The creation of several pulpit positions for American-born traditional rabbis in Harlem promised a more rewarding future for graduates of America's traditional religious seminaries.

The adoption by both German and East European congregations of almost identical policies in attempting to reach a similar Americanized constituency also foreshadowed future American Jewish communal structure. The acceptance of Seminary rabbis in synagogues ranging from the strictly East European Orthodox Ohab Zedek to the formerly staunchly German Reform Temple Mount Zion indicated that, at least in Harlem, forward-looking representatives of all Jewish denominations recognized the need to readjust Judaism to the impact of Americanization. Congregation Ohab Zedek's leaders understood, for example, that a homiletic discourse delivered in the vernacular German or Yiddish had no greater intrinsic holiness than one spoken in English, and Temple Mount Zion's people recognized that nineteenth-century Radical Reform principles might be too extreme for formerly Orthodox children of immigrants who desired membership in an American synagogue but who were repulsed by the totally nontraditional forms of Reform worship. And although each denomination would remain, to a great extent, theologically separated, they would be, from this point on, similarly engaged in the fight to construct new, enduring forms of Jewish life acceptable to a native-born Jewry.

These early efforts on behalf of Americanized Jewish young adults reached, however, only that limited segment of the next generation which was still more or less committed to religious life. None of these synagogues ever considered Jewish "missionary" work programs to reach those totally alienated from all forms of Jewish life. And as the numbers of American Jews began to grow during the second decade of the twentieth century, there were thousands of Harlem Jewish young people, whom the talmud torahs were never able to reach or failed to influence, who were growing up with no attachment to Judaism. One contemporary Christian student of American Jewish life described these young people as "the ones who, finding themselves unwilling to maintain the forms of Judaism and having a sort of instinctive dread of other religions are going without any religious expression or experience whatsoever." More ambitious rescue plans had to be drawn up to influence those falling away from Judaism.

The middle of the 1920s saw several similarly constituted rescue organizations established both in Harlem and in the other major Jewish sections of New York. Harlem's Young Men's Hebrew Orthodox League and Hebrew League, downtown's Young Israel synagogue, and Brownsville's Young Men's Hebrew League established synagogues and sponsored social activities on lines similar to Morais's early efforts.

The Harlem Young Men's Hebrew Orthodox League was founded in April 1915 by ten members of the Harry Fischel West Side Annex of the Uptown Talmud Torah, to provide the young adults of the community with an "institution which would create an Orthodox environment and teach the great principles of Orthodoxy." They perceived that even talmud-torah-educated young adults experienced a certain disaffection from Judaism "upon entering academic, professional, or business careers." And they understood that once on their own, few Jewish young adults continued to come in contact "during their spare time with a circle that reminds him of his obligations to his faith and people." The leaders of this league believed that they had the intellectual acumen to convince the second generation "that by study, Orthodox Judaism will be found to be entirely compatible with modern ideas."

They inaugurated their program by establishing model youth synagogues at the West Side Annex emphasizing decorum and congregational singing in services conducted by the young people themselves. In the fall of 1914, the new Harlem League conducted a Kehillah-sponsored "provisional synagogue." These provisional synagogues were organized throughout the city to combat the abuses of the "mushroom synagogues" established by private entrepreneurs in public halls and saloons to provide a place for unaffiliated Jews to attend High Holiday services. Many of these entrepreneurs were unscrupulous individuals who hired imposters as rabbis and generally exploited the public for commercial purposes. The provisional synagogues were designed to undercut the market served by "mushroom synagogues" by providing services at reasonable rates under reputable leadership to serve the High Holiday overflow crowd. The selection of the Young Men's Hebrew Orthodox League to serve the Lenox Avenue district of New York represented an early recognition by citywide authorities of the league's usefulness to the uptown community.

Thus established within the community, the Harlem Young Men's Hebrew Orthodox League quickly inaugurated numerous social and cultural activities and planned to maintain its own clubrooms, library, and gymnasium and to hold classes on Jewish topics. Among the lecturers in its early years were Rabbis Jacob Dolgenas, Bernard Drachman, and Herbert S. Goldstein. Goldstein, then associate rabbi at Yorkville's Congregation Kehilath Jeshurun, was elected honorary president of the league in recognition of his constant encouragement of its activities.

A second Harlem-based cultural institution created to attract Jewish young adults back to their faith was organized in September 1915. The Harlem Hebrew League was founded to "make known the ideals of Judaism" to uptown youths. League organizers established a headquarters for "Jewish men under Jewish refining influences" on Lenox Avenue where social and educational programs were held every weekday evening and on the Sabbath. This league offered its members lectures and debates in addition to its dignified modern Orthodox services. Rabbis Drachman, Goldstein, and Morais headed the list of speakers who addressed this youth organization as it began to gain support in the local community.

Uptown efforts to expand the scope of American synagogue life to include social, cultural, and recreational activities in the hope of making Judaism more relevant to neighborhood young people were paralleled on the Lower East Side by the activities of the founders of the Young Israel Synagogue. These advocates of traditional Judaism created in 1915 a model synagogue on East Broadway run according to the same principles as Morais's 1905 Harlem effort. Harry G. Fromberg, one of the founders of the movement, described their synagogue as a place "where every atom of our time-honored tradition could be observed and at the same time prove an attraction, particularly to young men and women: a synagogue where, with the exception of prayer, English would be used in the delivery of sermons and otherwise." The Young Israel synagogue emphasized congregational singing and decorum, outlawed all forms of commercialism in services, and sponsored a variety of social and cultural activities designed to keep the young people in the synagogue. Late in 1915, a federation of "organizations of young Jewry" composed of Harlem, downtown, and Brownsville youth leagues and synagogues was organized "to promote the welfare of Judaism" on a citywide basis.

For all the energy in this movement the founders of the Harlem Young Men's Hebrew Association still perceived them as too limited in scope and parochial in outlook to serve the majority of its community's young adults. These leaders argued that "Orthodox" Jews represented a relatively inconsequential proportion of the total population. They argued that there were thousands of young people whom the talmud torah never reached. These were young people "who never enter a synagogue and for them there must be some kind of training school" in Judaism. Yorkville's Ninety-Second Street Y, which many East Harlemites did attend, was nevertheless considered geographically inaccessible for the majority of uptown residents. And Yorkville leaders, for their part, were unwilling to expand their own activities to Harlem, describing themselves as an exclusively Yorkville institution. They preferred to support the establishment of a separate Harlem branch of their National Y.M.H.A. movement. Just such an institution, emphasizing social, cultural, and recreational activities and offering Jewish religious activities on a limited nondenominational basis was founded at an organizational meeting held at Temple Mount Zion in 1915. The Harlem Y received the support of several important local rabbinic and lay leaders including Rabbis Benjamin A. Tintner, Philip Klein, and Bernard Drachman, and Representative Isaac Siegel.

Rabbi Mordecai Kaplan failed to share his uptown colleagues' enthusiasm for the new Harlem Y. This former religious director of the Ninety-Second Street Y now argued that as presently organized, the YMHAs were no different from nonsectarian settlement houses, providing social and recreational activities for the youth of their communities in the hope of "keeping them off the streets." Kaplan charged that there was little that was "distinctly Jewish" in the content of YMHA programs which would set them off from other community-service organizations as a bulwark against "the possibility of Jews becoming assimilated." He characterized the YMHAs as "secular organizations" financed by Jewish money, and called upon the national movement to either drop the word "Hebrew" from its title and to openly declare itself a nonreligious organization or to immediately reconstitute itself as a "distinctly Jewish organization" committing itself wholeheartedly to the battle against assimilation.

Although he doubted that the YMHA would respond affirmatively to his criticism, Kaplan was not discouraged. For him, the future of Jewish life in America lay outside the hands of both the secular YMHA and the religious Orthodox and Hebrew leagues. Kaplan was convinced that the reconstructed synagogue was destined to play the crucial role in preserving Judaism in America. He believed that the primarily secular, social, cultural, and recreational activities of the Y could be effectively merged with modern religious-oriented programs of the leagues. The resulting synagogue-center movement would effectively influence the American Jewish young adult, who had graduated from the settlements and had outgrown his or her parents' immigrant synagogue culture, to identify with things Jewish. The synagogue center's social attractions would lure the unaffiliated into a religious surrounding, where they would be exposed to or reacquainted with the beauties, and ultimately, the values, of their ancestral faith. It was Kaplan's hope that with time and the proper programs, many Jews would eventually be drawn to the specifically religious activities of the institution and might ultimately attend their services conducted along the most modern Orthodox lines. Such an institution was to produce committed Jews from among the many religiously estranged young adults.

In fashioning his dream of a reconstructed synagogue, Kaplan drew heavily upon the educational philosophy espoused by his colleague Professor

John Dewey of Columbia University. Dewey believed that contemporary modern industrial society had thrust the school, in place of the home and neighborhood, into the role of society's major educative and socializing agent. It was, consequently, the job of modern educators not only to teach the traditional subject matter normally associated with the school but to create within the school an atmosphere conducive both to continued learning and to the personality development of each child/student. For Dewey—and the generation of progressive Jewish educators he trained and inspired—the final judgment on the usefulness of an educational program rested on its success in creating "a desire for continued growth" among its students. Adapting these principles to his proposed synagogue center, Kaplan argued that his new social and recreational activities would create the desired atmosphere conducive to continued identification with synagogue life and would eventually lead to greater interest in studying Judaism.

Kaplan first attempted to put these theories into practice in 1916 when he helped found the Central Jewish Institute organized by leaders of Yorkville's Congregation Kehilath Jeshurun, where he had earlier served as associate rabbi. This congregation and the community it served provided an exceptionally good testing ground for his programs to save affluent, Americanized second-generation Jews from assimilation. Kehilath Jeshurun members were drawn from among the most affluent element in the East European community: individuals who had succeeded in less than a generation in achieving a degree of economic advancement comparable to that of the Jews of Lenox Avenue. These Yorkville Jews were described by one official of the Central Jewish Institute as "bourgeois, well-to-do and distinctly conservative in contradistinction to the new Russian immigration which has a strong element of Radicalism and Yiddishism." Religiously, they were depicted as "Orthodox, which implies adherence to Jewish ceremonies and customs and an allegiance to Jewish life." Many were described as the scions of "families which were respected in the social life of the Eastern European ghetto, where learning was the distinguishing class mark."

Their affluent American-born children and their fellow Yorkville friends showed little of their ancestors' commitment to Jewish learning. On the contrary, these young people were observed by the same official to be a "half-baked second generation who knew little of Jewish life, tending to associate it merely with the ceremonies and especially with the prohibitions observed in the home. They are generally indifferent to, if not ashamed of Jewish life." The recipients of a public school education, these proficient English-speakers were also quick to regard themselves "as superior to their parents and everything associated with them." This same student of the community feared that these Yorkville Jews were representative of the disintegration of the ethnic and religious culture in the second generation and recognized the need for an "adequate agency to bridge the gap between the generations, to interpret the old traditions in terms of the new." Yorkville provided Rabbi Kaplan with a ready constituency for his Jewish "rescue" plans.

The Central Jewish Institute represented the first major attempt at amalgamating Jewish social, cultural, and recreational programs with religious educational activities under the auspices of an established Orthodox congregation. Institutional leadership emphasized the "harmonization of Jewish purpose with American life" as its *raison d'être*. It promoted with equal vigor its program of Jewish studies through a talmud torah and an extension school for "those who cannot be induced to enroll in the intensive work" and a center program whose activities "make for the physical and social well-being of the people who live in the neighborhood." Health and citizenship, it was declared, "are a part of, and not opposed to Judaism."

The Central Jewish Institute was not, however, the truly complete synagogue center envisioned by Kaplan. The single major component missing from its multifaceted program was, ironically, the synagogue itself. Although supported by the leadership of Kehilath Jeshurun and housed in an adjoining building, the C.J.I. lived an almost separate existence from its sponsoring institution. The synagogue failed to coordinate or update its traditional religious practices and rituals with the social and educational activities of the Institute. One critic of this Yorkville movement claimed that it possessed all the elements of a synagogue center "but only externally so. The three departments have no close contact because the synagogue element is not bold enough. The synagogue has not developed its full capacity and its influence is small." In 1918, Rabbi Kaplan, undoubtedly frustrated with the incompleteness of the C.J.I. program, severed his remaining ties with Yorkville's institutions and with the financial assistance of several of Kehilath Jeshurun's most affluent members, who had migrated to the elegant newly developed West Side neighborhood, established the Jewish Center Synagogue at 86th Street between Columbus and Amsterdam avenues. Now on his own, he was free to create a true synagogue-center program under Orthodox auspices which would serve as a model for hundreds of Jewish center–synagogues organized over the next several decades.

Rabbi Herbert S. Goldstein, founder of Harlem's Institutional Synagogue, shared Kaplan's critique of existing youth organizations and advocated an almost identical synagogue-centered program for attracting young people back to their faith. Goldstein was first directly exposed to Kaplan's philosophy in 1913, when as a senior at the Jewish Theological Seminary he was elected to succeed his teacher as English-speaking minister at Kehilath Jeshurun. He worked in close concert there with Kaplan in the founding and direction of the Central Jewish Institute and learned first-hand of the problems facing those committed to this new form of Jewish communal work. Goldstein first expressed his own dedication to meeting the challenges posed by the new generation of American Jews in June 1915, when he declared that the salvation of "the Judaism of the future" lay solely in the hands of the "young university-trained Orthodox Rabbis" like himself. In a public charge to his American-born, English-speaking colleagues, Goldstein argued that only they could help, for example, the "scientifically-trained, skeptical young Jew, reconcile what he learned in public school and college with the ancient doctrines of his faith." Goldstein believed that only those "reared on American soil, who have breathed the ideals of American democracy, who have been born and bred like other Americans, who have received a systematic scientific, secular education, and who are at the same time deeply saturated with a knowledge and desire of practicing the tenets of our faith" can understand the needs and desires of those eager "to break down ghetto walls . . . to live as their neighbors, their fellow citizens—the Americans." They alone "who have gone through this kind of youth" and remained true to Judaism can meet American Jewish men or women on their own level.

Goldstein called upon all Orthodox Jews to rally around these young zealots and directed established congregations to hire young men to their pulpits who would engage in missionary work among those "who have gone astray, to bring them back to Orthodox Judaism and keep and sustain those who are in the fold."

Goldstein outlined a concrete plan for what he called Jewish missionary work some fifteen months later when he called for the establishment of an Institutional Synagogue to serve second-generation American Jews. In a public letter to New York Jewry published in several local periodicals, Goldstein argued that all existing Jewish institutions were failing to influence young people toward Jewish observance. The relatively few modern educational institutes in existence reached, according to Goldstein, only 15 percent of Jewish youth. The religio-social landsmanshaft synagogues (the so-called "provincial synagogues," that expressed "local European mannerisms") were characterized as "un-American, antiquated and largely responsible for the great gap which now exists between the sons of the founders of the synagogues and the founders." The cheder education system, he declared, was a complete failure for its total inability "to impart to students the true meaning of the Jewish religion, nor inspire in them the proper love of their faith." The talmud torah movement, with which his father-in-law, Harry Fischel, and some of his own closest associates were intimately involved, Goldstein described as a worthy improvement over the earlier system. But he declared it too suffered from some important defects. The talmud torah movement had, he said, failed to overcome its East European roots. As a pauper's school, it failed to attract children of parents who could afford to pay tuition. In addition, the talmud torah movement's approach to Jewish youth was itself not ideal because "it is fractional in its work and divorces the child from the synagogue."

Goldstein expressed similar objection to the Y.M.H.A. movement, characterizing its efforts in the Jewish social field as "partial" because "it only takes the boy off the street and does not give him the education of a Jewish religious environment." Paralleling Kaplan's criticisms published a year earlier, Goldstein also stated that the YMHA's work was "negative" because it "failed to impart positive religion in the minds of the youth. It does not stand for positive religious conviction."

For Goldstein, just as for Kaplan, the "Institutional Synagogue–Jewish Center" concept represented Jewry's best chance to save a lost generation from voluntarily surrendering its Jewish identity. Goldstein too argued that historically "the synagogue of old was the center for prayer, study and the social life of the community all in one," and suggested that with the proper program, it could once again assume that traditional role. He envisioned a new multifaceted synagogue which would be "a place for study for adults in the evenings and for children in the afternoons." It would be a social and recreational center for young adults where "after plying their daily cares, they could spend a social hour in an Orthodox environment and in a truly Jewish atmosphere." This synagogue would also offer decorous modern Orthodox religious services designed specifically for an American congregation, while "keeping intact the Jewish ceremonies of our people." Goldstein was convinced that "if we desire to perpetuate the ideal Judaism of the past we must so shape Jewish spiritual activity that it will all find expression in one institution." He offered the Institutional Synagogue as that ideal Jewish social, religious, and cultural organization, embracing the best of the synagogue, talmud torah, and YMHA.

Goldstein submitted that he had both history and practicality on his side. From a purely financial standpoint it would be cheaper for local Jewish communities to build one large Institutional Synagogue, combining all the activities of a large congregation, talmud torah, and YMHA, than to support each separately. He also reasoned that the individual Jew could, for a little higher membership fee in the institutional synagogue, derive the benefits of three Jewish institutions. The three-in-one synagogue centers would have the additional advantage of making it possible for all members of a family to participate in their own age-group activities within the same religious institution and thereby bring back to family life "that religious unity and enthusiasm which is sorely lacking today."

Rabbi Goldstein's ambitious proposals for reviving Jewish youth were well received by the leaders of both the Harlem Young Men's Hebrew Orthodox League and the Harlem YMHA. Late in 1916, these men considered amalgamating their organizations to reach the youth of their neighborhood. The Harlem League, the smaller of the two organizations, with only thirty-five members on its rolls, was almost immediately taken by Goldstein's concepts; it decided several weeks after this published pronouncement to reorganize the organization and to "push with vigor its campaign for the establishment of a real Jewish center in Harlem." The League, which previously sponsored only religious and cultural activities, now announced its intention to construct a gymnasium and organize a library to attract a wider segment of uptown Jewry to its organization. The Harlem YMHA, seventy-five members strong, expressed its support of Goldstein's idea in April 1917, when it agreed under the leadership of its new president, Representative Isaac Siegel, to join Harlem League officials in inviting Rabbi Goldstein to coordinate uptown youth work. The rabbi was given the mandate of "bringing the message of Jewish Religious Revival to (Harlem) youth" through existing youth organizations reconstituted as the Institutional Synagogue.

Representative Siegel's leadership in the Harlem YMHA and his subsequent presidency of the Institutional Synagogue was the second instance of his direct involvement in local religious affairs. Almost a decade earlier, in 1908, Siegel had led a group of young protestors against Congregation Ohab Zedek, accusing this leading uptown synagogue of conducting organizational "business" on the Sabbath. Siegel's group claimed that on a given Sabbath several young men had attempted to gain admittance at the 116th Street sanctuary and were told by congregational leaders that only worshippers holding admission "tickets" could enter the synagogue. Siegel's young men were allegedly told that tickets could be purchased at a cigar store located across the street from the synagogue. Siegel publicly condemned this open commercialism and this obvious desecration of the Sabbath practiced by the religious "hypocrites" of Ohab Zedek.

Siegel's charges, which were published in a local Jewish periodical, were answered in print by a Mr. D. Berliner, an officer of the congregation. Berliner counterclaimed that admission tickets were "authorized solely to preseve order and decorum" in the services and vigorously denied that tickets were sold on the Sabbath. According to Berliner, tickets were needed to "keep back the mob of young men struggling to enter and the young dandies who came in merely to ogle women in the balcony."

Berliner's defense failed to move one contemporary editorialist who condemned Ohab Zedek for failing to recognize that a synagogue "has something more to do than to engage a chazan with a beautiful voice." "Where is the Rabbi?" this critic asked. "Where is the Hebrew and Religious School? What is the new Hungarian congregation doing for the community?" The editorialist went on to declare that the "Jewish community expects more" from its synagogues and commended Siegel for bringing this problem to public attention. Ohab Zedek's decision in 1909 to appoint Bernard Drachman to its uptown pulpit may well have been directed, to some extent, by communal pressure to modernize its approach to synagogue life, arising from this incident.

It is interesting, however, to note that Siegel deemed it inappropriate or impolitic to point to this early involvement in communal affairs when attacked by Rosenblatt as a "non-Jewish" representative in the fiercely contested 1916 congressional elections. It is possible that the candidate of the then "respectable element" in uptown Jewry did not want at that point to remind his most consistent supporters that he had once openly criticized the policies of one of Harlem's major religious establishments. By the same token, it is possible that Siegel's reawakened interest in communal activities may be attributed in part to his desire to still critics of his "Jewish" record. Whether the congressman's involvement in the Institutional Synagogue project was pietistic or political, it was Siegel who assumed the presidency of the merged organizations and who accepted the responsibility of contacting Rabbi Goldstein to invite him to assume the new Harlem pulpit.

Rabbi Goldstein accepted the call of uptown Jewry in April 1917 as an exciting challenge, making only two major requests of Harlem leaders: that he be granted life tenure as rabbi and leader of the Institutional Synagogue, and that the synagogue's constitution indicate that "no innovation in traditional Judaism may be inaugurated" into the synagogue's ritual "if there be one dissenting vote at a meeting of the corporation." His position thus secured, Goldstein immediately made plans for creating what he described as a "Jewish revival movement" in Harlem.

The new synagogue leased a private house near 116th Street and Lenox Avenue, described by Goldstein as the "heart of the most distressing Jewish conditions in the United States," for a synagogue, club, and schoolhouse. Goldstein announced plans for conducting "monster rallies" throughout Harlem to attract thousands of young people to his movement. He proposed the leasing of local theaters on Sunday mornings for services and lectures to reach "the large mass of young men and women who cannot be reached on Sabbath." In a related move, Goldstein suggested that Institutional Synagogue leaders approach leading Orthodox Jewish merchants in Harlem to solicit jobs for Jewish young people who themselves wished to keep the Sabbath.

Goldstein's Institutional Synagogue received an early spiritual boost in May 1917, when Henry S. Morais voiced his public support for this contemporary "youth synagogue." That same week saw the new project obtain its greatest financial assist when an anonymous supporter donated a five-story building at 116th Street between Lenox and Seventh avenues as a home for Goldstein's Jewish center-synagogue-school complex.

The new movement, through its Sunday revival meetings and its diversified program of youth activities, quickly gained the support of neighborhood people. By September 1917, after only five months of existence, the Institutional Synagogue attracted some 1,200 people to its Rosh Hashanah services, held at a public hall in Central Harlem. In January 1918, the synagogue reported a membership of 2,000 dues-paying members supporting thirty-one clubs and eight religious classes housed at the 116th Street building. A month later, the Institutional Synagogue, in conjunction with the Jewish Sabbath Association, opened a Harlem branch of the Association's employment bureau. Goldstein subsequently attempted to convince all Jewish shopkeepers in Harlem to close their stores on Saturday, in order to "arouse a Jewish spirit" in the neighborhood.

The Institutional Synagogue's most ambitious program remained its Jewish "missionary" work expressed through frequent "monster rallies." Mount Morris Theater, located only one-half block away from the synagogue, was the usual location for these meetings which often featured lectures by United States senators, congressmen and well-known local and national Jewish figures. Rabbi Goldstein explained the underlying purpose of these revival meetings when he declared that "every community needs an occasional soul-stirring reawakening and a revival of a religious interest from time to time. At our regular religious services we attract only those who are habitual synagogue-goers, but we must reach the wavering as well. This can only be done through revival meetings."

The Institutional Synagogue absorbed more than its share of criticism during its early years. The most frequently heard charges contended that this Orthodox institution was "elitist" in nature and was simply a recast, improved Harlem Hebrew League, of use only to those of that particular religious persuasion. The presence of the Harlem YMHA leaders on the board of the Institutional Synagogue apparently made little impression upon those who opposed Goldstein's efforts. Critics echoed the traditional National YMHA contention that "inasmuch as in a community there are young men of various religious beliefs and some of no religion at all, the problem cannot be solved by a temple or synagogue." While admitting that in theory the synagogue was the ideal, dissenters were quick to observe that "some people are not inspired by that ideal. Shall they come under no influence at all?"

Critics also noted the Institutional Synagogue's higher "three-in-one" membership fee as further proof of its fundamentally "elitist" nature. Goldstein's organization was described by one spokesman for the Yiddish press as "a private institution for the children coming from parents not necessarily wealthy, but from those who can afford to pay for instruction." Membership rates at the Institutional Synagogue, critics contended, "were prohibitive to the wage earner." Those who felt that the mass-oriented revival movement was not within the true spirit of Judaism also censured the new Harlem movement, and those who preferred rabbis to play a less activist role in community social problems deplored Rabbi Goldstein's decision to "resign as a minister of an established congregation to donate his entire time and energy to Billy Sundayism." Rabbi Goldstein was advised to "concentrate on religious education" and leave "sensationalism" to Christian evangelists.

Rabbi Goldstein responded by asserting that his movement was primarily religious and was pointed toward bringing the unaffiliated into the synagogue and leading those ignorant of Judaism toward the house of study. Goldstein also argued that there was nothing novel or radical in the concept of "Jewish revivalism." The prophets of old and the itinerant preachers of the East European settlement were all "revivalists" and all operated within the fabric of Jewish tradition. He asserted that his movement had both Jewish history and modern ministerial techniques on its side.

In considering Rabbi Goldstein's Institutional Synagogue and the other early youth organizations that operated both in Harlem and in the adjoining communities as forerunners of the Jewish Center movement of the 1920s and 1930s, one immediately notes that as early as 1910 or so, religious leaders were aware that rapid, complete Americanization brought with it profound challenges to the continuity of Jewish life in this country. They understood that even young adults who had been exposed as children to some Jewish education were not immune to the pressures imposed by general society to assimilate; to conform totally to majority cultural values. They feared for those Jews but even more so for those children of immigrants who received no training in Judaism and who were growing to maturity as Americans oblivious of the traditions of their people. And although American Jews still constituted but a relatively small proportion of their predominantly immigrant community, they understood that these people were the first wave of a second-generation American Jewish society that would grow to full maturity in later decades.

The Central Jewish Institute, the Jewish Center, and, of course, Harlem's Institutional Synagogue, which operated under Orthodox auspices, represented the first concerted efforts to deal with these problems and served as workable prototypes for later Conservative Jewish synagogue centers established in the soon-to-be constructed outlying neighborhoods by second-generation Jews. The Harlem and Yorkville youth organizations also influenced later communal developments by providing a forum for the emergence of the American-born or -educated, university-trained, traditional rabbi as a dominant force in communal life. Men like Drachman, Morais, Kaplan, and Goldstein represented the vanguard of a new generation of traditional American Jewish rabbis dedicated and equipped to tend to the spiritual needs of the American Jewish community. Jewish Theological Seminary teachers and rabbis who had made so little impact on the immigrant ghetto population found a small but enthusiastic group of followers within the Americanized segment of Harlem's German and East European communities. These rabbis and their successors were destined to become even more important factors in the life of their communities in the years to come. Many of the lessons learned in these uptown Orthodox institutions were readily applied to suburban Conservative congregations.

A high level of cooperation existed between the founders of the Conservative movement and their contemporary modern Orthodox counterparts. Indeed, it is often difficult to differentiate between the two. Both stood for traditional Judaism and preached similar messages to their Americanized congregants. A study of the early careers of Rabbis Herbert S. Goldstein and Mordecai M. Kaplan is highly instructive in this area. Before entering the seminary and earning his rabbinic degree from this American rabbinic institute, Goldstein was ordained as an Orthodox Rabbi by Rabbi S. Jaffee of Beth Ha-Midrash Ha-Gadol of Norfolk Street. Armed with this dual ordination, Goldstein was a logical choice as an English-speaking assistant rabbi under Rabbi Moses Z. Margolies, a leading East European Orthodox Rabbi who was sensitive to American problems and values. Margolies, it will be remembered, was a director of the Uptown Talmud Torah and supported local and Kehillah-sponsored efforts to update Jewish educational practices. Named to his post at Kehilath Jeshurun, Goldstein succeeded Rabbi Kaplan, a fellow seminary graduate, who had not earned Orthodox ordination prior to his rabbinic appointment but who nevertheless was deemed qualified to minister to an important traditional congregation. Margolies and Kaplan and, later, Margolies and Goldstein apparently worked harmoniously in the Yorkville pulpit. And they all seem to have cooperated successfully in the founding of the Central Jewish Institute, as the senior rabbi undoubtedly regarded both men as traditional rabbis and as skilled communal workers. The differences in their rabbinic training do not seem to have been a point of conflict among the three.

Both Goldstein and Kaplan severed their ties with the Kehilath Jeshurun community to establish similarly constituted youth-oriented synagogues in Harlem and on the West Side. Both institutions were organized and maintained according to traditional Orthodox guidelines. It is therefore interesting to observe, in retrospect, that the "Jewish Center–Institutional Synagogue" concept, which found its first expression within an Orthodox context controlled by seminary-trained rabbis, ultimately gained its greatest acceptance within the Conservative movement.

A final, enduring similarity between early modern Orthodoxy and Conservative Judaism may be seen from an examination of Rabbis Goldstein and Kaplan's later careers. Although Goldstein and Kaplan would ultimately go their separate theological and denominational ways, the former as a leader of both the Union of Orthodox Jewish Congregations of America and Yeshiva University, the latter as the founder and leader of the left-wing Conservative Jewish Reconstructionist movement, both remained united in their continued commitment to leading and inspiring that emerging heterogeneous group of modern Jewish religious leaders who sought, through similar homiletics and almost identically constituted socio-religious institutions, to serve the spiritual needs of a truly American Jewish community.

CHAPTER

15

No issue so divided the American Jewish community after World War I as did the issue of Zionism, the movement to create a Jewish state in the Land of Israel. On one side stood those who viewed Zionism as a return to tribalism, a negation of Judaism's mission to the world, and a dangerous slap at those countries that had made Jews feel welcome. On the other side stood those who viewed Zionism as a movement of Jewish spiritual uplift, the only solution to the rising problem of anti-Semitism, and a practical response to anti-immigration legislation everywhere.

Although some have seen the Zionist question in America as merely an extension of an older German–East European debate, the situation in fact was far more complicated. German Jews were far from being of one mind on the issue (the Reform Movement remained officially anti-Zionist until the 1930s, although individual Reform rabbis served as Zionist leaders), and prominent native Jews of German descent became Zionism's most ardent advocates. Such in fact was the case with Louis Brandeis, then a noted Boston lawyer with ties to the Brahmin elite, who not only converted to Zionism, but in 1914 agreed to assume the movement's leadership. Why Brandeis converted remains the subject of conjecture. What is clear is that he proceeded to translate Zionism into American terms: He stressed action over ideology, divorced Zionism from any personal commitment to immigrate to a Jewish state, and yoked the Zionist mission to America's mission—the outward spread of democratic ideals.

Can Brandeis's form of Zionism be denominated "American Zionism"? In one sense obviously not, since every permutation of European Zionism had its American counterpart, and a full range of Zionist dignitaries traveled to America in search of supporters. Non-Zionism—composed of people who aided the upbuilding of Palestine as a Jewish refuge but did not otherwise subscribe to any form of Zionist ideology—also claimed to be quintessentially American. Yet Melvin Urofsky, who has written major studies of both Louis Brandeis and American Zionism, argues here that what Brandeis espoused was American Zionism. Although many American Jews followed other Zionist doctrines, and many of Brandeis's ideas were derivative, he legiti-

209

mated Zionism in a new way—one firmly geared to American Jews' special needs.

American Zionism's challenge—similar to many we have seen before— was how to balance independence and interdependence, maintaining a separate American Jewish identity while remaining part of the larger worldwide Zionist movement. Brandeis more successfully than anyone else met this challenge. His writings and ideas, laced with characteristically American rhetoric, continued to dominate Zionist thinking in America long after 1948, when the State of Israel came into being.

Zionism: An American Experience

Melvin I. Urofsky

European Zionism resulted from the interaction of anti-Semitism, the nationalistic mood of the nineteenth century, and the age-old religious yearning for a return to Zion. Arguing that as long as Jews had no home of their own they would continuously be persecuted, Theodore Herzl declared that the only solution to the Jewish problem was the creation of a Jewish homeland. "The Jewish question exists wherever Jews live in perceptible numbers," he wrote. "Where it does not exist, it is carried by Jews in the course of their migrations. We naturally move to those places where we are not persecuted, and there our presence produces persecution. This is the case in every country, and will remain so . . . till the Jewish question finds a solution on a political basis." Although tempered to some extent by an insistence on cultural and religious priorities by theorists like Achad Ha-am, the Zionism of Herzl, Max Nordau, and even Chaim Weizmann was essentially secular. With the help and under the protection of the European powers, a geopolitical entity would be established in which Jews could build an autonomous society. There, all Jews who wanted to could come to live free from persecution.

As Joseph Adler has pointed out, Herzl intuitively heightened his nationalistic appeal by tying it to the ancient Jewish dream of messianic redemption. Although in the beginning he did not care where the Jewish state might be located, he ultimately realized that only Palestine would awaken the hearts of the people. This strain of messianism was particularly attractive to the East Europeans; for all of his scientific rationalism, it runs like a thread through the speeches and writings of Chaim Weizmann.

European Zionism, therefore, primarily addressed itself to the problem of anti-Semitism. "Everything depends on our propelling force," wrote Herzl. "And what is our propelling force? The misery of the Jews." Influenced by cultural and religious forces, especially messianism, Zionism was essentially a secular attempt to resolve that problem through the creation of a political

211

212   *Melvin I. Urofsky*

homeland. In crossing the ocean to America, however, Herzlian Zionism ran up against a completely different situation.

Most importantly, there had been no long history of anti-Semitism in the United States. Prior to the American Revolution, the Jewish population of the colonies had been relatively small and had encountered little resistance. In 1740 an act of Parliament permitted the naturalization of Jews in the British colonies; thus Jews in America enjoyed more freedom, legally and in fact, than their brethren any place else in the world. Moreover, Jews were not singled out any more specifically than other dissident religious groups, such as Catholics or Quakers. In the decades following independence, one state after another struck down religious qualifications for suffrage and office-holding. In 1845, David Levy Yulee entered the United States Senate from Florida, soon to be followed by Judah P. Benjamin. In 1859, Attorney General Jeremiah S. Black declared that "In regard to the protection of our citizens in their rights at home and abroad, we have no law which divides them into classes or makes any difference whatever between them." Secretary of State Lewis Cass reemphasized this in regard to protection of American citizens overseas. The object of the United States, according to Cass, was "not merely to protect a Catholic in a Protestant country, a Protestant in a Catholic country, a Jew in a Christian country, but an American in all countries."

The first significant expression of anti-Semitism was General Ulysses S. Grant's infamous Order No. 11, which, however, was quickly rescinded, and appropriate apologies made. But after the Civil War, anti-Jewish feeling seemed to increase perceptibly. The *Social Register* closed its lists to Jews, and fashionable hotels, resorts, and private schools followed suit; in 1892 the Union League Club blackballed Theodore Seligman, son of one of the club's founders. Yet even here, as John Higham and Ellis Rivkin have pointed out, American anti-Semitism was by and large unrelated to religion. Rather, it was part of wider American problems dealing with large-scale immigration and economic mal-distribution. The anti-Semitism of the late nineteenth century bore little relation to the centuries-old Jew-hatred of Europe; it grew out of distinctly American tensions, and affected other immigrant and religious groups as well. As these tensions rose or waned, so did the hostilities. Moreover, at no time were American Jews without defenders against prejudice, and their champions included such distinguished Gentiles as Zebulon B. Vance and Theodore Roosevelt. Modern nationalistic anti-Semitism has just not appeared in the United States. This is not to say that there is not or never has been anti-Semitism in this country, but rather that it has been of very low intensity, and of a much different type than in Europe.

Another condition unique to the United States was a widely held belief that America itself was a new Zion, an attitude dating back to the Puritans, who saw themselves as a seventeenth-century version of biblical Israel, come to build their "city upon a hill" in a wilderness Zion. Throughout American history, there have been continuous references to this country as unique, set apart, even as divinely inspired. This attitude has been shared not only by the dominant Christian society, but by Jews as well. In Europe, prospective emigrants equated the United States with Palestine as a land of hope and redemption, and once here pledged their complete loyalty. In the 1840s, the Jews of Charleston, South Carolina, plainly declared: "This country is our Palestine, this city our Jerusalem," a cry echoed constantly over the next century. Louis Marshall, celebrating 250 years of Jewish life in America, prayed that Jews "never forget . . . the gratitude that we owe to the God of our fathers, Who has led us out of Egypt into this land of freedom."

This concept of America as the new Zion dominated the thinking of the preeminent American Jewish religious and secular organizations, and especially of the American Jewish Committee. Unlike many European Jews who saw their native lands primarily as places of prejudice and repression, American Jews viewed this country as a bastion of freedom, where anti-Semitism was the exception rather than the rule. In Europe, Palestine was viewed as a symbolic and spiritual refuge; American Jews, especially if Reform, dismissed Eretz Yisroel as a barren wasteland, a relic of ancient history. In 1885 the Reform leadership explicitly denounced any desire to return to the land of their forefathers. Even those Orthodox and Conservative Jews who still prayed for redemption and annually chanted "Next year in Jerusalem" did so more out of religious habit and custom than from any real desire to go there. While they did not categorically deny Zion, in practice they too had chosen America as the land of redemption.

In this choice, they deferred, either temporarily or permanently, the personal commitment of "going up to Zion." Herzlian Zionism assumed that persecuted Jews would want to go to a Jewish homeland, choosing it in preference to any other nation, even the United States. (Since Herzl believed that Jews carried the seeds of anti-Semitism with them wherever they went, even America would ultimately oppress its Jews.) This contention became the focal point of anti-Zionist claims that Zionism and Americanism were incompatible. If one was a Zionist, he owed his ultimate loyalty to Palestine and not to America. The United States had up until then welcomed all immigrants, but demanded that once here, the newcomers give all their allegiance to their new home.

In such a setting one would not expect Zionism to flourish, and this indeed was the case prior to 1914. Pre-Herzlian Zionism consisted either of dreamers like Mordecai Noah or Warder Cresson, poets like Emma Lazarus, isolated units of Hoveve Zion or Shave Zion, and equally isolated pockets of Hebraicists. The advent of Herzl and the [Zionist] Congress coalesced many of these people into either the Federation of American Zionists (F.A.Z.) or one of several pro-Zionist fraternal orders, such as the Knights of Zion in the Midwest. None of these groups made much headway in building up large

Little pre-Herzl Zionism

memberships, raising funds for Zionist institutions, or in developing pro-Zionist sentiment in the Jewish or the general communities. On the eve of World War I, with a Jewish population of over 2.5 million, the Federation claimed only 12,000 members and operated on an annual budget of slightly more than $12,000. Zionism, as a force in the American Jewish community, was negligible.

Between 1897 and 1914, however, the United States underwent massive change. The industrialization following the Civil War had altered the nature of the economy and of the society. Millions of immigrants, responding to the demand for cheap factory labor, had poured into the country. But where earlier immigrants had been primarily Protestant, from Northern and Western Europe, and had settled mainly on the land, the newcomers were Jewish and Catholic, from Southern and Eastern Europe, who settled in the cities in ethnic enclaves. Slower to assimilate than the earlier immigrants, they tended to retain their ties to the old country and the old ways. Where the earlier Jewish immigrants had been German and Reform, the new wave came from Russia and Poland, and clung to their Orthodoxy. Moreover, they brought with them a basic sympathy for Zionism. They found themselves too busy earning a living and becoming Americanized to cultivate that sympathy, but when the time came, they would be ready to support a revivified Zionist movement in the United States.

Industrialization also created a number of social and cultural problems, and in the two decades prior to the war, a series of reform movements attempted to deal with those problems. The progressive impulse created new conditions in American society that would make it possible for an Americanized Zionism to flourish. The great achievements of the new leadership between 1914 and 1921 were (1) the reformulation of Zionist philosophy to make it complementary of American as well as Jewish hopes and ideals; (2) the identification of specific practical goals for which the movement and its sympathizers could work; and (3) the revitalization and reorganization of the administrative machinery. The war years marked a critical period for Zionism, both in Europe and in the United States, and the events shaping the movement came primarily from external, non-Jewish forces. The ability of Zionist leaders to respond to these forces determined the success of the cause.

The chief external factor was obviously the war that erupted in August 1914. The disruption and damage of battle affected all civilians, but bore down particularly hard on the Jews in Eastern Europe, the site of heavy fighting, and in Palestine, where the war disrupted normal economic routines. Responding to the distress of their brethren overseas, a number of Jewish organizations, all sympathetic to Zionism, convened in extraordinary session at the Hotel Marseilles in New York on August 30. The delegates formed a Provisional Executive Committee for General Zionist Affairs (P.E.C.), and, at the urging of Jacob de Haas, elected Louis D. Brandeis as chairman. The choice was a happy one, and Brandeis's assumption of the American Zionist leadership marked a turning point in the fortunes of the movement. Within six years a near-moribund movement had become the most powerful Zionist organization in the world.

Brandeis was a singularly gifted man, and undeniably those talents contributed greatly to the growth of American Zionism. Without detracting from his credit, however, it is obvious that conditions over which he had no control made it possible for him to mobilize American Jews and to win over a larger part of public opinion in favor of the cause. Drawing upon his experience as a reformer, and building upon the assumptions and techniques of those reforms, Brandeis molded the movement in the image of other progressive causes. By de-emphasizing the *Yiddishkeit* of Zionism, and enlarging upon its ethical and democratic ideals, he not only paved the way for Zionist acceptance and success in the United States but also set the stage for the later tension and struggle between European and American advocates of the movement.

Brandeis first set out to nullify the argument that Zionism was incompatible with Americanism; indeed, he declared just the opposite, that Zionism and Americanism shared the same basic beliefs in democracy and social justice. His efforts meshed perfectly with a growing reappraisal of the makeup and nature of American society.

The same large-scale immigration which had created a latent pool of pro-Zionist sympathy also called into question earlier assumptions about assimilation and Americanization. Because earlier immigrants seemingly had joined the general population so effortlessly, and also seemingly had shed their old world traits, most Americans subscribed to the so-called "melting pot" philosophy of assimilation. Once here, this theory assumed, every immigrant would want to speak only English, drop all vestiges of prior cultures and loyalties, and work to be as American in appearance and behavior as native-born sons. In a line stretching back to J. Hector St. John de Crèvecoeur, writers argued that Americanization involved homogenization, and that true patriotism demanded a single-minded loyalty to the United States. Theodore Roosevelt's polemics against "hyphenated" Americans was the last anguished cry of a theory that by 1910 was breaking upon the failure of millions of new-wave immigrants to lose their Old World ways and attachments.

The progressives, especially those concerned with education, wrestled mightily with this problem, and gradually a new philosophy emerged that turned necessity into virtue. Led by settlement-house workers like Jane Addams and academics like Horace Kallen, these theorists argued that America's strength lay not in a bland uniformity but in a vibrant heterogeneity of dozens of different cultures. Immigrants should be encouraged to learn English, assume American ways, and be loyal to American institutions, but they should also value the heritage and customs of their ancestral homes. Cultural pluralism undermined the argument that one could or should be loyal to only one country or culture; by doing so it also helped to undercut the anti-Zionists' claim that Zionism contradicted Americanism.

Brandeis shifted away from assimilationism

In his appeal for Zionist support, Brandeis rang numerous changes on this theme, even though up until 1910 he had himself vehemently attacked dual loyalties. There was no room in this country for "hyphenated Americans," he had once proclaimed. "Habits of living or of thought which tend to keep alive differences of origin or classify men according to their religious beliefs are inconsistent with the American ideal of brotherhood, and are disloyal." In 1915, he summed up his new beliefs when he argued that dual loyalties were only objectionable if inconsistent; if the objectives of different loyalties were similar, then they supported one another. Zionism and Americanism shared many basic assumptions, and "every American Jew who aids in advancing the Jewish settlement in Palestine . . . will be a better man and a better American for doing so." Assimilation he now denounced as "national suicide," and American Jews owed it to America as well as to themselves to preserve their distinctive identity.

This assertion that Zionism and Americanism shared similar values is the clue both to Brandeis's involvement in the cause and to his success as its leader. Stephen S. Wise, Julian W. Mack, Felix Frankfurter, and other members of the Brandeis group shared a deep commitment to American ideals and culture. What attracted them to Zionism was not just the need for a haven from persecution—since they themselves did not suffer from oppression—but rather the possibility that a Jewish state could be established based on the ethical tenets of Judaism, principles they viewed as closely akin to American ideals. Addressing the 1915 American Zionist convention, Brandeis said: "The highest Jewish ideals are essentially American in a very important particular. It is Democracy that Zionism represents. It is Social Justice which Zionism represents, and every bit of that is the American ideal of the twentieth century." Both in public and in private, Brandeis emphasized the closeness of these two: "Zionism is the Pilgrims' inspiration and impulse over again"; "the ideals for America should prevail likewise in the Jewish State"; "we [Zionists] stand for democracy and social justice. And what have been made fundamentals of American law, namely, life, liberty, and the pursuit of happiness are all essentially Judaistic and have been taught by them for thousands of years."

To those who had been disheartened by the failure of the United States to achieve those ideals, and who believed that industrialization and growing economic giantism undermined democracy, Zionism offered a new opportunity. With their passion for equality, progressive reformers sympathized with the plight of a people unjustly persecuted for nearly two thousand years. The demand for a Jewish homeland meshed not only with the Zeitgeist of nineteenth-century nationalism, but with American reform ideals of self-deter-

Brandeis = Amer. + Zion share values .

mination. For those American Jews who believed in the humane ethics of Judaism, rather than in its ritual and theology, the Zionist goals represented a logical union of secular and religious beliefs.

The Brandeisian synthesis also rejected the personal commitment to "go up to Zion," which had been a major weapon in the arsenal of those who claimed that Zionism contradicted patriotism, since if each Zionist was expected to leave for the promised land, then in truth one could not be a good American and a good Zionist at the same time. Moreover, the anti-Zionists worried that the creation of a Jewish state might give rise to anti-Semitic forces demanding the removal of all Jews to the new homeland.

The personal commitment had been integral to European Zionism, but American leaders of the F.A.Z. had immediately rejected it, realizing the difficulties it would raise in the United States. A Richard Gottheil or a Harry Friedenwald, however, lacked the stature and prestige of a Brandeis. Their protestations that no Jew would be forced to go to Palestine had been ignored, and in 1914 the anti-Zionist press still argued that Zionism meant the removal of all Jews from the United States.

Brandeis constantly emphasized that no Jews would be forced to go to Palestine. "The place is made ready; legal right of habitation is secured; and any who wish are free to go. But it is of the essence of Zionism that there shall be no compulsion." Brandeis considered Palestine spiritually necessary for the American Jews, but those being persecuted in Europe, especially in Russia, still had need of a haven; and growing pressure to restrict immigration to the United States made it likely that this country would no longer be a refuge for those seeking to escape oppression in the old world. American Jews had found their Zion, but they still owed it to their less fortunate brethren in Europe to secure a Zion for them. American Jews had the responsibility to build up Palestine, not primarily for themselves, but as an asylum for other Jews.

Yonathan Shapiro has termed this shift of emphasis "Palestinianism," and has condemned the Brandeis group for diverting energy from a commitment to Zionist ideology and principle to a pragmatic and expedient philanthropism. It is true that the American Zionists were more interested in practical work than in ideas, but here again, this is very typical of the entire progressive movement. It is noteworthy that the most important philosophic movement this country has ever produced is pragmatism, and the basic ideas of William James, John Dewey, Charles S. Peirce, and others were receiving wide attention at this time. And pragmatism, we may recall, was once defined less as a philosophy than as a means of doing without one. Americans have always been more interested in specific practical work than in ideas, and the emphasis on building up Palestine appealed to the American need to *do* rather than to *analyze*. By identifying specific tasks, by aiming for concrete accomplishments, Zionism made itself attractive and understandable to those

American Jews in whom the American cultural traits outweighed the European Jewish antecedents. It made it possible for Jacob Schiff and Louis Marshall to join in the upbuilding of Palestine, although each proclaimed to his death that he was not a "Zionist."

At the same time that Brandeis was emphasizing the similarity of Zionist and American beliefs, he reshaped the organizational structure of the movement along lines he had earlier developed in reform battles in New England. Prior to 1914, no single Zionist group had been able to claim primacy in the United States. Although the Federation of American Zionists had continuously proclaimed that it officially represented the World Zionist organization, other American Zionist groups almost totally ignored the F.A.Z. A number of fraternal and religious orders collected monies for various Zionist projects, and the W.Z.O., fearful of losing any funds or alienating any supporters, dealt with them all on a more or less equal basis. Herzl, and Max Nordau after him, consistently refused pleas by F.A.Z. leaders to deal with it as the official American arm, and this refusal undercut periodic attempts to unite all American Zionists into one organization.

The trauma of the war, the obvious need for unified action, and the national prestige of Brandeis and his lieutenants set the stage for the unification of the American movement, a process culminating in 1918 with the creation of the Zionist Organization of America. Brandeis from the start, however, insisted upon organizational reform that would channel Zionist sentiment into one powerful force, and though his actions undeniably created that force, they also alienated some who preferred the autonomy of local clubs and an independence from the interference of national leaders.

Many of the men and women assembled at the Hotel Marseilles assumed that they were merely establishing a fund-raising operation, and saw Brandeis more as a "name" than as a leader. In accepting the chairmanship, he at first seemed to confirm this view. He apologized that he lacked a greater familiarity with American Jewish affairs, emphasized the great need for relief funds, and opened the drive with a personal donation of $1,000. As many of the delegates prepared to leave, they were jolted when Brandeis called upon them to stay and prepare reports on the status of their organizations, how many members they had, their annual budgets, and how much work they were prepared to undertake. In the next two days Brandeis must have been equally as shocked when he learned of the chaotic conditions and disarray among those he was now expected to lead.

The first thing he did was to establish a full-time office staff and impose strict accounting procedures. He expected and demanded almost daily reports on amounts of money raised, new members enrolled, and propaganda produced. Despite his concurrent involvement in national political affairs, Brandeis found time to oversee practically every detail of Zionist activity. No matter how large or small a donation to the relief fund, a personal note of thanks should be sent, and Zionist propaganda enclosed. Had a local branch pledged a specific amount; if so, was the pledge met, and what was being done to raise more money? Even the print size of the Hadassah newsletter came in for his scrutiny, and the format ultimately changed. To prevent conflicts of directions and energies, he made it clear to the Actions Committee of the W.Z.O. that in the future it would have to deal with American Zionists solely through the Provisional Committee.

Within a year after he had assumed the chairmanship, Brandeis had revitalized the movement, and created for the first time an efficient and functioning organizational apparatus. He secured the cooperation and active involvement of a number of prominent American Jews who had previously eschewed Zionist interests, such as Julian W. Mack and Felix Frankfurter, and he brought Stephen Wise back to a central role in the movement. Moreover, he spurred an intense effort to recruit college students and graduates into Zionist organizations like the Menorah Society and the Intercollegiate Zionist groups, emphasizing that this body of educated Americans was the future hope of the cause. While recent European immigrants formed the mass support now, future growth depended on recruiting Americanized Jews to the movement.

Even as the movement grew, some voices questioned what had happened to the problems of ideology. They saw reports on dollars and cents, on numbers of members, on pieces of literature, but who was paying attention to what it all meant? The old-line European Zionists and Socialist Zionists were especially aggrieved at what they considered an abandonment of philosophy. Here again, Brandeis molded the movement to specific American needs and assumptions. Despite their distrust of gigantic corporations, Americans insisted that civic enterprises operate on sound, efficient business principles. The F.A.Z. had been a sloppy organization: literature had been mailed irregularly, collections for shekel stamps haphazard, and stock certificates of the Jewish Colonial Trust mislaid for months. If the principles of European Zionism were unacceptable to many Americans, so were its operating procedures. We do not wish to imply, however, that Brandeis had no interest in philosophy or principles. Like most progressive reformers, he held a deep commitment to a well-defined set of first principles; but these he considered constant and eternal verities, not open to discussion or analysis. Once the progressives determined upon these principles, they acted upon them; no one has ever accused these reformers of being introspective.

To Brandeis, the first principles of Zionism had been well defined by Herzl (with, of course, the American modifications) and to a lesser degree by Achad Ha-am. In the crisis of the war the important thing was not to debate endlessly on minute questions of philosophy, but to work for specific and attainable goals. Brandeis considered one of the most important of these goals to be the development of a well-organized, well-disciplined and influential Zionist movement in America. His motto, repeated time and again, of "Members! Money! Discipline!" emphasized the practical rather than the theoretical, the doing rather than the saying.

This is neither the time nor the place to explore in detail the inner workings of the American Zionist organization during the war years, nor the ensuing conflict with Chaim Weizmann that ultimately erupted at the Cleveland convention in 1921. Research so far confirms the contention that the movement during the whole of the Brandeis leadership faithfully reflected the prevailing ethos of progressivism, the faith in equality and the perfectability of man, the need for identification of specific and attainable goals, the assumption that organization was necessary for action. By recasting American Zionism along these lines, Americanized Jews like Brandeis, Mack, and Frankfurter took a fringe cult and made it part of the mainstream of American reform. One could, in fact, say that they made it respectable.

Many Jews, however, did not view the Americanization of the movement as a blessing. For them, the Brandeisian synthesis weakened Zionism by diverting attention from important ideological considerations toward mundane practical work. The immigrants who had brought their Zionism to America with them were at first thrilled by the advent of "real" Americans as leaders, but they eventually came to fear and resent the dilution of the Jewish component. The Brandeis leadership was frankly American; it lacked *Yiddishkeit*. If it had been more Jewish, however, it is doubtful whether it could have adapted the movement to American circumstances.

By the end of 1918, rebellion was brewing in the immigrant ranks, fanned by the resentment of some of the older F.A.Z. leaders like Louis Lipsky who had been shunted aside by the new men. When Chaim Weizmann made his move to assume the complete leadership of the world movement, he provided a nucleus around which the anti-Brandeis resentment could form. The fight over the Keren Hayesod (Development Fund) in 1921, which led to the resignation of the American leadership, was only in part a power struggle between two strong personalities, neither of whom could play a secondary role. It also marked the divergence in methods and philosophy between two factions, one which saw itself principally as Jewish and one which considered itself primarily as American.

In the 1920s, the Zionist Organization of America fell away drastically from its peak membership and budgets of the war years. Some of this undeniably was the letdown following the war crisis, a letdown shared by all segments of the society. But it also saw the rank-and-file membership demand the return of the "American" leaders, and the adoption by Weizmann and his American lieutenants of practically the entire Brandeis program. With the return of Julian Mack and Robert Szold to leadership in the 1930s, the American Zionists sealed their adherence to a philosophy that gave precedence to American customs and ideals. The shock of the Holocaust confirmed them even further in their devotion to America at the same time it spurred them on to the final practical attainment of the Jewish state.

CHAPTER

16 The nineteen thirties, the decade of the Great Depression, was a period of stress and ferment, with poverty, fear, and hopelessness stalking the American landscape and dark clouds looming on the European horizon. From a Jewish point of view the situation looked especially bleak. Doubly burdened in the depression, Jews faced not only economic privations but anti-Semitism as well.

Just at the moment when the American dream seemed to be failing so painfully, a whole new generation of American Jews—the children of the East European immigrants—came of age. Sometime during the 1930s, as Lloyd P. Gartner, a leading student of British and American Jewish history points out in his article here, the majority of Jews living in America became American born. Old leaders and old established patterns no longer seemed relevant. Rather than being concerned about natives and immigrants, American Jews now worried far more about economics and ideology.

Two features of the 1930s merit special attention: the emergence of Jews in American public life, and the first flourishing of American Jewish intellectuals and literati. Both signified in different ways Jewish educational achievements. Both also foreshadowed the post–World War II rise of Jews to the crest of American public life and culture. Yet for all their similarities, these two features also evidenced two diametrically opposite trends in American Jewish life. One saw Jews seeking entry into the centers of American power and influence. The other saw them firmly committed to remaining on the outside, as critics, gadflies, and advocates of revolutionary change.

The New Deal, coupled with President Franklin D. Roosevelt's penchant for talent, opened the door for the "best and the brightest" in Jewish life (and those in other minority groups as well) to enter government service for the first time. Felix Frankfurter, Samuel I. Rosenman, Ben Cohen, Bernard Baruch, David Niles, Henry Morgenthau, Sidney Hillman, David Lilienthal, Abe Fortas, and countless other Jews played prominent and behind-the-scenes roles in the Roosevelt administration as policymakers and implementers. Never before had Jews been active in government to such a large extent. In the wake of the New Deal, Roosevelt became a Jewish hero, and Jewish ties to the Democratic party were secured for a generation or more.

At the same time as some Jews were gaining prominence for their work in the nation's capital, other Jews—more radical in background—were gathering in New York. These New York Jewish intellectuals, as they came to be known, advocated more drastic responses to the social and economic crises of the depression years; many openly espoused communism. Their critical analyses of American life and society—sometimes brilliant, sometimes doctrinaire—

marked them as outsiders; they thought "dangerous thoughts" and sometimes acted in dangerous ways.

The most creative and lasting works produced by these figures were novels, volumes such as Henry Roth's Call It Sleep *and Michael Gold's* Jews Without Money. *These books, drawn from the lives of Jewish immigrants and their children, featured elements that would characterize American Jewish fiction for decades afterward, even into the 1980s. "The patterns of Jewish speech, the experiences of Jewish childhood and adolescence, the smells and tastes of the Jewish kitchen, the sounds of the Jewish synagogue"—these, according to Leslie A. Fiedler, have become "staples" of American Jewish literature since the 1930s. Irving Howe has compared American Jewish literature throughout this period to a regional culture breaking through into national consciousness. It is regional, he explains,*

> *in that it derives from and deals overwhelmingly with one locale, usually the streets and tenements of the immigrant Jewish neighborhoods or the "better" neighborhoods to which the children of the immigrants have moved; regional in that it offers exotic or curious local customs for the inspection of native readers; and regional in that it comes to us as an outburst of literary consciousness resulting from an encounter between an immigrant group and the host culture of America.*

American Jewish literature, like so much else, thus harkens back to the experience of those who passed through "the midpassage of American Jewry," the dark years of the depression. From the creative ferment of this period, in all its bleakness, the contemporary American Jewish community arose.

The Midpassage of
American Jewry

Lloyd P. Gartner

Zurich, August 1929. The reconstruction of the Jewish world after World War I came to fullness when, after years of negotiation, non-Zionist notables entered into the "Pact of Glory" with the Zionist movement to found the Jewish Agency for Palestine. The agreement was joyously made official at the Zionist Congress, held as usual in Switzerland. Then, after a few heady days, began the rapid, steep, and almost uninterrupted descent. Louis Marshall, the recognized head of American Jewry and main negotiator with Chaim Weizmann, fell ill after the Jewish Agency assembly and was dead in three weeks. As Marshall lay dying, a bloody onslaught by Arabs on the Jewish National Home exposed its physical weakness and made clear a depth of Arab hostility that few had reckoned with. Great Britain started its long retreat from the promise of the Balfour Declaration and the stipulations of the Palestine Mandate. The disturbing summer of 1929 ended with the first massive crack in the United States stock market, and other cracks followed until the securities market lay in ruins. Unemployment and business failures increased monthly, while banks collapsed and the world's financial system came into peril. The international dimensions of the economic crisis gave point to the alarming reports being received from Germany over the rising power of the Nazi movement.

The new agenda of American Jewry was outlined during that summer and autumn of 1929, while the death of Marshall symbolized the weakening of its patrician leadership. Depression in America on a scale never known before had to turn the concerns even of prosperous American Jews to making a living and holding on to what they had. The world depression helped the Nazis into power in 1933, and the hideous twelve years' chronicle of European Jewry began. Where lay hope? It was not a propitious time to wager on America's liberal democracy. Soviet Russia, many urgently argued, was the future and it worked. Depression in America, Nazism in Germany, the Jewish

National Home, and the sinking fortunes of East European Jewry became the agenda of American Jewry after 1929, and a hesitant, uncertain leadership had to cope with it all. Fifteen years earlier, in 1914, it is hard to imagine anyone foreseeing even a small part of this agenda. Fifteen years after it ended, in 1960, did not many sense that their world was so different that what had happened between 1929 and 1945 was a nightmare, or some portion of it a matter decent enough for nostalgia? So different had the times become, and that much had the public affairs of American Jewry changed. Historians generally stress continuity beneath the surface of change, but we had better look upon these years as a time of abrupt and drastic alterations in the regularities and tempo of American Jewish life. It is not only that the events of these years were stark, horrifying, and sometimes thrilling. In 1929, American Jewry was still dominated by its immigrant experience, the end of which had been decreed only four years earlier by the Johnson Act. Yiddish in its varied uses, Jewish trade unions, and *landsmanshaften* all reflected publicly the kind of life led in thousands of Jewish households. Thousands more studiously kept apart from the immigrant milieu in which they had grown up, or rebelled against it. Sixteen years later, in 1945, the immigrant world was shriveled or gone, and so was the complex of attitudes toward it. The years when this happened were American Jewry's eventful, trying midpassage.

How can we recount what happened to the Jewish people between 1929 and 1945 without seeking the wrath of Amos, the grandeur of Isaiah, the despair of Jeremiah? There is no hope I can do this. Let me attempt something modest by comparison: What lay before American Jews in their country? How did they attempt to cope with their public agenda? And how did their domestic affairs influence their foreign activities?

During the first thirty years of the twentieth century American Jews had progressed materially to an astonishing degree. Neither the foreignness of most of them as East European immigrants nor xenophobia nor anti-Semitism kept them from improving their lot with the general prosperity of the age, marked only by brief setbacks. The Jews quit the Lower East Side and its counterparts in practically every city and moved to better neighborhoods. They left proletarian occupations and peddling to become shopkeepers, petty entrepreneurs, and white-collar workers. Those who remained garment workers were fortified in strong unions. There were high hopes for the economic advance of the children. A good many Jews were teachers, accountants, lawyers, and physicians. From 1929 all that changed. As large enterprises laid off their workers en masse and small firms closed down, unemployment rose to levels never imagined: In major industrial cities like Pittsburgh, Cleveland, and Detroit it ranged between 30 percent and 35 percent of the labor force, besides those who could find only part-time work. Unemployment also struck the Jews hard. With the cessation of building in the boom city of Los Angeles, "two hundred Jewish carpenters cannot find work, or to put it in milder terms sixty percent of the Jewish carpenters belonging to this group have been out of employment . . . for many, many months." We learn of a man with a wife and three young children who was "working as a presser irregularly, averaging $3.50 per week." Jewish needleworkers' unions could do nothing against their employers' going out of business or cutting back severely. The old days of sweatshops and piece work seemed to be returning as wages and hours fell back to what they had been twenty-five years before. Voluntary wage cuts and industry-wide strikes accomplished little before the New Deal's programs. Many dispossessed shopkeepers and men out of work took to door-to-door peddling, which underwent a revival owing to the desperate efforts of men to support themselves. Ruined businessmen presented an "insistent and increasing demand" for relief to Jewish agencies:

> Our Jewish people have asked help later because they are tradesmen. They will buy and sell as long as there are those to trade with. Coming to us now in increasing numbers [in 1931] are the small merchant, the builder and real estate dealer. In fact, a new clientele is being created—the so-called "white collar" class.

The Jewish merchant could hold out longer, but to return to business was harder than for the worker, who needed no capital but only a job. Jewish institutions suffered harshly as contributions dwindled. Perhaps the worst off were schools, especially those with ambitious programs whose following was mainly among the Orthodox, then the least prosperous segment of the Jewish community. Tuition could not be collected and other income was scarce. For the unfortunate teachers there were frequent payless paydays, and months of waiting for even partial payment of arrears of salary.

A generation inured to the psychic trials of prosperity might be reminded of those that came from poverty:

> . . . a period such as we are passing through takes its toll in various forms of physical illnesses, particularly that of undernourished children, to say nothing of mental conflict and mental illness, depression and despondency and the increasing number of problems of delinquency.

And a veteran social worker sighed:

> As I observe the young people in this fourth year of the depression [1934] I am appalled by their cynical acceptance of things as they are. They are not avid for tools of understanding: they reject opportunities for vocational preparation, seeing, as they do, that fitness is no guarantee of work. . . .

Young people went to college but with faint prospect of employment. Alfred Kazin's mood was typical: "One hot afternoon, in June, 1934, deep in the depression, I had just completed my college course for the year and was desolately on my way home to Brooklyn." Early in the depression it was possible to declare, as did the director of a Jewish employment bureau, that "We should face our employment situation as a people and solve our problems within the group," in the spirit of the apologetic pride that "Jews take care of their own." However, the dimensions of the problem became so huge that Jews no longer even made the attempt. Until the New Deal made the relief of unemployment a federal responsibility, there were sad and sometimes stormy scenes in Jewish agencies which, like other private charities, were the funnel through which state unemployment relief appropriations were doled out to recipients. The New Deal unemployment burden relieved Jewish and private charities of an impossible burden. Even in 1938 there was heavy Jewish unemployment, said to be 14.7 percent of the Jewish labor force in Pittsburgh, 5.2 percent in Buffalo, and 8.8 percent of experienced Jewish workers in San Francisco; in Detroit, three years before, it had stood at 14.7 percent. In the New York metropolis, the percentage was 12 to 13 percent in 1935–1937. The rapid shifting of Jewish neighborhoods which accompanied upward mobility lessened or ceased.

So shattering was the depression and the wave of economic anti-Semitism it released that the economic future of the Jews in the United States seemed in question:

> Unlike Americans as a whole, the Jewish group does not possess a balanced economic distribution which allows economic gains and losses, strains and tensions, to be spread evenly among their number. Jews are not represented on the farms or in manual jobs. The needle trades have employed large numbers, although even here other nationalities have been supplanting them in recent decades. The heavy industries engage few Jews either among employers or workers. Banking, stock brokering, moving pictures and other forms of amusement, real estate, and the distributive trades account for most of our Jewish wealth. The professions, small business and white-collar occupations yield our large Jewish middle class.

The middle class, and precisely its mercantile and white-collar segment in which Jews sought their place, seemed the most endangered in the long range, although, as it happened, it was rather less afflicted by unemployment than was unskilled and proletarian labor. Thus, unemployment among Jews was proportionately less severe. Perhaps, it was argued, Jews were "overrepresented" in trade and the professions, and their youth should be directed to become farmers, technicians, and skilled craftsmen. By no means was it clear when representation became overrepresentation. More or less it meant fields where there were many Jews or against which anti-Semites complained. These proposals for vocational shifts, in retrospect, were attuned more to public relations than to economic realities. Young Jews disregarded them, and continued along to college with an eye on independent business and the professions, preparing without realizing it for the opportunities which opened wide in the 1940s.

What disturbed Jews deepest was not the high unemployment and economic insecurity they shared with the American population at large, but the dangerously anti-Semitic atmosphere fostered by the depression which might last many more years. Father Charles E. Coughlin broadcast nationally from Detroit, and his anti-Semitism became more explicit with each weekly talk. At street-corner meetings in upper Manhattan hatred of Jews was spewed and in subway stations beneath they could be assaulted. The Nazis of the German-American Bund sought to carry on like their mentors in Germany. There was a plethora of anti-Semitic organizations. All the time American Jews had in mind the ravaging of the Jews in Germany, like themselves educated, acculturated, patriotic, economically successful. *It Can't Happen Here* was the ironic title of Sinclair Lewis's popular novel of 1935 which imagined how "it" did happen. There was reassurance that the American people largely detested Nazism, yet impossible to suggest any easing of restrictions on the immigration of its Jewish or other victims. President Roosevelt did not choose to try. A proposal for freer immigration was likely to generate a popular counterproposal to halt all immigration to the United States during a period of mass unemployment.

All Jews knew of the large areas of the labor market that were practically shut to them. They had almost no chance in banks, insurance firms—except as brokers selling policies to other Jews—large corporations, department stores, as lawyers in large law firms, as scholars in universities or as physicians in hospitals. To make matters look cleaner, some of these enterprises would hire token Jews who would not be advanced. There were Jewish employers who followed the trend and did not hire Jews. But during a time of desperate job-seeking, many employers did not have to bother with excuses—they didn't want Jews working for them. Most private universities, particularly the most distinguished, had quotas on Jewish admissions. Notorious were the medical schools, whose anti-Semitic policies compelled hundreds of Jewish medical students to emigrate to foreign schools, notably Edinburgh in Scotland.

The large cities knew sharp interethnic tensions. In Boston and New York there was friction between Jews and Irish, as the Jews competed hard and often successfully for jobs in which the Irish had long predominated. These included white-collar work, positions in the school system, and a share in the control of the Democratic party machine with its vast job-giving powers, from street cleaners to judges. The dramatic mayoralty of Fiorello H. LaGuardia in New York City meant the decline of Irish municipal power entrenched in Tammany Hall, and the rise of Jews and Italians. Irish anger at the Jewish challenge also had an ideological basis, with the Jews strongly

ROOSEVELT

supporting the Spanish Republicans during the Civil War in Spain and the Catholics—meaning mainly Irish, especially at the level of the hierarchy—strong for the insurgents. Jews opposed the Catholic and Irish desire for some religious influence in the public schools. Before Pearl Harbor, the Irish generally opposed aid to their homeland's old oppressor Great Britain, while most Jews advocated aid to Hitler's enemies. Communism rather than Nazism was the great enemy to many Catholics.

Against this bleak setting of economic trouble, anti-Semitism, and concern for Jews overseas, the presidency of Franklin Delano Roosevelt held a meaning which was not only tangible and political. Even today, almost fifty years after he entered the White House for the longest and most dynamic and eventful tenure in American history, Roosevelt appears so much more vivid a figure than any of his successors that it is easy to realize what he meant to the electorate which four times sent him to the White House. As William E. Leuchtenburg observes:

> When Roosevelt took office, the country to a very large degree responded to the will of a single element: the white, Anglo-Saxon, Protestant property-holding class. Under the New Deal, new groups took their place in the sun. It was not merely that they received benefits they had not had before but that they were "recognized" as having a place in the commonwealth.

The New Deal, that vast, quite unplanned aggregation of relief and reform measures, many of which owed something to Jewish economists and social workers, to the Jewish labor movement and the Lower East Side of New York, became part of the fabric of American life. The mass of Jews embraced it enthusiastically. Yet important as they were, these measures were not the reason for the support of Roosevelt which at times surpassed even adoration to become idolatry. This old American Protestant aristocrat, a type Jews have often supported politically, smiling and supremely affable, placed Jews at the political nerve center in his victorious coalition of ethnic urban groups, proletarian workers, Blacks, and deprived farmers. He openly loathed Nazism and Fascism. He appointed Jews to high office, and it was learned with appreciation that he brushed aside the pleas of some prominent Jews not to raise the Jewish political profile in the dangerous year of 1939, and replaced the revered Brandeis on the Supreme Court with Felix Frankfurter. Eighty to 90 percent of the Jews voted for Roosevelt in his four elections, each time in a higher proportion. The lowest was in the 1932 election when many Jews voted Socialist and Communist. The vote for these parties of the left declined with succeeding presidential elections, and the Jews, like most of the other voters, switched to Roosevelt. One might also suggest a kind of Manichean politics. The embodiment of evil, Adolf Hitler, required the embodiment of good against him, and that had to be Franklin Delano Roosevelt, except for those who insisted in seeing the embodiment in Josef Stalin. Roosevelt was supported in New York by such Jewish favorites as Herbert H. Lehman, Robert F. Wagner, and Fiorello H. LaGuardia.

The evident failure of American capitalism in a liberal, democratic state to fulfill the American promise of mass prosperity led to movements leftward and rightward, for abandoning democracy as the right demanded, or for doing away with capitalism as the left demanded. Jews, of course, gravitated to the left, especially because the far right was anti-Semitic. American literature, including the Jewish writers who were beginning to figure prominently in it, was saturated with the social questions of the time. Jewish writing and thinking moved generally to the left along with American thought and letters at large. The numerous novels of Jewish immigrant life were as a rule autobiographical. They were critical, often harshly so, of the immigrant world and of those who rose within it to worldly success. Now their attitude of rejection extended to the inhospitable social order. One scholar has enumerated seventy radical proletarian novels appearing between 1930 and 1940 by fifty-three authors of whom seventeen appear to be Jewish. Jewish prominence in American literature really begins with these novels of radical protest of which few, to be sure, are good literature.   ·

Social problems were conceived by the intellectual consensus of the time in general social and economic terms, and answers to them were provided in the same frame. There were thus no distinct or specific Jewish problems, and it was unscientific and ethnocentric to assume otherwise. Anti-Semitism had to be regarded as a disease of capitalist society, and the Jews were victims on account of their economic stratification and minority status. Two things were required: a drastic change in capitalism or its abolition, and the participation of the Jews in the forces which were to bring this about, whether these were Socialists or Communists or the new industrial union movement. It was a specious universalism, for it denied that the Jews constituted a group which, whatever else they were part of, was also whole in itself and merited serious attention as such; whatever society did to solve its problems as a whole would not as an automatic consequence solve the problems of the Jews. The universalist Jews naturally sought their place in universalist social and political movements where they frequently found that quite a high proportion of their fellow universalists were also Jews. Many were writers and teachers, as well as social workers who were often employed by institutions within the Jewish community.

It was during the 1930s, at a point in time which cannot be determined, that the majority of Jews became American born. Moreover, American Jews became an older group as their birthrate continued to decline. The immigrant world and its Yiddish press, speech, synagogues, theatre, and literature was passing, and so was the Jewish character of the trade unions they had built. *Landsmanshaften* were shriveling, while "Americanization" activities lost their point except to serve the limited number of refugees from Germany. Religious and cultural life was dominated by the quest for an American form of religious tradition and by the effort to maintain institutions unaided by government or federations of Jewish philanthropies. The characteristic face of Orthodoxy was the postimmigrant neighborhood synagogue, most of whose members were but superficially observant. Major Orthodox leaders arrived from Europe during this time—Rabbis Soloveitchik, Feinstein, Breuer, and Schneerson in chronological order—but their impact was felt only in later years. Reform Judaism, financially better established and long past its adaptation to the American scene, began very tentatively to examine the possibilities of a renewal of religious tradition. It adopted a pro-Zionist policy, but with a forceful anti-Zionist minority in opposition, and also devoted much attention to general social questions. Conservative Judaism was not yet a powerful third force on the religious scene. Yet its Reconstructionist wing, led by Mordecai M. Kaplan, combined theological radicalism with traditional ritual practice, Zionism with the social gospel, and obtained much attention and some influence among rabbis and Jewish communal intelligentsia.

At the level of the organized Jewish community as a whole, except for local Jewish charities, fund-raising faded into the background because so little could be raised for overseas needs. The antiseptic words of the *American Jewish Year Book* for 1931–1932 described the situation:

> Economic conditions in the United States during the past year were such as to compel the Jewish community to apply by far the greater part of its energies to the solution of its own domestic problems, including those of continuing the activities and, in some cases, preventing the dissolution of institutions and agencies which had been created by the community in previous years. American Jewry was prevented therefore from taking as active an interest in its sister communities overseas as in former years, especially as far as material aid was concerned.

The Joint Distribution Committee, supported by the older German-Jewish wealth, saw its income shrink from $4,583,000 in 1927 to $1,632,000 in 1929 and to $385,000 in 1932. The disaster of German Jewry brought a great increase, to $1,151,000 in 1933 and to $1,402,000 in 1934. From 1936 the income of the JDC went up steadily, but still lagged far behind the needs. The combined income of the two main funds for Palestine, the Jewish National Fund and the Palestine Foundation Fund, fell even lower than the JDC. From a mere $723,000 in 1930 it sagged to $339,000 in 1933, and then climbed gradually to $3,489,000 in 1939. Hadassah, however, managed to maintain its income fairly well. During the depressed 1930s the permanent overseas aid structure was built. The Jewish National Fund, the Palestine Foundation Fund, and a few smaller bodies joined to form the United Palestine Appeal in 1935. Four year later the financially successful UPA entered into an agreement with the Joint Distribution Committee and the National Refugee Service, renewable annually, to establish the United Jewish Appeal. There was little about the United Jewish Appeal's early years to foretell that after World War II it would become the largest voluntary philanthropy in history. The partners fought one another constantly over the proportionate distribution of UJA funds. The leaders of the Joint insisted that European Jewry required assistance for physical survival, while the Zionists argued that only by developing Palestine could there be a sure and certain solution to Jewish persecution and homelessness which philanthropy could never provide. Individual communities that conducted combined campaigns were vexed by debates over the proportions to be retained for local needs and those to be sent for overseas requirements.

The time appeared ripe during the 1930s for power within American Jewry to pass into the hands of the East European stock. Numerically, they constituted the vast majority. They were rising fast in political recognition, thanks especially to the New Deal and its local counterparts. The disillusion with America's political and economic leaders of the 1920s included the affluent stockbrokers, bankers, merchants, and lawyers, mainly Republicans of the German-Jewish stock who had controlled the American Jewish community. Louis Marshall, had he lived, would have been out of his element in the 1930s. The old patriciate was vulnerable on other scores. Some of them lost their wealth or much of it, while many patrician heirs were but faintly Jewish when they were Jewish at all. The patriciate had placed its faith in emancipation as the full and sufficient cure for Jewish needs, and in philanthropy, preferably nonsectarian, as their highest expression as Jews. Nazism shattered the first article, while the New Deal made the second expendable. Shorn of their prestige, and in some cases of their wealth and Judaism, their deepest beliefs challenged, it is no surprise that the old leaders hardly led. Their circumspection in Jewish matters domestic and foreign, and their fear and dislike of public agitation ran counter to the eagerness of American Jewry for forceful, passionate demonstration and protest. These were the tactics of the pro-Zionist, pro-New Deal American Jewish Congress, revived in 1930 by Rabbi Stephen S. Wise, and they were deplored by the American Jewish Committee, spokesman of the diminished patriciate. In most local communities Jewish Community Councils were established, functioning as a council of local organizations with a degree of moral suasion but little real power.

Yet the East European stock failed to take over the American Jewish community nationally during the 1930s. They had the numbers but not the money, and men of means are always indispensable in a voluntarily organized community. Perhaps the East Europeans lacked the confidence and the men. Behind the veteran Wise, not an East European himself, one does not find a cadre of potential national leaders of note waiting in the wings, except a few rabbis of whom the most notable was acknowledged to be the brilliant, dominating Abba Hillel Silver of Cleveland. Thus, the old order of the patrici- ate was gravely weakened during the 1930s, but the newer stock was unable to take over. There was a vacuum of national Jewish leadership at the most critical moment. It was upon this troubled, hesitant Jewish community of some five million souls that war descended in December 1941.

FOR FURTHER READING

The two best surveys of American Jewish history between the two world wars are Judd L. Teller's *Strangers and Natives* (1968), which describes "the evolution of the American Jew from 1921 to the present," and Lucy S. Dawidowicz's *On Equal Terms* (1982), which covers American Jewish life during the past century. Oscar Janowsky (ed.), *The American Jew: A Composite Portrait* (1942) contains insightful articles on the period by contemporaries. For in-depth study, the annual volumes of the *American Jewish Year Book* are indispensable.

Nathan C. Belth has surveyed American anti-Semitism, emphasizing the twentieth century in his *A Promise to Keep* (1979). More focused analytical studies have been anthologized by Leonard Dinnerstein (ed.), *Antisemitism in the United States* (1971), and in John Higham's *Send These to Me* (1975), where his own seminal essays are collected. The most thoroughly documented incident of twentieth-century American anti-Semitism is the subject of Leonard Dinnerstein's *The Leo Frank Case* (1966); for recent revelations clearing Frank, see *The New York Times* (March 8, 1982). Other studies include Hyman Berman, "Political Anti-Semitism in Minnesota During the Great Depression," *Jewish Social Studies* 38 (1976), pp. 247–264, and Burton Boxerman, "Rise of Anti-Semitism in St. Louis, 1944–1945," *YIVO Annual* 14 (1969), pp. 251–269. Robert Singerman's *Antisemitic Propaganda: An Annotated Bibliography and Research Guide* (1982) covers primary and secondary sources, including a great deal of material dealing with this period.

Jewish religious developments in twentieth-century America are treated broadly in Nathan Glazer's *American Judaism* (1972) and Joseph L. Blau's *Judaism in America* (1976). Various important articles are gathered in Jacob Neusner (ed.), *Understanding American Judaism* (2 vols., 1975). The emergence of the American rabbinate over the past century, but especially in this period, is analyzed from three Jewish religious perspectives in a special issue of *American Jewish Archives* 35 (November 1983). For other religious developments, see Deborah Dash Moore's *At Home in America: Second Generation New York Jews* (1981); and Arnold M. Eisen's *The Chosen People in America* (1983), the first serious study of Jewish religious ideology in America. Specific denominational developments can be traced in Sefton Temkin, "A Century of Reform Judaism in America," *American Jewish Year Book* 74

(1973), pp. 3–75; Joseph Blau (ed.), *Reform Judaism: A Historical Perspective* (1973); Marshall Sklare, *Conservative Judaism* (1972), a classic sociological study of the movement's rise; Charles S. Liebman, "Reconstructionism in American Jewish Life," *American Jewish Year Book* 71 (1970), pp. 3–99; Louis Bernstein, *Challenge and Mission: The Emergence of the English Speaking Orthodox Rabbinate* (1982); and Charles S. Liebman, "Orthodoxy in American Jewish Life," *American Jewish Year Book* 66 (1965), pp. 21–97.

The Zionist movement in America has spawned a vast literature. Melvin I. Urofsky, *American Zionism from Herzl to the Holocaust* (1976) and Naomi W. Cohen, *American Jews and the Zionist Idea* (1975) are the best synthetic treatments, both with extensive references to other sources. Urofsky's *A Mind of One Piece* (1971), dealing with Louis Brandeis, and his *A Voice That Spoke for Justice* (1982), a biography of Stephen S. Wise, also contain much on Zionism during this period. Yonathan Shapiro, *Leadership of the American Zionist Organization* (1971), and Samuel Halperin, *The Political World of American Zionism* (1961) deal more broadly with the American Zionist leadership. A special issue of *American Jewish History* 69 (September 1979) contains several valuable articles, two of which challenge the Brandeis-centered historiography of recent years. Stuart Knee, *The Concept of Zionist Dissent in the American Mind* (1979) offers the first serious look at a range of Zionism's American critics. For articles on other specialized themes see the *Herzl Year Book* and the journal *Studies in Zionism*.

The relationship between American Reform Judaism and Zionism has attracted particular attention in recent years: see David Polish, *Renew Our Days: The Zionist Issue in Reform Judaism* (1976); Howard R. Greenstein, *Turning Point: Zionism and Reform Judaism* (1981); Michael A. Meyer, "American Reform Judaism and Zionism: Early Efforts at Ideological Rapprochement," *Studies in Zionism* 7 (1983), pp. 49–64; and Gary P. Zola, "Reform Judaism's Pioneer Zionist: Maximilian Heller," *American Jewish History* 73 (June 1984), pp. 375–397. On the relationship between the American government and the Zionist movement, see Zvi Ganin, *Truman, American Jewry and Israel* (1979) and the review essay by Ian Bickerton in *American Jewish Archives* 33 (April 1981), pp. 141–152. For the subsequent history of America-Israel relations see Nadav Safran, *Israel: The Embattled Ally* (1981).

The problems faced by individual Jews and Jewish communities in the depression have not yet been systematically studied. Lloyd P. Gartner presents important data on the Jews of Cleveland in his history of that community (1978), and other Jewish community histories deal briefly with the subject as well. "Jews in the New Deal" is the subject of an article by Leonard Dinnerstein in the special issue of *American Jewish History* 72 (June 1983) devoted to "The Centennial of Roosevelt's Birth." Years ago, Abraham Cronbach argued that Jews' pioneering role in American social welfare influenced New Deal legislation; see his "Jewish Pioneering in American Social Welfare," *American Jewish Archives* 3 (June 1951), pp. 51–78.

American Jewish literature has a large bibliography of its own. See Ira B. Nadel, *Jewish Writers of North America: A Guide to Information Sources* (1981); Stanley F. Chyet, "American Jewish Literary Productivity: A Selected Bicentennial Bibliography," *Studies in Bibliography and Booklore* 2 (1975–1976), pp. 5–24; and Jackson R. Bryer's checklist in I. Malin (ed.), *Contemporary American Jewish Literature* (1973). Book-length surveys include Louis Harap, *The Image of the Jew in American Literature: From Early Republic to Mass Immigration* (1974), which covers the early literature and ends with Abraham Cahan; Leslie A. Fiedler, *To The Gentiles* (1972); Alan Guttmann, *The Jewish Writer in America* (1971); Irving Malin, *Jews and Americans* (1965); and Samuel Girgus, *The New Covenant* (1984). For Irving Howe's stimulating interpretation, see the introduction to his *Jewish-American Stories* (1977).

PART FIVE

THE HOLOCAUST AND BEYOND

Three major developments shaped American Jewish life in the decades following World War II. The first, the Holocaust—the mass murder of six million Jews by the Nazis—had the most immediate effect. With European centers of Judaism destroyed, America remained the only major culturally vibrant Jewish center left in the Diaspora. As a result, smaller Jewish communities in Europe and around the world turned increasingly to American Jewry for guidance and support. Thousands of Jewish refugees likewise turned to America, and under more liberal immigration procedures many gained admission. Within a few years, some had contributed in vital ways to American cultural, scientific, and intellectual life. Others, especially Hungarian and Hassidic Jews, added fresh dimensions to American Judaism, and helped to promote Orthodoxy's postwar revitalization.

The second major development to have an impact on American Jewish life came in 1948 with the creation of the State of Israel. Before long, support for Israel became a fundamental tenet of American Jewish life, the main focus of American Jewish charities, and a basic standard by which American Jews judged their political allies. The precise relationship between American Jews and Israel remained ill-defined, particularly as Israel emerged as an independent center of worldwide Jewish life. Still, the two Jewish communities came to share and experience a growing emotional feeling of interdependence—perennial disagreements notwithstanding.

The final development that changed postwar Jewish life was the spectacular rise of American Jews to positions of authority and respect within the general American community. Burgeoning economic growth, the postwar decline of anti-Semitism, increasing popular acceptance of religious and cultural pluralism, the high educational achievements of native-born Jews, and an overpowering desire on the part of many Jews to "make it" in America all contributed to this extraordinary success. The result was a community more at home in America than ever before: more self-assured, more confident about expressing its Judaism in public, more willing to use the political arena to fight for issues of communal concern. Jews did, to be sure, still continue to monitor anti-Semitism and to express concern whenever it arose. But they worried far more about assimilation, for as anti-Semitism declined intermarriage rates rose. The question Jews faced as they entered their fourth century on American soil—a perennial question, as we have seen—was how to *balance* assimilation and identity; how to be at home in two worlds, American and Jewish, without having to forsake one for the other.

CHAPTER

17

The word "Holocaust" came to refer to the mass Nazi extermination of six million Jews only in the early 1960s. It was then that the trial of Adolf Eichmann, the writings of Elie Wiesel, and, slightly later, Arthur Morse's bestseller, While Six Million Died, brought home to many just how awesome the effects of the catastrophe had been, and how many unresolved questions it left in its wake. Since that time, the Holocaust in all its dimensions has been closely studied, and volumes concerned with the subject have multiplied. But some of the most sensitive questions relating to the Holocaust remain unanswered. They are still passionately debated today.

From the point of view of American Jewish history one critical question stands out: Could American Jewry have done more to save their brethren in need? Many say yes. They blame Jewish leaders for doing too little too late, argue that American Jews generally should have applied greater pressure on the government, and point accusingly at missed opportunities—actions that if taken might have made a difference. Their bill of indictment is a long one, and includes some of American Jewry's best respected leaders.

But there is also another side to the question, ably argued here by Henry L. Feingold, one of the foremost scholars in the Holocaust field. He concludes—sadly—that given the realities of the day much more could not have been done. America's highest priority was to win the war; that, President Roosevelt argued, was the best way to rescue Jews. As for admitting Jewish refugees outside the normal quota, nativist feelings ran so high that even a bill to admit refugee children failed to pass the Congress. Efforts to admit hundreds of thousands of Jews were foredoomed. Of course, Americans failed to fully appreciate what the Final Solution meant. Even those who did read about it in their newspapers could not have comprehended it; nothing on such a scale had ever happened before. While Feingold agrees that Jewish leaders might have been more united, and probably put too much faith in the President's goodwill, he points out that they could hardly have opposed the President in wartime, even if they had wanted to. The lesson he draws is clear: American Jews, indeed Jews everywhere in the Diaspora, were far less powerful than they or their enemies believed.

Who Shall Bear Guilt
for the Holocaust?
The Human Dilemma
(1979)

Henry L. Feingold

A simple searing truth emerges from the vast body of research and writing on the Holocaust. It is that European Jewry was ground to dust between the twin millstones of a murderous Nazi intent and a callous Allied indifference. It is a truth with which the living seem unable to come to terms. Historians expect that as time moves us away from a cataclysmic event our passions will subside and our historical judgment of it will mellow. But that tempered judgment is hardly in evidence in the historical examination of the Holocaust. Instead, time has merely produced a longer list of what might have been done and an indictment that grows more damning. There are after all six million pieces of evidence to demonstrate that the world did not do enough. Can anything more be said?

Given that emotionally charged context, it seems at the least foolhardy and at the most blasphemous to question whether the characterization of the Holocaust's witnesses as callously indifferent does full justice to the historical reality of their posture during those bitter years. There is a strange disjuncture in the emerging history of the witnesses. Researchers pile fact upon fact to show that they did almost nothing to save Jewish lives. And yet if the key decision makers could speak today they would be puzzled by the indictment, since they rarely thought about Jews at all. Roosevelt might admit to some weakness at Yalta, and Churchill might admit that the Italian campaign was a mistake. But if they recalled Auschwitz at all it would probably be vague in their memories.

Historical research in the area of the Holocaust is beset with problems of no ordinary kind. It seems as if the memory of that man-made catastrophe is as deadly to the spirit of scholarship as was the actual experience to those who underwent its agony. The answers we are receiving are so muddled. The perpetrators have been found to be at once incredibly demonic but also banal. The suspicion that the victims were less than courageous, that they supposedly went "like sheep to the slaughter," has produced a minor myth about heroic resistance in the Warsaw ghetto and the forests of eastern Europe to prove that it wasn't so. Like the resistance apologetic, the indictment against the witnesses is as predictable as it is irresistible.

That is so because in theory, at least, witnessing nations and agencies had choices, and there is ample evidence that the choices made were not dictated by human concern as we think they should have been. In the case of America the charge of indifference is heard most clearly in the work of Arthur Morse, who found the rescue activities of the Roosevelt administration insufficient and filled with duplicity, and Saul Friedman, who allowed his anger to pour over into an indictment of American Jewry and its leadership. One ought not to dismiss such works out of hand. And yet it is necessary to recognize that they are as much cries of pain as they are serious history.

The list of grievances is well known. The Roosevelt administration could have offered a haven between the years 1938 and 1941. Had that been done, had there been more largess, there is some reason to believe that the decision for systematic slaughter taken in Berlin might not have been made or at least might have been delayed. There could have been threats of retribution and other forms of psychological warfare which would have signaled to those in Berlin and in the Nazi satellites that the Final Solution entailed punishment. Recently the question of bombing the concentration camps and the rail lines leading to them has received special attention. The assumption is that physical intercession from the air might have slowed the killing process. American Jewry has been subject to particularly serious charges of not having done enough, of not using its considerable political leverage during the New Deal to help its brethren. Other witnesses also have been judged wanting. Britain imposed a White Paper limiting migration to Palestine in the worst of the refugee crisis, the Pope failed to use his great moral power against the Nazis, the International Red Cross showed little daring in interpreting its role vis-à-vis the persecution of the Jews. The list documenting the witnesses' failure of spirit and mind could be extended; but that would take us away from the core problem faced by the historian dealing with the subject.

He must determine what the possibilities of rescue actually were. Failure cannot be determined until we have some agreement on what was realistically possible. There is little agreement among historians on what these possibilities were, given Nazi fanaticism on the Jewish question. Lucy Dawidowicz, for example, argues compellingly that once the ideological and physical war were merged in the Nazi invasion of Russia in June 1941, the possibilities for rescue were minimal. That, incidentally, was the position also taken by Earl Winterton, who for a time represented Britain on the Intergovernmental Committee, and Breckinridge Long, the undersecretary of state responsible for the potpourri of programs that made up the American rescue effort during the crisis. Other historians, including myself, have pointed out that the Nazi *Gleichshaltung* on the Jewish question was nowhere near so efficient as generally assumed. The war mobilization of their economy, for example, was not achieved until 1944. Opportunities for rescue were present especially during the refugee phase, when the Final Solution had not yet been decided upon and possibilities of bribery and ransom existed. It was the momentum of this initial failure during the refugee phase that carried over into the killing phase.

The point is that in the absence of agreement on possibilities, historians are merely repeating the debate between power holders and rescue advocates which took place during the crisis. The latter group insisted that not enough was being done and the former insisted that the best way to save the Jews was to win the war as quickly as possible. Nothing could be done to interfere with that objective—including, ironically, the rescue of the Jews. When Stephen Wise pointed out that by the time victory came there would be no Jews left in Europe, he exposed what the argument between rescue advocates and their opponents in fact was about. It concerned priorities, and beyond that, the war aims that ordered those priorities. What rescue advocates were asking then, and what the historians of the role of witness are asking today, is: Why was not the Jewish question central to the concern of the witnesses as it was to the Nazis who spoke about it incessantly? But we cannot solve that question of priorities until we have some answer to the question of what World War II was all about, and what role the so-called "Jewish question" played in it.

Clearly, Allied war leaders were wary of accepting the Nazi priority on the Jewish question. The war was not one to save the Jews, and they would not allow war strategy and propaganda to be aimed in that direction. None of the conferences that worked out war aims and strategy—the Argentina meeting which produced the Atlantic Charter (August 1941), the several visits of Churchill to Washington, the Casablanca Conference (January 1943), the Quebec Conference (August 1943), the Moscow Conference (October 1943), the Teheran Conference in November, and finally the Yalta and Potsdam conferences in 1945—had anything to say about the fate of the Jews. The silence was not solely a consequence of the fact that Allied leaders did not remotely fathom the special significance of what was happening to Jews in Nazi concentration camps. Even had they understood, it is doubtful that they would have acknowledged the centrality of the Final Solution. To have done so would have played into Nazi hands and perhaps interfered with a full mobilization for war. Hence Roosevelt's insistence on using a euphemistic vocabulary to handle what Berlin called the Jewish problem. There was distress in the Oval Office when George Rublee, who had unexpectedly negotiated a "Statement of Agreement" with Hjalmar Schacht and Helmut Wohlthat in the spring of 1939, spoke of Jews rather than the "political refugees," the preferred euphemism. The two agencies concerned with Jews, the Intergovernmental Committee for Political Refugees which grew out of the Evian Conference, and the War Refugee Board, carefully avoided the use of the word Jew in their titles. When the American restrictive immigration law was finally circumvented in the spring of 1944 and a handful of refugees were to be interned in Oswego outside the quota system, just as had been done for thousands of suspected Axis agents active in Latin America, Robert Murphy was cautioned to be certain to select a "good mix" from the refugees who had found a precarious haven in North Africa. Undoubtedly what Roosevelt meant was not too many Jews. The crucible of the Jews under the Nazi yoke was effectively concealed behind the camouflage terminology conceived by the Nazi bureaucracy and the Allies. Even today in eastern Europe unwilling-ness persists to recognize the special furor the Nazis reserved for the Jews and the relationship of the Jews to the Holocaust. The Soviet government does not acknowledge that it was Jews who were slaughtered at Babi Yar; and in Poland the Jewish victims have become in death what they were never in life, honored citizens of that nation. In the East it became the Great Patriotic War and in the West it was ultimately dubbed the Great Crusade, never a war to save the Jews. Those who examine the history textbooks continually note with despair that the Holocaust is barely mentioned at all.

The low level of concern about the fate of the Jews had a direct effect in strengthening the hands of those in Berlin responsible for implementing the Final Solution. They became convinced that the democracies secretly agreed with their plan to rid the world of the Jewish scourge. "At bottom," Goebbels wrote in his diary on December 13, 1942, "I believe both the English and the Americans are happy that we are exterminating the Jewish riff-raff." It was not difficult even for those less imaginative than Goebbels to entertain such a fantasy. Each Jew sent to the East meant, in effect, one fewer refugee in need of a haven and succor. Inadvertently the Final Solution was solving a problem for the Allies as well. Nazi propaganda frequently took note in the early years of the war of the reluctance of the receiving nations to welcome Jews. They watched London's policy of curtailing immigration to Palestine, American refusal to receive the number of refugees that might have been legally admit-ted under the quota system, the Pope's silence. Goebbels' impression was after all not so far from the truth. Smull Zygelbojm, the Bundist representa-tive to the Polish Government-in-Exile, came to much the same conclusion shortly before his suicide.

Yet Zygelbojm, who was very close to the crisis, was bedeviled by the dilemma of what to do. He was dismayed by the assumption underlying a request for action that he received from Warsaw in the spring of 1943. The message demanded that Jewish leaders "go to all important English and American agencies. Tell them not to leave until they have obtained guarantees that a way has been decided upon to save the Jews. Let them accept no food or drink, let them die a slow death while the world looks on. This may shake the conscience of the world." "It is utterly impossible," Zygelbojm wrote to a friend, "they would never let me die a slow lingering death. They would simply bring in two policemen and have me dragged away to an institution." The bitter irony was that while Zygelbojm had come to have grave doubts about the existence of a "conscience of the world," his former colleagues in Warsaw, who were aware of the fate that awaited Jews at Treblinka, could still speak of it as if it were a reality.

Once such priorities were in place it proved relatively easy for State Department officers like Breckinridge Long to build what one historian has called a "paper wall"—a series of all but insurmountable administrative regulations to keep Jewish refugees out of America. "We can delay and effectively stop for a temporary period of indefinite length," he informed Adolf A. Berle and James C. Dunn on June 26, 1940, "the number of immigrants into the U.S. We could do this by simply advising our consuls to put every obstacle in the way and resort to various administrative advices [sic] which would postpone and postpone." That is precisely what was done; only in the year 1939 were the relevant quotas filled. During the initial phase the mere existence of strong restrictionist sentiment reinforced by the depression proved sufficient. After the war started, the notion that the Nazis had infiltrated spies into the refugee stream was used. The creation of a veritable security psychosis concerning refugees triggered the creation of a screening procedure so rigid that after June 1940 it was more difficult for a refugee to gain entrance to the neutral United States than to wartime Britain. During the war a similar low priority for the rescue of Jews might be noted in the neutral nations of Latin America and Europe, the Vatican and the International Red Cross. There was no agency of international standing which could press the Jewish case specifically. But that is a well-known story that need not be retold here.

The question is, why did not the witnessing nations and agencies sense that the systematic killing in the death camps by means of production processes developed in the West was at the ideological heart of World War II, and therefore required a response? Why were they unable to fathom that Auschwitz meant more than the mass destruction of European Jewry? It perverted the values at the heart of their own civilization; if allowed to proceed unhampered, it meant that their world would never be the same again. Roosevelt, Churchill, and Pius XII understood that they were locked in mortal combat with an incredibly demonic foe. But as the leaders of World War I sent millions to their death with little idea of the long-range consequences, these leaders never had the moral insight to understand that the destruction of the Jews would also destroy something central to their way of life. Even today few thinkers have made the link between the demoralization and loss of confidence in the West and the chimneys of the death camps. The Holocaust has a relatively low priority in the history texts used in our schools. It is merely another in a long litany of atrocities. Today as yesterday, few understand that a new order of events occurred in Auschwitz, and that our lives can never be the same again.

Yet how could it have been different? If the key decision makers at the time were told what Auschwitz really meant, would it have made a difference? They would have dismissed the notion that they could make decisions on the basis of abstract philosophy even if the long-range continuance of their own nations were at stake. They were concerned with concrete reality, with survival for another day. Until the early months of 1943 it looked to them as if their enterprise would surely fail. And if that happened, what matter abstract notions about the sanctity of life? The sense that *all* life, not merely Jewish life, was in jeopardy may have been less urgently felt in America, which even after Pearl Harbor was geographically removed from the physical destruction wrought by war. In America it was business as usual. What was being done to Jews was a European affair. Roosevelt viewed the admission of refugees in the domestic political context, the only one he really knew and could control to some extent. He understood that the American people would never understand the admission of thousands, perhaps millions, of refugees while "one third of the nation was ill housed, ill fed and ill clad." In case he dared forget, Senator Reynolds, a Democrat from North Carolina in the forefront of the struggle to keep refugees out, was there to remind him, and did so by using the President's own ringing phrases.

That brings us to the most bitter ironies of all concerning the role of America. The Roosevelt administration's inability to move on the refugee front was a classic case of democracy at work, the democracy which American Jewry revered so highly. The American people, including its Jewish component before 1938, did not welcome refugees. So strong was this sentiment that it would have taken an act of extraordinary political courage to thwart the popular will. Had Roosevelt done so there was a good chance, as Rep. Samuel Dickstein, the Jewish chairman of the House Committee on Immigration and Naturalization pointed out, that there would have occurred a congressional reaction of even more restrictive laws in the face of the crisis. Roosevelt was occasionally capable of such political courage, especially on a major issue. Witness his action on the destroyer-bases deal which he implemented by executive order in September 1940. But in the case of refugees, even Jewish refugee children, he chose to be more the fox than the lion. He settled first for a politics of gestures. That is perhaps the key to the mystery of the invitation of thirty-two nations to Evian extended in March 1938 to consider the refugee problem. The invitation was carefully hedged. It stated that the United States would not alter its immigration regulations and did not expect other states to do so. That of course consigned the Evian conference to failure.

Soon the "politics of gestures" became more elaborate. It featured among other things an enthusiasm for mass resettlement schemes. That usually amounted to tucking away a highly urbanized Jewish minority in some tropical equatorial rain forest or desert to "pioneer." The Jews predictably could not muster much passion for it. Resettlement imposed on Jews, whether conceived in Berlin or Washington, they understood as a concealed form of group dissolution, and they would have little to do with it. Thus it was doomed to failure.

By the time Henry Morgenthau, Jr., Roosevelt's secretary of the treasury and perhaps his closest Jewish friend, was enlisted in the rescue effort, it was already late in the game. Morgenthau did succeed in convincing the President to establish the War Refugee Board in January 1944. He prepared a highly secret brief which demonstrated that the State Department had deliberately and consistently sabotaged efforts to rescue Jews. It was a devastating document, and the WRB which it brought into existence did play an important role in saving those Hungarian Jews in Budapest who survived the war. But it was created too late to save the millions.

Similar practical concerns dictated the response of other witnessing nations and agencies. Pressed unwillingly into a life-and-death struggle for survival, British leaders predictably viewed German anti-Jewish depredations within the context of their own national survival. It was a foregone conclusion that in balancing the needs of the Jews against their own need for Arab loyalty and oil should there be a war, the latter would win out. Within that context they were, according to one researcher, more generous to Jewish refugees than the United States. Apparently moral considerations did bother some British leaders after the betrayal of the White Paper. It was partly that which led to the hedged offer of British Guiana for a small resettlement scheme. That colony had been the scene of two prior resettlement failures, and posed many other problems, so that except for some territorialists like Josef Rosen, Jews did not welcome it with enthusiasm and Zionists certainly did not see it as a substitute for Palestine. The indifferent response of Jewish leaders exasperated Sir Herbert Emerson, chairman of the Intergovernmental Refugee Committee. The subtle anti-Semitism in his reaction was not uncommon among middle-echelon bureaucrats in London and Washington: "The trouble with the refugee affair was the trouble with the Jews and most eastern people," he complained in Washington in October 1939. "There was always some other scheme in the background for which they were prepared to sacrifice schemes already in hand."

The problem with assessing the role of the Vatican as witness is made complex by the fact that such power as it had was in the spiritual rather than the temporal realm; and yet the Pope faced a problem of survival which was physical, involving as it did the institution of the Church. Just as we expected the leader who introduced the welfare state in America to demonstrate a special sensitivity to the plight of the Jews, so the Pope, who ostensibly embodied in his person the moral conscience of a good part of the Christian world, was expected to speak out, to use his power. He did not, and it does not require a special study of Church politics to realize that its priorities were ordered by crucial requirements in the temporal rather than the spiritual sphere. During World War II it also sensed that it faced a struggle for mere survival. The Vatican probably possessed more precise information on the actual workings of the Final Solution than did any other state. And while the Pope had none of the divisions Stalin later sought, he had an extensive, brilliantly organized infrastructure which might have been brought into play for rescue work and a voice that had a profound influence with millions in occupied Europe. Yet the Pope remained silent, even while the Jews of Rome were deported "from under his window." That posture contrasted sharply with the activities of certain Dutch and French bishops and some lesser officials like Cardinal Roncalli, later Pope John, who were active in the rescue effort. But these did not bear the responsibility for the survival of the institution of the Church itself.

One need not search out the reason for the Pope's silence in his Germanophilia or in his oversensitivity to the threat the Church faced from the Left. The latter had been demonstrated under the Calles and Cardenas regime in Mexico and during the Civil War in Spain. But observing that the Church genuinely felt the threat of "Godless Communism" is a long way from concluding that therefore Pius XII accepted the Nazis' line that they were the staunchest opponents of a Communist conspiracy which was somehow Jewish in nature. The immediate threat to the Church during the years of the Holocaust emanated from Berlin, and we know today that Hitler did indeed intend to settle matters with the Church after hostilities were over.

The Nazi ideology not only posed a physical threat, but also divided the Catholic flock. Over 42 percent of the SS were Catholic, and many top-ranking Nazi leaders, including Hitler, Himmler, Heydrich, and Eichmann, were at least nominally so. The war itself had placed the Vatican in a delicate position since Catholics fought on both sides. The Pope's primary problem was how to walk that delicate tightrope. The determination not to speak out on Jews, which was at the very center of Nazi cosmology, should be viewed in that light. His choice was not basically different from that of the British in the Middle East or of Roosevelt on refugee policy.

The International Red Cross also thought in terms of its viability as an agency whose effectiveness was based on its ability to maintain a strict neutrality. It faced a legal dilemma, for although the Nazis spoke endlessly about the threat of "international Jewry" the Jews of Germany were legally an "internal" problem during the refugee phase. After the deportation and internment in camps began, their status became even more difficult to define. When Denmark requested the Red Cross to investigate the fate of Danish Jews deported to Theresienstadt, it could do so since the request indicated that Denmark continued to recognize them as Danish citizens. But such requests were not forthcoming from other occupied countries. And the

Danish request set the stage for one of the cruelest hoaxes of the war. The Red Cross delegation which visited Theresienstadt to carry out that charge apparently was totally taken in by the Potemkin village techniques, and gave the "model" camp a clean bill of health even while inmates were starving to death and being deported to Auschwitz behind the facade. Overly sensitive to the fact that it was a voluntary agency whose operation depended on the goodwill of all parties, it did not press with determination the case concerning Jews. Food parcels were not delivered to camps until 1944, nor did it press for a change of classification of certain Jewish inmates to prisoners of war. That tactic, suggested by the World Jewish Congress, might have saved many lives. It was for that reason that Leon Kubowitzki, the leading rescue proponent of the World Jewish Congress, found that "the persistent silence of the Red Cross in the face of various stages of the extermination policy, of which it was well informed, will remain one of the troubling and distressing riddles of the Second World War." Yet here too one can observe how the integrity and well-being of the agency took precedence over the rescue of the Jews. It may well be that the priorities of nations and international agencies are directed first and foremost to their own well-being and cannot readily be transferred for altruistic reasons to a vulnerable minority facing the threat of mass murder.

We come next to a question which embodies at once all the frustrations we feel at the failure of the witnesses and which is for that reason posed with increasing frequency in Holocaust symposia and in publications on the catastrophe. The question of bombing Auschwitz and the rail lines leading to the camp raises the twin problems of assessing the failure of the witnesses and of determining the range of possibilities and their relationship to strategic priorities. The assumption is that interdiction from the air was, in the absence of physical control of the death camps, the best practical way to interrupt the killing process.

A recent article in *Commentary* by Professor David Wyman and another by Roger M. Williams in *Commonweal* demonstrate beyond doubt that by the spring of 1944 the bombing of Auschwitz was feasible. Thousands of Hungarian and Slovakian Jews might have been saved had the American 15th Air Force, stationed in Italy and already bombing the synthetic oil and rubber works not five miles from the gas chambers, been allowed to do so. Moreover, by the fall of 1944 Auschwitz was well within the range of Russian dive bombers. Given that context, the note by Assistant Secretary of the Army John J. McCloy that bombing was of "doubtful efficacy" and the Soviet rejection of the idea are the most horrendously inhuman acts by witnesses during the years of the Holocaust. All that was required was a relatively minor change in the priority assigned to the rescue of Jews.

Yet a perceptive historian cannot long remain unaware of the seductive element in the bombing alternative. All one had to do, it seems, was to destroy the death chambers or the railroad lines leading to them, and the "production" of death would cease or at least be delayed. Things were not that simple. Jewish rescue advocates were late in picking up the signals emanating from Hungary for bombing, and even then there was little unanimity on its effectiveness. It was the World Jewish Congress which transmitted the request for bombing to the Roosevelt administration; but its own agent, A. Leon Kubowitzki, held strong reservations about bombing since he did not want the Jewish inmates of the camps to be the first victims of Allied intercession from the air. There were then and continue to be today genuine doubts that, given German fanaticism on the Jewish question and the technical difficulties involved in precision bombing, bombing the camps could have stopped the killing. The *Einzatsgruppen*, the special killing squads which followed behind German lines after the invasion of Russia, killed greater numbers in shorter order than the camps. The Germans were able to repair rail lines and bridges with remarkable speed. And, of course, Auschwitz was only one of the several camps where organized killing took place.

Most important, the bombing-of-Auschwitz alternative, so highly touted today, does not come to grips with the question of the fear that the Germans would escalate the terror and involve the Allies in a contest in which the Germans held all the cards. In a recent interview, McCloy cited this reason rather than the unwillingness to assign war resources to missions that were not directly involved in winning the war as the reason uppermost in Roosevelt's mind when the bombing alternative was rejected. An almost unnoticed sub-theme in McCloy's August 14 note spoke of the fear that bombing might "provoke even more vindictive action by the Germans." Survivors and rescue advocates might well wonder what "more vindictive action" than Auschwitz was possible. But that views the bombing alternative from the vantage of the Jewish victims—which, as we have seen, is precisely what non-Jewish decision makers could not do, given their different order of priorities and sense of what was possible. The people who conceived of the Final Solution could in fact have escalated terror. They could have staged mass executions of prisoners of war or of hostages in occupied countries or the summary execution of shot-down bomber crews for "war crimes." Their imagination rarely failed when it came to conceiving new forms of terror, nor did they seem to possess such normal moral restraints as one might find in the Allied camp. That was one of the reasons that the Final Solution could be implemented by them.

Nevertheless, one can hardly escape the conclusion that bombing deserved to be tried and might conceivably have saved lives. The failure to do so, however, is best viewed in the larger framework of the bombing question. It began with a collective *démarche* delivered by the governments-in-exile to the Allied high command in December 1942. That request did not ask for the bombing of the camps, but for something called "retaliatory bombing." That notion too was rejected because of the fear of an escalation of terror, and rescue advocates did not pick up the idea until it was all but too late. There is good reason to believe that retaliatory bombing offered even greater hope for rescue than the bombing of the camps themselves.

In 1943, when the death mills of Auschwitz and other death camps ground on relentlessly, bombing was in fact not feasible but retaliatory bombing was. That was the year when the heavy saturation bombing of German cities was in full swing. In one sense the bombing of Hamburg in July 1943 and the savaging of other German cities, including the bombing of Dresden, which many Germans consider a separate war atrocity, make sense today only when considered in the context of the death camps. Albert Speer and our own postwar evaluation of saturation bombing inform us that it had almost no effect on curtailing German war production. Not until one industry, fuel or ball bearings, was target-centered did the Nazi war machine feel the pinch. Yet it might have furnished rescue advocates with an instrument to break through the "wall of silence" which surrounded what was happening to Jews. Even bombing interpreted as retaliatory could have remarkable effects, especially in the satellites. When Miklos Horthy, the Hungarian regent, called a halt to the deportations on July 7, 1944, he did so in part out of fear that Budapest would be subject to more heavy raids, as it had been on June 2. It was the bombing of Budapest, not Auschwitz, that had the desired effect. We know that Goebbels in his perverse way fully expected such a *quid pro quo* and had even taken the precaution of planning a massive counter-atrocity campaign should the Allies make a connection between bombing and the death camps. Himmler also had already made the link. We find him addressing his officers on June 21, 1944, on the great difficulties encountered in implementing the Final Solution. He told the gathered group that if their hearts were ever softened by pity, let them remember that the savage bombing of German cities "was after all organized in the last analysis by the Jews."

Yet the natural link between bombing and the Final Solution made by Nazi leaders was not shared by Allied leadership or by Jewish rescue advocates. Had they done so, it is not inconceivable that the fear of disaffection and the terrible price the Reich was paying might have led more rational-minded leaders in the Nazi hierarchy to a reevaluation of the Final Solution, which was after all a purely ideological goal. Not all Nazis were convinced that the murder of the Jews was worth the ruin of a single German city. We do not know if such a rearrangement of Nazi priorities was possible; the theme of retaliatory bombing was not fully picked up by rescue advocates, and by the time the notion of bombing the camps came to the fore in March 1944, millions of Jews already were in ashes. That is why the twelve-point rescue program which came out of the giant Madison Square Garden protest rally in March 1943 is as startling in its own way as McCloy's later response to the plea to bomb Auschwitz. It was silent on the question of bombing. It seems clear that the researchers into the role of the witnesses in the future will have to place failure of mind next to failure of spirit to account for their inaction during the Holocaust.

I have saved the discussion of the role of American Jewry for the end because it is the most problematic of all. For those who remain convinced that American Jewry failed, how the problem is posed does not really matter, since the answer is always the same. Still, how did it happen that American Jewry—possessing what was perhaps the richest organizational infrastructure of any hyphenate group in America, experienced in projecting pressure on government on behalf of their coreligionists since the Damascus blood libel of 1840, emerging from the depression faster than any other ethnic group, boasting a disproportionate number of influential Jews in Roosevelt's inner circle, and chairing the three major committees in Congress concerned with rescue—despite all this was unable to appreciably move the Roosevelt administration on the rescue question?

Stated in this way, the question provides not the slightest suggestion of the real problem which must be addressed if an adequate history of the role of American Jewry during the Holocaust is ever to emerge. For even if all these assets in the possession of American Jewry were present, one still cannot avoid the conclusion that American Jewry's political power did not match the responsibilities assigned to it by yesterday's rescue advocates and today's historians. We need to know much more about the character and structure of American Jewry during the thirties, the political context of the host culture in which it was compelled to act, and the ability of hyphenate or ethnic groups to influence public policy.

The political and organizational weaknesses of American Jewry during the thirties have been amply documented. It seems clear that the precipitous shift of the mantle of leadership of world Jewry found American Jewry unprepared. A communal base for unified action did not exist. Instead there was fragmentation, lack of coherence in the message projected to policy makers, profound disagreement on what might be done in the face of the crisis, and strife among the leaders of the myriad political and religious factions that constituted the community. It may well be that the assumption of contemporary historians that there existed a single Jewish community held together by a common sense of its history and a desire for joint enterprise is the product of a messianic imagination.

One is hard-pressed to find such a community on the American scene during the thirties. Even those delicate strands that sometimes did allow the "uptown" and "downtown" divisions to act together vanished during the crisis. The issues that caused the disruption stemmed from the crisis and seem appallingly irrelevant today. There was disagreement on the actual nature of the Nazi threat, the efficacy of the anti-Nazi boycott, the creation of a Jewish army, the commonwealth resolution of the Biltmore Conference, the activities of the Peter Bergson group, and the way rescue activities were actually carried out around the periphery of occupied Europe. There was something tragic in the way each separate Jewish constituency was compelled in the absence of a unified front to go to Washington to plead separately for its particular refugee clientele. In 1944 Rabbi Jacob Rosenheim, director of the Vaad Ha-Hatzala, the rescue committee of the Orthodox wing, explained why he found it better to act alone. He observed that the rescue scene "was a dog eat dog world [in which] the interest of religious Jews [is] always menaced by the preponderance of the wealthy and privileged Jewish organizations especially the Agency and the Joint." Clearly for Rosenheim the Nazis were not the only enemy. It did not take long for the unfriendly officials in the State Department to learn about the strife within the community. In 1944 we find Breckinridge Long writing in his diary: "The Jewish organizations are all divided amidst controversies. . . .there is no cohesion nor any sympathetic collaboration [but] . . . rather rivalry, jealousy and antagonism." It was a fairly accurate observation.

Yet one can have doubts whether the administration's rescue policy would have been appreciably changed had the Jews had a Pope, as Roosevelt once wished in a moment of exasperation. In the American historical experience the ability of pressure groups to reorder policy priorities has been fairly circumscribed. The Irish-Americans, perhaps the most politically astute of all hyphenate groups, tried to use American power to "twist the lion's tail" in the nineteenth and twentieth centuries. Yet with all their political talent they were unable to prevent the Anglo-American rapprochement which developed gradually after 1895. During the years before World War I the German-Americans were a larger and more cohesive group than American Jewry during the thirties. Yet they failed to prevent the entrance of America into war against their former fatherland. And adamant opposition of Polish-Americans did not prevent the "Crime of Crimea," the surrender of part of Poland to the Soviet Union at Yalta.

More examples could be cited to establish the fact that hyphenate pressure has not been distinctly successful in pulling foreign policy out of its channels once it has been firmly established that a given policy serves the national interest. Despite the rantings of the former head of the Joint Chiefs of Staff and others, Jews have done no better than other groups in this regard. That it is thought to be otherwise is part of the anti-Semitic imagination, which has always assigned Jews far more power and importance behind the scenes than they possessed. It is one of the great ironies of our time that many Jews share the belief that they possess such secret power. It is a comforting thought for a weak and vulnerable people. It should be apparent to any Jew living in the time-space between Kishinev and Auschwitz that such can hardly be the case. A powerful people does not lose one third of its adherents while the rest of the world looks on.

The charge that American Jewry was indifferent to the survival of its brethren during the Holocaust is not only untrue, but would have been highly uncharacteristic from a historical perspective. Much of American Jewry's organizational resources in the nineteenth and twentieth centuries—the Board of Delegates of American Israelites, the American Jewish Committee, the Joint Distribution Committee and the various philanthropic organizations which preceded it, the American Jewish Congress, the various Zionist organizations and appeals—were structured in relation to Jewish communities and problems abroad. From its colonial beginnings, when American Jewry welcomed "messengers" from Palestine, it has consistently demonstrated a strong attachment to Jewish communities overseas. The Holocaust years did not mark a sudden change in that pattern. A close perusal would indicate that virtually every means of public pressure, from delegations to the White House to giant public demonstrations—techniques later adopted by the civil rights movement—were initially used by American Jewry during the war years to bring their message to American political leaders. They were not terribly effective because leaders were not fully attuned to Jewish objectives, and because the war itself tended to mute the cry of pain of a group trying vainly to convince America that its suffering was inordinate and required special attention.

Given the circumstances, American Jewry seemed bound to fail. Sometimes one is tempted to believe that such was the case with everything related to the Holocaust, including the writing of its history. Those who despair of the role of American Jewry forget that throughout the war years the actual physical control of the scene of the slaughter remained in Nazi hands. Wresting that physical control from them, the most certain means of rescue, required a basic redirecting of war strategy to save the Jews. Even under the best of circumstances, military strategists never would have accepted such restrictions. British historian Bernard Wasserstein, searching through recently declassified British documents, discovered that at one point, as the war drew to a close, Churchill and Eden actually favored a direct military effort to save the Jews. But they did not succeed in breaking through the middle echelons of the bureaucracy and the military command to effect it. That is the reason why the American failure during the refugee phase (1938–1941), and the failure to support the notion of retaliatory bombing and the bombing of the camps and rail lines leading to them looms so large today. Such steps were impossible without a massive redirecting of strategy and without great sacrifice of lives and material. Aside from the possibility of ransoming proposals, which came at the beginning and end of the Holocaust, there seemed to be no other way to rescue appreciable numbers.

Besides the lack of precedent for responding to such a situation, American Jewry was plagued by its inability to get the fact of systematized mass murder believed. Few could fathom that a modern nation with a culture that had produced Goethe, Heine, Bach, and Beethoven, the German *Kulturgebiet* which Jews especially linked to progress and enlightenment, had embarked on such a program. It beggared the imagination. The immense problem of gaining credibility was never solved during the crisis and contributed notably to the failure to activate decision makers to mount a more strenuous rescue effort. The role of the State Department in deliberately attempting to suppress the story of the Final Solution, a now well-known and separate tragedy, made breaking through the credibility barrier even more difficult.

It is in that context that the role of Rabbi Stephen Wise in asking Sumner Welles to confirm the Riegner cable, which contained the first details of the operation of the Final Solution, is best viewed. American Jewish leadership might be accused of ignorance, ineffectiveness, or just sheer lack of stature, as Nahum Goldmann recently observed, but the charge of betrayal is unwarranted and unfair. The contents of the Riegner cable, which spoke of the use of prussic acid and the production of soap from the fat of the cadavers, was so horrendous that to have publicized it without confirmation would have resulted in widening the credibility gap. Middle-echelon State Department officials were not remiss in accusing Jewish leaders of atrocity mongering. In the context of the history of the thirties that charge was far from innocent. The notion that Americans had been skillfully manipulated by British propaganda into entering World War I was common fare in the revisionist history that made its debut in the thirties. A warning that British and Jewish interests were plotting to bring America into World War II had been a major theme in a speech delivered in September 1941 in Des Moines by Charles Lindbergh, a greatly esteemed national folk hero. It was but a small jump for the isolationist-minded American public to believe that it was happening all over again. The neutrality laws passed by Congress in the thirties were based on the same supposition.

Although the delay of several months in publicizing the Riegner report was probably costly, it was necessary to gain credibility. Moreover, a duplicate cable had been forwarded to the British branch of the World Jewish Congress, so that there was little danger that the story could have been permanently suppressed by the State Department. Eventually even the department's attempt to cut off the flow of information at the source was discovered and used to remove its hand from the rescue levers.

The inability to believe the unbelievable was not confined to Washington policymakers. It plagued Jewish leaders who were right on top of the operation and had every reason to believe it. The strategies developed by the Jewish councils in eastern Europe, "rescue through work" and "rescue through bribery," and eventually the surrender of the aged and the infirm in the hope that the Nazis did not intend to liquidate useful Jews, was based on the assumption that the Nazis did not intend to kill *all* the Jews.

Even after the press made public news of the Final Solution, most

Americans, including many Jews, simply did not absorb the fact of what was happening. A poll of Americans in January 1943, when an estimated one million Jews already had been killed, indicated that less than half the population believed that mass murder was occurring. Most thought it was just a rumor. By December 1944, when much more detail was available, the picture had not drastically altered. Seventy-five percent now believed that the Germans had murdered many people in concentration camps. But when asked to estimate how many, most answered one hundred thousand or less. By May 1945, when Americans already had seen pictures of the camps, the median estimate rose to one million, and 85 percent were now able to acknowledge that systematic mass murder had taken place. But the public was oblivious to the fact that the victims were largely Jewish. The inability to understand the immensity of the crime extended to the Jewish observers around the periphery of occupied Europe. They underestimated the number who had lost their lives by a million and a half. The figure of six million was not fully established until the early months of 1946.

The credibility problem was at the very core of the reaction of the witnesses: they could not react to something they did not know or believe. The problem of credibility takes us out of the realm of history. We need to know much more about how such facts enter the public conscience. How does one get people to believe the unbelievable? Rescue advocates did not succeed in solving that problem during those bitter years; and that, in some measure, is at the root of their failure to move governments and rescue agencies. In democracies it requires an aroused public opinion to move governments to action. Without that there is little hope that governments who are naturally reluctant to act would do so.

Thus far no historians have probed the role of Jewish political culture, those assumptions and qualities of style and habit that shape relationships to power and power holders, in accounting for the Jewish response. To be sure there are some untested observations in Raul Hilberg's *The Destruction of European Jewry* and Lucy Dawidowicz's *The War Against the Jews*. But no systematic study of its workings during the Holocaust years has been published. It is such an elusive subject that one can seriously wonder if it can be examined by modern scholarship. Yet it is precisely in that area that one of the keys to our conundrum regarding the Jewish response may lie.

Underlying the response of Jewish victims and witnesses at the time is an assumption about the world order so pervasive that we tend to forget that it is there at all. Jews believed then that there existed somewhere in the world, whether in the Oval Office or the Vatican or Downing Street, a spirit of civilization whose moral concern could be mobilized to save the Jews. The failure to arouse and mobilize that concern is the cause of the current despair regarding the role of the Jewish witness, and which leads to the search for betrayers. It is an assumption that continues to hold sway in Jewish political culture, despite the fact that there is little in recent Jewish experience that might confirm the existence of such a force in human affairs.

To some extent that despair is present in most literary works dealing with the Holocaust, especially in the speeches and works of one of the leading spokesmen for the victims, Elie Wiesel. It is a contemporary echo of what the Jewish victims felt before they were forced to enter the gas chambers. Emmanuel Ringelblum and others recorded it in their diaries. They wondered why no one came to their rescue and often assumed that the civilized world would not allow such a thing to happen. It can be heard most clearly in the message sent to Smull Zygelbojm which asked Jewish leaders to starve themselves to death if necessary in order to "shake the conscience of the world." The assumption was and continues to be that there is a "conscience of the world."

American Jewry, no less than others, shared that belief. Most of them were convinced that Roosevelt's welfare state, which reflected their own humanitarian proclivities, was a manifestation of that spirit of concern. That is why they loved him so; after 1936, even while other hyphenates began to decline in their political support, American Jewry raised the proportion of its pro-FDR vote to over 90 percent. Yet if they searched for deeds which actually helped their coreligionists, they would have found only rhetoric. That and their support of FDR's domestic program proved sufficient to hold them even after he had passed from the scene.

It may be that the Jewish voter had not resolved in his own mind the problem of possibilities of rescue or even the need for it. He assumed in his private way that the "authorities" were doing all that could be done. American Jewish leaders who were aware of the previous dismal record of government intercession in the Jewish interest nevertheless were hard-pressed for an alternative. They might have recalled how hard Jews had fought for an equal-rights clause in the Roumanian Constitution at the Congress of Berlin in 1878, only to see it almost immediately thwarted by the Roumanian government. They surely were aware that dozens of diplomatic intercessions on behalf of Russian Jews at the turn of the century had come to nothing. Surely they knew that the most successful single effort to bring better treatment for their coreligionists, the abrogation of the Treaty of 1832 with Czarist Russia in 1911, had come to nothing. They might have recalled that when Louis Marshall turned to the Vatican in 1915 with a request that it use its influence to halt the anti-Jewish depredations in Poland, the response had been indifferent. The League of Nations, which many Jews imagined would house the spirit of humanity and even amplify it, had become a dismal failure by the thirties. They must have noted Roosevelt's niggardly response to the refugee crisis and Britain's reneging on the promise contained in the Balfour Declaration. They must have seen how drastically the situation had deteriorated even since World War I. At that time one could at least hint that Berlin would do for Jews what London would not and gain concessions. In short, they could not have failed to understand that for Jews living in the thirties the world had become less secure and benevolent than ever. But living with the knowledge of total vulnerability in an increasingly atavistic world is a reality almost too painful to face. One had to choose sides, and clearly Roosevelt with all his shortcomings was still better than the alternatives. There were in fact no alternatives, not on the domestic political scene and not in the international arena. The truth was that during the years of the Holocaust Jewish communities were caught in the classic condition of powerlessness which by definition means lack of options. That was true of American Jewry as well.

In that context the central assumption of pre-Holocaust Jewish political culture becomes understandable. It was based as much on powerlessness as on residual messianic fervor, or the universalism of democratic socialism which large numbers in the community adhered to. As a general rule it is precisely the weak and vulnerable who call for justice and righteousness in the world. The powerful are more inclined to speak of order and harmony. It is in the interest of the weak to have a caring spirit of civilization intercede for them. That may explain why Jews especially called on a threatened world to be better than it wanted to be.

For American Jewry the notion of benevolence and concern in the world was not totally out of touch with reality. Bereft of specific power, they did in fact make astounding economic and political advances in the eighteenth, nineteenth, and twentieth centuries. Despite occasional setbacks, the idea that progress was possible, even inevitable, was deeply ingrained in American Jewry's historical experience. More than other Jewries who lived in the West, they had to some degree been disarmed by their history so that they never fully understood the signs that all was not well in the secular nation-state system. The most important of these signs was the relative ease with which the nations ordered and accepted the incredible carnage of World War I. That experience contained many of the portents of the Holocaust, including the use of gas and the cheapening of human life. The rise of totalitarian systems in the interwar period which extended further the demeaning of individual human dignity was not part of their experience, so they did not understand what the massive bloodletting in the Soviet Union and the transferring of populations like so many herds of cattle signified. They did not understand that the nation-state was dangerously out of control, that all moral and ethical restraints had vanished and only countervailing power held it in check.

Many Jews still looked to the nations for succor; they sought restraints. "We fell victims to our faith in mankind," writes Alexander Donat, "our belief that humanity had set limits to the degradation and persecution of one's fellow man." The countering facts were of too recent a vintage to seep into their historical consciousness and alter their visions and assumptions about the world in which they lived. Jewish leaders and rank and file blithely disregarded the mounting evidence that states and other forms of human organization, even those like the Holy See, which professed to a humanizing mission through Christian love, were less than ever able to fulfill such a role. The behavioral cues of states came from within and were determined by the need of the organization to survive at all costs. With a few notable exceptions the rescue of Jews during the years of the Holocaust did not fit in with such objectives, and they were allowed to perish like so much excess human cargo on a lifeboat.

The indictment of the witnesses is based on the old assumption that there exists such a spirit of civilization, a sense of humanitarian concern in the world, which could have been mobilized to save Jewish lives during the Holocaust. It indicts the Roosevelt administration, the Vatican, the British government, and all other witnessing nations and agencies for not acting, for not caring, and it reserves a special indignation for American Jewry's failure to mobilize a spirit that did not in fact exist. It is an indictment which cannot produce authentic history. Perhaps that cannot really be written until the pain subsides.

CHAPTER

18

With the terrible destruction of the major European centers of Judaism, America assumed the mantle of Disaspora Jewish leadership. It now stood unrivaled as the largest, richest, and politically most important Jewish community in the world. The State of Israel, created in 1948, served as world Jewry's spiritual homeland. It became the focal point of American Jewish life and philanthropy, and the symbol around which American Jews united. But for years it remained dependent on American Jewry's massive economic and political support. For leadership, American Jews continued to rely on their own resources.

Taking their new responsibilities seriously, and shaken by the mass destruction of Jewish culture in Europe, American Jews worked in the decades following World War II to reinvigorate their country's Jewish culture. They gave money to American Jewish cultural institutions, encouraged the publication of books in English dealing with Jewish themes, and set up programs in Jewish studies at hundreds of American universities. Significantly, some of the most popular courses in Jewish studies at the university level dealt with the Holocaust and the State of Israel. Together, as Jacob Neusner has pointed out, these came to be the "principal components" in the mythic life of American Jews, the symbols used by Jews "to explain to themselves the meaning of their distinctive existence as a group, and of their individual participation in that group."

Yet critical as the Holocaust and the State of Israel have been in shaping postwar American Jewish life, there were in addition ongoing domestic trends that also left their impact. The most important of these, as Deborah Dash Moore points out, was the persistence of ethnicity, the continued feeling on the part of second and third generation American Jews that being Jewish matters, that it is something worth holding onto. Although the New York Jews whom Moore studied felt thoroughly at home in America, had succeeded economically, and faced relatively little anti-Semitism, they did not assimilate in the way that so many had predicted. Instead, they continued to express their Judaism through their life-styles and politics. Even those who maintained only tenuous connections to the synagogue still lived and acted in ways that defined them as Jews, and set them apart—but not too far apart—from their non-Jewish neighbors.

At Home in America

Deborah Dash Moore

In the 1950s second-generation Jews continued to nourish a world of unself-conscious Jewishness in their neighborhoods. They turned to their neighborhoods to translate what Jewishness meant into a livable reality and to their public institutions to give expression to the varied content of Jewish ethnicity. New York Jews experienced a sense of community in their neighborhoods. They felt at home where they lived. Through residential concentration, New York Jews often acquired a psychological attitude of a majority, in a country where they were a small minority. The clustering of thousands of Jews into city neighborhoods made Jewish living comfortable and natural.

Second-generation Jews fit into the urban landscape of their lives, and most third-generation Jews who followed them sought a similar sense of being at home. "Generally the Jew still lives in what are called Jewish neighborhoods—or now, Jewish suburbs," sociologist Herbert Gans observed in 1956. Furthermore, "his best friends are almost certain to be Jewish; and his wife likes to have the children play with other Jewish children wherever possible." Although in the postwar period second-generation Jews left the old neighborhoods of Flatbush for the fresh newness of Forest Hills, or moved up from the Grand Concourse to the hills of Riverdale, they quickly introduced into these areas the visible signs of Jewish ethnic group life. As Jews filled Riverdale's modern apartment buildings, they also tenanted its shops, opening bakeries and butchershops, clothing and book stores, delicatessens and delicacy shops. Yet not all Jews moved at the same speed. Moving to a new apartment or house required a rising income which the elderly did not often possess. Some Jews lingered in the old neighborhoods because they were ideologically committed to Orthodoxy or Yiddish radicalism and they wanted to remain close to their local institutions. The influx of refugees in the 1940s also strengthened these second-generation neighborhoods and contributed to their longevity.

The postwar apartment shortage in New York City pushed Jews into the suburbs of Westchester, Long Island, and New Jersey as well as into new urban neighborhoods. But Jews chose suburbia and home ownership reluctantly. "Of course those Jews who moved into the mass-produced Levittown-type suburbs found that though they lived in separate houses their neighbors were still close by. On the other hand," Marshall Sklare notes perceptively, "there were no hallways or lobbies, as in apartment houses, for chance meetings, no elevators for quick exchanges of gossip and news, no corner luncheonettes for ready sociability, no street life to speak of. For many," he concludes, "the absence of these staples of the Jewish urban scene was a real deprivation." Yet even in the suburbs of Westchester or Long Island, where the signs of ethnicity were homogenized, Jews developed shorthand symbols of their presence. Real estate agents understood the codes. As Sklare points out, they came "to know what to stress in showing a suburban house to a prospective Jewish buyer—comfort, modernization, good schools, and easy access to shopping, transportation, and 'people.' Thus, even when Jews seemingly embrace suburbia, they still look for the urban virtues—convenience, cultural and social opportunities."

The networks of builders and real estate operators, so important in directing Jewish residential dispersion in the 1920s, continued to operate effectively. By word of mouth as well as from advertising, Jews came to know that Trump built solid homes in Brooklyn or in Queens, and that Levitt offered substantial value on Long Island. Similarly "Abraham Kazan, having managed the Amalgamated Co-ops successfully through the depression, played the major role in launching post-war co-ops in the city. The success of these," Glazer and Moynihan point out, "led to other large co-operative developments, which have anchored large groups of middle income citizens to the inner city."

Moving into new neighborhoods, second and third generation Jews participated in the city's expansion following the Second World War. The New York metropolitan district grew to include the surrounding suburban areas, even parts of New Jersey. But the suburban sprawl only spotlighted the centrality of Manhattan. Residence in such formerly exclusive areas as Forest Hills or Riverdale did not erase the old dichotomy between New York and the ethnic neighborhood. The American, cosmopolitan city eluded second-generation Jews and their children. The problem of residential exclusion also remained. Although second and third generation Jews took to the courts for redress more successfully than those who tried in the 1920s, gentlemen's agreements effectively kept Jews out of certain parts of the suburbs.

Yet if the postwar residential dispersion conformed to many of the precedents set by second-generation Jews in the 1920s, it also diverged in some aspects. Unlike the urban growth of Queens, the suburban expansion followed highways rather than subway tracks. The automobile determined the structure of these new suburbs and in the process changed the basis of community. In 1959 sociologist Amitai Etzioni, with one eye on the modern suburbs, reviewed a reissue of Wirth's *The Ghetto*, arguing that "a group can maintain its cultural and social integration and identity" without having a neighborhood locus. Etzioni considered suburban American Jews to be a reference group based upon "a common identity, tradition, values, and consciousness" which is "maintained by communication and activated in limited social situations and core institutions." Etzioni provided an alternative explanation for the persistence of Jewish ethnicity. Looking at the Jewish suburban dispersion, Etzioni concluded that residential contiguity no longer functioned as a factor in maintaining Jewishness. Yet while "private automobiles and telephones make it possible to have greater dispersion than previously," Nathan Kantrowitz shows that few New Yorkers took advantage of this technology to forego residential concentration. Furthermore, residential segregation was characteristic of many ethnic groups in the multiethnic metropolis. If the suburbs changed the structure of Jewish residential concentration, they did not obliterate the fact of segregation. "The history of the Jews in the United States," C. Bezalel Sherman observed in the 1950s (with only a touch of exaggeration) "may be written on the basis of the exchange of one area of compact Jewish settlement for another." Residential concentration, the product of "internal desire and external avoidance," continued to provide the territorial foundation for Jewish ethnic community.

Within the new neighborhoods New York Jews again built institutions. Looking at Queens in 1955, Morris Freedman discovered that "for many Jewish families, settling here seems to have involved a new adventure in Jewishness, expressing itself in formal affiliation, for the first time in their lives, with a Jewish community institution. The most obvious manifestation of this phenomenon," he continued, "is the burgeoning of 'community centers' throughout the borough, especially in the more recently developed areas." Postwar synagogue building eclipsed even the 1920s boom. Million-dollar synagogue centers of modern architectural design attracted attention and comment. Freedman found on Queens Boulevard

> two impressive centers in quick succession: in Rego Park, one of the first fashionable sections of the apartment belt, is a great white building looking somewhat like a bank, with a huge Star of David on one blank wall and flanked by stores; a little farther east is a substantial building, recently completed, reminiscent of a modern college auditorium—plain, high, out-thrust front with rows of steps leading up—which houses the Forest Hills Jewish Center.

Jews appeared to be participating in the widely discussed national religious revival.

To some observers, the bright shiny synagogue centers suggested the final transformation of third-generation Jews into an American religious group. Will Herberg attributed the change to the third generation, the one which wanted to remember all that the second generation tried to forget. According to Herberg, Jewish ethnicity, the bane of second-generation existence, went underground and reeemerged with the third generation as Jewish religion, an American faith. As Marshall Sklare argued, the Jews became a middle-class ethnic church, "a fellowship whose members are differentiated from those belonging to other denominations by virtue of their special *descent* as well as by their doctrines or practices. In America the uniqueness of this type of church," Sklare wrote, "is its articulation of ethnicity and religiosity in a multi-ethnic society where ethnic groups are essentially minority groups, i.e., subordinate to a majority group presumed to be non-ethnic." Especially in the suburbs, synagogues served as ethnic facilities, with religious services often taking a back seat to recreational and educational activities. Increasingly, as all religions became Americanized, they came to share common values.

These analyses of the postwar synagogue center suggest that it did not differ significantly from its earlier model. Third-generation Jews—even more than their parents—established the synagogue center as the key local Jewish institution in the suburbs. The tangle of religion and ethnicity institutionalized in the synagogue center could not be unraveled. And, as attendance figures soon revealed, Jews' participation in worship services still did not come close to approximating the percentages reached by the religious revival in the Christian churches. If third-generation Jews were now members of an American religious faith, they behaved in a most peculiar and unreligious manner. Gans called the Jewish revival " not a return to the observance of traditional Judaism, but a manifestation in the main of the new symbolic Judaism." An aspect of Jewish ethnicity, this new version of Jewish religion served "as a symbol for the expression of Jewishness." Third-generation Jews coupled symbolic Judaism with a staunch belief in an American civil religion. Indeed, their civil religious fundamentalism brought them into open conflict with their neighbors over the character of the local public schools.

Second and third generation suburban Jews fought the battle of separation of church and state with renewed vigor in the 1950s. Unlike the inconclusive skirmishes before the war, the struggles to ban prayer and to remove Christmas celebrations from the public schools often passed into the courts, occasionally reaching the Supreme Court. Jewish efforts to purge the public schools of Christian characteristics accompanied a fervent drive to promote faith in American civil religion. Second and third generation Jews often turned into a creed the constitutional clause separating church and state and the parallel article protecting religious freedom. They came to feel that, in Charles Liebman's words, "only separation of church and state assures the existence of religiously neutral areas of life where the Jew can function with his Jewish status as a matter of irrelevance." As the theories of progressive education had supported the efforts of second-generation Jews to legitimate their ethnic separateness and their pluralist vision of American democracy, so the new concept of an American civil religion buttressed Jewish efforts to achieve respect and recognition from public school authorities. Similarly, Jews often accepted Christmas-Chanukah celebrations as a valid compromise, since this synthesis articulated America's supposed Judeo-Christian heritage.

The attempt to gain acceptance from public school authorities paralleled a renewed struggle against discrimination in higher education. Armed with laws prohibiting discrimination in college admissions, New York Jews also pressed for an expanded state university system to accommodate those who flocked to college after the war. In this environment, the idea of a Jewish university reappeared. Under the energetic supervision of Dr. Samuel Belkin, Revel's successor, Yeshiva College further expanded into a university, adding new schools of graduate study as well as a college for women, Stern College. Yeshiva University also founded a medical school, named, ironically, not in honor of a famous Jewish doctor like Moses Maimonides, but for the world renowned physicist Albert Einstein. Unlike the College, the graduate schools were open to Jews and Gentiles alike. Thus Yeshiva University institutionalized a nonsectarian liberal educational ideal friendly to Jews but accessible to Gentiles, a goal which had been articulated by some early supporters of the College. Yeshiva University countered the effects of academic discrimination against Jews and underlined the valuable Jewish contribution to American higher education. It also symbolized the maturing of the second generation and reflected its love of American secular society. The building of this institution of higher learning represented the creative commitment of second-generation American Jews.

Such creative expressions of Jewish ethnicity simultaneously strengthened communal philanthropy. The scope of philanthropy expanded in the postwar era as demands for funds escalated. In the wake of the Holocaust and the tension surrounding the creation of Israel, American Jews mobilized to provide financial assistance to their brethren. The tremendous need for money in turn boosted the prestige of philanthropy and restored its communal influence, even when the fund-raising supported only local organizations, as was the case of New York Federation. During the 1950s New York Federation and the more recently established United Jewish Appeal refused to combine their fund-raising. In maintaining its independence, Federation held on to its pretensions to represent the New York Jewish community, but it also sought to broaden its constituency by establishing a separate neighborhood division for fund-raising. And, as the study of religion became a subject of scientific inquiry divorced from religious profession or practice, Federation inaugurated a department of religious affairs. Thus Federation leaders successfully maintained the primacy of philanthropy as the representative voice of the organized New York Jewish community.

Similarly undaunted by postwar developments, Jewish liberalism continued to reign as the ideology of American Jewish ethnicity. But the Cold War environment eroded the middle ground on which Jewish liberalism stood. The attack on Jewish Communists by organizations within the Jewish world as well as the anti-Communist hysteria provoked by Senator Joseph McCarthy disrupted Jewish radical activities. Although McCarthy and others succeeded in discrediting communism (as socialism had been routed in New York after World War I), they did not break most second-generation Jews' ties to liberalism. Indeed, "McCarthy may have pushed Jews toward the Democratic party." Even ideological liberals like Alex Rose and David Dubinsky held on to their synthesis. In 1944 Rose and Dubinsky created the Liberal Party in New York when they lost control of the American Labor Party. They refused to join the Democrats or the Communists. Similarly, Jewish support for civil liberties, civil rights, the welfare state, and internationalism did not waver. Indeed, many second-generation Jews continued to see their liberal ideology as an expression of their Jewishness. From their American experience, these Jews discovered an apparently integral relationship between Jewishness and liberalism, and on occasion even used the latter to define the former. As the editor of *Commentary* observed, they believed "that the essence of Judaism is the struggle for universal justice and human brotherhood" and asserted "that anyone who fights for this ideal is to that degree more Jewish than a man who merely observes the rituals or identifies himself with the Jewish community." But the dwindling of a radical alternative effectively realigned Jewish liberalism into an ideology associated with the left rather than with a more conservative American alternative to socialism. The new position of Jewish liberalism on the left wing meant that Jews stood farther from the American political consensus as the 1950s progressed. While middle-class American Jewish liberalism developed as a synthesis of Jewish ethnic concerns with the pragmatic tradition of American urban politics, the loyalty of second-generation Jews to liberalism in the years after World War II anchored them to the liberal wing of post–New Deal Democratic politics. In this situation, Jewish support of liberalism buttressed Jewish ethnicity in an enduring fashion.

The persistence of Jewish ethnicity after World War II suggests, in Liebman's words, that "the essence of American Jewish identity, the core meaning of Judaism for many American Jews, may very well be their social ties to one another." This pattern of Jewish associationalism "exists independently of other attributes of Jewish identity. It is a pattern found among all types of Jews and in all types of Jewish communities, urban and suburban, wealthy and poor, first-generation and third-generation American." Jewish associationalism, institutionally nurtured by the middle-class urban neighborhoods of New York and supported by occupational concentration, gave birth to varied expressions of Jewish ethnicity. As a group, second-generation Jews

Liebman

"associationalism"

acculturated thoroughly while preserving strong communal boundaries. "Some writers have regarded the flight from the Jewish community as typical for a large part of second-generation Jewry," Gans writes. "However, while many intellectuals may have tried to escape, the great mass of Jews in this country never even considered the possibility. They became middle class almost as a matter of course, assimilating culturally to the majority but continuing to live among Jews without questioning their own Jewishness or its ineluctability." While the synthesis involved the adaptation of American characteristics, the second generation assimilated these middle-class values into its ethnic identity. Indeed, so intensively did second-generation Jews cultivate selected American values that their idiosyncratic American pantheon came to define their new Jewishness. The emergent Jewish culture was organizationally rooted in the fertile structures of New York life.

The appearance of an American Jewish ethnicity with the second generation highlights the important structural basis of Jewish life. Jewish values have never existed as the abstract expressions of a static religion. On the contrary, the dynamic of Jewish values appears in the structural context of community culture itself. Second-generation Jews reconstructed that context through the urban neighborhood. They strengthened the neighborhood's associational patterns with a network of ethnic occupational ties. Such a base supported many ways to be Jewish and sustained diverse expressions of moral community. It nourished individual freedom in the context of rich institutional complexity. Middle-class Jewish ethnicity extended the ideal of a pluralist society as it rewove the web of urban community.

CHAPTER

19

That some now speak of a "golden age" of American Jewish culture comes as something of a surprise. For years, down to World War II, leading European Jews pictured America as a Jewish cultural wilderness, a land barren of creative Jewish expression. Overall achievements, though not absent, were few and far between, and what was produced was rarely American Jewish—it was usually one or the other without any attempt at synthesis.

Only in the postwar decades did Jews emerge in a formidable way on the American cultural scene. Many of America's best-known late twentieth century novels have been written by Jews (Saul Bellow, Bernard Malamud, Norman Mailer, Philip Roth), and Jews have figured disproportionately in the ranks of America's university professors and foremost intellectuals. But whether this evidences an American Jewish culture renaissance or merely American Jews' assimilation into the cultural mainstream remains unclear. While some see a distinctive American Jewish culture aborning, others insist that there exists only a general American culture to which Jews and non-Jews contribute.

In defining American Jewish culture, minimalists look first to language. Anything not written in a Jewish language like Hebrew or Yiddish is to their mind automatically excluded as not truly Jewish. Maximalists, by contrast, include under "American Jewish" anything created by an American of Jewish extraction, whether it has a Jewish theme or not. In between are those who search for certain defining commonalities in American Jewish culture. American Jewish culture to them involves Jewish ideals, the universal application of Jewish experiences, and the employment of what may be seen as a distinctive American Jewish style—shaped by immigration, urbanization, Yiddish culture, and rapid social mobility.

Robert Alter, professor of literature at the University of California at Berkeley, argues here that American Jewish culture, to be true to its name, must display authentic continuity with the Jewish past as well as distinctive American qualities. He finds American Jewish literature wanting since it only articulates "the ambivalences of a confused cultural identity" but never resolves them. The situation is different, he suggests, in the realm of American

Jewish scholarship. There he finds burgeoning evidence of cultural vitality: works of serious Jewish content, informed by Jewish tradition, and distinctively American in methodology, orientation, and mode of expression. Alter refuses to side either with those who see recent decades as a "golden age," or with those who find nothing creative in American Jewish life at all. Instead, he strikes a cautious note, wary of exuberance, but still watching eagerly "to detect at least an occasional glimmering of an American Jewish culture in the making."

The Jew Who Didn't Get Away: On the Possibility of an American Jewish Culture

Robert Alter

Is there an American Jewish culture? The question is nearly imponderable because each of its component terms is so clearly problematic. Let us assume, however daunting the assumption may be, that for this issue culture means high culture rather than the sort of collective behavior studied by the ethnographer (say, Maimonides and the Vilna Gaon rather than bagels and lox); that Jewish implies a relation of authentic continuity with the Jewish past; and that American means distinctively American. Having defined the question in this uncompromising manner, we can readily see that only the last term can be taken with any assurance as an accomplished fact, for there has been no other major Diaspora community in which the Jews have been so completely integrated into the life of the country, where they have felt so much at home, and, therefore, so natural about making the local cultural idiom their own. But the attainment of distinctive American identity is, of course, precisely what casts doubt on the realization of the Jewish component of our question.

    The quandary of a possible Jewish culture in this country is felt most acutely as a linguistic problem, though it is certainly not exhausted by considerations of language. Kafka, contemplating the partly analogous phenomenon of German Jewish writing, stated the matter with characteristic trenchancy in a remarkable letter to Max Brod written in June 1921. The German Jewish writer, he proposed, was inexorably confronted with three impossibilities: "The impossibility of not writing, the impossibility of writing German, the impossibility of writing differently." Some American Jewish writers have been locked into just this three-sided dilemma (and, in what follows, I shall concentrate on prose fiction, where the use of the language is implicated in the representation of social milieu), though it must also be said that for a good many others the dilemma has rather easily dissolved. This latter alternative is more feasible in America than it could have been in Kafka's German-speaking world because in this country the wide-open gates of assimilation do not have a hidden trip-wire inside. An American writer of Jewish extraction can become, let us say, Norman Mailer, making himself heir to the literary legacy of Hemingway, O'Farrell, Dos Passos, cultivating the moral stance and style of the American tough guy and loner, scrupulously avoiding, among all possible self-images (as Mailer would observe at the beginning of *Armies of the Night*) that of the Jewish boy from Brooklyn with the adenoidal voice, suffering from too much mother-love—in other words, being anything but Alexander Portnoy.

There was a time, and perhaps for some American Jews it is not yet over, when many felt that Portnoy and his swarming brood of fictional cousins might be the expression of a distinctive Jewish literary culture in this country. This feeling, I suspect, was all along chiefly a reflection of the need of American Jews to be sustained by the illusion of possessing a culture of their own, as they drifted away from their immigrant origins; and as such it was closely cognate with the nostalgia for the old East Side and the world of the *shtetl*. American Jewish genre fiction is, of course, still being written by the ream today, but for the most part it seems to have slipped to the level of the popular commercial novel, Jewish family sagas being especially prominent in the last few years, and there is not much sense now that it stands high on the agenda of serious American writing. The illusion of a Jewish literary renaissance in America is a phenomenon of the early postwar period, and, with a few minor qualifications, can be set within a span of a dozen years. One might date its beginning from the publication in 1953 of *The Adventures of Augie March*, Saul Bellow's ambitious picaresque novel rooted in the Jewish immigrant milieu of Chicago and proclaiming itself, in the manifesto of its opening sentence, an unabashedly American work ("I am an American, Chicago-born," Augie announces at the very outset). In the new cultural pluralism of the postwar years, that manifesto was readily accepted: *Augie March* was given the National Book Award for Fiction and was thought by many to have inaugurated a new era in the American novel. By the end of the 1950s, the output of prestigious Jewish fiction had built to a crescendo: In 1958, Bernard Malamud's striking collection of stories, *The Magic Barrel*, was published; in 1959, Philip Roth's first volume of fiction, *Goodbye, Columbus*, appeared; and almost as though such honors from the American literary world were to be expected as a matter of course, each was accorded the National Book Award for Fiction. I would place the peak of this whole vogue in 1964, which saw the publication of Bellow's *Herzog* (once again, a winner of the National Book Award) and the softcover reissue of Henry Roth's *Call It Sleep*, a masterpiece largely neglected for thirty years and now a paperback best-seller, proclaimed a great American novel on the front page of the *New York Times Book Review*. After the mid-sixties, the movement gradually ebbed, and while Jewish genre writing continues to be written, it no longer seems, as I have said, to be the central impulse in American letters that it once appeared to some observers.

Interestingly, some American Jewish writing after that false springtime from the 1950s through the early 1960s has turned to sober self-reflection on the nature of this sort of literature and the kind of cultural predicament it embodies. Perhaps the single most instructive document in this regard is Philip Roth's short novel, *The Ghost Writer* (1979), not so much for its success as a piece of fiction (I find it rather schematic) but for the critical argument it makes. Though *The Ghost Writer* is not, strictly speaking, a *roman à clef,* Roth does try to delineate the range of possibilities of American Jewish fiction by offering us fictitious extrapolations of its holy trinity: Bellow, Malamud, and Roth himself. The narrator, Nathan Zuckerman, a character who first appeared in *My Life As a Man* (1974), is patently a stand-in for the young Philip Roth. Felix Abravanel, a writer who does not actually appear in the novel but who is repeatedly mentioned, would seem to be the Bellow figure here (perhaps with a touch of Mailer)—churning with energy and extravagant egotism, flaunting his parade of wives and his alimony woes, creating passionate larger-than-life characters that recall the exuberance of Isaac Babel's Odessa stories. The central literary figure in the book is the short-story writer E. I. Lonoff, to whose rural New England home the young Zuckerman comes as a worshipful disciple. Lonoff is transparently projected out of the life and work of Bernard Malamud. Here, for example, are some characteristic remarks by Zuckerman about his own perception of Lonoff's fiction:

> I first came upon Lonoff's thwarted, secretive, imprisoned souls, and realized that out of everything humbling from which my own striving, troubled father had labored to elevate us all, a literature of such dour wit and poignancy could be shamelessly conceived.

And Zuckerman, the bright English major, goes on to cite his own celebration of Lonoff in a senior essay which spoke of Lonoff's

> vaudevillian's feel for legend and landscape . . . his "translated" English to lend a mildly ironic flavor to even the most commonplace expression; . . . his cryptic, muted, dreamy resonance.

But why should Lonoff-Malamud be a Jewish writer at all? the narrator is led to wonder, and this question leads us to the heart of the larger issue we are trying to understand. Though there may be odd little echoes of Yiddish in his prose, he writes, after all, in American English, is thought of (in the period in which the story is set, the late 1950s) as an important new presence in American literature, and he lives in the New England woods with his gentile wife and his fair-haired children. "I think of you," Zuckerman-Roth, oppressed by the parochialism of his own Jewish upbringing, tells Lonoff-Malamud, "as the Jew who got away." And yet, as the narrator recognizes, a

Lonoff story without a Jew is unthinkable, and somehow, for all his absorp-tion into the American landscape, the tonalities of his work remain stub-bornly Jewish. Lonoff might ideally like to simplify matters by putting Jewish origins entirely behind him—one could cite the actual instances of Malamud's first novel, *The Natural*, set in the world of the great American game, and Roth's own facsimile Wasp novel, *When She Was Good*—but no writer can sever himself with such surgical neatness from his own formative past; and, so, Lonoff quite properly responds to Zuckerman: "Well, the Jew who got away didn't get away altogether."

Now, for Kafka, with whom I began, this amphibian character of the Jewish writer is an intolerable predicament, an "impossibility," as he says, but what is noteworthy about Roth's novel is that it tries to convert the predica-ment into a positive virtue. I can recall no other work of American Jewish fiction that makes such a strenuous effort to validate its own enterprise by establishing a literary tradition for it. Unfortunately, there happen to be only two European Jewish fiction writers in non-Jewish languages of unquestion-ably major structure, Kafka and Babel; so Roth must make a great deal of them as forebears and models for his Lonoff-Malamud, adding Chekhov, Gogol, and a general sense of East European literary modes which the American Jewish writer of East European immigrant background is supposed to possess and assimilate artistically in order to shape his special contribution to American literature. All this is rather touching as a writer's confession of his need for a distinctive cultural context, but it is not very convincing as literary history. To state matters bluntly in the case of the real Malamud, as a writer he is really a gifted eccentric who, early on, invented a narrow but brilliant mode of short fiction peculiar to himself, connected only in the most tenuous way either with Jewish experience or with European literature; and having exhausted that limited vein, he has been floundering for nearly two decades. The fictional Lonoff, of course, is not obliged to jibe in all respects with the actual Malamud, but the disparity between what is claimed for the former and the actuality of the latter suggests how much the ideal of an international modern Jewish literary tradition in Western languages is an alluring fantasy and no more.

Perhaps the central fact about American Jewish fiction is that it is an expression of Jews in transition (we should not forget Kafka's three impos-sibilities), and by virtue of that problematic fact it cannot really meet our test of authentic Jewishness or powerful high culture. Indeed, I would argue that some of the best pieces of fiction by American Jewish writers have served mainly to articulate the ambivalences of a confused cultural identity, or the reflex of guilt in the transition from one identity to another. This is, let me hasten to add, an important function for imaginative literature to perform—not only for the writer confessionally, on behalf of himself, but for large numbers of his readers, who, whether consciously or not, find in the fiction a potent speaking image of their own unsettled and unsettling conflicts. The exploration of ambivalent identity, however, does not uncover firm enough or deep enough ground for the creation of what we would like to think of as a culture.

Let me briefly illustrate this use of fiction as a vehicle for ventilating ambivalence from the early and widely read work of Roth and Malamud, for I think that the imagination of ambivalence is what really connects them and other Jewish writers rather than any modern Jewish literary tradition. The most striking paradigm for this kind of fiction is provided by Roth's story, "Eli the Fanatic." Eli, it will be recalled, a successful young lawyer in a highly assimilated suburban Jewish community, is given the task of diplomatically asking a yeshiva which has invaded the genteel town to move to a more appropriate neighborhood. The black-garbed yeshiva teacher in the story is a concentration-camp survivor who, it is intimated, has been castrated by the Nazis. When Eli encounters stubborn resistance from the yeshiva, he gets the notion of at least making the intruders less offensive to the American eye by putting them in modern dress, and so he sends one of his Brooks Brothers suits for the teacher to wear. Then he finds a cardboard box at his back door with the teacher's clothes sent him in exchange, exuding a terrible, oppressive dank blackness which is also somehow alluring. The neurotic Eli discovers he cannot resist that allure, and he dons the whole black outfit, not even omitting the *arba kanfos*, the fringed ritual undergarment, and he goes marching down the main street of Woodenton to the hospital where his wife is giving birth to a son. Obviously, a chief element of the pressure of guilt that impels him to this bizarre act is that he must assume the role of Jewish father in place of the sterilized refugee. Throughout the story, the relationship between the yeshiva types and Eli and his friends has been defined as a relationship between Jew and other: when Eli first steps outside his house in the black suit, a neighbor frantically phones to say, "Eli, there's a Jew at your door," and he tries to explain, *"That's me."* It hardly needs to be said that the exchange of clothing is an exchange of identities. The only thing that links American Eli, the comfortable denizen of postwar suburbia, to the Jew from the ancestral world is Eli's sense of guilt over his own affluent assimilation, over his not having been a victim. This is no basis for identity, only for a frantic gesture of sheer craziness: I can remain an American, or I can renounce my American world and swathe myself in patriarchal blackness, become the other who is the Jew. There is no middle ground.

Malamud, in his own fashion, has written exactly the same story, or at any rate a story that has the same thematic substructure, even using the same central symbol. I have in mind "The Last Mohican," where the American art student Fidelman, newly arrived in Rome to write his dissertation, is confronted by another sort of Old World Jew and Holocaust survivor, the professional *schnorrer* Susskind. Not satisfied with a mere handout, Susskind wants

Fidelman to give him his second suit. When the American indignantly refuses, Susskind steals his research notes, and the outraged Fidelman begins a
frantic search for him all over Rome. At the very end, after a dream in which
Fidelman sees a Giotto painting of Saint Francis giving his robe to a poor
knight, the art student goes chasing after the refugee, who still eludes him.
Fidelman is last heard shouting, "The suit is yours. All is forgiven." This is
not, I would say, a story about the importance of charity, as the invocation of
the model of Saint Francis might lead one to believe, but, more essentially, a
story about the ambiguities of Jewish solidarity in a world after Hitler, about
the tight and narrow nexus of guilt that connects the comfortable American
with the European survivor. Fidelman never manages to give his suit to
Susskind; Eli effects an exchange of garments and by so doing yields to an
episode of madness; in both cases, the fiction is devoted to tracing the squirm
of ambivalence between two thoroughly incompatible identities, one of which
has actually been rejected by the writer except as a hypothesis to play out in
the story.

Elsewhere, Malamud has invented other situations to express the same
dilemma: "The Lady of the Lake," where the American hiding his Jewish
identity falls in love with a supposed Italian noblewoman, who turns out to
be a concentration-camp survivor and who rejects him because she thinks he
is a Gentile; "The Jewbird," a fantasy where a Yiddish-accented bird visitor
with the smell of herring on his breath is finally cast out to die in the wintry
cold because his vulgar presence is felt to be intrusive by the American Jewish
paterfamilias. (This, of course, is once again the plot of "Eli the Fanatic" with a
different ending.) And *The Ghost Writer* itself tries to engage the guilty ambivalences of the American Jew after the European genocide in still another
way through Zuckerman's fantasy of meeting the real Anne Frank and at last
justifying himself in the eyes of his censorious Jewish readers by joining his
destiny with hers.

I would like to propose as a limiting case in this general use of American
Jewish fiction as an instrument for the expression of conflicts in identity
Cynthia Ozick's brilliant novella, *Envy; or, Yiddish in America* (1969). It is a story
that has, as I shall try to explain, resonances lacking in the Roth and Malamud
pieces we have been considering, but, finally, it is controlled by the same
problematic. Like *The Ghost Writer,* it is a self-reflexive fiction that extrapolates
from the actual careers of well-known writers in order to ponder the possibilities of Jewish culture in this country. In this case, as most readers
recognized at once, the writers in question are Yiddish: Ostrover, the spec-
tacularly successful novelist whose work is full of sex and demons obviously
corresponding to I. B. Singer, and the envious neglected poet Edelshtein,
from whose point of view the story is told, corresponding to Yakov Glatstein.
There is something inspired in the way Cynthia Ozick invents, out of the
careers of Singer and Glatstein, a painful confrontation of opposite literary

and cultural alternatives (indeed, nothing else she has written goes this deep). Ostrover, in the story, is a cruel egotist and a shameless trickster in life and in art, but it is also intimated that he has genius, a sort of genius happily perceptible through the veil of translation and also in tune with modern sensibilities. His extraordinary success, however repugnant to the rest of the Yiddish world, is finally justified by real achievement. There has been some debate among readers as to whether Edelshtein is equally to be thought of as a great poet or, rather, as a self-deluded second-rater merely envious of a more popular and more gifted rival. I would conclude that we are clearly meant to assume greatness in Edelshtein, not only because of the allusion to Glatstein (surely a major modern poet) but also because of the power of his culminating interior monologues, the evidence of his poetry briefly quoted in the story (which is as good as Cynthia Ozick can make it), and because a central thematic tension would disappear if he were a poet without talent.

Edelshtein, the rancorous old man hungering to be known through translation by the great world, becomes emblematic of the fate of indigenous Jewish culture, which may be subtle and profound and vibrant in its use of its own distinctive idiom, but which, in relation to the vast mainstream of global culture, is doomed to be a tiny rivulet trickling off into the backwaters of oblivion. Edelshtein's trenchant verdict on the new American Jewish writers may be all too justified—"Spawned in America, pogroms a rumor, *mamaloshen* a stranger, history a vacuum"—but it is they, and by an accident of cultural fashion, Ostrover, who are read, not he.

The tension, then, between the acclaimed Ostrover and the unsung Edelshtein is a poignant and historically suggestive one, and there is no counterpart for it in the work of Roth, Malamud, and the more typical American Jewish writers, who tend, as we have seen, to imagine the unassimilated Jewish cultural community as a monolith of otherness without internal conflicts and divergent possibilities. There is, however, a second line of thematic tension in *Envy* which brings it close to the paradigm of "Eli the Fanatic." Between Ostrover and Edelshtein stands Hannah, an American-born girl majoring in English at Barnard who happens to have learned Yiddish from her grandfather. She is one of the drove of translators enlisted by Ostrover, and on the terrible winter night when the story takes place, Edelshtein is consumed by the fantasy that she can be persuaded to become his translator and so convey his achievement to the great world. When importuned by the poet at the end of the story, she responds with a furious tirade, denouncing the Yiddishists as a swarm of parasitic old men, obsessed with suffering, whom she would like to see die and leave her in peace to enjoy the breadth and liveliness of modern Western culture. (The story, it should be noted, continually associates Jewishness, as much American Jewish fiction has done, with oppressive images of old age—decrepit, sagging, hairy bodies, aches and wheezes, dressers crowded with unguents and medications.) This resentful side of Hannah's ambivalence brings us back, more or less, to the expulsion of the Jewbird, to Eli's attempted exorcism of the black-suited yeshiva bunch. More or less, because there is a significant element of "more" that is worth noting.

The Jew from the ancestral world here is not merely a dybbuk from the past pursuing the ambivalent American but a figure given its own reverberant voice. Just before the end of the story, Edelshtein, brooding over Hannah's eagerness to be part of a larger history, suddenly proposes to himself the idea of viewing the issue of particularism and universalism from the other end of the telescope, mindful of the three thousand continuous years of vision and turmoil and national greatness that the Jews carry with them:

> I'm at home only in a prison, history is my prison, the ravine [at Babi Yar] my house—only listen—suppose it turns out that the destiny of the Jews is vast, open, eternal, and that Western Civilization is meant to dwindle, shrivel, shrink into the ghetto of the world—what of history then?

This is, I would imagine, as far as one can go in using fiction as a means of articulating the ambivalence of the American Jew's cultural identity. It goes farther than Malamud, Roth, and others because there is an informed sense that the ancestral world has its own powerful claims to make, is more than a mere projection of the vaguely and intermittently guilty consciousness of the assimilated American Jew. But this remains a story about living between two or three impossibilities. Elsewhere, in a moment of unguarded and rather fanciful optimism, Cynthia Ozick has entertained the notion that American Jewish writers might be in the process of creating a "new Yiddish" in their work—a language drawn from American as Yiddish once was drawn from German but infused with Jewish specificity in its nuances of feeling, its range of idioms, images, and syntactic maneuvers. In the past, of course, Jews could create a Yiddish because they possessed a language of their own, Hebrew, with which they were able to interweave and refashion the Germanic borrowings, but this is hardly the case for most American Jews. The literary evidence, moveover, points rather toward an impulse of assimilation into the larger American tradition. American Jewish writing, including Cynthia Ozick's own, seems largely a phenomenon of transition, and in that regard we would do well to note another characterization of this sort of phenomenon by Kafka—it is one of his disturbing animal images—in the letter to Max Brod from which I quoted earlier:

> Most young Jews who began to write German wanted to leave Jewishness behind them. . . .But with their posterior legs they were still glued to their fathers' Jewishness and with their waving anterior legs they found no new ground. The ensuing despair became their inspiration.

Perhaps one or two modifications should be made to adapt this disquieting image to the American situation. Given the general differentness of the American Diaspora, given especially the recent American openness to the voices of minority cultures, the straddling four-legged beast seems often to feel not despair but a kind of antic exuberance in its awkward sprawl between two cultures, one a memory, an idea, recurrent twinge of guilt, the other a reality, and therefore, finally solid ground to set foot on.

If I appear to have been painting a rather gloomy picture, that is only because in some quarters of the American Jewish community since the Second World War there have been unreasonable expectations of what a literature written in the English language on this continent might do for the Jews—expectations, it should be said, neither shared nor encouraged by very many of the writers. From a historical viewpoint, it is important to keep in mind that though Jews have lived in many very different cultures and have been profoundly influenced by them, they have never created a distinctive imaginative literature except in indigenous Jewish languages. When it comes to writing poetry and fiction, the logic of the literature seems to go along with the logic of the language. If you choose to write in Russian or German or Arabic, the ultimate horizon by which your work is oriented, whatever its Jewish emphases, is the tradition of Russian or German or Arabic literature. Judah Halevi could write *The Kuzari* in Arabic (using Hebrew characters, as was the practice) because in his period one naturally wrote philosophy in Arabic—all the modes of conceptualization were drawn from the Arabic universe of discourse. But when, for example, he wrote his astonishingly beautiful sea poems, it is inconceivable that he could have used any medium but Hebrew: both *The Kuzari* and the poems are powerful expression of Jewish culture, but the latter, as a manifestation of literary culture, required an indigenous language.

The instance of the bilingual writers of medieval Spain may suggest that, in fact, what we ought to be doing is to look elsewhere than at poetry and fiction for signs of a nascent Jewish culture in this country. There is hardly room for blithe optimism on this score, but I myself remain rather hopeful, especially about what has been happening over the last decade, and I point to a perhaps surprising arena that has been showing encouraging signs of Jewish life—the academy. As a matter of historical coincidence, at just about the time when the vogue of American Jewish fiction was peaking in the mid-sixties, a new generation of American-born, American-trained Jewish scholars was beginning to come into its own. By the late 1960s, a serious professional organization had been established, the Association for Jewish Studies, which now has many hundreds of members, an intellectually lively and various annual meeting, and a scholarly journal of its own. More important, mature, and original scholarly work by this native generation has been appearing with growing frequency, work that is free, by the nature of the discourse involved, from the linguistic "impossibilities" observable in belletristic writing, for one does not need the medium of Hebrew or a "new Yiddish" to write a history of rabbinic literature, a study of Jewish thought in the Hellenistic world, an account of the Marranos.

In invoking Jewish scholarship as evidence of cultural vitality, I don't want to seem to be indulging in an illusion I once publicly criticized in others—the illusion that the presence of Jewish studies on American campuses can somehow compensate for the grave deficiencies of the Jewish home and Jewish primary education and can imbue students with a cohesive sense of identity as Jews. I still maintain that the university classroom, as a matter of both principle and of practical fact, is not a place for the forging of ethnic, religious, or national identities, and that the perspective brought to bear on materials there has to be chiefly one of dispassionate analysis, not empassioned commitment. What I have in mind in the present context is not the influence of teachers of Judaica on the young, but rather, the published work of those teachers as products of American Jewish life, as shaping instances of what could be one important facet of a possible Jewish culture in this country. I would like to contemplate, in other words, the sundry studies that have been appearing of biblical literature, the Talmud, medieval Jewish philosophy, the Kabbalah, Hasidism, Zionism, and so forth, as alternatives of original cultural expression to the stories and novels we have up to now been considering.

It might be objected that historical scholarship is, after all, an antiquarian enterprise which has little to do with the contemporary urgency of the more primary creations that make up literature. It is true that, for a long time, a certain musty antiquarianism attached itself to a good deal of Jewish historical research and, in the egregious instance of the nineteenth-century German *Wissenschaft des Judentums*, some scholars were consciously motivated by the desire to give Judaism an honorable burial. All that has dramatically changed in the new generation of American Jewish scholars, as I shall try briefly to explain.

Through the first half of this century, perhaps until as late as the 1960s, Jewish scholarship in this country was characterized by two basic external conditions: with very few and marginal exceptions, its centers were in the Jewish seminaries and, with virtually no exceptions, its practitioners were European-born, usually also European-trained. To reduce this situation to a rough formula: Jewish scholarship in this country was essentially the old *Wissenschaft*, with most of its methods, assumptions, and mental set transplanted to American soil. It is hardly surprising that this sort of scholarship should have had only limited connections with American culture in general or with the distinctive forms of Jewish life that might be emerging in this country. By the end of the 1960s, most of the action had moved from the seminaries to the university campuses and was being carried on by scholars who had grown up in America and received their academic training here. These two changes, in themselves, have resulted in a much fuller interplay between Jewish scholarship and the larger American intellectual realm, and it has been a very productive interplay.

As for the scholars themselves, in virtually every instance I can think of, the decision to devote a career to the rigorous understanding of some aspect of the Jewish historical experience has been directly connected with an existential choice to affirm a cultural identity as a Jew. The typical earlier pattern among Jewish scholars was an Orthodox upbringing, including talmudic training in a traditional yeshiva, which the scholar then carried with him into the Western world of Ph.D.'s and footnoted publications, sometimes maintaining a version of the early Orthodoxy, more often showing rather a kind of intellectual nostalgia for Orthodoxy's world of learning. There are still occasional instances of this pattern among the postwar generation of American Jewish scholars, but it is far more common to find people who were raised in homes whose Jewish character ranged from inconsistent to dilute or vestigial, and who at some early point made a conscious decision to express their Jewishness in a different way from that of their parents, intently studying Jewish tradition, mastering its languages, perhaps adopting a personal observance of it in one fashion or another. Many of these scholars represent, in other words, a new kind of Jew, distinctly made in America. One can detect, in much of their work, however disparate their methods and their topics, an enlivening sense of personal recovery of the Jewish past which is expressed through a bold intellectual recuperation of major texts, figures, and historical eras.

To make this generalization more concrete, let me mention four exemplary publications that have appeared recently—three books and a new journal. The three books are *Tormented Master: A Life of Rabbi Nahman of Bratslav* by Arthur Green (1979), *Introduction to the Code of Maimonides* by Isadore Twersky (1980), and *Judaism: The Evidence of the Mishnah* by Jacob Neusner. The Journal is *Prooftexts*, descriptively subtitled "A Journal of Jewish Literary History," and published by the Johns Hopkins University Press (the books as well, it might be noted, are all published by university presses, not by Jewish houses). The three books in question could scarcely be more different from one another, and the Jewish background and sensibility of the three writers are equally divergent. Green was educated at Brandeis; did his doctorate with Brandeis's senior Jewish historian, Alexander Altmann; was long active in the *havurah* movement; and comes to the academic study of Hasidism out of a personal, albeit non-Orthodox, involvement in Jewish mysticism. Neusner was educated at Harvard, then at the Jewish Theological Seminary and Columbia, and completed his doctorate under the guidance of Morton Smith, Columbia's distinguished historian of early Christianity and Hellenistic Jewry. Twersky, unlike the other two, was reared in a traditionally devout home, the scion of a Hasidic rabbinic line. He has never removed himself from that sphere of pious origins, but at Harvard he became the leading disciple of Harry Wolfson, the eminent expositor of Philo, Spinoza, and medieval Jewish philosophy. Green's biography of Rabbi Nahman is his first book; Neusner's and Twersky's books are culminating works by scholars in their late forties. Yet all three studies share an ability to restore their materials to a dense historical context and to make the internal dynamics of their subjects fully accessible to the modern mind without modernizing distortion. What Twersky says of his own aim could equally be applied to what Green has done with Rabbi Nahman and what Neusner has done with Mishnaic Judaism, however different their respective approaches:

> to extricate Maimonides from the domain of historical anonymity, where his identity is blurred and beclouded and to delineate his individual contours: his methods and achievements, critical attitudes, and traditional convictions.

If scholarly works likes these meet two of our initial specifications—an informed connection with the Jewish past and the seriousness of high culture—do they reflect any noticeable American component as expressions of American Jewish culture? I think it is safe to say that all three, at the very least in the nuances of their formulation and probably in more substantive ways, could have been thought out and written only in America. Even Twersky's book, which is the most traditional in method, being the systematic exposition of one complex work, the *Mishneh Torah*, reflects the orientation of the discipline of intellectual history in which the author was trained, and it is surely revelatory that the first few paragraphs of the preface should cite A. N. Whitehead, Henry James, and René Wellek (the Harvard-Yale connection stands out) as methodological guides for this investigation of a Jewish legal-philosophical text. Green's *Tormented Master* would not have the shape and substance it does without the model of Erik Erikson's *Young Man Luther* and the general American genre of biography. Neusner's discrimination of historical stages in the evolution of the Mishnah and his bold inference of a set of urgent philosophical and historical issues implicit in this mass of concrete legal formulations could not have been achieved without his very American feeling for the unity of historical studies as a discipline and without what he has learned from historians working on topics other than Jewish ones, sometimes in far-removed periods. All three of these books, then, are marked in varying degree and manner by a sense of staking out new territory in the understanding of the Jewish past, with methods and an élan that have American origins.

Finally, I would like to suggest that the excitement of primary discovery which informs these three works is also perceptible on a smaller scale in the first three issues of *Prooftexts*. The journal, though it includes an occasional Israeli contributor, is manifestly a homemade American product. Almost all its editors are Americans in their thirties, one or two even younger, and one senses in virtually all the articles an energetic impulse to seize the great Jewish texts, ancient, medieval, and modern, and to put them in a new, vital focus. Not surprisingly, a few of the articles have been disappointing or even exasperating, but, in three modest-sized issues, *Prooftexts* has already published several really admirable pieces, and altogether it reflects a feeling of intellectual effervescence that one does not readily associate with Jewish learned journals. These sundry readings, moreover, of biblical literature, rabbinic texts, modern Hebrew and Yiddish literature, would not have taken the forms they did without such various local models as the New York critics of the forties and fifties, the New Critics, the Harvard theorists of oral-formulaic poetry, the recent American recensions of structuralist thinking on literature.

These allusive remarks about recent American Jewish scholarhip have been made, not by way of summing up, but in an effort to look around and point forward. The disappearance of the American Jew has been a prediction solemnly intoned for the past several decades, with or without demographic data, and with varying emphases; but I am increasingly impressed by the stubborn insistence of surprising numbers of American Jews about finding ways—sometimes, perhaps rather peculiar ways—to assert themselves as Jews. With such insistence, one ought to be able to detect at least an occasional glimmering of an American Jewish culture in the making. My guess is that such glimmerings will brighten and multiply in several directions over the next decade or two. For the moment, it would be well to remember that the length and breadth of Jewish culture in this country need not be defined by the bleak curve running between *A Mother's Kisses* and *To an Early Grave*, that there are other, perhaps more encouraging directions in which to look.

CHAPTER

20

The experience of the past quarter of a century has confirmed many American Jews in their long-standing belief that "America is different"—in America they can feel secure. There have been moments of doubt, particularly when anti-Semitism has reared up, or when those who call for a "Christian America" have seemed to be gaining ground. But for the most part Jews have been reassured. Anti-Jewish manifestations, whenever they have occurred, have met with widespread condemnation and heartfelt expressions of outrage.

While this Jewish love affair with America continues, the Jewish community itself has been changing—in ways described here by Stephen J. Whitfield of Brandeis University. Whitfield first stresses the shattering impact of the Holocaust on American Jews; before it everything else pales. He also calls attention to the 1967 Six-Day War and its effects (in its wake Jewish political and financial support for Israel soared) as well as to the larger meaning of the American Jewish movement to aid Soviet Jews. Both reveal much about Jewish political effectiveness and about the new Jewish activism of young people, who were formerly alienated from American Jewish life.

More might be said about two other recent trends in the American Jewish community: the turn toward neoconservatism in politics, and the religious awakening that has reinvigorated forces of tradition throughout Jewish life. In both cases American Jews have clearly been influenced by the world around them. Yet as Whitfield points out, the torch of Jewish liberalism, in religion no less than in politics, continues to burn brightly. Feminism has thus made deep inroads in Jewish life, as witnessed by the growing number of Reform and Reconstructionist women rabbis and the recent ordination of the first Conservative woman rabbi. At the same time, Jews as a group continue to support liberal political causes to a far greater extent than do others of their socioeconomic class.

There is one final question that Whitfield confronts, perhaps the most important question of all: Will the American Jewish community survive? Negative assessments are common, but predictions of American Jewry's imminent disappearance have now lasted through several generations. At least to date, the community has shown itself to be far more resilient than its critics ever believed. Yet what of the future? Will conversions to Judaism mitigate future losses from intermarriage? Will the Jewish birthrate increase? Will the current "Jewish awakening" reinvigorate American Judaism and American Jewish identity? Or will assimilation take its inexorable toll, reducing American Jewry to a population of only a few hundred thousand in the twenty-first century? The past offers many lessons, but never a sure single answer. What happens in the future will actually depend on those who shape it.

American Jews: Their Story Continues

(1983)

Stephen J. Whitfield

Ever since Abraham left Ur of the Chaldees, no spot on earth has attracted more of his descendants than the United States. Almost six million Jews currently reside here, making 42 percent of the world Jewry Americans. And yet they are a statistically insignificant minority within the nation, constituting under 2.5 percent of its population. If the impression they have made on the public culture, the economic foundations, and artistic vision of the United States is nevertheless so much greater than a glance at their numbers would warrant, that may be due to the more ancient and tenacious heritage which American Jews are themselves both perpetuating and transforming. How they have done so since 1961 can best be appreciated from the perspectives of both American and Jewish history.

The record of the American experiment in self-government has continued to justify the belief that here, unlike elsewhere in the Diaspora, minority rights and individual liberties would be secure. The hope that America would be different has been strikingly confirmed. If anything, the political system has proven even more receptive since 1961 to the extension of civil rights and to the incessant struggle for a more just society. Although nearly all Americans are Christians, Judaism has been frequently honored as one of the three great faiths; and adherence to it has not only been accepted but publicly celebrated by both Protestants and Catholics. Rabbis are asked to join ministers and priests in blessing or dignifying the rites of popular sovereignty. Earlier fears associated with the specter of "bloc voting" have also evaporated so completely that aspirants to national office need *yarmulkes* for their ethnic rallies almost as much as makeup for their television appearances.

The constitutional prohibition against a religious test for public office has permitted Jews to participate in the nation's service, which has recently included half a dozen seats in the Senate and five times that number in the

284

ica from the seventies of the nineteenth century until the thirties of the twentieth. In an article that he published in *Sinai* in 1859, Einhorn wrote: "German research and knowledge constitute the source of the Jewish Reform idea, and *German* Jewry possesses the mission to gain life and currency for this idea upon American soil." Without it, American Jews might well give up their ceremonial laws and their old customs, but they would do so out of accommodation, not within a principled system that affirmed a modernized Judaism even as it rejected outdated forms. Only German Jews, nurtured on German-Jewish religious thought, could have any conception of Judaism's historical development or its universal character. At least for the present, Einhorn believed the Reform idea still required the German umbilical cord; it was too young in America, too much in ferment to divest itself of its original German shell. Only after the German-Jewish heritage would be fully absorbed could American Jewry seek to be more independent, to substitute the English language for the German, and to embark on its own course. In but one important respect was Einhorn very American: He spoke out on controversial issues—such as slavery—from the pulpit, a venture rarely if ever undertaken by rabbis in Germany in the nineteenth century. Although Einhorn's devotion to the spiritual heritage of the German nation remained undiminished to his final sermon in 1879, his respect for Jewish thinkers in Germany, especially those who called themselves Reformers, had begun to decline precipitously a decade earlier. By the 1870s not just the Americanizers, but he and other Germanists among the radical Reformers were seriously questioning whether Philippson, Geiger, and other German Reformers could still serve as guides for the Jewish religion in America. A revolt was underway and even Einhorn became a part of it.

"A Revolt was underway..."

As the radical Reformers' views on German Jewry soured, they began to approximate those of that most enthusiastically American among the American Jewish Reformers, Isaac Mayer Wise. Bereft of all nostalgia for Europe, Wise did not identify himself actively as a German Jew or encourage others to do so. He consistently took pride in his coreligionists' capacity to acculturate rapidly in America, leaving behind foreign attachments while clinging the more fervently to their inherited identity as Jews. Modernization, in Wise's writing, was associated with America, not Germany. In the United States, Jews faced new challenges which he believed they had not had to deal with abroad. Forced to respond to a throng of propagandizing missionaries and to raucous atheists, the "thoughtless ceremonial Jew" was transformed into the "thinking and enlightened Israelite." As early as the 1850s, American Jewry had already shown its mettle. In 1855, the Cleveland Conference brought together a handful of moderate Reformers and traditionalists to declare their belief in the divine origin of the Bible and in the Talmud as its authoritative

expositor. Wise, who was a participant, immediately insisted that this conference had done more than the German rabbinical assemblies of the 1840s
and the current meetings in Giessen and Wiesbaden. It had defined principles, not just dealt with specific practices. Moreover, the American meeting
had done more good than "the dry historical investigations of [Zacharias]
Frankel's school. The latter, however much we appreciate their scientific
labor, entirely neglect the wants of the time; writing the biographies of the old
Talmudists, they forget the questions of the day and the disunion and dishar-
mony that tears the congregations asunder." As synagogues became more
German in the early 1860s, Wise struggled against the trend. Sarcastically he
wrote, "The Alexandrine Hebrews had a Greek ritual, the Babylonians
adopted the Chaldean, and the American Israelites, in the midst of an English
speaking community, should be German. They call that reform, we call it
retrogression." Yet in those years, even Wise was forced to preach in German
in his Cincinnati congregation at least every other week.

For Wise, Europe represented, above all, oppression. He felt no loyalty
whatever to the Austrian Empire of his origins. In America, Jews preached
upon occasion from Christian pulpits; in 1860, Rabbi Morris Raphall had
opened a session of Congress with a prayer. The equivalent in Germany
would be hard to imagine. What contemporary German culture offered, Wise
held in the seventies, was not religious idealism, but such enemies of religion
as materialism and Darwinism. America, by contrast, had given the Jews
liberty. Here they were free to participate in its great and manifest destiny,
here Jewish religious values could find a fertile soil. The Jewish leadership in
Germany, Wise believed, had failed to appreciate the virtues either of America or of its Jewry. Men like Ludwig Philippson used every occasion to put it
in its place. They could not grasp "the significance of American Jewry for all
Israel."

Let us note that Wise's assessment of the critical attitude shared by the
Jewish leadership in Germany was no exaggeration. Ludwig Philippson expected that the men he recommended for American pulpits and teaching
positions would continue to write appreciative letters. When they did not, he
accused some of "gross ingratitude" and claimed that others were "purposely
seeking to estrange Jews there completely from German Judaism." According
to Philippson, American Jewry could lay no claim to significant religious
creativity. Its entire religious development was "either brought along or
imported from Germany." To argue otherwise was "absurd presumption." It
was the daughter raising herself above her mother to whom she owes everything; it was the self-flattery of insisting "we savages are after all better men."

Zacharias Frankel's position was not so possessive or so crudely stated,
but in its own way it was even more devastating. In an article in his *Mon-
atsschrift*, Frankel related a few facts about the Jewish settlement in America,
but then noted—still in 1863—that beyond this American Jewry really had no

House of Representatives. In the past two decades, they have chaired the Council of Economic Advisors, the Federal Reserve Board, and the National Security Council. Had it not been for a scandal, Abe Fortas would have become the first Jew to serve as chief justice of the United States. The Jewish community was not offended when President Reagan appointed none of its members to his cabinet, nor was any concern felt when several of his predecessors enlisted more than one Jew in their cabinets. That Jewish birth mattered so little was one sign of how fully the American promise of equal opportunity has been fulfilled. Special mention should be made here of Henry Kissinger, whose spectacular career as national security advisor and then secretary of state under Richard Nixon and Gerald Ford seemed to eclipse the reputations of the two Presidents he served. That a foreign-born Jewish intellectual was designated to represent the United States in negotiations with Mao and Brezhnev was unusual enough. But Kissinger captured not only a Nobel Peace Prize but the popular imagination as well; and at one foreign policy breakfast meeting in Chicago, the serving of Special K cereal confirmed his status as a folk hero.

In only one respect did public policy seem to abrogate the promise of equal rights. The principle of affirmative action, by which no citizen could suffer discrimination on account of race, national origin, or sex, was sometimes implemented in a way that was indistinguishable from the establishment of quotas. Many Jewish organizations and communal leaders opposed what they considered a distortion of the aim of ensuring justice in a pluralistic society. But whatever the extent of such preferential hiring practices, the general status of Jews in American society so far appears to have been unaffected.

The hospitality of the public culture to the aspirations of individual Jews and to the practice of Judaism is astonishing enough, in contrast to the melancholy history of earlier Diaspora communities. The extent to which civil rights and liberties have been enlarged in the past two decades should elicit pride as well as gratitude. To an unprecedented degree, Jews have been able to move freely within the wider society, and the opportunity to pursue individual happiness has beckoned as never before. Yet despite the abolition of public discrimination, about three-fourths of American Jews still form their closest friendships with other Jews. The process of acculturation may have blurred distinctions between Jews and their gentile neighbors, but a sense of peoplehood has not been surrendered. Guaranteed freedom of association, American Jews have generally continued to affirm membership in k'lal yisrael (the community of Israel). Even as they have fought for the right to be equal, they have exercised the freedom to be different. The latter trend deserves emphasis.

The American populace has increasingly located itself in urban areas—the Jews, more so. Over 95 percent of American Jewry lives in a city or its immediate surroundings, and four Jews out of every five live in only ten population centers. One out of every three Jews still lives in the New York area, but Los Angeles has replaced Chicago as the second-largest concentration of Jews in the United States. In fact, since more Jews prefer to live in Los Angeles than in Tel Aviv (despite the similarities which satirists have observed), the California city serves as the second-largest Jewish community in the world.

Americans live as comfortably as any people on the planet—the Jews, more so. At the dawn of the twentieth century, according to one government report, the typical Jewish immigrant from Eastern Europe landed with nine dollars. By 1961, that immigrant's children and grandchildren had become firmly entrenched in the middle class. Jews ascended more rapidly into that class than any other immigrant group, and now rank near or above certain Asian-American groups in affluence. Average Jewish incomes exceed those of the Episcopalians and Congregationalists who founded most of the New World colonies over three centuries ago. But deprivation still persists. According to 1973 and 1981 surveys, about 15 percent of New York's Jews lived at or near the poverty level; and figures elsewhere are comparable. But even when most Jews belonged to the working class, they tended to encourage middle-class ambitions among their children, so that even in the garment trade unions Jews are more likely to remain among their leaders than their members. The son of the current president of the International Ladies Garment Workers Union is himself a dress manufacturer.

Many Americans have believed in education as the precondition of status and prosperity—the Jews, more so. American schools have long been noted for their efforts to accommodate the masses. But it would scarcely be possible for more Jews to be attending college than at present, since over six out of every seven of college age can currently be found on campus. The Jew is more likely than his gentile neighbor to hold an advanced degree, and to have entered the professions, one of which is education itself. By 1970, the proportion of Jews serving on university faculties was over three times their percentage of the general population. And the better the reputation of the university, the more likely Jews were teaching there; in the most prestigious institutions of higher learning, 30 percent of the faculty is Jewish. Since 1961 Jews have become presidents of several Ivy League colleges and of other distinguished universities, and they have remained disproportionately represented in the nation's scientific elite.

Americans have continued to dominate the international competition for Nobel Prizes, and Jews have become laureates so frequently it is odd that the feverish anti-Semitic imagination had not located the center of international conspiracy in Stockholm. While continuing to receive honors in the sciences and medicine, Jews have won almost half the total number of Memorial Prizes that Americans have earned in economics. The last two American laureates in literature have been Saul Bellow (1976) and Isaac Bashevis Singer (1978). Since the Second World War, the story of cultural and intellectual life in America would scarcely be intelligible without acknowledging the contributions of Jews in virtually all the arts and perhaps most branches of learning. And while Jews have continued to exert a considerable influence on the national imagination through their roles as entertainers and entrepreneurs in popular culture, a noticeable change has occurred in recent decades. The fresh appreciation of ethnic differences that began in the mid-1960s has included the celebration of Jewish identity in many best-selling novels, in serious analyses of *Yiddishkeit* such as Irving Howe's *World of Our Fathers* (1976), in musicals like *Fiddler on the Roof* (1964), and in films too numerous to mention. No longer would actors and actresses feel obliged to disguise their ethnic origins by altering their surnames; no longer would they wish to emulate the comedian who admitted to have "cut off my nose to spite my race." Indeed the exotic appeal that ethnicity offered to the participants in mass culture seemed even to put the dominant white Anglo-Saxon Protestant group on the defensive.

Nostalgia and sentimentality were not the only responses that the Jewish past evoked, however; and the memory of the most desolate chapter in all of Jewish experience came to the surface. In 1961 the term "Holocaust" was barely, if at all, in circulation; and the catastrophe to which it referred was infrequently mentioned. It was as though a numbing had been inflicted too painful for American Jewry to acknowledge, a wound too deep for language itself to start to heal. But even then that reaction to the murder of most of the Jews of Europe was beginning to be replaced by a more direct and explicit grappling with the nightmare of the Holocaust. Here books were decisive. In 1960 the memoir of a survivor of Auschwitz and Buchenwald was translated from the French, and Elie Wiesel became the best-known and perhaps most articulate witness to attempt to impose his memories and visions of the horror that American Jews had been lucky enough to escape. It was one index of his impact that he later became chairman of a government-sponsored Holocaust Memorial Council. A year after Wiesel's *Night* was published, Raul Hilberg's *The Destruction of the European Jews* became the first major work in English to take scholarly account of the disaster. The memoirs, histories, and fiction that have been published thereafter defy tabulation. They also challenge the capacity of ordinary, decent, common-sensical readers to absorb their message.

But writers were not alone in haunting the consciousness of American Jewry. In 1960 Israeli agents captured Adolf Eichmann in Argentina. The following year the former S.S. lieutenant colonel was put on trial in Jerusalem, and in 1962 a hangman executed the man who had been responsible for transporting the Jews of Nazi-occupied Europe to their deaths. The judicial procedures and revelations not only seared Israeli society but also helped make it possible for the Holocaust to shadow the agenda and the idiom of organized Jewry in the United States. Whether in the curriculum of Jewish education, whether in observance of Yom Hashoah (Holocaust Rembrance Day), whether in forums and symposia and speeches reverberating through the institutional life of American Jewry, the recollection of how over one-third of world Jewry was extinguished has become an inextricable part of the Jewish mentality in the United States.

How deeply this sense of cataclysm has become embedded was revealed in 1967. Early in June the threat posed to Israel by Arab encirclement seemed to call into question once more the capacity of the Jewish people itself to survive, and the Six-Day War tapped fears that once again American Jewry would be unable to help beleaguered brethren to avert a Holocaust. That war was probably a turning point in modern Jewish history, primarily because the stunning victory of the Israel Defense Forces made it possible for Jerusalem to be reunited under Jewish sovereignty, and because the West Bank and Gaza fell under an occupation that still defies a political solution. The war also disclosed how central the welfare of Israel was to the Diaspora. Despite the persistently low levels of American *aliyah* (emigration to Israel) that were a rebuke to classical Zionist ideology, Jews in the United States discovered—perhaps more poignantly than they had realized—how devoted they were to the perpetuation and security of the State of Israel. Support for it has remained the most urgent cause around which American Jewry, for all its disparate tendencies, has rallied.

The 1967 war also inaugurated an outpouring of philanthropic support that was unprecedented in the annals of American Jewish generosity. Sustaining that level of philanthropy has remained the challenge of the fund-raising agencies—and the envy of other American charities. But that challenge has generally been met. The annual budget of the United Jewish Appeal, for example, is one-third the budget of the national United Way (to which Jews of course also contribute). In 1981 the U.J.A. raised $543 million, and in 1982 received pledges of $567 million. Such figures need to be placed in perspective: the U.J.A. raises more money per year than the combined efforts of the American Cancer Society, the American Heart Association, the Muscular Dystrophy Association, the March of Dimes, and the National Easter Seal Society. The reasons for such generosity are too complex to be recorded here. But solicitors who work through the primary agencies of Jewish philanthropy, the federations from 227 communities that constitute the Council of Jewish Federations and Welfare Funds, attribute pride in Israeli accomplishments as an important motivation. American Jewry also freely elects to tax itself to support the young and old, the ill and the needy, under the auspices of social welfare institutions throughout the United States. Many contributors also believe that only viable Jewish institutions can combat anti-Semitic sentiments in the United States, and that—since the terrible ordeal of the Second

World War—American Jewry could not be dormant while brethren were in danger.

Another effect of the Six-Day War was to arouse sentiments of Jewish nationalism within the U.S.S.R. In the aftermath of the Israeli victory, some Jews attempted to dramatize their plight by "hijacking" a plane from Leningrad. They were captured, tried, and convicted in 1970; but they stirred the admiration of other Soviet Jews and troubled the consciences of many American Jews. Pressures within and outside the Soviet Union led its government to relax its grip on Jews seeking to emigrate to Israel and to the West. Since 1970 about 256,000 Soviet Jews have managed to emigrate, although that grip tightened again early in the 1980s.

To varying degrees most American Jewish institutions took an interest in the struggle of Russian coreligionists to emancipate themselves. That interest resonated within the American government itself, with the Jackson-Vanik amendment of 1973–1974 and the Helsinki agreement of 1975 linking the bestowal of most-favored-nation status on the Soviet Union to the relaxation of emigration restrictions. Although Soviet compliance was widely regarded as unsatisfactory by American Jewish activists, such efforts reflected the political effectiveness of a tiny minority whose own position in the United States was so secure that it could devote itself to the assistance of Jewry overseas. Another instance of the capacity of American Jews to communicate their concern was the swap of prisoners in 1979 that demonstrated the commitment of the Carter administration to human rights. The F.B.I. had arrested two Soviet spies operating on American soil. The spies were exchanged not for Americans in Soviet custody but for five Soviet nationals who were political prisoners, including two Jews convicted in the Leningrad trial nine years earlier. For American diplomacy to deem non-American lives as so precious was a pointed contrast to its failures before and during the Holocaust. The episode was nevertheless an inspiring breakthrough for the human rights movement, in which the influence of American Jews has been decisive.

Memory and hope thus conspired to spur the struggle for *pidyon shevuyim* (the release of captives), and the combination of bitter recollections and idealistic moralism is probably the most succinct description of the distinctive political profile of American Jewry. Ever since the emancipation of European Jewry, their hostility to the privileges of church and aristocracy led them to be receptive to the Left, where progressive dreams often seemed a modern version of Prophetic demands for social justice. In the United States the memories of Old World discrimination still lingered. The confrontation of the Roosevelt administration with the unparalleled crisis of American capitalism and with the formidable military threat of the Axis powers attracted the allegiance of up to 90 percent of American Jewry, and most of them have remained liberal Democrats. By the 1960s and 1970s, the original ranks that made up the Roosevelt coalition became depleted. The Jews did not break ranks.

Whatever the future portends, the recent historical evidence is irrefutable. In 1960 the proportion of Jews voting for John F. Kennedy exceeded the proportion of Catholics and equaled the percentage of blacks. In 1964 relatively more Jews voted against Barry Goldwater, the champion of the G.O.P. right wing, than did any other group of whites, regardless of income. In 1968 the percentage of the Jewish vote for Hubert Humphrey could have been mistaken for the turnout of the poorest racial minorities. When George Wallace campaigned outside the South, Jews found his candidacy about as repugnant as blacks did. Even in 1972, while Richard Nixon was winning the support of three-fourths of all residents of high socioeconomic areas, while he was enlisting the loyalty of the majority of all groups of white ethnics, the Jews were again exceptional. They cast two-thirds of their vote for the liberal, Democratic candidate. In fact, if the rest of the electorate had voted the way the Jews did, George McGovern would have triumphed in the greatest landslide in the history of the American presidency. In 1976, had it not been for the black vote, Jimmy Carter would have lost every Southern state except his native Georgia. But he did attract 72 percent of Jewish ballots. In 1980 Ronald Reagan managed to prevent the Democratic candidate for President from winning the majority of Jewish votes. Carter won only a plurality, even as he was decisively beaten in the general election; and when the third-party candidacy of John Anderson is taken into account, the Jews still maintained—though at a considerably low level of enthusiasm—their tradition of liberalism.

Their dedication to liberalism has also incorporated feminism, surely the most pervasive and important of the social and political causes to have erupted in the United States since 1961. If any one book was responsible for igniting the revival of feminism, it was *The Feminine Mystique*, published in 1963 by Betty Friedan (*née* Goldstein). Other women of Jewish birth have been prominent in both the moderate and radical wings of the movement, and have made an incalculable impact upon the very texture of national life. The Jewish world has also been affected. The Reconstructionist seminary accepted women ever since its founding in 1968, and the Reform movement ordained women rabbis beginning with Sally Priesand in 1972. Soon thereafter, the Jewish Theological Seminary voted against the ordination of women as Conservative rabbis, but it later reversed this stance. Women have won increased responsibilities in all the religious movements, including Orthodoxy. Organizations dominated by female volunteers continued to affect Jewish life; Hadassah, for example, remained the largest women's voluntary organization in the United States, period. Here too Israel helped affect attitudes. The contributions of women to its *Kibbutzim* and to its defense forces were part of its international image, and one popular American feminist poster showed Prime Minister Golda Meir above the caption: "But can she type?" According to opinion polls, a man who is Jewish was slightly more likely to have favored passage of the Equal Rights Amendment than a woman who is gentile. As if further proof of the liberalism distinguishing American Jews were needed.

Exercising the freedom to be different has not, oddly enough, irritated bigots, who have remained on the discredited perimeters of the social order. Anti-Semitism has enjoyed no respectable constituency, and has been widely understood to be both undemocratic and un-American. But the disreputable still perpetrated synagogue and cemetery desecrations, and epithets and canards have been publicly uttered. And even though civil rights and defense agencies have learned to assume that their victories may not be permanent, even though many Jews continue to surmise that familiar expressions of anti-Semitism are not only of the past, the very limited scope of such prejudice has been a noteworthy—and praiseworthy—facet of the American scene.

Public opinion polls have also consistently shown a large reservoir of goodwill among gentile Americans toward the State of Israel. Since Anwar Sadat's visit to Jerusalem in 1977, Egypt has been the sole Arab state to galvanize comparable expressions of benevolence and trust. Nevertheless the sharp criticism of Israel voiced in international forums, particularly the United Nations, has vexed and angered so many American Jews that anti-Zionism has appeared a greater menace than traditional versions of anti-Semitism. Indeed, since pro-Israel sentiments are so integral to the political and psychological orientation of American Jewry, anti-Zionism increasingly came to be defined as anti-Semitism. This definition is one clue to the importance that American Jews have continued to attach to the legitimacy and security of the only member of the community of nations whose existence has seemed open to debate. The political attacks upon its sovereignty and viability could not be easily separated from the history of earlier forms of hostility to Jewry, and the most important of Diaspora communities therefore felt a special intimacy and concern for the fate of Israel.

American Jews have historically been far better attuned to the problems of persecution overseas than to the challenge that their own special identity might pose, but even the most benign account of their recent past must be tempered by recognition of a demographic danger. Looming large in the history of the Jewish people, its American component is nevertheless faced with possible depletion of its human resources; and ever since the early 1960s omens about the survival of the community itself have been sounded.

Three factors have commanded attention. American Jewish history could be told in terms of the waves of immigration that have not only washed across the nation itself but have also replenished the life of the community. Only about two thousand Sephardim lived here during the Revolution; and the second wave of German Jews was large enough to check some of the effects of assimilation, even as the far more massive wave of Eastern Europeans performed the same function by the turn of the century. Immigrants from the Soviet Union, Israel, and Latin America also arrived here in the 1960s and 1970s. But they have registered a less resonant impact than their predecessors. The Holocaust devastated the source of further immigration and obliterated precisely those communities where Jewish religious and cultural life was most creative and radiant. American Jewry will therefore be required to perpetuate itself rather than to depend, as in the past, on other Diaspora communities where the forces of secularization and assimilation might be more retarded than here.

The second factor is the birthrate. Jews have been admired for many attributes—their industriousness and their intelligence, their economic skills and their ethical sensitivity. Planned parenthood organizations should also honor them for achieving what amounts to zero population growth in the past couple of decades. However exemplary the practice of limiting children once was in accelerating the ascent from poverty, however similar this practice has been among other families in the middle class, the Jews' efficiency in methods of birth control has instilled fears about group survival itself.

The third factor is the most uncertain, the most problematic, the least susceptible to a policy consensus within the community itself: intermarriage. At the beginning of the twentieth century, the statistical probability that a Jew would wed a Gentile was so low (about 1 percent) that it was only slightly less likely that a white would marry a black. Only in the last two decades however has the increase in intermarriage rates been so dramatic that alarms have been widely voiced. By the early 1980s, in many cities and towns, about one out of every three Jews who chooses a spouse chooses a Gentile. Such rates demonstrate the degree to which Jews have become integrated within the host society, the extent to which accidents of birth have not hampered the national promises of self-fulfillment and the pursuit of happiness and of romantic love. Such high rates may suggest the disappearance of distinctive traits separating Jews from their neighbors—or the opposite, since Jews may be valued in the marriage market because of a reputation for stability and sobriety, for being good providers and good homemakers. But whatever the reasons, many rabbis and other communal leaders have warned that, at present rates, the pool of Jews from which Gentiles can select eligible mates may be destined to disappear. Nor have the rates of conversion to Judaism been high enough to quash such fears.

Can *Look* Magazine therefore be credited with some foresight? In 1964 it published an article ominously entitled "The Vanishing American Jew." Since then, of course, the American Jew has not vanished (although *Look* itself did); and there is comfort in the knowledge that the evidence is not yet in, the precincts have not all reported. Whatever the future holds, American Jews have already made an extraordinary contribution to the enhancement of their

country, and have achieved a synthesis of their citizenship and their peoplehood that must fascinate the student of Jewish history as well. That past is
burdened with ample enough evidence of injustice, pain, and waste, with the
needless suffering and blasted hopes that have proven to be the fate of our
entire species. But human struggles and aspirations have sometimes been
rewarded too, and here the American experience is relevant. That is why
history need not be a source of despair but can also be its antidote.

FOR FURTHER READING

The gnawing problem of America and the Holocaust has attracted a wide range of scholars since Arthur Morse penned his indictment of American policy in *While Six Million Died* (1967). Book-length studies include Henry L. Feingold, *The Politics of Rescue* (1970); David S. Wyman, *Paper Walls: America and the Refugee Crisis 1938–1941* (1971); Saul Friedman, *No Haven for the Oppressed* (1973); Yehuda Bauer, *American Jewry and the Holocaust* (1981); Monty N. Penkower, *The Jews Were Expendable* (1983); and the best of them all, David S. Wyman, *The Abandonment of the Jews* (1984). Sander A. Diamond, *The Nazi Movement in the United States* (1974) and Moshe R. Gottlieb, *American Anti-Nazi Resistance* (1982) cover pro- and anti-Nazi activities in the United States before Pearl Harbor. Robert W. Ross, *So It Was True* (1980) chronicles American Protestant press reactions to Nazi persecutions. Leonard Dinnerstein, *America and the Survivors of the Holocaust* (1982) moves beyond World War II and analyzes postwar attitudes toward Jewish refugees. Leon A. Jick, "The Holocaust: Its Use and Abuse Within the American Public," *Yad Vashem Studies* 14 (1981), pp. 303–318, and Stephen J. Whitfield's "American Jewish Intellectuals and Totalitarianism" and "The Holocaust in the American Jewish Mind" reprinted in his *Voices of Jacob, Hands of Esau* (1984) trace the impact of the Holocaust over the past four decades.

Bernard Martin (ed.), *Movements and Issues in American Judaism* (1978) covers a wide range of developments on the Jewish scene since 1945, arranged both chronologically and topically. Perceptive articles on recent trends can also be found in Oscar I. Janowsky (ed.), *The American Jew: A Reappraisal* (1964); Peter I. Rose (ed.), *The Ghetto and Beyond* (1969); David Sidorsky (ed.), *The Future of the Jewish Community in America* (1973); and Marshall Sklare (ed.), *The Jewish Community in America* (1974) and *The Jew in American Society* (1974). For bibliographical essays covering the major areas of contemporary American Jewish life see Marshall Sklare (ed.), *Understanding American Jewry* (1982). Daniel Elazar analyzes how the American Jewish community operates from a political-science point of view in his path-breaking *Community and Polity* (1976). The single best synthesis of recent American Jewish history and sociology is Chaim I. Waxman's *American Jews in Transition* (1983).

Jewish identity in contemporary America has been examined

from the perspective of social psychology by Simon Herman, *Jewish Identity* (1977), and sociologically by Arnold Dashefsky and Howard Shapiro, *Ethnic Identification Among American Jews* (1974). For a perceptive review of other research see Harold S. Himmelfarb, "Research on American Jewish Identity and Identification: Progress, Pitfalls, and Prospects," in Sklare's *Understanding American Jewry*. Charles S. Liebman, *The Ambivalent American Jew* (1973) and Jacob Neusner, *Stranger at Home* (1981) comment on broader and sometimes contradictory patterns found in contemporary Jewish identities and belief structures. Jonathan D. Sarna, "The Great American Jewish Awakening," *Midstream* 28 (October 1982), pp. 30–34, examines renewed interest in tradition and ritual in American Jewish life.

The impact of the Six-Day War on American Jews was described a year later by Marshall Sklare, "Lakeville and Israel: The Six-Day War and Its Aftermath," *Midstream* 14 (October 1968), and is viewed in the context of subsequent events in Moshe Davis (ed.), *The Yom Kippur War, Israel, and the Jewish People* (1974). For its impact on American Jewish settlement in Israel, see Gerald Engel, "North American Settlers in Israel," *American Jewish Year Book* 71 (1970), pp. 161–187. Israeli immigration to the United States, a more sensitive subject, has been studied by Dov Elizur, "Israelis in the United States: Motives, Attitudes and Intentions," *American Jewish Year Book* 80 (1980), pp. 53–67.

The immigration of Russian Jews to the United States since the Six-Day War forms the subject of Dan N. Jacobs and Ellen F. Paul (eds.), *Studies of the Third Wave* (1981), a collection of the best articles on the subject. For other studies see the *Journal of Jewish Communal Service*. William W. Orbach, *The American Movement to Aid Soviet Jews* (1979) analyzes the movement from the point of view of its meaning for American Jews.

Studies relevant to the changing nature of American Jewish life regularly appear in the annual volumes of the *American Jewish Year Book*. See also Sefton D. Temkin's survey of "Jewish Life in the United States 1972–1982" in *Encyclopaedia Judaica Decennial Book, 1973–1982* (Jerusalem, 1983).

APPENDIX 1

THE GROWTH OF THE AMERICAN JEWISH POPULATION

	Estimated totals (low—high)	Percentage of total population
1660	50	—
1700	200–300	—
1776	1,000–2,500	.04–.10
1790	1,300–3,000	.03–.08
1800	1,600–2,500	.03–.04
1820	2,700–3,000	.03
1830	4,000–6,000	.03–.05
1840	15,000	.09
1850	50,000	.22
1860	125,000–150,000	.40–.48
1880	230,000–280,000	.46–.56
1890	400,000–450,000	.64–.71
1900	938,000–1,058,000	1.23–1.39
1910	1,508,000–2,044,000	1.63–2.22
1920	3,300,000–3,600,000	3.12–3.41
1930	4,228,000–4,400,000	3.44–3.58
1940	4,771,000–4,831,000	3.63–3.68
1950	4,500,000–5,000,000	2.98–3.31
1960	5,367,000–5,531,000	2.99–3.08
1970	5,370,000–6,000,000	2.64–2.95
1980	5,500,000–5,921,000	2.42–2.61

Source: Contemporary and retrospective estimates for nineteenth century; for twentieth century see Jack J. Diamond, "A Reader in Demography," *American Jewish Yearbook* 77 (1977), pp. 251–319, and Abraham J. Karp, *Haven and Home* (New York, 1985), p. 374.

APPENDIX 2

A CENTURY OF JEWISH IMMIGRATION TO THE UNITED STATES

	Total Jewish	Annual average	Jews as percentage of total
1881–1889	204,300	22,700	4.3
1890–1898	366,600	40,700	10.8
1899–1902	214,000	53,500	11.3
1903–1907	615,200	123,000	12.1
1908–1914	656,500	93,800	9.8
1881–1914	2,056,600	60,488	9.4
1915–1919	65,700	13,140	5.6
1920–1924	286,500	57,300	10.3
1925–1929	56,200	11,240	3.7
1930–1934	26,500	5,300	6.2
1935–1939	85,800	17,160	31.5
1940–1944	78,400	15,680	38.4
1945–1949	105,100	21,020	16.1
1950–1954	48,400	9,680	4.4
1955–1959	36,000	7,200	2.6
1960–1964	43,000	8,600	3.0
1965–1969	39,000	7,800	2.2
1970–1974	34,700	6,940	1.8

Source: Simon Kuznets, "Immigration of Russian Jews to the United States: Background and Structure," *Perspectives in American History* 9 (1975), pp. 35–124; *American Jewish Year Book* 77 (1977), p. 319.

REFERENCE SOURCES IN AMERICAN JEWISH HISTORY

Bibliographical Guides

William W. Brickman. *The Jewish Community in America: An Annotated and Classified Bibliographical Guide* (1977)
Jeffrey Gurock. *American Jewish History: A Bibliographical Guide* (1983)
Moses Rischin. *An Inventory of American Jewish History* (1954)

Encyclopedias

Encyclopaedia Judaica (1971–1972)
The Jewish Encyclopedia (1906)
Universal Jewish Encyclopedia (1939–1943)

Leading Periodicals

American Jewish Archives (1948–) [Index to vols. 1–24 (1979)]
American Jewish History (1978–); formerly *Publications of the American Jewish Historical Society* (1892–1961) and *American Jewish Historical Quarterly* (1961–1968)
American Jewish Year Book (1899–) [Index to vols. 1–50 (1967)]
Jewish Journal of Sociology (1959–)
Jewish Social Studies (1939–) [Index to vols. 1–25 (1967)]
Leo Baeck Institute Yearbook (1958–) [Index to vols. 1–20 (1982)]
Modern Judaism (1981–)
Rhode Island Jewish Historical Notes (1954–) [Index to vols. 1–7 (1984)]
Western States Jewish Historical Quarterly (1968–) [Index to vols. 1–12 (1981)]
YIVO Annual of Jewish Social Science (1946–)

Indexes

Index to Jewish Periodicals (1969–)
The Jewish Experience in America (1983) [abstracts of articles in scholarly journals, 1973–1979]

Jacob R. Marcus. *An Index to Scientific Articles on American Jewish History* (1971)[indexes major articles 1888–1968]

Selected Subject Bibliographies

John M. Cohn. "Demographic Studies of Jewish Communities in the United States: A Bibliographic Introduction and Survey." *American Jewish Archives* 32 (April 1980), pp. 35–51

Daniel Elazar. "Jewish Community Studies: A Selected Bibliography." *Community and Polity* (1976), pp. 394–399

Rudolf Glanz. *The German Jew in America: An Annotated Bibliography* (1969)

Samuel C. Heilman. "The Sociology of American Jewry: The Last Ten Years." *Annual Review of Sociology* 8 (1982), pp. 135–160

Ezekiel Lifschutz. *Bibliography of American and Canadian Jewish Memoirs and Autobiographies* (1970)

Harry Lurie. "[Bibliography] On the History of the Jewish Communities in the United States and Canada." *A Heritage Affirmed* (1961), pp. 457–467

Ira Nadel. *Jewish Writers of North America: A Guide to Information Sources* (1981)

Robert Singerman. *Antisemitic Propaganda: An Annotated Bibliography and Research Guide* (1982)

Malcolm H. Stern. "American Reform Judaism: A Bibliography." *American Jewish Historical Quarterly* 63 (1973), pp. 120–137

Herbert A. Strauss. *Jewish Immigrants of the Nazi Period in the U.S.A.* (1978–)

Textbooks

Henry L. Feingold. *Zion in America* (1974)

Nathan Glazer. *American Judaism* (1972)

Arthur A. Goren. *The American Jews* (1982)

Abraham J. Karp. *Haven and Home* (1984)

Rufus Learsi [Israel Goldberg]. *The Jews in America* (1972)

INDEX

Abbot, Francis E., 93
Adams, John Q., 34
Adler, Felix, 50, 89, 110
Amalgamated Clothing Workers Union, 159
American Jewish Committee, 150, 213, 232,
American Jewish Congress, 152, 153, 232
American Society for Meliorating the Condition of the Jews, 33
Americanization, 122–130, 162, 164, 171, 193–208, 215, 230
Anti-Semitism, 12, 58, 60, 62–71, 95, 121, 156, 159, 165–166, 173–190, 209, 211, 212, 222, 228, 230, 238, 246, 252, 261, 264, 282
Ararat, 32
Assimilation, 14, 37, 48, 53, 196–197, 238, 276, 283, 292
Association for Jewish Studies, 277
Auschwitz, 248–249

B'nai B'rith, 49
B'nai Jeshurun (New York), 35
Bache, Semon, 74
Backus, Isaac, 23
Badeau, Adam, 70
Barondess, Joseph, 137
Baruch, Bernard, 185
Belkin, Samuel, 264
Bellow, Saul, 270
Bene Israel (Cincinnati), 36
Benjamin, Judah P., 60
Bergh, Harry, 71
Bernstein, Herman, 177, 183–184, 185
Beth Elohim (Charleston), 35, 51
Beth Shalome (Richmond), 26–27
Bingham, Theodore A., 147
Birmingham, Stephen, 72
Blaustein, David, 107, 126, 138
Brandeis, Louis D., 152, 163, 178, 209, 214–221
Brisbane, Arthur, 186–187

Cahan, Abraham, 103, 122
Cameron, William J., 176–190
Cass, Lewis, 212
Central Jewish Institute, 201

Channing, William E., 91
Chaplains, 60
Charity, 122
Charleston, 7, 21
Cincinnati, 36
Civil religion, 263–264
Civil War, 60–71, 76, 86, 113
Cleveland Conference, 53
Clothing industry, 112–117, 158, 164
Cohen, Barrow E., 35
Cohen, Jacob I., 34
Cohen, Jacob R., 25
Collyer, Robert, 91
Colonial Period, 5–17
Communism, 222, 265
Conservative Judaism, 191, 207–208, 231
Constitution, 18, 24, 25, 26
Conway, Moncure D., 91
Coughlin, Charles E., 228
Culture, 49, 59, 222, 259, 267–281

Daniel, Annie S., 114, 117
Daniels, C. C., 178
De La Motta, Jacob, 34
Dearborn Independent, 176–190
Democratic Party, 64–69, 222, 290
Depression, 222–233
Dewey, John, 200
Dissenters, Protestant, 23
Dolgenas, Jacob, 197
Drachman, Bernard, 50, 193, 195, 197, 204
Dubinsky, David, 161
Dubois, John V., 63

East European Jews, 59, 99–155
Economic life, 8–9, 21, 62, 73–86, 103, 112–117, 135–146, 225–228, 237, 286
Education, 11–12, 129, 153–154, 286
Educational Alliance, 124–125
Einhorn, David, 46, 48, 52, 56, 87
Emanu-El (New York), 52, 121
Ethical Culture, 163
Ethnicity, 155, 259, 260–266, 287
Etting, Solomon, 34
Evian Conference, 245

Federal Council of Churches, 183
Federation of American Zionists, 213–214

Federation of Jewish Philanthropies, 151
Felsenthal, Bernhard, 47, 50, 57, 91, 92, 95
Fiction, 270–277
Filene, A. Lincoln, 163
Fischel, Harry, 202
Ford, Henry, 174–190
Fortas, Abe, 285
Frank, Leo, 173
Frankel, Zacharis, 51
Frankfurter, Felix, 216, 219, 222, 229
Franklin, Leo, 177, 183, 189
Free Religious Association, 90, 92
Freud, Sigmund, 174
Friedan, Betty, 290
Friedenwald, Harry, 217
Frontier, 5

Gallagher, William Henry, 185–186
Geiger, Abraham, 55, 65
General Orders No. 11, 60–71
German Period, 44ff.
Germany, 43, 46, 85–86
Glatstein, Yakov, 274
Godlove, Lewis, 89
Gold, Michael, 107
Goldman, Marcus, 74
Goldstein, Herbert S., 197–198, 201, 203, 204, 205, 206–208
Gompers, Samuel, 159
Gottheil, Gustav, 121
Gottheil, Richard, 217
Grant, Jesse, 65–66
Grant, Madison, 189
Grant, Ulysses S., 60–71
Gratz, Barnard, 34
Gratz, Rebecca, 33, 57
Green, Arthur, 279
Guggenheim, Meyer, 75

Halleck, Henry W., 64
Hapgood, Hutchins, 162
Har Sinai (Baltimore), 51
Harby, Isaac, 35
Harlem, New York, 192
Harmonie Club, 79
Hart, Isaac, 20
Hart, Moses, 34
Hausman, Gustav, 195
Hebrew Emigrant Aid Society, 122
Hebrew Union College, 41–44
Heidelbach, Philip, 75
Heilprin, Michael, 60
Herzl, Theodore, 211
Hessians, 20
Hirsch, Emil G., 50, 87, 92, 95
Hollander, Jacob H., 123

Holocaust, 237–259, 287, 292
Howe, Irving, 156

Immigration, 31, 36, 41, 45, 73, 99–155, 158–159, 291–292
Intermarriage, 29, 80, 132, 191, 238, 283, 292
International Ladies Garment Worker's Union, 161
Isaac Elchanan Theological Seminary, 191
Isaacs, Samuel M., 68
Israel, 237, 259, 288

Jackson, Solomon H., 33, 34
Jastrow, Morris, 50
Jefferson, Thomas, 24, 34
Jewish Community Centers, 191, 262
Jewish Community Council, 232
Jewish Encyclopedia, 59
Jewish Labor Movement, 135–146
Jewish Theological Seminary of America, 151, 191, 195, 201
Joint Distribution Committee, 231

Kallen, Horace, 215
Kaplan, Mordecai, 151, 155, 199, 200, 201, 203, 231
Kashrut, 133–155
Kaskel, Ceasar, 64
Kehillah, 147–155, 169
Kennedy, Thomas, 22, 34
Kissinger, Henry, 285
Klein, Philip, 147, 195
Kohler, Kaufmann, 55, 58
Kohn, Jacob, 195
Kuhn, Abraham, 75

Labor movement, 156–166
Landsmanshafts, 127, 195, 230
Lawrence, David, 184
Lazarus, Emma, 121
Leeser, Isaac, 35, 43, 46, 50, 51
Lehman, Henry, 75
Lehman, Herbert, 165
Leibold, Ernest G., 176–190
Leipzig Synod, 55
Levantine Jews, 128–129
Levi, Moses E., 33
Levy, Asser, 38
Lilienthal, Max, 47
Lincoln, Abraham, 60, 64
Lindbergh, Charles, 254
Lipsky, Louis, 152, 220
Literature, 223, 230
Loeb, Solomon, 75
Long, Breckinridge, 241, 244
Lost Ten Tribes, 36

Louis, Minnie D., 123, 129
Lowell, A. Lawrence, 175

Machzike Talmud Torah, 129
Mack, Julian W., 165, 216, 219, 221
Magnes, Judah, 147, 149–155
Malamud, Bernard, 270, 272, 273–274
Margolies, Moses Z., 208
Marranos, 6
Marshall, Louis, 118, 150, 154, 163, 181,
    183, 187, 190, 213, 218, 224, 256
Maryland "Jew Bill", 34
Masliansky, Zevi H., 126
Meat Boycott, 135–146
Medill, Joseph, 66–67
Mendes, H. P., 193
Meyer, Eugene Jr., 185
Mikveh Israel (Philadelphia), 35, 43
Monroe, James, 34
Morais, Henry S., 194, 205
Morgenthau, Henry Jr., 246
Morse, Arthur, 239–241
Moses, Adolph, 70
Myers, Moses, 32
Myers, Samuel, 32–33

Nazism, 224, 228, 232
Neusner, Jacob, 259, 279
New Deal, 161, 222, 227, 229
New York, 3, 6, 7, 101–117, 118–132, 135–
    146, 193–208, 222, 259–266
Newport, RI, 7, 21
Noah, Mordecai, 29, 32, 34

Orthodox Judaism, 87, 151, 191, 193–208,
    194, 195, 197, 231, 237
Ozick, Cynthia 274

Parker, Theodore, 91
Peddlers, 74
Philadelphia, 7, 21
Philadelphia Conference, 55
Philanthropy, 126–131, 162, 264, 288
Phillips, Jonas, 22
Pipp, E. G., 176–190
Pittsburgh Platform, 89
Politics, 61, 135–146, 251–258, 265, 282, 290
Posnanski, Gustav, 51
Price, George, 112, 114, 116
Price, Julius J., 195
Prooftexts, 279
Protocol of Peace, 156, 163
Protocols of the Learned Elders of Zion,
    175–176

Rabbis, 10, 89–96, 193–208
Radin, Adolph N., 125, 142

Raphall, Morris J., 60
Reagan, Ronald, 285
Recife, Brazil, 3
Reconstructionist Judaism, 231
Red Cross, 247–248
Reed, James A., 186
Reform Judaism, 44, 51–53, 81, 87, 213, 231
Reformed Society of Israelites, 35
Rehine, Zalma, 36
Religious life, 9–11, 21–22, 26–27, 43–44,
    50–59, 87–96, 143, 161, 191–208, 231,
    262–263
Revolution, 18–28
Richmond, VA, 26
Riegner, Gerhardt, 254
Riis, Jacob, 111
Roberts, Kenneth, 175
Roosevelt, Franklin D., 222, 229, 240, 241–
    258
Rosenwald, Julius, 165
Rosenwald, Samuel, 75
Roth, Henry, 270
Roth, Philip, 270–272, 273

Sachs, Michael, 51
Salomon, Edward S., 67
Salomon, Haym, 18, 21
Sapiro, Aaron, 185
Savannah, 7, 21
Schiff, Jacob, 77–78, 80, 84, 123, 126, 150,
    163, 165, 181, 218
Schiff, Mortimer, 79
Schindler, Solomon, 92, 95
Scholarship, 278–281
Scholle, William, 75
Second generation, 171, 191, 200, 260–266
Seixas, Gershom, 21, 27
Seligman, Joseph, 73, 84–85
Sephardim, 10
Seymour, Horatio, 65
Shearith Israel, 20–21, 25, 26, 27, 35
Siegel, Isaac, 204
Silver, Abba Hillel, 233
Simons, George A., 175
Singer, I. B., 274
Six-Day War, 288
Slavery, 9, 60
Solis, Jacob S., 36
Sombart, Werner, 177
Sonneschein, Solomon H., 89, 92, 95
Speyer, Philip, 77
Steffens, Lincoln, 122
Stoddard, Lothrop, 175
Straus, Lazarus, 75
Straus, Oscar, 81
Strong, Josiah, 189
Stuyvesant, Peter, 7

Suburbanization, 261
Sulzberger, Cyrus L., 150
Synagogues, 10, 191–208, 262–263
Syrkin, Nachman, 152
Szold, Benjamin, 87
Szold, Robert, 221

Tenements, 107–112
Tintner, Benjamin A., 195
Touro, Isaac, 20
Triangle fire, 115
Turner, F. J., 5, 14
Twersky, Isidor, 279

Unitarianism, 87–96
United Hebrew Charities, 122–123, 130, 132
United Hebrew Trades, 159

Vance, Zebulon B., 212
Voorsanger, Jacob, 58

Wald, Lillian, 117, 165
Warburg, Felix, 150, 165
Warburg, Paul, 180, 181
Washington, George, 25, 28
Weinstein, Gregory, 114

Weizmann, Chaim, 220
Wendt, Charles W., 92
Wiesel, Elie, 287
Williams, Roger, 23
Wise, Isaac Mayer, 44, 49, 50, 52, 53, 58–59, 68, 71, 92, 93, 95
Wise, Stephen S., 152, 216, 219, 232, 242, 254
Wolf, Simon, 70
Women, 56, 133–146, 194, 282, 290
World Jewish Congress, 247
World War I, 147, 171, 173, 209

Yeshiva Etz Chaim, 129
Yeshiva Isaac Elchanan, 129
Yeshiva University, 191
Yezierska, Anzia, 104
Yiddish, 121, 160
Young Men's and Young Women's Hebrew Associations, 191, 199, 203
Yulee, David, 36, 60

Zionism, 81, 130, 151, 153, 182, 209–221, 224
Zuntz, Alexander, 20
Zygelbojm, Smull, 243–244, 256